The Indians and Brazil

Published in Cooperation with the
Center for Latin American Studies at the
University of Florida

The Indians and Brazil

Mercio P. Gomes

Translated by John W. Moon

University Press of Florida

Gainesville · Tallahassee · Tampa · Boca Raton
Pensacola · Orlando · Miami · Jacksonville

Third edition (first English-language edition) 2000

The Indians and Brazil was first published in Portuguese as *Os Indios e o Brasil,*
copyright 1988 by Mercio P. Gomes, published by Editoria Vozes Ltda. Second
edition, copyright 1991 by Mercio P. Gomes, published by Editoria Vozes Ltda.
For further information, write Editoria Vozes Ltda, Rua Frei Luís, 100, 25689
Petrópolis, RJ, Brazil.

05 04 03 02 01 00   6 5 4 3 2 1

Library of Congress Cataloging-in-Publication Data
Gomes, Mércio Pereira, 1950–
[Indios e o Brasil. English]
The Indians and Brazil / Mercio P. Gomes ; translated by John W. Moon.
p   cm.
Translation of: Os indios e o Brasil.
"Published in cooperation with the Center for Latin American Studies
at the University of Florida"—Half t.p. verso.
Includes bibliographical references.
ISBN 0-8130-1720-3 (cloth : acid-free paper)
1. Indians of South American—Brazil—Government relations.
2. Indians of South America—Brazil—Social conditions. I. Title.
F2519.3.G6G6613   2000
981'.00498—dc21   99-38728

The University Press of Florida is the scholarly publishing agency for the State
University System of Florida, comprising Florida A&M University, Florida
Atlantic University, Florida International University, Florida State University,
University of Central Florida, University of Florida, University of North Florida,
University of South Florida, and University of West Florida.

University Press of Florida
15 Northwest 15th Street
Gainesville, FL 32611
http://www.upf.com

In Memoriam
Charles Wagley, Eduardo Galvão, and Darcy Ribeiro
Anthropologists who made a difference in the
destiny of the Brazilian Indians

Contents

Preface   ix

Introduction   1

1. The Indian in History   28

2. Indian Policies   57

3. What We Think about the Indians   100

4. Who Are the Indians?   132

5. The Indians Today   175

6. The Future of the Indians   221

Appendix A. Indian Lands   247

Appendix B. Indian Historic Demography   249

Appendix C. Indian Ethnies, Language Families, and Populations   250

Notes   259

Bibliography   283

Preface to the English Edition

The Indians and Brazil is an anthropological study of the history of the relations between the aboriginal populations of Brazil and the Brazilian society and polity that were formed upon the Indians' territory and over their lives and livelihood. When it was first written and published in 1988, this book also had a cultural and political purpose, which seems to me to be just as valid for an English-reading public today: it carried the message, still unrecognized by most people, that the living Brazilian Indian "ethnie" (ethnic groups), against all odds and all predictions to the contrary, are not on the verge of extinction.[1] On the contrary, they have been growing in numbers since the mid-1950s and have increased their odds for success in their struggle for a lasting permanence in the world. Three decades ago, most anthropologists did not think of that as a serious possibility, not because they did not see in their research signs of population increase and the rise of ethnic affirmation, but because the set of theories they used to interpret their data—which I have called here the paradigm of acculturation—did not concede the possibility of survival for the Indians of the Americas and, for that matter, for nonstate-level, egalitarian, "primitive," societies over the world.

The general public—in this case, the Brazilian public—realized something was going on from the uproar raised around and by the Indians from the mid-1970s on. People certainly kept thinking that the Indians' defiant protests and the appearance of charismatic Indian leaders on the national political scene could only represent a kind of swan song, the last desperate outcry of a despairing people. In response, the public was divided. They either felt sorry for and lent their sympathy to the Indian cause—one more lost cause to uphold—or shrugged their shoulders in dismissal, indifferent to the consummation of a long-expected outcome.

I myself took ten years, from the time I did my first fieldwork with a Brazilian Indian ethnie in 1975, before I fully realized that it was not only that ethnie, the Tenetehara (also known as Guajajara), that had survived and was growing in numbers but nearly all ethnies in Brazil. The only visible exceptions were those that had recently come into contact with segments of the national society and were undergoing the terrible process of being infected by foreign, devastating diseases with consequent heavy population losses. The new evidence for this surprising population growth—what I have called the Indian demographic turnaround—was there, but how to explain it? The extinction of the Brazilian Indian ethnies had for over two centuries been taken as historical fact, accountable by all modes of theory, as unrefutable as a dogma, something taken for granted by anthropology and very much ingrained in the spirit and the imagination of the Western civilization. As I sifted through the accumulating new data that anthropologists, linguists, and the Brazilian Indian agency were turning out, I pursued a new course of analysis and interpretation to account for this wondrous phenomenon. If it was not a miracle it must be found in history.

First of all, it became clear to me that the paradigm of acculturation accounted for only half the picture. The theories and models within this paradigm accord that, as two ethnies meet, the stronger one, unless they are equally matched, tends to overpower the weaker one. The outcome is eventually the absorption (either by integration or assimilation, if those notions can be considered dissimilar) of the weaker into the stronger's fold. However, the paradigm of acculturation disregarded the possibility that the smaller, weaker part can, in many cases, set up a reaction against the imposition of the stronger part. Eventually this dominated ethnie might preserve enough of its character to maintain its self-identity and accommodate itself to the new situation, without necessarily diluting itself into nothing. In the 1970s, it became evident that this mechanism was developing among the Brazilian Indians, as well as among other ethnies in the world.[2]

Second, the reason such an absolute consensus seemed to prevail concerning the extermination of egalitarian peoples lay not so much in the historical evidence, although it was very persuasive, but in the ideological makeup of Western civilization as it expanded and proceeded to control the world. As with all cultures, Western civilization fabricates its self-image partly by contrasting itself with others. However, it has been doing that in relation not just to some but to all others in the world. As it has placed itself on top of an ascending scale, it has expected that the rest of the world should, for its own good, move up in due course to become like Western civilization itself. Those cultures that could not make it would eventually disappear, as so many had done through history, and make room for the expansion of the dominating civilization. The theory of evolution captured this sentiment and justified it for the scientific mind during the nineteenth century and until the rise of modern anthropological thinking. In the 1930s, the theory of acculturation defined this sentiment in terms of a functional process but did not change it substantially. One way or another, an inexorable fate awaited the weaker part.

What makes the difference now is that Western self-assurance and notions of superiority seem to have cracked in some places. My hunch is that the explosion of the A-bomb in 1945 was the symbolic turning point that opened the way for self-doubt and consequently for the acceptance of other worldviews in the core of the Western mind. As new ways of life began to gain respect, the Indians, egalitarian peoples, began to be seen as something more than the representation of the past. There is no doubt that in the public mind they are still perceived as exotic, perhaps nature-bound, more instinctive than rational, but no longer are they perceived as merely savage and brutish. Thus they obtained a new chance to come forward into the political arena and fight for their lives on less unfriendly grounds.

Third, there is the objective matter of a qualitative change in the health conditions of humankind. In the last forty or fifty years, there has occurred a continuing lessening in the virulence of diseases that had once been the scourge of humanity and particularly of the aboriginal populations of the Americas and Oceania. Smallpox, probably the most devastating of all, has been eradicated as an epidemic in most places since the mid-1950s and completely wiped out as a disease by the late 1970s. Most other diseases have also been controlled and have become much less virulent than before. Of course, new diseases have cropped up in the 1980s and others have staged a rather nasty comeback, but nevertheless they are still relatively under control. The Indians in Brazil have indeed benefitted from this new condition of public health, independently of the sanitary measures taken by the Brazilian Indian agency.

As I aligned these factors as arguments, it became somewhat easier to demonstrate how well the Brazilian Indians were faring in the process of survival. I began to receive positive response from anthropologist friends to whom I presented these matters. Particularly important to me were the discussions I had with Carlos Moreira Neto, the esteemed Brazilian ethnohistorian; José Luiz dos Santos, from the University of Campinas; and the late Darcy Ribeiro, whose book on Brazilian Indians predicted their extinction.

So this book was written to come to terms with a new world phenomenon. It focuses on demonstrating that the Indian ethnies living in the Brazilian territory, the Brazilian Indians, if you will, who had survived through the 1950s, are now steadfastly increasing in population and are showing signs that they might not be on the wane after all. I consider this fact one of the most surprising and important social phenomena in the last five hundred years. The consequences will, it is hoped, be positive also for the Brazilian nation as a whole.

In many parts of the world the same phenomenon is occurring or has occurred conclusively. I believe the three main reasons just stated should be applicable elsewhere. However, they take place in historical contexts, so there is a story to be told about each of them. Our story here is how this came about within the formation of the Brazilian nation as an expansion of Western civilization. Therefore, much of this book deals with the history of Brazil, although from a minor but unique perspective, that of the survival, not the demise, of the aboriginal Indian populations. For most historians this perspective could only be promptly dismissed as an anthropologist's daydream. For were not the Tupinambá, the largest tribe on the coast, completely wiped out in about a century of colonization? Were not black slaves brought from Africa to substitute for the dying Indians? Are they not but a small minority in Brazil? These are acceptable readings of an undeniable reality, but the fact of matter is that since a good number of the Brazilian ethnies did survive somehow or other, something must have happened in the course of that history to make possible such an event. As we look into that history with the trained eye of an anthropologist, we can focus better on the importance of the Indian ethnies in the formation of the Brazilian nation. In this book I present data and arguments that point to a different, new reading of the rather ambiguous relationship between Brazilians and Brazilian Indians. I hope that this new perspective might shed some light into our present and perhaps on the years to come. That is the political as much as the anthropological purpose of this book. The survival of the Indians might even turn out to be a factor in influencing the destiny of Brazil.

In coming to terms with this new reality I have developed, if not a method, a style of anthropology in which the notion of prospectiveness is incorporated in both theory and practice. That is, I have come to feel that whenever an anthropologist makes a statement about a living subject, he should be willing to make himself accountable for the results of his assertion in the future. That, I believe, is the proof of the pudding in social science. My proposition that the Indians have survived and will have a new place in the world means not only that I think that the situation is so, empirically and theoretically, but also that I wish it to be so and will do as much as I can for it to come to pass. A methodological consequence is the need to imagine scenarios for the future, a task that is certainly not in the regular purview of traditional anthropology. At any rate, although my general scenario for the Indians is not completely rosy, at least it is devoid of the dark gray hues that were so present in the conclusions found within the paradigm of acculturation.

Among the many new obstacles that one can envision for the continuing survival of the Indians in the future, several have appeared in recent years and are of particular concern to the anthropologist. One is a waning interest in Indians and in the Indian cause among formerly enthusiastic or sympathetic supporters within the Brazilian and international public. This circumstance can be detected in several ways: decrease in media coverage, departure of Indian supporters from government posts, dissolution of many NGOs (nongovernmental organizations) for the defense of Indian, tacit acceptance by both the Brazilian congress and the press of anti-Indian public policies, and a discernible scaling back in the professional training of anthropologists to work with Indians. Another obstacle can be perceived within the general crisis of identity (philosophical, epistemological, psychological, and especially professional) that anthropology has been experiencing in the last twenty years or so. In part this crisis is due to the rise of a sentiment of loss of the legitimacy that anthropologists had acquired in their relation to egalitarian peoples. Anthropologists' former role of speaking out on behalf of the Indians has paled precisely because of the rise of indigenous peoples with their own voices and political legitimacy. With that change, anthropologists have grown reticent and insecure about what they say about such peoples, which has not only paralyzed field research but also silenced most anthropologists' voices.

Reflecting this crisis, postmodernist critique brought forth a new style of doing anthropology and in particular of writing about Indians and egalitarian societies. Instead of speaking for or about, this most fashionable trend purports to speak *with* the Indian. Here we find works in which the anthropologist engages in a personal, confessional analysis of his relationship with some real or constructed native about an event or an aspect of his life that might shed some light on his culture. This kind of discourse usually purports to bring about and elevate the native's view of the world, but oftentimes the result is rather self-serving. It seems in many cases that the more one speaks with the native, the more one speaks about oneself. In fact, it is hard to imagine what postmodernist authors think about the future of egalitarian societies, although I would concede that they outwardly wish them well.

There is no doubt that the bulk of our ethnographic and anthropological literature still reflects a continuing concern with natives and their physical, material, and cultural well-being, yet as egalitarian peoples they remain a long distance from us. Their cultures might seem as viable as they are, but not so in the long run. Their future does not sound promising, and there lingers a feeling that there is very little one can do about it, though one wishes one could help. Let us recall here that one of Claude Lévi-Strauss's most widely read books, *Tristes Tropiques,* has been published in English with the title *A World on the Wane.*

This mixed feeling of sympathy and helplessness can possibly be detected in anthropology as early as in the monographs published by the Smithsonian Institution in the last quarter of the nineteenth century, at a time when the theory of evolution was dominant everywhere. The advent of culture relativism did not much change the scene in the case of Brazilian Indians, although in the 1940s and 1950s we find anthropologists such as Charles Wagley, Kalervo Oberg, Herbert Baldus, Darcy Ribeiro, Alfred Métraux, and Eduardo Galvão—all inspired by the work of Curt Nimuendaju—making practical policy propositions and even working for official agencies in an effort to help save the Indians. In the 1960s there was a swelling of field research coming from the United States, as well as France, England, and Brazil, that went hand in hand with the practical purpose of doing something for the Indians. In the 1970s many anthropologists actually went out of their way to urge their governments and their fellow citizens to take interest in and feel responsible for the destiny of the Indians. Many social organizations, such as Culture Survival (founded in Boston by anthropologist David Maybury-Lewis), International Survival (founded in London), and IWGH (based in Norway), led important campaigns on behalf of many Indian and egalitarian peoples' organizations from all corners of the world. They paved the way for the blossoming of many such organizations, which obtained the warm support of many more people in the 1980s. The Indian issue gained in interest when it was purposely mixed with ecological ones, and the Indians were presented to the public as erstwhile versions of the good savage.

However, it seems that, in this last decade of the millennium, this sentiment of sympathy has begun to wane. Is this a sign that people feel the Indians have survived and now they should fend for themselves? Whatever it may be, I truly miss the presence of a new generation of anthropologists interested in doing fieldwork with the intention of contributing to the survival and permanence of the Indians. It seems that the last ones are working for NGOs or the World Bank.

Apart from the influence of postmodernist critique, the anthropological literature on Brazilian Indians in the 1990s continues to follow the paths opened by either the materialist renewal of the 1960s or the powerful establishment of the Lévi-Strauss structuralist paradigm. The sort of French-derived Marxist paradigm that had some popularity in the 1970s has not prospered much since. A great part of this literature and almost all of this theoretical makeup is taken into account in this book insofar as it pertains to the understanding of the process of ethnic survival.

As for the political role that anthropologists can have in regard to the issue of Indian survival, it is important to place it within the larger process of the formation of the new self-consciousness of Western civilization. There is no doubt that we anthropologists have contributed to this process as proponents of ideas and as critics of our civilization. Perhaps nowadays our role is no longer as important as when we stood out as spokespersons for the Indians. In those times we spoke out for what we thought the Indians were like, and we managed to convince a good portion of our fellow citizens of the value of egalitarian peoples.

The rise of Indian political consciousness and their presence in the media detracted from the voice of the wise anthropologist. At best, he became an expert behind the scenes. It could not be any other way. But the consequence is that it smothered the voice of anthropology to murmuring and muttering. Perhaps this drastic drop in self-confidence and loss of legitimacy to speak out for someone other than oneself has been one of the main reasons for the rise of postmodernist rambling and the paralysis seen among anthropologists who no longer find it necessary to go out into the field and actually work with people and issues, which is important not only for them but also for their discipline and, in a lesser sense, for humanity.

There is much still that anthropology can do to create and expand on its theoretical and practical view of the world by studying the Indians. The reevaluation of the paradigm of acculturation should be an important step in coming to terms with the new cultural reality brought about by the survival of peoples who, a few decades ago, everyone believed would be extinct. The reevaluation of the paradigm primitive/civilized, one that was established by the theory of evolution but that cultural relativism was rather keen in eschewing, is a demand whose repercussions will help reshape our view of the future of humankind.

Most important, we anthropologists should join together in an effort to tackle the daunting challenge of finding viable ways and means to increase the productivity of egalitarian economies without changing them so much as to cause the destruction of their originality, although it is a task that almost everyone—Marxists and capitalists, evolutionists and cultural relativists, materialists and idealists, hard-core scientists and postmodernists—agree is nearly impossible. Would that not be a worthy motivation to help us get out of the trap in which anthropology presently finds itself? For all these considerations, this book can be seen as both an analysis of a cultural-political situation as well as a calling for action in both theory and practice.

Introduction

Although it may not be fair to charge Brazil of being innately against the Indians who live in its territory, it is at any rate hard to associate the two in any other way than a zero sum. Surely the histories of each are in an inverse relation: as one grows big and powerful, the other dwindles and becomes weaker and weaker. In appraising the reports and the news that have come out in the media in the last twenty or thirty years concerning the predicament of the Indians in Brazil we may arrive at the conclusion that their lot is with the tormented and the forsaken. Here the Indians have endured the wrongdoings of mining companies and wayward miners, plantation owners and their hired gunmen, poor land squatters, lumber companies, and multinational corporations whose exclusive interest is land speculation. They have also endured neglect, misunderstanding, and insensitiveness from the government that is responsible for their welfare. All things considered, there seems to be no place for the Indians in Brazil—certainly not in modern Brazil.

The fact is, however, that the Brazil of today is no worse to the Indians than the Brazil of thirty years ago, or of the nineteenth century. Ill will on the part of government authorities, a persisting paternalistic attitude, a reckless economic policy, and the lack of human solidarity all weigh heavily against the autochtonous inhabitants of Brazil in our day, as it did in the past. The country reveals its vile side in the disposition of a significant number of Brazilians who insist on deprecating the Indians and on reputing them and their cultures to be liabilities to the Brazilian society and Western civilization. On the other hand, there are a fair number of Brazilians who hold the highest sympathy toward the Indians, support them as the original and legitimate holders of the territories they inhabit, and consider that the nation as a whole owes them a historical debt.[1]

We may rejoice that this empathy does not come about as commiseration, but as the dawning of a new, committed understanding that sees the Indians as full, but special, partners and allies of the Brazilian nation. There is no doubt that Brazilians know more about Indians today and that this knowledge is a determining factor in increasing their level of cultural and political awareness. They are beginning to realize that the Indians' relentless struggle for survival has a political value in itself, and is not unlike the parallel movements in which Brazilians have engaged for the enlargement of their fundamental rights as citizens of a modern nation.

As the process of democratization pushes on, however slowly, in the Brazilian sociopolitical arena, the relationship between the Indians and Brazil also changes, but perhaps at a different pace. The fact is that—independent of any other cultural or political variable—in the last thirty or forty years the Indians have been experiencing a new, unexpected, and extraordinary development that we may unabashedly call "the Indian demographic turnaround." This notion is meant to express the fact that most extant Indian peoples have interrupted their former propensity to lose population and have actually been growing in numbers, thus lending hope that a historical reversion will occur in their demographic formation. It may be hasty to conclude that the Indians have survived for good, that this demographic turnaround has become a concrete, permanent reality. Indeed, it might still be too early to stress the notion of an irreversible survival when we are presented with a historical scenario in which 95 percent of an entire population was wiped out over a period of five centuries in which there are only a few decades of consistent recovery. For most people the most appropriate expression to characterize the present situation of the surviving Indians is to consider them remnant populations, as many, if not most, of the surviving ethnic groups have smaller populations than they did in the past. Today, at the turn of the millennium, there are some 350,000 Indians in Brazil, whereas there were 5 million in 1500. Not only did millions of human beings perish, but some 500 or more distinct ethnic groups, the end-products of thousands of years of evolution and adaptation, were extinguished forever. They succumbed, but all of humanity also lost for it. For not only was our collective memory deprived of the values and knowledge amassed by these peoples, but we also suffered a reduction in the biological diversity that warrants *Homo sapiens* greater chances of survival.[2]

Nonetheless, for all the doubts and wariness we might still have, we should not downplay the strong evidence that the surviving Indian peoples have been growing during these last four decades. As this evidence becomes unequivocal, the Indian demographic turnaround posits a new challenge to the alarmist expectations of a great number of people, including anthropologists, historians, indigenists, and demographers. Some ethnic groups, such as the Guarani, Terena, Guajajara, Tikuna, Kaingang, and Makuxi,[3] who have been living through more than two hundred years of permanent contact with the Luso-Brazilian world, seem to have acquired the biological and cultural reinforcement necessary to defend themselves from the most brutal adversities that have been imposed upon them until now. Their populations number in the lower tens of thousands and are growing at faster rates than the general Brazilian population. Other smaller groups are witnessing their populations grow also at constant rates, as is happening with the Karajá, Munduruku, Maué, Xavante, Canela, and Kayapó. Still others, such as the Urubu-Kaapor, Bororo, Xikrin, Krikati, the Xinguano groups, the Nambiquara, the Tapirapé, and most of the Pano-speaking groups (who had been considered as late as the mid-1950s on the way to extinction), have recovered from their demographic downslide and reached a sound level of biological and cultural stability.

There are still a few ethnic groups who have not yet made their demographic turnaround and continue to suffer population losses to the point of endangering their survival. Such is the case of the Avá-Canoeiro, the Guajá, the Assurini, the Juma, and the Urueuauau. According to an analysis made in the mid-1950s, some sixty-five ethnic groups had become extinct in the first half of the twentieth century alone.[4] However, as it turned out, several of those groups did recover from their severe population losses and are still around, such as the Canela Apanyekra, Krikati, Karipuna, Waiãpi, and even the elusive Guató.[5] Other groups such as the Xetá, Xipaya, Krêjé, Kamakan, Oti-Xavante, and Kepkiriwat waned until their ultimate extinction. The most dramatic case known is that of two adult male Indians who were found in the mid-1980s near a tributary of the Tocantins River, in eastern Amazon. They were taken to visit all the tribes around that area and although their language was recognized as a Tupi language, it was unintelligible to everyone they spoke with. They may indeed be the last survivors of a tribe that has ceased to exist.

Today the surviving Brazilian Indians live in a wide range of situations in relation to the encompassing society at large. This range extends all the way from the very acculturated Indians of the Brazilian northeast, all of whom are engaged in the regional socioeconomic system, to the Indians whom we might call *autonomous,* because they live apart from the dominant cultural and economic system. The Indian agency as well as most anthropologists prefer to categorize these Indians as "isolated"—as if this condition were their most important cultural characteristic, rather than a consequence of a self-conscious political decision. All the same, from whatever condition they may be in, the Indian peoples must fight in their own fashion for a place of their own not only in Brazil but also in the common-wealth of peoples. They are engaged in a fierce and unrelenting war for physical as well as for existential survival; a war fought in the dark—for they certainly do not have control over the weapons at hand, nor do they know just what the outcome might be.

Neither do we know—we who, from the other side, the safer side, are attempting to understand the meaning and the direction of human history, in particular the history of Brazil. All we know is that the prediction that the Indian case was a terminal one—as many had augured and some had even wished—has not been fulfilled. As we try to delineate a scenario of the near-future to propose a strategy that would help secure the perma-nence of Indian peoples in Brazil, we realize how complex and cunning the problems are. The Indian question is moved by contradictory forces of great destructive power, is supported by considerably less powerful allies, and is influenced by baffling events—usually negative ones—that occur in con-texts that require swiftness in the process of political decision making.

For instance, should the Indians be allowed to sell their high-priced hard-woods, or should they be given subsidies to keep them on the ground and off the market? What would happen in the long run to an Indian group that decides to accept cash money into their economy from royalties based on the exploitation of minerals or timber found on their lands? Would that cause the capitalization of their economies or the eventual destruction of their cultures? Should we support them in that decision or not?

In the mid-1980s this question was actually put to the Kayapó Indians of Pará state, Indians who control a vast territory of tropical forest with rich timber and alluvial gold. The leaders of the young adults age group made the decision for everyone and concurred with the idea of the entry of gold prospectors and logging companies. Today, after having been through an outbreak of uncontrolled consumerism that entailed many cultural changes in their villages, including the taste for industrialized foods—such as soda pop and canned meat—the Kayapó are now in the process of licking their wounds. Some of their most important rivers, such as the Fresco, have been contaminated with the mercury left by the process of retrieving gold. Their waters have become a health hazard. Furthermore, Kayapó society has confronted itself with the emergence of social differences it had never experienced before.

Similar social problems apply also to the Cintas-Largas of Rondônia state, whose self-appointed leaders opened their forests to timber companies in exchange for goods that benefit only a small number of them. In Maranhão state, it took less than ten years for the Guajajara to be left without a single mahogany or cedar tree on their formerly rich lands, and they have become no richer for letting their forests be devastated. The Yanomami represent the most dramatic case of recent devastation. In the past fifteen years their lands have been repeatedly invaded by thousands of gold prospectors, who not only have polluted the rivers but also have brought and spread among those defenseless Indians the most virulent strains of malaria, oncocercosis, tuberculosis, and other diseases.

The present situation of Indian peoples in Brazil is in many ways unsettling. To understand it as it stands today we must try to trace the history of the relationship they have engaged in with the Brazilian society. The dynamics of this relationship indicate an involvement with virtually every segment of the nation, from the early colonists, Jesuit priests, and royal administrators of colonial times, to the poor backwoodsman, the manager of a modern agribusiness company, the politicians and college students of today, and especially international public opinion.

The Indians constitute, therefore, a question of national and even international scope and interest. Brazil, whatever its political inclinations may be, cannot escape from the Indian, not even as it aspires to become a world power. As we keep this in mind we propose to study the Indians in terms of their broadest relationships with people both near them and far away and to discuss the paths and means that might help them not only to survive but also to have a rightful place in the Brazilian nation—as an autonomous, essential, and constituent element of its people. This is what I call "the Indian question."

THE SCOPE OF THE INDIAN QUESTION

The Indian question is concurrent with the discovery and establishment of Europeans and Africans in Brazil and in America in general, and it will continue to exist as long as a single Indian remains alive. This question can best be characterized according to the kind of relationship the Indians have engaged in with the world that has been growing around them and against their volition. Ironically, and often fatally, this overpowering world has compelled them into the condition of becoming strangers in their own homeland. The Indian is at the center of the Indian question, around which almost all the national segments revolve, be it by opposition, by complementarity, or even by subordination. The Indian question is as dynamic as the course of history. In the early years of colonization it was basically a military question, as the Indians were considered a threat to the Portuguese colonial establishment. Subsequently, many of the Indian groups were reduced to conditions of slavery and servitude, and the Indian question became an economic matter. As they became less and less numerous, but still important economically and socially in some areas, they began to be treated as clients in a paternalistic way. This kind of relationship has proved to be resilient and long-lasting, as it engaged everyone who has come in contact with the Indians since the mid-1800s, including not only the regular folks who live near the Indians but also government policy makers and even anthropologists.

However, in the last few decades some important changes in the Indians' cultural demeanor and political attitude, as well as in the ideological makeup of Brazil (and the world) have begun to undermine the prevailing paternalism. We may be witnessing the beginning of a new kind of relationship between Indians and Brazilians, perhaps a less violent, less dominating one, but surely no less tense and not without new tinges of ambiguity.

In many ways, the Indian question has accompanied step by step the course of the formation of Brazil as a new nation, but seemingly in an inverse relation—and therein lies the meaning of its tragedy. Why this has been so may be easy to demonstrate. But why this contradiction should be considered a normal and inexorable fact can only be explained as a process of rationalization that is rooted in both scientific and popular thinking. To understand the process of rationalization that has consciously or unconsciously put down the Indians, we must once again track it into the past, to follow its line of discourse as it meanders through different arguments and disparate considerations; we must observe the sources of its dynamics and the points in which there was some equilibrium between the pros and the cons (but never of harmony between the parts). If we can, perhaps we should try to extract from all this the lessons that might point to new and better possibilities for the fair and wise resolution of the Indian question.

In a deeper and long-lasting sense, the Indian question has been unfolding in a broader historical sweep than that which defines Brazilian history or even the history of the Americas. It is the political and ideological outcome of an untimely encounter that happened as a clash between two types of civilization, two great complexes of human possibilities.

On one hand stands the Old World civilization, a 10,000-year-old synthesis and a dispersing core of the cultural experiences of hundreds of different cultures and peoples. In one way or another—usually through war, but sometimes through dialogue and the diffusion of knowledge—Europe developed a dynamic cultural complex that has produced an indomitable drive for expansion since the fifteenth century. This civilization was formed originally beyond Europe itself, having aggregated the contributions of cultures and political entities of Asia, the Middle East, and Mediterranean Africa. This historical development becomes very clear not only in terms of culture and political institutions but also because its people, its human stock, however varied in its makeup, evolved a common immunological system. This kind of biological unity was fundamental in the confrontation with the peoples they found in their way to expansion.

On the other hand, there stands the civilization of the New World, a cultural formation with perhaps an identical timetable of development, but which did not obtain a complete integration of all its components. The great Mexican, Guatemalan, and Andean cultural complexes did not expand beyond their frontiers, and they interconnected neither with themselves nor with intermediary complexes, such as the cultures of the North American desert or the chiefdoms of Central America and the northern Andes.

By the sixteenth century the empires of the Aztecs and the Incas were indeed expansionist and both sought to reach new frontiers, but neither of them achieved permanent results. The Aztecs had military and trading outposts to the north and the south, but they were constantly being challenged. The Inca attempted to penetrate into the Amazon, but their drive for colonization was unproductive. Only at the cost of much military force were they able to secure some positions on the Bolivian plateau and on the headwaters of the Amazon River. As for the great majority of American peoples, they lived mostly in egalitarian and nonhierarchical political systems and defended their liberty by all possible means.

There are many reasons the New World did not reach the same level of political power as the Old World polities. At the risk of sounding simplistic I may venture to mention the fact that America lacked the horse (which had become extinct here in 10,000 B.C.), did not smelt iron, and although they knew of the concept, they did not make practical use of the wheel. But the American peoples ultimately lost the great battle against the incoming Europeans for a different reason: because they had no contact with the Old World, especially with its diseases, their immunological system was unprepared for the terrible bacteria, viruses, and parasites that had been the scourge of Eurasia for generations. When European colonists brought these pestilences to the New World, they carried along their mightiest weapon.

This universal and far-reaching aspect of the Indian question seems to many observers to be in its concluding phase. Perhaps a new civilization, a new cultural complex, is being formed on our continent, certainly with the preponderant influence of the victors. There remain, however, some enclaves of the original civilization in the Andes, in Mexico, in the American desert, and finally, even in Brazil. Those who see the inert force contained in the faces of the Quechua and Aymara Indians of Peru, Bolivia, and Ecuador can feel that perhaps not all the chips have been counted. But for now, not much attention is being paid to them.

As for Brazil, the 220 peoples who have endured perhaps do not carry as much weight in the making of this new civilization. It seems that few believe in them as a possibility for historic continuity or cultural renewal. They are survivors of an ethnic tragedy that was carried out in the form of a long-lasting holocaust within the boundaries of a territory, for the purpose of forming a nation. Their current political, ideological, and cultural status, as has been the case for many years, surely cannot be estimated by their numbers but by the quality they lend to the sentiment of Brazilian nationality.

An Ideological Question

The lasting permanence and relative importance of the Indian question in Brazil today is due not only to a kind of historical tribute, to the presence of the survivors—in short, to the continuity of its elements and structure—but also to the ideological influence it has had upon the formation of Brazilian nationality. Despite the magnitude of the violence that was carried out against the Indians by the state, the colonists, and the members of the new nation, this violence was never totally consensual. It is interesting to note that many institutions and segments of the European civilization, including Christendom and the Portuguese, had terrible doubts and strong guilt feelings about what they were doing or saw others doing to destroy or reduce the Indians to the condition of inferior beings. The Catholic Church (which, from a historical point of view, was part of the Portuguese colonial project and promoted it in its fashion), the Portuguese Crown (that is, the king and the state bureaucracy), and even, occasionally, the colonists (particularly once they realized the danger was under control), occasionally demonstrated a non-economic, humane interest for the Indians. In comparison with the way Europeans looked upon African blacks, the Indians received a more subtle and less cruel treatment. Somehow they conceded to the Indians certain rights.

The first set of Portuguese precepts pertaining to the Indians were included in the Regulations of 1548, which were given by King Pedro III to the first appointed governor-general of Brazil, Tomé de Souza. They explicitly declared that the Indians should be dealt with on terms of respect and friendship, unless they acted against the interests of the Portuguese, in which case they should be treated as enemies.[6] We will see that the main characteristic of the Indian policy of the Portuguese Crown can be read as an attitude of bad faith in relation to the position that the Indians should have in the colonial project. Policies changed frequently, from condemning Indian slavery as illegal and immoral to the other extreme of condoning it. The bottom line of it all was that the Indians could stay as they were so long as they accepted the conditions of subdued vassals.

This incongruity also characterizes the church, both secular and monastic. It acted at times arm-in-arm with the enemies of the Indians; at other times it would defend the Indians at the risk of Christian lives. All the while, the colonists pursued their own private interests, which aimed at the enlargement of their economic and political power. They perceived the Indians as strange, savage people with little disposition to work, as well as a barrier to their expansion. Nevertheless, they could not at times avoid the recognition that the Indians were people and had the right to be free. But as the colonists needed the Indians' labor power or their lands, the colonists most frequently reduced the Indians to the level of being semi-human, creatures of nature, in order to guiltlessly attack them and conquer new possessions. Once that was done, laws could be issued and upheld to guarantee the little that was left for the Indians and to integrate them into the colonial realm.

This dubious attitude became more sharply defined when Brazil broke from Portugal and became independent as a nation, in 1822. The forefathers and ideologues of the new nation felt an urgent need to create a national identity and to design a national agenda for it. The most important of them all was José Bonifácio de Andrade e Silva, who became known as the "Patriarch of Independence." In 1819 he wrote a paper entitled "Notes on the Civilization of the Barbarian Indians of Brazil" and presented it to the Constituent Assembly of 1823, thus initiating the Brazilian concern for finding an adequate place for the Indians both in the national sentiment as well as in the national territory. From that time on liberals and conservatives, landowners, and the small middle class that was being formed began to engage themselves in a battle of ideas and concepts that ended up producing an array of laws, dispositions, biases, and idealizations about the Indians, some of which still echo in our time.[7]

In the beginning, the discussions and proposals were centered around the Brazilian Historic and Geographical Institute (IHGB), founded in 1838 in Rio de Janeiro, then the capital of the nation. There Brazilian and foreign scholars published their views on the history of and prospects for the new nation, most of the time taking account of the Indians as part of it. The German naturalist Karl von Martius, who had been in Brazil on a scientific expedition from 1817 to 1821, introduced for the first time the image that the Brazilian people were like a great river formed by three tributaries, the Indians, the whites, and the blacks. For better or for worse, this image and its variations have since been ingrained in the national consciousness in an indelible fashion. It is employed even by those who are clearly anti-indigenist, such as the historian Francisco Adolpho de Varnhagen, the scientist Hermann von Ihering, and many others who join in the belief that the Indians are historically unfeasible in Brazil.[8] Liberals, romantics, positivists, militarymen, clergymen, in short, the so-called civil society, and even the state itself have been, at one moment or another, great defenders of Indian interests. Friends one day, enemies the next.

In comparison with such countries as Argentina, Venezuela, Colombia, and the United States, Brazil presents itself with a pattern of indigenist ideology and policies that is ambivalent and unstable. This situation may demonstrate that the country is searching for a resolution of the Indian question and may also reflect its pursuit of a cultural identity. (Comparisons with other countries, such as Paraguay, Bolivia, Peru, Ecuador, and Mexico, are more difficult to make because of the diverse ethnic compositions and densities of those countries as opposed to the Brazilian case.)

Independence from Portugal in 1822 resulted in the establishment of a monarchical regime known as the Empire of Brazil, which was ruled by two princes of Portuguese descent and lasted until 1889. As far as the Indians were concerned this regime meant the continuation of the general Portuguese attitude that had prevailed until then, for the ideas of Bonifácio were not accepted immediately. Although one of the last Portuguese pieces of legislation concerning the Indians had been a royal edict that allowed anyone to carry out a private war and enslave certain Indian tribes, the new nation took notice of it and in 1831 abolished that law and any form of enslavement of Indians.

Since then Brazil has disavowed any sort of policy of extermination, as Argentina and the United States had in effect done during the nineteenth century.[9] The Indian policy that prevailed during the Empire was conceptualized by a law in 1831 and set up by a royal decree issued in 1845. It became known as the Regiment of the Missions and was enforced by a central agency called the Directorate General of the Indians, seated in the capital of the Empire, Rio de Janeiro, with offices in all the nation's provinces. This policy was based on a set of principles and guidelines that meant both to protect the Indians against oppression and to lead them toward full integration with the rest of the population. The general idea shared by everyone at that time was that the Indians could eventually reach an acceptable level of civilization to be integrated but only by means of Christianization. Thus the guiding motto of this policy was to "civilize and catechize" the Indians. Every Brazilian province (now called *state*) had its own director general who was appointed by the governors (then called *presidents*). Each director general of the Indians supervised the so-called "partial directories," a kind of Indian post that assisted a set of Indian villages, as well as "Indian colonies," which were better equipped to speed the Indians to the condition of civilization. By the 1850s the provincial Indian agencies had mapped out in their territories who the Indians were, where they lived, and how they were doing.

Yet this policy proved incapable of defending the Indians against a much more effective and detrimental law for Brazil, the infamous Law of the Lands, issued in 1850. It simply stated that any piece of land could be considered someone's property only if it were registered in official land registrars. Otherwise it would be considered no-man's-land and, consequently, state property. The powerful landowners hastened to register their claimed and alleged properties and whoever else's they could obtain. Most Brazilian peasants missed their chance to become landowners. Some Indian tribes found out about the law and tried to have their lands registered, including by appealing directly to the emperor. A few actually succeeded in having their lands granted. Most tribes, however, never received news of the law and its consequences. By the 1860s, many Indian villages were left without their previously held lands, and the Indians were forcibly thrown into the assimilation process, forfeiting their ethnic identities and dissolving into the peasant population.

In the following years, a few Brazilian provinces concocted a devious procedure not only for usurping Indian lands but also for doing away with Indian groups. Instead of making use of firearms, the presidents of such provinces as Ceará, São Paulo, and Sergipe simply issued bureaucratic measures that declared there no longer existed any Indians in their provinces. That way they eschewed having to comply with the Regiment of the Missions. Thus the local partial directories were extinguished, and the lands used by the Indians were considered of public utility. The village lands were thrown up for grabs, and the Indians were condemned to live as squatters on other people's lands. In short, with the stroke of a pen as many Indians were extinguished as were killed off in other countries by firearms.

Although the Empire's Indian policy was not efficacious in defending the Indians against imperial land policy, the fact that the government had an explicit nonviolent policy eventually did make a difference. It left a mark that the following generations of policy makers were obliged to uphold. When, in the early years of the twentieth century, Brazil was accused in the International Congress of Americanists, held in Vienna, of condoning the killing of Indians, it felt obliged to respond, and it did so by creating a new Indian agency, the Indian Protection Service (SPI). Its first director, Colonel Cândido Rondon, inscribed as its motto the pledge "die if necessary; kill, never," representing the firm decision that no violence should be perpetrated against any Indian people with whom contact was to be made, even if the Indians should respond with violence. This policy was firmly applied in practice by the Indian agents in the years to come. The records show that more than a few such men not only closely followed the dictates of this motto but actually died in its service. This legacy of self-sacrifice undoubtedly constitutes a contribution to a philosophy of humanism and to a sentiment of native solidarity in the country.

In short, the ideological dimension of the Brazilian version of indigenism—which can be defined as the set of laws, ideologies, and attitudes present in both the Brazilian state and its Indian agencies as well as in the Brazilian imagination—is crucial to an understanding of the current issues pervading the Indian question. The Indians cannot be measured by their numbers alone, nor by the size of the territories they hold; one must also take into account their part in the history of the country and in the minds of its countrymen. In a sense, one can say that the Indians are at the core of the Brazilian self-image and consciousness. Therein may lie both their greatest strength and chance for survival as well as their ultimate weakness and source of instability, for this consciousness does not always square with the economic and social realities that dominate the country.[10]

The Current Situation

The Indian question has unfolded in Brazilian history with an outrageously negative outcome for the Indians. The Brazilian nation was built with the blood and sweat, and upon the native territories, of the five million Indians who lived there. For this unholy sacrifice, the surviving Indians have been entitled to take their place in the country's lowest social rankings, with the further penalty of retaining, in most cases, only a small fraction of their original lands. Father Antônio Vieira, the seventeenth-century Jesuit Indian defender who witnessed the destruction of the Indians in the Amazon, called this process the Portuguese greed for "red gold." Nowadays, Indian labor is no longer necessary for the country, but the lands are still eagerly coveted. While living in hunger, with their overall health conditions deteriorating, many Indians remain vulnerable to the epidemics that once devastated them. Pressured not to be what they are, some 50 of the 220 ethnic groups lost their original languages. However, a significant number of Indians still keep themselves apart from contact with Brazilian society, living as autonomous peoples who govern themselves by their own customs, free from external interference.

The factors that make up the Indian question at present are many and varied. The Indian peoples themselves, the state, the church, the level and intensity of socioeconomic development, the disputing economic interests, the military establishment, intellectuals (anthropologists, journalists, writers, lawyers, etc.), the urban middle class, landowners, ranchers, and land squatters—all make up a dynamic structure in motion. What motivates this dynamism varies in time: scarcity of labor, self-protection during war, the value of land, or extractive goods.

It is more than clear to everyone that land, particularly forest land and its natural resources—which can be turned into commodities, production factors, or reserve of value—is currently the great fulcrum of the Indian question. The Indians have as their constitutional right the actual possession—recognized officially or in the process of recognition—of about 10 percent of the national territory. This amounts to over 890,000 square kilometers of land. As owners of valuable lands, the Indians thus defy all sorts of authoritarian developmental policies, including those financed by international agencies such as the World Bank, mining and lumbering interests, agribusiness and ranching corporations, and last but not least, all manner of national and multinational land speculation.

These dominant interests constitute powerful lobbies in congress, the federal administration, and the media. In a direct manner or by political maneuvering, they corrode attempts by the government or organizations in the civil society to create a real dialogue with the Indians. Such dialogue would be possible only if it began with the political determination to demarcate all Indian lands once and for all. As anti-Indian interests work to indefinitely delay such a dialogue, they have in mind the continued economic exploitation of rich lands in the future without undue interference from their legitimate owners. In addition, hydroelectric projects, mineral prospecting, lumber exploitation, the policy of national security, and the opening of forest lands to landless peasants and agribusiness complete the panorama of current problems.

The National Indian Foundation (FUNAI), which was created by the government with the express task of demarcating all Indian lands (originally by 1978, a date that was reset by the Brazilian Constitution of 1988 for 1993) obviously has not fulfilled its mission. Thus it is incapable of giving form to an Indian policy that might establish a new place and a new role for the Indians on the national scene. Brazil is also behind in the need to change the legal status of the Indians. According to the Civil Code of 1918, they are considered as "relatively capable" persons, on the same level with legal minors and the mentally deficient. Notwithstanding this, Indian leaders are often received with honors at national and international events. One of them was elected a member of the National Congress by an important state of the Union, though this was, juridically speaking, a discrepancy that the new constitution was unable to resolve.

In the past twenty years the Indians have achieved a fairly respected position with national and international public opinion. No doubt they represent something people long for, but they have also gained empathy for the conscious struggle they wage for their rights to land and self-government. However, it seems that in recent years they have been losing part of the public esteem as their demands are confounded by the moral disruption of the Indian agency and the diversionist claims of some urbanized Indians. Indian policy is the loser in all this. We are living through a very special historic moment for the Indian question, a time that brings new hopes but also unexpected dangers, a period of transition whose outcome we cannot yet clearly foresee.

A Bibliographical and Methodological Note

This book seeks to fulfill the task of reinterpreting the relations between the Indians and the Brazilian nation in light of the most important historical data of recent years—the Indian demographic turnaround. It intends to analyze and scientifically announce this event of great significance to the Indians, to Brazil, and to the rest of the world.

This does not mean that I am writing a revision of Brazilian Indian history. I am simply going deeper into some aspects of it so as to extract the sociological and anthropological foundations that might permit us to describe how and why the great majority of Indian peoples were obliterated from the face of the earth and how, nevertheless, a small number of them survived. I will also try to demonstrate how the Indians are determined to revive their cultural power and redesign their history.

I start with a methodological approach that focuses on history not from the point of view of Brazilian society, but from the point of view of the Indians who have survived. This is what motivated the writing of this book. I shall then follow the pathways of the history of Brazil with the eyes of one who lives between two worlds: that of a common Brazilian who is engaged in the intellectual and political conflicts of his time, and that of the Indian—or rather, whatever one can fathom of that world through more than twenty years of field and archival research, personal contacts, meetings, and political activities with individuals of several ethnic groups. For an anthropologist who has lived for months at a time in the villages of the Guajajara (who have more than 380 years of acquaintance with Luso-Brazilian civilization), the Urubu-Kaapor (first contacted in 1928), and among various bands of the Guajá (some of whom still remain autonomous, living away from the control of FUNAI), a rereading of Brazilian history with regard to the Indians reveals a more intimate meaning. The most obscure data, the least informative description, even the fabrications of chroniclers and the bad faith of historians may be understood and interpreted with greater confidence as to the content and the meaning of the Indian presence in this history.

Of course, the perceptive historian is capable of discerning the significance of events to Indian history even without having had personal knowledge of Indian cultures. In Brazil some scholars have done this, specifically João Capistrano de Abreu, João Francisco Lisboa, and Sérgio Buarque de Holanda. But there is much more to be said about the actual experience of living a prolonged residence in an Indian village; of accompanying for weeks the forced march of a people through the forest as they are moved from one territory to another; of attending with the scantiest of medical resources to a flu epidemic that devastates and destroys a handful of men, women, and children; of witnessing the comings and goings of an old Capuchin friar doing missionary work in Indian as well as peasant villages; of sharing the social panic of a people faced with the threat of an imminent attack by local invaders of their land; of becoming involved in altercations with ranchers and small town shopkeepers who are disputing with Indians whom they normally exploit as a matter of course; of attempting to convince stonewalling authorities and bureaucrats of the need for action to help a people survive through hard times; and of living through the tense and ambivalent relationship between Indians and landless farmers. All these experiences have magnified my understanding of facts involving Indian peoples in the history of Brazil. Their presence and weight in the social formation of Brazil become a tangible reality and one's interpretation grows richer and more complete. One can better understand the nature of a "descent," that is, the mass transference of at times more than 1,500 Indians from their lands to Luso-Brazilian towns, as happened so many times during the first three centuries of colonization. Missionary work, wars of extermination, population decreases, the formation of the Brazilian peasantry on the ruins of Indian groups—all these historical events become more legible as if they were contemporary realities.

At any rate, these experiences have become virtually a necessity for anthropological work in the past forty years. To live through them has not always been easy, but it is certainly a cultural privilege that a few of us from this generation of Brazilians (and non-Brazilians) have enjoyed this unique chance of experiencing such intense kinds of fieldwork. One can only expect that it will help advance knowledge of our cultural reality. Often we do not realize that this constitutes a methodological factor of transcendental importance, as it forces the researcher to live in practically one single moment the whole of a historic reality.

It seems no longer necessary, although our anthropology departments insist on following the antiquated model, that anthropological work should begin with a temporary tour de force in the field and conclude with the preparation of a dissertation. Today, in Brazil, one's living objects of research are easy to find, not more than a few hours away by plane, at the most a few days away by boat. They are on the outskirts of cities, in hospitals and medical centers, and even in the corridors of the National Congress. They can be found in the writings and accounts of anthropologists, adventurers, politicians, indigenists, and even the Indians themselves. One should not hurry too much because they will also be available in the future.

This new reality is so lively and compelling that it is disturbing the research strategies and results of accomplished scholars from other countries. Formerly they would come to Brazil with the fantasy of being the first to study a certain people and would return imagining they would be the last ones to write about them, for good or ill. Quite often they disdained any previous information about "his or her people," even data that had been elaborated according to the canons of official methodology. It should come as no surprise, therefore, that years later the living objects of their research step forward to complain that what was said of them is not exactly the case, or has not been so for many years. Knowledge of the ways of a people or of the structure of a society demands renewal, not only because history imposes changes but also because cultures change at their own pace. As a consequence, one cannot avoid using a dialectical approach to anthropological research because both reality and knowledge of reality are dialectic. In addition, one cannot escape from the subjective bias carried by the anthropologist and the time in which he or she is living. Taking these things into consideration, one has to conclude that every social analysis necessarily becomes an interpretation.

On the whole we can feel confident in announcing that in our time Brazilian Indian anthropology can be more daring in the production of knowledge as well as in proposing action to intervene in the Indian reality. Although the production of knowledge is multinational, we should not feel pushed to maintain the same old methodologies as those used for other contexts. The social and political reality involving the Indians is so special that it demands the development of its own methods of knowledge.

THE BRAZILIAN ANTHROPOLOGICAL TRADITION

The state of the art of our knowledge of Brazilian Indians and of their relationship with Brazil is based on the previous work of many people, both from Brazil and from other countries. Brazilian anthropology has a tradition that is rooted in certain basic themes and maintains a clear line of continuity. To begin with we should single out the pioneer work of Curt Unkel Nimuendaju as the modern basis of Brazilian anthropology.

Nimuendaju was a German-born worker who became fascinated with Indians as he read about them in the library of his hometown. He came to Brazil in 1904 and spent the next forty years of his life traveling through an enormous expanse of Brazil's territory. He personally came to know a great number of the extant Indian tribes and witnessed the demise of a few of them. He read widely in Brazilian history, did archival research in many cities throughout the country, and battled incessantly in all possible instances for the Indian cause. His lifelong commitment to the Indians was such that as he became a naturalized Brazilian citizen he adopted as his last name the word *nimuendaju,* which means "the one who made himself a home." In all this, he did not neglect to register the most precious information about these peoples and their histories and to write some of the most fertile analyses and interpretations to be found in Indian anthropological literature.

For many years Nimuendaju exchanged correspondence with several anthropologists throughout the world, especially Robert Lowie of the University of California at Berkeley. Lowie edited and published Nimuendaju's studies on the Eastern Timbira, the Xerente, and the Apinayé, and several articles on these and other Indian groups in the *Handbook of South American Indians.* These classic monographs have become the indispensable groundwork from which dozens of doctoral dissertations and books have been elaborated by Brazilian and American anthropologists. When he died in 1945, in a village of the Tikuna Indians on the upper Amazon River, Nimuendaju left a rich and precious collection of works, the majority of which remain unpublished in Brazil. His monographs on the Guarani, Xerente, Timbira, Apinayé, and Tikuna, and his *Ethnographic Map* constitute the foundations of anthropological knowledge about the Indian peoples. Nimuendaju's life and works provide the keystone for the special research methodology we are now experiencing and represent the exceptional figure of an activist anthropologist.[11]

The other pillar of Indian anthropology, Herbert Baldus, is also a German-Brazilian. Although Nimuendaju had diligently researched Indian history, it was Baldus, working in the Paulista Museum, who dedicated himself to the task of systematizing the sources of Indian history. Besides his many field trips and the publication of scholarly articles and books, especially his work on the Tapirapé, Baldus is best known for the two volumes of his *Critical Bibliography of Brazilian Ethnology* (1951–68).[12] Practically everything published about Indians up to that time is discussed and indexed in this work. Both Baldus and Nimuendaju are pioneers in placing the Indians in the histories that involve them not in an illustrative fashion, as was done in the anthropology practiced at that time, but as an integral part. Indians are studied in their struggles for survival, they are shown losing ground and reacting, being extinguished or fleeing, or changing themselves in function of their own cultural ways and as a result of the duress they are forced to endure.

This conception of anthropology outlined a path to be followed from the late 1940s, and upon which we find the notable work of Florestan Fernandes on the Tupinambá Indians. In his two main books, *The Social Organization of the Tupinambá Indians* and *The Social Function of War in Tupinambá Society,* and in other articles, the Tupinambá are interpreted superficially from a functionalist viewpoint, as if to pay dues to the dominant school of the time, but in fact we see them through a historical methodology. In Fernandes's work the various social institutions of the Tupinambá are analyzed within the complexity of the whole cultural and historic structures that involve them, including their physical and social environment and the confrontation with the newly arrived Portuguese and French. These works convincingly prove that the Tupinambá were not passive in the face of the arriving invaders, but reacted valiantly, and were defeated for reasons that shall be discussed later.[13]

Darcy Ribeiro and Eduardo Galvão are two Brazilian anthropologists who consolidate this Nimuendaju/Baldus tradition in their research and in their dedication to the Indian cause. Besides doing fieldwork as anthropologists they have both worked in the Indian Protection Service (SPI), during the time Marshal Cândido Rondon was still alive. They organized and promoted research projects in many Indian areas and made a point of systematizing ethnographic, historical, cinematographical, and statistical material from SPI Indian posts. They also tried to convince SPI indigenist agents to adopt more anthropologically oriented methods and practices in their day to day activities.

Darcy Ribeiro spent ten years with the SPI (1947–56), during which time he did extensive research on topics relating to religion, art, culture change, and inter-ethnic relations among the Guarani, Xokleng, Kadiwéu, Bororo, Urubu-Kaapor, and Oti-Xavante. In 1953 he founded, as an integral part of the SPI, the Museum of the Indian, whose basic purpose was to confront current and historic anti-Indian prejudice in Brazil. He wrote the arguments for the foundation of the Xingu National Park, a landmark of Brazilian indigenist policy in the 1950s—it constituted the first time that Brazil recognized as Indian territory a large stretch of land of more than three million hectares. The conception of this Indian park highlighted state responsibility toward the survival of the Indians in conjunction with the preservation of the environmental heritage of the nation as a whole.

Ribeiro's main accomplishment at the SPI was to balance the aspirations of the scholar with the action-orientation of the administrator, without making a value judgment as to which should be more emphasized.

The anthropologists who were with him had the same sort of balanced sense of purpose; they were determined to be both anthropologists and indigenists. This was the reason for the fruitfulness of the indigenism practiced in that period. In 1967 the SPI was abolished and replaced by FUNAI, and the combination of anthropologist-indigenist was deliberately split by the military regime. The idea was to facilitate conditions for the manipulation of public opinion and, obviously, to weaken the pro-Indian forces in the country.

Darcy Ribeiro's main work on Indian anthropology, *The Indians and Civilization,* conceived during the mid-1950s but published in 1970, constitutes what is perhaps the most notable interpretative synthesis of knowledge about the Indian peoples and their relations to the formation and development of Brazil in the twentieth century. Its main thesis is based on the general anthropological notion that Indian cultures are a part of the evolutionary process of human societies, but that they are not fossils of former eras of human evolution. They are self-sufficient and integrated by a logic of their own. As they come in contact with different types of culture that may be considered superior from the point of view of economic production, Indian cultures tend to develop or adjust their institutions to integrate them socially and economically with those cultures and societies. This process generally occurs in an unbalanced way where the most powerful society has the upper hand and encroaches upon the weaker one's modes of existence. Indian cultures do indeed change, not in a passive way but as a "transfiguration" that still maintains a core structure of self-identity. They do not assimilate themselves to the dominating culture, for that would be a form of self-destruction. They may be destroyed in that process, however.[14]

The conceptual framework and methodology used in this book can be placed within the scope of the anthropological tradition that we might call the *acculturation paradigm,* a varied set of ideas, propositions, preconceptions, intuitions, analyses, theories, sentiments, and attitudes about the relation between the so-called primitive and the civilized domains. Its origins go back to the Enlightenment, when the *bon sauvage* became a reality in Western thought. Then it passes through and absorbs new themes contained in the theory of evolution, in Darwin, Marx, Durkheim and Malinowski, in positivism, liberalism, and in the idea of progress. Finally it reaches the twentieth century and merges with the conceptions of the new schools of anthropological thought. The acculturation paradigm incorporates all the different propositions that in so many ways announce the eventual and inevitable extinction of Indian cultures and societies as they are confronted with the implacable expansion of Western civilization. Accordingly, Ribeiro's analyses and interpretations are guided by this spirit, as are, for that matter, all studies from this period. Nevertheless, his book is pervaded by a sentiment of indignation and grief, of dismay and hopelessness. In every conclusion reached one can discern the zest of scientific rigor mingled with the humanistic restlessness of the author.

In this context one can understand how and why the concept of *ethnic transfiguration* was formulated. It purports to state that, no matter what they went through, Indian peoples would never be assimilated by Brazilian society. Most of them became acculturated, but as they went through this process they re-created themselves in new cultural syntheses. By emphasizing the capacity to change and maintain an identity of their own, Ribeiro was unconsciously trying to transcend the straightjacket of the acculturation paradigm. With this reasoning he opens the way to rebutting the inevitability of extinction, suggests forms of permanent accommodation to political, economic, and cultural domination, and hopes for a better fate for the Indians.

We cannot disregard the fact that most of Ribeiro's book deals precisely with the description of the many cases of extinction of Indian peoples and that he probably had no idea that the population of many Indian groups was on the increase. It is thus all the more surprising that he concocted a concept that theoretically perceives the possibility for survival among Indian peoples.

However, the concept of ethnic transfiguration was never fully discussed and utilized by other anthropologists. Other ideas and themes that also attempted to explain the new conditions of ethnic survival ended up dominating the studies of interethnic relations in the following years.

Eduardo Galvão is best known for his studies on the religious system of the Amazonian peasant—the *caboclo*—and on his classification of Brazilian Indians in culture areas. Like Nimuendaju, he was a great field researcher, passionate in his craft. He became an anthropologist in practical terms at the age of 18, when, in 1940, the National Museum sent him to deliver documentation supplies to the anthropologist Charles Wagley, who was doing fieldwork with the Tapirapé Indians in the remote Araguaia River region. Galvão and Wagley became friends and from then on they engaged in an intellectual association that was to result in various joint and individual works. Charles Wagley's influence on Brazilian anthropology was to extend for three generations. From the 1940s through the 1970s he did research with the Tapirapé Indians, and he sent many graduate students from Columbia University and the University of Florida to do their theses on Brazilian themes. He visited Brazil almost every year and went around the country organizing joint research projects with Brazilian anthropologists such as Thales de Azevedo, Herbert Baldus, Florestan Fernandes, and Darcy Ribeiro, and with such educators as Anísio Teixeira and Maria Yedda Linhares.

Almost up to his death in 1976, Galvão studied Indian cultures and protested against the military government for ignoring the Indians in its purposes of building highways and hydroelectric plants in the Amazon, and opening up the forest for lumber companies, gold miners, and real estate speculators. He was particularly concerned with the Indians of the Xingu National Park because of the consequences that would ensue from a projected highway that would cross it, and with the infamous TransAmazon Highway, which eventually crossed Indian territories and imposed immediate contact with several of them. In the late 1970s most anthropologists followed suit in this protest, which helped establish in Brazil the view that the Indians are part of the nation, that they deserve to be protected, and that their lands must be maintained.

Galvão's best-known studies concern the question of acculturation and culture change among the Indians of the upper Negro and upper Xingu Rivers. In these two areas several different Indian cultural traditions have established a basic modus vivendi that is shared by all. To explain how this came about, Galvão developed the notion of "cultural compression." He also studied the production and diffusion of material culture traits, such as the bull-roarer, ceramic styles, and some of the principal South American crops. His research on the Amazonian *caboclos* demonstrated that there is a direct relation between their cultural system and that of the Indians from whom they are descended. Some of his articles were published posthumously in the book *Encounter of Societies: Indians and Whites in Brazil*. In one of his most influential articles he classifies Brazilian Indian peoples by cultural areas, a notion created by North American anthropology that sought to understand the similarity of cultures that have different histories and linguistic origins. Taking into account only the extant Indian groups, he proposed eleven culture areas for Brazil. To define culture area he used such criteria as cultural similarity, but not language affiliation, interethnic relations, cultural compression, ecological adaptation, and external contact. He published his study on the Amazonian caboclo in *Saints and Ghosts,* and, together with Charles Wagley, a monograph on the Tenetehara Indians entitled *The Tenetehara Indians: A Culture in Transition*.

While working in the SPI between 1952 and 1955 Galvão, along with Darcy Ribeiro, helped institute the first graduate course in anthropology in Brazil, at the Museum of the Indian. In 1963 he founded and was the first director of the Institute for Human Sciences at the newly created University of Brasília, from which he resigned in 1965, after having been stripped of his political rights.[15]

For our purposes, Galvão's importance resides in his status as the first Brazilian anthropologist and one of the first in the world to explicitly place in doubt the inexorability of the process of extinction of the Indian peoples. This apparently happened in the mid-1950s when he was translating into Portuguese the book that he and Charles Wagley had published on the Tenetehara in 1949. This is how he rephrased the introduction to the translation:

> We concluded then with the statement that within the lifetime of a generation, or a little more, the process of change of this Indian tribal culture to a regional, Brazilian-like one would be just about concluded. This statement attracted quite a bit of criticism. Some considered it optimistic, while others raised serious doubts about the possibility of an assimilative process being carried out. The doubts are well founded. *Many Indian tribes exist today because they have resisted (and there are no indications that they will not resist in the future), the process of integration into the Brazilian peasantry.* In many situations of contact, the outcome is not necessarily an assimilation of the type we have described for the Tenetehara, but a depopulation and demoralization of the Indian society, which, unable to resist the trauma of such an adverse situation, simply disintegrates. The brutal diminution of Indian populations, today reduced to some 100,000 individuals, is an example. Other tribes, thanks to a minimum of favorable conditions, maintain their own culture and organizations, albeit with many elements modified by the influence of Brazilians. It is necessary to put our minds to study the special cases of resistance as well as those of assimilation.[16]

Along with this brilliant insight, Galvão proposed as a program of studies the themes of assimilation and resistance. As it turned out, in the 1950s and 1960s the majority of studies on interethnic relations dealt with questions of assimilation or acculturation. They were done with a more critical perspective and based on a historical and sociological approach of greater density than the classical studies on acculturation and social change of

Anglo-American anthropology. Later on, however, Indian research interests changed to the processes of resistance and ethnic survival, in which the Indians are seen a priori as victors, or at least not as inevitable losers.

In the 1970s Brazilian Indian anthropology had in Roberto Cardoso de Oliveira its most prominent figure, not only because of his publications but mainly because of his influence as a professor and as an important person in the official granting agencies. In the late 1960s he was called to replace Galvão at the Anthropology Department of the University of Brasília. There he coordinated several research projects until he retired and moved to the State University of Campinas. The first type of research projects he directed concerned the theme of assimilation and "caboclization," that is, the process by which Indians become Brazilian backwoodsmen (*caboclos*),which he designated as "studies in interethnic friction." Later he moved to the theme of ethnic resistance, which he pursued through the concept of *ethnic identity.* He proposed that the maintenance of one's ethnic identity should be seen as the basic factor of resistance and survival of Indian peoples.[17]

Many interesting studies were done on Indian ethnic identity in the 1970s and early 1980s. They represent early attempts to explain both the undisclosed Indian demographic turnaround and the rise of Indian political consciousness that was aroused by the encroaching Brazilian economy and society. The theoretical approaches of these studies varied between interactionism and structuralism. Some studies put their emphasis on the search for the cultural or social traits called "diacritical marks," which an ethnic group eventually chooses to distinguish itself and set it apart from others in contexts of interaction—an emphasis defended by the Norwegian anthropologist Fredrik Barth. Others took the structuralist variant raised in the works of Claude Lévi-Strauss and his disciples, according to which social or ethnic identity can be found as a collective extension of the anthropological notion of person. The problem, then, was how to construe this notion in an ethnic group or in any cultural institution.

The concept of ethnic identity served as a basic framework for the studies not only of Indian societies but also of other minorities in the country. A plethora of books and articles were produced to define the notion of a rural community, and to examine what it means to be black in Brazil, what distinguishes an urban cultural niche from another, how sexual minorities fare in a sexist society, and where the new social and political movements are going. Such was the interest and so many were the studies in those years that today people ask whether the fixation with identity was not more of an issue for Brazilians than a problem for the Indians.[18]

The preponderance of studies produced in the 1970s and early 1980s on ethnic identity as a factor of resistance against the homogenizing avalanche of Western culture, although theoretically structuralist or ahistorical in most of the analyses, could not in the end ignore the fact that interethnic relations exist in historical contexts. Manuela Carneiro da Cunha, who carried out her first studies on the notions of person and death among the Krahô Indians, availed herself of a historical approach in her later studies.

Going against the structuralist current and against the Brazilian anthropological establishment we can pinpoint the work of the Marxist-oriented anthropologist Carlos de Araújo Moreira Neto. In the book *Indians in Amazônia: From Majority to Minority,* and in a number of studies that are still unpublished or little known, Moreira Neto analyzes the demise of Indian peoples as a result of a deliberate policy of the colonial project, something he feels is still going on in the present. His method is to present the Indians acting and reacting to the external world with a partial consciousness of their reality, but in a way that is not much different from ours. From this point of view one should try to understand the Indians by an act of self-reflection and in an open dialogue with them. The Indians may be considered different and be regarded as the Other, as structuralists purport, but they are also similar to us. Like ourselves, they are inside history, somewhat at a loss in figuring out how to be free of it.[19]

There is no doubt that Brazilian anthropology, with regard to the study of inter-ethnic relations, has reached a valuable level of analysis and interpretation. Making allowances for the differing proportions in size of ethnic populations and the respective political weights thereof, it measures up to Mexican anthropology, even regarding the political commitment to the objects of research. However, as we examine it more closely, we can see that Brazilian anthropology reveals a significant gap that needs to be filled or repaired. In the last twenty years comparatively few monographs have been written with the traditional purpose of describing Indian cultures. Moreover, they concentrate on a restricted number of Indian peoples and deal with singular aspects of their cultures. Many of the recent monographs are variations or revisitations of older studies, such as those produced by Nimuendaju during his many years of research among the Timbira, Xerente, Tikuna, and Guarani. Quite often it seems as if they are written to argue or demonstrate some fashionable theoretical novelty of doubtful relevance that few people are interested in. The result is that we end up having information that is less trustworthy than that which existed previously.

There are several reasons why we suffer this gap. We should recognize, to begin with, that good ethnographies can only be made with good linguistic studies, and many anthropology departments lack the proficiency in that discipline to teach their students. Another reason stems from the fact that in recent years there has arisen a concentrated effort on the part of the anthropologist-citizen with studies to bring to light the survival potentialities of the Indians. All the same, there is an important reason why this ethnographic gap has not been bridged: it is because the Indians and the Indian movements have begun to feel and demonstrate a certain rejection of anthropologists, be they Brazilian or foreign. Doing research frequently takes much longer than was originally deemed necessary simply because the anthropologist becomes involved with political issues, takes sides, has to leave the village, or finds it difficult to negotiate his or her residence back in the village.

There are dozens of Brazilian Indian groups that need to be examined more closely, in terms of what they think of their world, of the knowledge they produce, of their lifestyles, and undoubtedly in terms of their perspectives for survival. The task of writing monographs, one of the fundamental poles of anthropological knowledge, does not necessarily have to be done in the traditional mold conceived and formalized at the beginning of the century. To better understand present-day Indian peoples it is necessary to include in one's theoretical framework the political and cultural conditions of Brazil, including the analyses made within the Brazilian anthropological tradition. A more workable methodology must be conceptualized and forged to work as an instrument to integrate history and structure not only in the analyses and theories about interethnic relations, but about culture itself.

An ethnography need not be exclusively descriptive and static, nor must it be dominated by an excessive search for ethnographic novelties. This virtual mania of our discipline sometimes makes it impossible for another anthropologist to gauge the data collected because of their exotic and bizarre contents. The singularity of cultures and peoples should be understood as part of human diversity, but one also has to take into account their universality.

In this book we conceive of culture as a human relation with both conscious and unconscious conditions, controlled both by a collectivity and by individuals. As we contextualize this dialectic within a historical perspective, we transcend those theories that make a point of differentiating Indians from civilized peoples, of reducing the former to the status of inferior beings, and of stating that they are dominated by prelogical forms of thought or by immutable and historic precepts.

This book does not mean to defend a theoretical proposition, but it does not see itself as a mere description of events. It has the purpose of demonstrating that a historical and dialectic approach can explain more adequately the meaning and the consequences of the existence and permanence of the Indian peoples in Brazil. I have applied the expression "Indian question" to represent the totality of the process of relationship between the Indian peoples and the social forces that surround them, in Brazil and elsewhere. These two confronting entities are conceived to be linked to one another, forming a structure of relations on a temporal axis. The Indian question derives meaning from history, from a conscious and an unconscious self-reflection, and from connections with the entire range of peoples and cultures of the world. The explanation for the survival of the Indian or for his or her extermination is a regional matter, but follows from this conceptual framework.

Here I intend to analyze what happened to the Indians in times past. It is not an edifying story to tell. I shall look into their struggles, their defeats, and also their small, but significant, victories. I want to read this history from the point of view of both the Indians and Brazilian civilization. Most of all, I am concerned with the Indians in terms of their present and future perspectives. This is a book that is necessarily impregnated with sentiments of indignation and a refusal to accept the present situation. It wishes to point encouragingly to a glimmer of hope. Based on recent data and on a new historic interpretation I feel confident in announcing that the Indians are not going to die out. Having this in mind, our duty is to face the negative and positive sides of the status quo and try to perceive the possibilities for the future.

1

The Indian in History

A Living Paradise

The discovery of America unleashed ancient fears and renewed hopes for Europeans. Living in a time that had not yet liberated itself from Catholic hegemony and grappling with religious conflicts that presaged more constraints and less freedom, the European beheld this vision of a new humanity as something dazzling and out of this world. Brazil was discovered on April 22, 1500, by a Portuguese armada commanded by Pedro Álvares Cabral. Also with this armada was the official chronicler Pero Vaz de Caminha, who reported to King Manuel with the first account of the newly found land. He could not contain himself with what he beheld: the shimmering beaches, the dense forests, the serene river mouths, the bounteousness of the land, the amazing men and women striding around in their natural nudity, laughing openly and candidly proposing a dialogue.[1]

This enchantment was intense but short-lived. It lasted precisely until the moment when the sojourning became business. It was barely sufficient to kindle among Europeans the recurrence of their subliminal dreams of felicity and plenitude. French, Norman, Breton, Dutch, English, Irish, and German sailors who one way or another landed on this tropical land brought back to their countries impressive tales of this paradise that seemed without malice or dishonor, filled with tranquillity and abundance, with equality and generosity of all and for all. However, there was a strange blemish: the Indians practiced anthropophagy, or cannibalism—the ritual killing and eating of an enemy. This custom appeared to European eyes as not only aberrant in nature, but also naive and senseless.

Thomas More, in his *Utopia* (1518), was the first European to epitomize the paradigm of social happiness as a lost ideal to be found on some far-off, tropical island in the Atlantic. The way of life he described was based on the stories he collected from sailors coming back from the Brazilian coast, as well as from the letters of Amerigo Vespucci, which had become widely read in the early 1500s. Many other writers would take up their pens in a similar vein, using data they had themselves gathered or borrowed from others. As they likened this vision to their own existence, they related it to their past and projected it onto a fancied future.

The insightful essay by French philosopher Michel de Montaigne, "On Cannibals" (1574), was perhaps the most remarkable humanistic and relativistic analysis ever written on the Tupinambá and drew a fascinating profile of these Indians. Contrasting their anthropophagy with the massacres and tortures that were occurring in Europe because of the wars between Catholics and Protestants, Montaigne could not help coming to a judgment more favorable to the Tupinambá custom. Although Europeans were steadfastly beginning to focus on the rest of the world through their own image and likeness, Montaigne's surprising discernment was to remain on the scene and influence a continuous stream of thinkers down to the Enlightenment and beyond. They were to uphold the ideals of freedom and brotherhood, the spirit of tolerance, respect, and intellectual curiosity that became the secular additions to the millennial traditions of the Old World.[2] Thus was created the utopian myth.

For the Indians, the paradise was not a myth. It was a physical and cultural reality made up of hundreds of ethnically diversified but socially similar groups that were in political turmoil. It had taken several thousand years for them to develop to that point of demographic expansion and political complexity, but in previous times they had had more hierarchical cultures, especially in the lower Amazon.[3] Many distinct ethnic groups were living in a situation of trade and close contact, each at its own pace and mode of development, moved by an impelling force that still eludes modern anthropology.

All along the Brazilian coast, from the mouth of the Amazon down to Patos Lagoon, and on the lower reaches of the main rivers there were around one million Tupinambá.[4] They dominated this expanse of land living in villages of between three hundred and one thousand persons. Each village was economically self-sufficient and banded together with the rhythm of an ineffable sentiment of tradition and fidelity, a set of rules of kinship, and the immediate interest of mutual defense. Several factors worked against the formation of tight-knit alliances and in favor of dispersion and autarchy. For one, the economic self-sufficiency of villages was bound to an extensive ecological uniformity that discouraged economic specialization. Second, the lack of any seriously menacing foes sustained the Tupinambá in this enormous geographical expanse with a large but scattered population. These factors lowered the pressure for organizing themselves into more complex and regimented forms of social life. As a consequence, fighting occurred mostly within the ethnic group itself, and took on airs of ritualized feuding and then cannibalism. Alliances between villages were of short duration, easily broken at one end only to be remade along other lines, with other partners. The Portuguese, French, and Dutch did not take long to find out about this situation and soon learned how to take advantage of it. Lack of cohesive alliances was indeed the most vulnerable point of the Tupinambá political system.

Tupinambá infighting was intense. By the early 1500s they were the indisputable lords of whatever region they occupied. Fighting one another without any purpose of conquering new territories or making slaves may have been the main reason for the appearance of cannibalism. Tupinambá cannibalism thus functioned as a kind of refined endocide, since the preferred victims were one's fellow compatriots. Prisoners were secured in battles or sorties by the simple gesture of touching their shoulder with one's hand. With this the warrior would become a captive and be taken to the village of his captor, who became his master. For as long as he lived in the village, until the day of his death agony (or of his supreme honor, as the occasion was perceived), the captive was treated as a brother-in-law by his master and as an affinal relative by the rest of the villagers. He was given a woman to help him in his chores and share his hammock, and she might conceive a child by him, even fall in love with him. He would never choose to flee to his home village: should he do so, he would be very badly received by his relatives, as a poltroon and unworthy of the moral fiber of a Tupinambá.

Some weeks or months after the capture a feast would be summoned for the anthropophagic ritual. Messages would be sent to allied villages, and on the set day they would be received with full honors. The captive knew his day was coming by the arrangements that were made preceding the ceremony. When everything was prepared, he had his body painted suitably. His executioner was dressed in full attire. The ritual would begin with a stylized duel between the victim and his executioner in the arena of the village. The slayer held a powerful war club, while the captive was tied at the waist by a rope held by two opposite parties of men, so that he might not escape nor have much room to dodge the blows. The victim had the right to insult all present calling them mean and weak, pledging vengeance from his relatives, and if possible throwing rocks and sand upon his executioner. As he faltered and weakened a powerful club would strike his head and, if necessary, a coup de grace was performed. Afterwards, the frenzied crowd would yell in excitement around the fallen body, which would be immediately cleansed, gutted, and butchered like game and set to roast over a slow fire. The captive's flesh was avidly craved—above all, it is said, by the old women. Since it was shared by all the participants, not more than a morsel would be available to each person.[5]

Such a custom could only function if the captive-victim agreed to these terms. A member of any other Indian group that did not share the same ideals and sentiments would have not the slightest scruple in absconding from this temporary good life and returning home as a hero. With the Portuguese and other Europeans as victims, the cannibalistic ritual became a kind of farce, and it was with contempt that the Tupinambá dispatched these whimpering, kneeling implorers.

The living paradise of the Tupinambá provided them with an abundance of nurture both to meet their vital needs and for the sheer joy of living. It allowed them to laugh at the French who came from so far away to gather red dyewood.[6] The Atlantic coast of Brazil was apparently so rich and boundless that the Tupinambá could afford to suddenly abandon everything—villages, fields, hunting and fishing grounds—and take the paths to the west in search of Marey Y, the "Land Without Evil." The social paradise was constituted by a system of economic equanimity, wide personal freedom, and shared power that gave opportunities to everyone, by age or by merit, to reach the most acclaimed positions. This paradise contained its own negation, however: the absence of a mechanism with the capacity to bring together autarchic forces, to provide them with a stronger sense of nationality, and to create a more cohesive and less fragmented social and political system. The Tupinambá were unable to do what other peoples with smaller populations managed to accomplish.

Upon the arrival of the Portuguese, the Tupinambá's internecine wars and cannibalism intensified. They sometimes refrained because of the presence of the famous caraíbas or pajé-guaçu, their great shamans or prophets, who had the right to sojourn in any village, and thus to travel without any constraints. The political role of the caraíbas in sixteenth-century Tupinambá society is still cause for controversy. Did they function as prophets of a new, more hierarchized era, or were they the society's voice against the war chiefs who represented a new type of power, that is, the possibility of the formation of chiefdom? As a caraíba went around the villages of a certain region he might prophesy a better life in some place to the west, perhaps in heaven, and exhort everyone to join and take up the holy quest by means of dancing, singing, and fasting. There are accounts of several exoduses, and many others must have occurred without being registered in history. One of them began in the early1530s, from the Pernambuco coast, with some ten thousand to fourteen thousand people. They crossed the whole expanse of northern Brazil, traversed the Amazon river, where other Indians attacked them, and, in 1538, they finally reached the Andes at Chachapoya, no more than three hundred strong.

The search for a heavenly paradise meant that something was amiss in the earthly one. Such was the political conundrum the Indians experienced. Nonetheless, it can be said that the life of the Tupinambá was in many senses qualitatively superior to that of the majority of the Portuguese people.[7] It was, by any measure, a life of abundance and personal gratification. Tupinambá elders lived to advanced ages (up to 100 or 120 years, as some chroniclers naively report). Every man had the right to stand up and speak in the assemblies and councils. Between leader and follower there reigned such equality that the greatest honor for a war chief was simply "to walk in front of his men"[8] and have several wives, the latter not being an exclusive privilege. Furthermore, their level of economic production satisfied their wants without damaging the quality of their environment.

The wide distribution of the Tupinambá was recognized by all who visited them. Their culture was incredibly homogeneous, as was their language. Names such as Carijó, Tamoio, Tupiniquim, Temiminó, Caeté, Potiguara, Tobajara, or Tabajara, were almost all patronymic or terms for familial relationships. For instance, tamoio means "grandfather"; temiminó, "grandson." The word tupy means "first father," that is, ancestor, and tupinambá probably means "relative of the ancestors." Why the Portuguese and French chose to call some local groups "Tupinambá," and others "Tupiniquins" or "Tamoios" is not clear, and it has definitely made things confusing. However, it seems to be linguistically adequate and proper that the generic names of these Indians have remained in history as "Tupy" and "Tupinambá."

At any rate, never did any of these terms represent separate nations or peoples, nor geographic subdivisions or political units. On some occasions political alliances with some degree of stability were formed, such as the famous Tamoio Confederation, a confederation of Tupinambá villages that fought against the Portuguese in Rio de Janeiro, or the union of villages of the island of São Luís in present-day Maranhão. These political arrangements showed possibilities for a greater degree of hierarchy, but such never came about. The example of São Luís island reveals the heterogeneous composition of the federated villages. Some had come from the Potengi, on the northeast coast, and others from Itamaracá, approximately three hundred kilometers to the south. They could have been enemies in their former territories. The unstable character of this federation revealed itself when, once defeated by the Portuguese and their Indian allies, the villages broke up and dispersed across the forests of Pará.

On the other hand, names such as Aimorés, Goitacazes, Guaianases, Janduis, Cariris—in short, the *Tapuia,* as the Tupinambá and Portuguese called them in colonial times—and, later, the Puris, Coroados, Botocudos, Kayapó, and others were not Tupinambá. Their languages and cultures were different and their populations were smaller, although some Kayapó villages are said to have as many as two thousand people. They were no match for the Tupinambá. In fact, according to Indian lore of the sixteenth century, several of these peoples were the earlier inhabitants of the coast and had been expelled from there by the Tupinambá. Most of them moved inland and, in consequence, few made contact or alliance with the Europeans.

In the Amazon, there were many non-Tupinambá peoples living in denser populations who controlled strategic stretches of bountiful land. Some of them made alliances with the English, Irish, and Dutch who attempted to establish colonies and commercial outposts there during the first three decades of the seventeenth century. In the northeast, non-Tupinambá peoples lived in the backlands. They were of Jê and Kariri linguistic affiliation and became known by names such as Jandui, Otchukayana, Jeicó, Inhamuns, and others. Some descriptions of these people were made by Dutch backwoodsmen and by Capuchin friars, but the ethnographic accounts that did survive are rather poor in quality. Thus we know relatively little about Tapuia peoples. We would have to wait practically until the nineteenth century for the naturalists to renew the ethnographic curiosity of Europeans and Brazilians vis-à-vis the Indians.

Without full comprehensive knowledge, it can nonetheless be said that socially and politically the Tapuia were not all that different from the Tupinambá. They were no match in warfare, but defended themselves as best they could and as their population contingents allowed. According to the accounts of such chroniclers as Gabriel Soares de Souza (1587), André Thevet (1560), Fernão Cardim (1584), and others, they were numerous as autonomous peoples, but their demographic density was not impressive. Soares de Souza enumerates more than 150 peoples, the great majority of them Tapuia, merely in the regions he knew, such as the backlands of Bahia, Pernambuco, and parts of the captaincies of Rio de Janeiro, São Paulo, Ceará, and Piauí. If we include all the other regions of Brazil except the Amazon, we may hypothetically calculate this population at more than one million people.

The Amazon, by the accounts of the navigators of the great river beginning with the Spanish adventurer Francisco Orellana, was very densely populated. Three million persons is not an exaggerated number. As a total, therefore, we can hypothetically estimate that there were some five million Indians living in the territory of what is now Brazil.[9]

On the island of Marajó, at the mouth of the Amazon River, and on the lower Tapajós River, the Aruans, Nheengaíbas, Tapajós, and other Indians were descendants of peoples who had sustained more complex cultures than those existing in the sixteenth century. Ceramics and ceremonial structures that survived deterioration for five to ten centuries were sophisticated and expressive, reflexes perhaps of more cohesive and ranked political organizations. When the Europeans arrived, however, these cultures no longer existed. The reasons behind their demise are still unclear, much as are the reasons behind the downfall of Mayan civilization. The record shows divergent archeological explanations and even supernatural speculations.[10] In the early 1600s, when Irish, Dutch, and Portuguese attempted to establish trading posts in this territory, the populations of the lower Amazon tribes, as well as those along the Amazon, were still high. They benefitted from a high level of agricultural productivity, with fields irrigated by the ebb and flow of the rivers, from a high intake of fish, and even the semi-domestication of river turtles.[11]

In sum, from the Tapajós and Omáguas Indians of the Amazon region (organized economically and politically at a level that went beyond the tribal but did not quite reach the chiefdom level), to the classically tribal Tupinambá along the Atlantic seaboard, the Tapuya of the Brazilian hinterland, and the scattered bands of Aimorés and Puris of the forests of eastern Brazil (with an itinerant agriculture and a strong dependence on hunting), there were many differences to be noted, even by uninterested administrators and missionaries. Cultural and social differences were also perceived by the Indians themselves. For centuries, these were the only differences they knew of between humankind and nature.

The arrival of the Europeans changed things radically for the Indians as well as for the Europeans. A new world, full of temptations, goods, power, and unspeakable sufferings opened before them. What we know of the journey of the Tupinambá to the Andes, as well as the connection of Inca civilization with tropical peoples by means of the Bolivian Chaco and the Amazon tributaries, makes it evident that there was a political dynamism on the South American continent that was certainly more intense than what is commonly supposed today.

Even the distant coastal Tupinambá knew, at least from hearsay, of Inca civilization and of other forms of intermediary political organization. It would be useless to speculate on whether or not, if left undisturbed for a longer period of time, the Tupinambá might have evolved in the direction of a hierarchical social structure. What is certain is that it was not a matter of political decision to change one's social condition. To be a tribal agriculturist or a nomadic hunter depended on many highly dynamic and interdependent factors. Population size, competition for territory, technological innovations and adaptations, the vastness and broad uniformity of the land, and other factors fused with existing social forms that emphasized freedom and autarchy of local groups whose main lines of organization were flexible kinship rules and the need for self-defense. That is why the Tupinambá, dominant as they were along the coast, maintained their social and cultural ways even at the high price of self-violence.

Freedom and war have been said to be the two poles of tribal philosophy. Freedom from social hierarchy could only be maintained by means of constant warfare. This state of being can be characterized, following Pierre Clastres, by the expression "society against the state"; that is to say, in such cultures the desire to maintain freedom and social equality is stronger than the pressure to accept coercive power and social hierarchy. Thus they repudiate any sort of political institution that might threaten their status quo.[12] If this assertion sounds far-fetched, we can at least recognize that the paradise of freedom and equality is a self-conscious, self-sufficient, and self-sustaining production of human activity. Unfortunately, it is too fragile when confronted by hierarchical power. The Indians of Brazil resisted desperately but were defeated in a little more than a century. Their last great chance for securing some measure of autonomy occurred during the great rebellion known as the Cabanagem (1838–41) when the lower Amazon groups, by then transfigured into a syncretic culture from their long years of missionization and servitude to the colonial regime, fought desperately against the forces of that regime. They were subjugated and their earthly paradise was vanquished, and the Indians remained to survive at best in purgatory.

EXPERIENCES OF COEXISTENCE

The iron ax landed on the new continent as a technological marvel of the enchanted strangers. A widely disseminated myth among various Indian peoples places their culture's hero, their demiurge, as the keeper of agriculture, more precisely as the owner of the axes. In olden times the task of cutting down trees for swidden plots was done automatically by the axes at the command of the demiurge. Humans only had to collect the products as they ripened. Because of the curiosity of a woman, the demiurge stopped ordering the axes to work, and humans had to do the task thenceforth. Another myth relates how the Indians were presented by their demiurge with the option of choosing between iron and wood implements. The trusting Indians preferred the bow, while the whites chose the gun and the machete. Several ergonomic studies have proved that the use of iron axes reduces by more than two thirds the labor time of a stone ax in the task of clearing a swidden plot, for example.[13] Of course, the utility and efficiency of iron tools have always been obvious to the Indians.

Utilitarian iron pulled the Indian toward contact and cohabitation with, and dependence upon, civilization. With this relationship came scissors, knives, mirrors, and colored glass beads. Nothing escaped the interest of the Indian. As these new items were incorporated into the Indian's universe of knowledge and technology, their natural curiosity and eagerness to discover more new things was enhanced.

The Europeans never paid much attention to the reasons and motivations that moved the Indians to relate with them. For Europeans, however, the main motive was economic. Brazilwood was, for the first fifty years after the discovery, the primary source of wealth for those adventurers. The Indians were cajoled with trinkets into working long hours and days to cut down and carry the precious logs of wood to the coast to be loaded onto ships. Even then, however, Portuguese captains began the practice of enslaving Indians they had taken in battles or by buying captives from other tribes. On more than a few occasions, captive Indian slaves were transported to Europe. In 1512, for example, the ledger of the ship *Bretoa* commanded by Cristóvão Pires listed 35 Indian slaves among the ship's merchandise bound for Lisbon. Extant records of expeditions by other non-Portuguese Europeans do not indicate slave transactions, at least not as an item for export. It is possible that they enslaved prisoners of war, but it is more probable that the insecurity of their trade outposts did not allow chattel slavery to become a common type of economic exploitation.[14]

Before installing a general government in Bahia in 1549, the Portuguese tried to establish permanent colonies along the Brazilian coast through a political and administrative system known as *hereditary captaincies*. The country was divided into fifteen areas, which were bestowed as hereditary grants to twelve patricians, including rich bankers, merchants, and nobles, who received the title of *captain*. Only two captaincies ever amounted to much: that of Duarte Coelho, in present-day Pernambuco, and that of Martim Afonso de Souza, in São Vicente, on the coast of São Paulo state. These captains were able to transport and settle colonists on their own, establish the first sugarcane plantations, and bend the neighboring Indians to their power.

In São Vicente, Europeans made alliance with the Tupiniquim Indians through the good offices of João Ramalho, a Portuguese sailor who had somehow been left ashore in the early 1500s. Ramalho had been wise enough to ingratiate himself with the Indians and in his more than forty years of living with them he had actually gone native, having many wives, sons, and daughters, and consequently considerable power. In Pernambuco, there was no alliance, rather the Tabajara Indians were beaten mercilessly. Most of them fled westward.

The other captaincies did not take root, mostly because they were not able to do away with the Indian problem. An example is the captaincy of Porto Seguro, in southern Bahia. For years the captain and his settlers fought the Tupiniquim. But when they seemed to have mastered the situation, the Aimoré Indians, using small, guerrilla-like bands, made incursions to the coast from their territory further inland. These Indian invaders simply responded to the vacuum effectively created by the expelled Tupiniquim, who had moved south to Espírito Santo. Throughout the 1500s the Aimoré were the target of war parties officially appointed by the governor-general. At one point the Portuguese Crown determined that they were "uncivilizable" and could only be dealt with by the force of arms.[15]

On the other hand, most other European adventurers kept their purposes restricted to trading in areas where they could harbor a ship, load it, and set sail as quickly as possible. Usually they would leave some adventurers behind, so that at their return they would have wood ready to load. They tried to keep their trading partners happy and loyal, which was no easy task. The Indians supplied them with logs of Brazilwood and *tatajuba* wood (which yields a yellow dye), cotton fiber, and pets such as monkeys, parrots, and macaws; in exchange they got axes, knives, scissors, glass beads, mirrors, combs, and occasionally cloth and hats.[16] Similar collections of odds and ends are still used as allurement today by the FUNAI teams that attempt to make contact with autonomous Indian groups—an irrefutable proof of Indian fascination with such objects and also of the unchanging character of European-Indian relations.

Many Brazilians are of the opinion that had Brazil been colonized by the French or the Dutch—as could have happened—relations with the Indians might have been less violent, as is supposedly attested by the latter's peaceful conduct in those early years. Indeed, the nature of early French colonization may indicate that there was more dialogue with the Indians than the Portuguese ever had. However, the two more permanent colonization projects they attempted were short-lived. The first one was called "Antarctic France" and was established on Guanabara Bay in present-day Rio de Janeiro; it lasted from 1560 to 1565. The second one was known as "Equinoctial France" and was settled on the São Luís island, in Maranhão state, lasting from 1612 to 1615.

With a time span of fifty years between them, both settlements had similar policies with regard to the Indians. They were both preceded by long years of close trading contact and even of mutual visiting. For instance, in 1555 thirty Tupinambá Indians from Guanabara Bay were taken to Rouen, where they were treated with respect and curiosity. With the assistance of French sailors who knew them they staged an impressive theatrical battle for the delight of the nobility of France. Three of these Tupinambá were baptized and married French wives, and their heirs were recognized with some distinction until at least the following century. Tupinambá from São Luís island were also invited to visit France and some of their young were brought to be educated there.

The Antarctic French colony was settled first by a levy of rugged Bretons and Normans of Catholic extraction. They strove to adapt to Tupinambá culture, taking wives among the young women and participating in tribal life. Some Tupinambá were taken to France, where they were shown off to prospective investors, and they returned to Brazil feigning French airs. It seemed that the colony would take root. The second group of settlers were Protestants sent by the religious leader John Calvin in an agreement with the director of the project. Apparently Calvin had great hopes that a religious community could be created in the New World. As could be expected, the newly arriving Protestants immediately found fault with their Catholic patricians and dispute ensued. On the other hand, it seems that the Tupinambá, some 8,000 strong who at first gladly worked for the French, began to feel encroached upon and voiced their dissatisfaction with the colonists. It is therefore probable that over time the balance of mutual good will would have been lost there.[17]

The same can be said for the colony of Equinoctial France, on the São Luís island. There were 10,000 Tupinambá on the island and 35,000 to 40,000 more along the coast. They too at first seemed contented with the presence of the French but never to the point of completely trusting them. Most of the Tupinambá had had earlier experiences with the Portuguese and knew what could come of it. The accounts published after the demise of the colony by two French Capuchin friars suggest that here the relationship between colonists and Indians would probably also have eventually soured.[18] In short, the French may have been more equanimous with the Indians at first, but if we consider what came to happen in their colonies in the Caribbean and elsewhere, her legacy cannot be said to be in the least enviable.

The Dutch were more successful in establishing a foothold in Brazil. After a frustrated assault in 1621 on Salvador da Bahia, then the capital of Brazil, they managed to conquer a few years later the important port city of Olinda, the capital of the captaincy of Pernambuco, which prided itself of having the most successful sugar-export industry. Sugar at that time was the most profitable commodity—next to slave traffic—in the world. By 1640 the Dutch joint enterprise, banked by both capitalists and the Dutch state, had been so successful that one of their governors, Mauricius of Nassau, founded a new port city, New Amsterdam, which later became known as Recife. From there they spread their power to the captaincies of Alagoas, Paraíba, Rio Grande do Norte, Ceará, and to the northern state of Maranhão.

Despite religious differences and strong mutual biases, the Dutch administrators related fairly well to the established Portuguese elite of plantation owners and tried to build a political alliance with the inland Indians. At that time most of the Tabajara, Potiguara, and Caeté Indians, all of them Tupinambá in culture, who had numbered 150,000 in the sixteenth century, had either been killed off or had migrated to Maranhão and Pará. By 1631 there were only 4,000 male Indians on the coast, from Alagoas to Rio Grande do Norte,[19] and many of those were slaves imported by the Portuguese from the conquest wars in Pará some years before.[20] Thus, the Dutch had actually very little to do with the mighty Tupinambá. It was with the indomitable Tapuia, who lived in the dry backlands of northeast Brazil, that the Dutch entered into political alliance. By the late 1630s a few Dutch backwoodsmen were sent to make contact and get to know these tribes in order to consolidate alliances with them. When the Luso-Brazilian landowners began to organize guerrilla war parties to fight the Dutch, Governor Mauricius of Nassau tried to straighten out the ties with the Tapuia. In 1847 the Dutch convened an assembly of Indians in the town of Itapecerica, near Recife.[21] There was little time left, however, for the Dutch to count on those Indians to fight the Luso-Brazilians, and consequently such a political experiment did not endure.

Contrary to the concepts and practices of the English in North America, the Portuguese never treated the Indians as nations (although the term was used in the royal charts), but as vassals. However, on two occasions the Portuguese Crown found it necessary to sign formal pacts with Indians. The first happened when some villages of the Janduí Indians, the most powerful Tapuia tribe and a former ally of the Dutch, sent a delegation to Bahia to negotiate a peace agreement putting an end to the assaults they had been suffering since the expulsion of the Dutch in 1654. These assaults were planned and ordered by the Portuguese Crown and were so persistent that they became known in Brazilian historiography as the War of the Barbarians. It lasted from the 1650s until 1714, when the last resisting Indian bastion was crushed and the inhabitants killed, enslaved, or gathered in missions and official villages. In 1691 the Janduí delegation traveled a thousand miles to Salvador and formally signed a peace treaty that included the preservation of their lands.[22] Nevertheless, the Luso-Brazilian ranchers who were expanding their cattle estates into Janduí territory took no notice of this treaty, and the Portuguese Crown continued to issue royal charts to pursue Indians who rebelled against their strict orders to keep quiet.

The second occasion for an accord occurred one century later, in 1791. This time it was with the so-called Horseback Indians (Índios Cavaleiros, or Guaicuru, now known as Kadiwéu) and the governor-general of Brazil, who was located by then in the city of Rio de Janeiro.[23] The Portuguese had a strategic interest in maintaining Guaicuru territory, in what is now the state of Mato Grosso do Sul, within Brazilian borders. The Horseback Indians, in the fashion of the Plains Indians of North America, were absolute and unbeatable masters of that territory. The treaty backfired on the Indians and shortly thereafter their lands began to be invaded by cattle ranchers and gold prospectors. They brought with them new strains of smallpox and other diseases that caused a decline in Guaicuru population and consequently their political subjugation. Today the Kadiwéu still maintain a part of their original territory in the Pantanal (the wetlands region of west central Brazil), because of the role as allies they played for Brazil in its war against Paraguay (1865–70). Their present land was granted by Emperor Dom Pedro II as retribution and was confirmed by the Indian agency in the 1920s. However, large tracts of this land are presently rented out to cattle ranchers in the Pantanal. As for the Janduí, they are no more.

WARS OF EXTERMINATION

The most purposeful and prolonged war of extermination in Brazilian history was the War of the Barbarians. After the Portuguese had recovered their independence from Spain in 1642, some of the new king's councilors, especially Father Antônio Vieira, had considered selling off the whole of Northeast Brazil to the Dutch. But the Luso-Brazilian, Creole plantation owners, together with both Indians and free blacks as allies, put up guerrilla resistance against the Dutch until they were able to expel them from their rich sugarcane lands. The Dutch's Indian allies, the Janduí, Jeicó, Otchukayana, and others, were declared traitors and supporters of a possible Dutch comeback. Furthermore, their territory began to be valued by the expanding cattle frontier that was burgeoning after the decline of sugar prices. As conflict broke out, the Crown issued orders to subjugate and even wipe out these Indians. Many official expeditions were sent out and much damage was inflicted upon many of their villages, although they continued to remain strong enough to cause concern to the authorities. At one point, the captain-general of Pernambuco called upon Domingos Jorge Velho, a rambunctious and powerful *bandeirante,* or Indian slaver, to be military commander for the whole captaincy.

Born of São Paulo, Velho had a numerous company of Indian *mamelucos,* or half-castes, and had already carried out significant carnage throughout the country, especially in the scrublands of Piauí, where he had conquered more territory for himself than he had been awarded in prizes and land grants.[24] However, although Velho went into Indian territory and made a few assaults upon scattered villages, he did not finish with the rebellious Indians because his mission was diverted to attack and destroy runaway slave settlements that had been established in Alagoas. The famous Quilombo dos Palmares, a confederacy of villages organized by black leaders, was razed to the ground by Velho after nearly seventy years of existence.

After destroying Palmares, Velho went back to Piauí, where he set up cattle ranches and went on destroying Indian villages. Other equally violent Indian slavers continued Velho's tradition in the following two centuries. The Gueguês, Acroás, Pimenteiras, Gamelas, and Xavante endured the brunt of extermination wars through the 1700s and early 1800s. Some tribes like the Gamela and Xavante fled westward toward the captaincy of Maranhão and beyond. Most often when Indian villages were attacked, the adult males would be killed, while the young and women would be taken as slaves and distributed among cattle ranches. Many of these ranches became the property of the Jesuit Order, received in bequest by the family of the famous Casa da Torre, which at the time encompassed a large part of Piauí.[25]

In colonial times, wars against Indians were carried out to obtain slaves and/or to castigate audacious Indian groups, but their main purpose was to clear land for colonization. Although only in the case of Indians considered "uncivilizable" were wars explicitly referred to as wars of extermination, most wars had the purpose not only of breaking down Indian resistance but also of wiping out entire ethnic groups or settlements in a given region.

In each territory explored and slated for colonization there ensued new wars of extermination. The first such explicit war began in Bahia in 1558, when governor-general of Brazil Mem de Sá crushed Tupinambá rebellion, killing between 15,000 and 30,000, with the complacency and encouragement of all.[26] After the expulsion of the French from Rio de Janeiro in 1565, there followed a war of extermination against the Tupinambá of Cabo Frio and the Paraíba do Sul valley.[27] In northeast Brazil the conquest of Paraíba, beginning in 1585, required the incitement of Tupinambá rivalries, and finally the persecution and killing off of the rival faction that had previously been allied with French traders.[28] The conquest of Maranhão, beginning in 1614, led a few years later to the massacre of some 30,000 Tupinambá Indians who lived between the island of São Luís and what is now the city of Belém. In the words of an official chronicler, the Portuguese man of arms and later captain-general of the state of Maranhão and Grão Pará, Bento Maciel Parente, had, with the slaughter perpetrated against those Tupinambá, "extinguished the last relics of that people."[29]

For the conquest of the lower Amazon, it was necessary to make use of all the ways and means acquired during the previous century regarding techniques of war, imprisonment, and instigation of Indian rivalries. Jesuit Father Antônio Vieira accuses the Portuguese of having wiped out two million Indians in four hundred villages in the period between 1616 and 1656,[30] but there could not have been that many Indians in the region designated. One-fourth of that number is possible, if we take into account the reports of Orellana and others who first visited the Amazon River a century before.[31] On the island of Marajó alone, there were still some forty thousand Indians when Vieira attempted to promote peace during the decade he lived in that region. By then there had already been many deaths, since those Indians had previously served as a shield against the intentions of the Irish and the Dutch of establishing trade posts and colonies in the region.[32]

The tragedy of the Indians of the lower Amazon and the lower Rio Negro rivers was completed with the Cabanagem in 1841, when the defeat of that rebellion led to one of the greatest bloodbaths in Brazilian history. At its end, only the Maué remained as a surviving Indian group living along the lower Amazon, a situation that can only be compared to the northeast after the War of the Barbarians.[33]

In short, wars of extermination were part of Portuguese Indian policies from beginning to end. In the last years of colonization, as the Portuguese Crown fled toward Brazil upon Napoleon's invasion of Lisbon, prince regent Dom João issued several royal charters to promote the so-called "War Against the Botocudos" of the Doce and Mucuri river valleys, in the present states of Minas Gerais, Espírito Santo, and Bahia. The charters determined that any person was allowed to set up a war party to find and kill these Indians, to take them as captives and slaves for fifteen years, and to usurp their lands. New charters were issued against the Timbira Indians of Maranhão and the so-called Coroados of Paraná, whose lands were in the way of new economic frontiers.[34]

These royal measures remained valid during the first years after independence. Several of the new provinces that had rebellious Indians organized official war parties and promoted private campaigns against them. Once again the term "uncivilizable" was used for the Mura of the middle Amazon and the Avá-Canoeiro of the upper Tocantins River, in the state of Goiás, even after the charters had been revoked, in 1831. Later in that century, the Coroado Indians, now known as Kaingang and Xokleng, in southern Brazil, suffered intermittent assaults by the so called *bugreiros*, or "Injun hunters," a type of vigilante death squad specializing in Indians.[35] Indian groups living in areas of tree gums, native rubber, Brazilnuts, and other extractive products were battered by similar groups throughout the nineteenth century and up until the first decades of this century. In all cases these forays were financed by private companies and local potentates.[36] In rangeland areas, such as the scrublands of Goiás and Maranhão, expeditions by ranchers were frequent and devastating. In 1913, of a village of 130 Canela Indians in southern Maranhão, some 60 of them were killed by gunshot and machete blows, after local ranchers had gathered them up for a party of barbecue and drinking.[37]

I do not intend to recount all the massacres that have been perpetrated against Indians in this century, nor number the attempts that were frustrated or only partially successful. One cannot affirm that history continues to repeat itself, but the records show that there is not a complete cut-off from the past. A few examples will suffice to make the point clear.

A most poignant case is that of the Avá-Canoeiro Indians of the scrublands of Goiás. In the early 1800s they numbered some 2,000 people living on the banks of the upper Tocantins River, a region that had been little populated until the previous thirty to forty years. They were then declared uncivilizable by the Crown and from then on suffered periodic attacks by official war expeditions. Their numbers decreased to some 450 people by the beginning of the twentieth century. They continued to be hit by local ranchers and their hired hands, and their numbers continued decreasing, as did their control over their territory. The Indian agency tried to make contact with them from 1920 until the late 1950s but was unsuccessful. As late as 1961, when Brasília, the country's new capital, was being built some 130 miles to the south, a new wave of ranchers and settlers came into Avá-Canoeiro territory. The result was new conflict and more massacres, none of which was ever deemed to be cause for criminal prosecution. A small group of 13 Avá-Canoeiro was contacted in 1973, but half of them have died since. Another small group of 4 was contacted in 1983 and they now number only 6 people. It is probable that there are still three or four very small groups wandering around the remote reaches of those lands that are now in the hands of Brazilians.

Another well-known case is the massacre of the Cintas-Largas Indians of the state of Rondônia, in western Amazon. It happened in 1963, when a group of *bugreiros* led by a former employee of the Indian agency was hired by lumber and rubber companies to finish the job of exterminating a village of Cintas-Largas Indians. The village was first attacked by an airplane that dropped dynamite bombs; a few days later the gunmen showed up. Three years later, photos of Indians being butchered appeared in the press, causing great public indignation. An inquiry commission was set up in the Congress to investigate the origins of this and other scandals. In the end, the military government found it easier to extinguish the Indian agency, the SPI, and substitute a new one, FUNAI, and the case was closed.[38]

More recently there have occurred the 1987 killing of fourteen Tikuna Indians by loggers of the upper Amazon river, and the massacre of eighteen Yanomami, in July, 1993, by gold prospectors. All of these crimes—old and new, official and private—are recognized today as ethnocide. They imply not only the destruction of human beings, but of the cultural bases that constitute them and give their lives meaning and support.

DEADLY EPIDEMICS

More devastating yet, according to the appraisal of historians, were the epidemics of diseases brought by Europeans and Africans. Smallpox, measles, chicken pox—with their indelible pockmarks—tuberculosis, yellow fever, and the various strains of flu devastated entire villages, entire peoples. Many times these victimized peoples did not even come into contact with the primary sources of contamination. They would receive the viruses and bacteria secondhand through contact with other Indians, often times in the most casual of encounters.

The American peoples—who originated from a few migrant bands that crossed the Bering Strait land bridge from Asia, probably during a period between 30,000 and 60,000 years ago—evolved their immunological system in a different fashion from that of the inhabitants of other continents, who through the ages maintained contact with each other. Since America was virtually an isolated continent, its inhabitants did not develop resistance to diseases originating in other parts of the world. This situation led to their tragic fragility.[39]

To account for the virulence in the diseases cited above, it is critical to link this biological factor of destruction with an important sociological factor. Devastating epidemics occur in the context of social convulsions that undoubtedly intensify the epidemics' potency. Thus, whenever their occurrence was associated with wars of extermination or enslavement, the results were always worse for the Indian. For example, during the five years or more in which the French lived in Guanabara Bay with Tupinambá allies, only one epidemic is reported to have caused any significant human damage. After the Portuguese attacked the French and their Tupinambá allies in a war of extermination, however, epidemics broke out with great virulence. Likewise, the great epidemics in Bahia were more devastating following the war of extermination carried out by Mem de Sá. The same is true for the major epidemics that took place in São Paulo, Maranhão, and Pará.[40]

Even in periods without war, epidemics broke out frequently and some lingered for years. One is reported to have lasted from 1743 to 1750 in all the immediate region of the lower Amazon.[41] The potency of an epidemic is, of course, enhanced when it erupts in times of food scarcity. Starvation can easily hasten the death of the ailing and weaken the healthy. Some anthropologists and Indian agents have witnessed such tragic moments. Darcy Ribeiro describes a dramatic case of a measles epidemic he witnessed among the Ka'apor Indians in 1949. Of an original population of 600, some 180 died in two months' time, and many more would have died if it had not been for the aid he and other researchers were able to provide.[42]

Epidemics still occur but generally with less virulence, probably for two reasons. One is that the surviving Indians have acquired a better adapted immunological system than their ancestors. Second, in Brazil—and elsewhere for that matter—today's sanitary control of epidemics is far superior due to the many vaccination campaigns undertaken in the last fifty years.

When the etiology of epidemics and the means of contamination were discovered, Portuguese and Brazilians felt no scruples in making use of this knowledge to promote the extermination of Indian peoples who stood in their path. This most cruel type of warfare is known today as bacteriological warfare. The first time it was employed in Brazil was in 1815, in the town of Caxias, Maranhão, the native land of the famous Indianist poet, Gonçalves Dias. A smallpox epidemic was spreading through the region when a band of Canela Indians (Capiekrans) came to town on a visit. Local authorities made a distribution of gifts and clothes previously contaminated by the sick. The Indians contracted the disease, and on becoming aware of the nature of their contagion, fled into the forest. The survivors contaminated others, and months later the epidemic had reached the Indians living in the Tocantins region.[43]

At the end of the nineteenth century, bugreiros of Santa Catarina and Paraná, hired by immigration companies, adopted the method of leaving blankets infected with measles and smallpox at trading points as gifts to the autonomous Indians of the region.[44] Thus the Indians would be killed and land would be cleared for new settlers.

Programmed outbreaks of epidemics truly represent the apex of a perverse spirit of extermination and ethnocide. That this was done in Brazil against its original inhabitants is an ignominious illustration of the country's amoral political character.

SLAVERY AND SERVITUDE

An honorable fate did not await the survivors imprisoned in wars. Personal slavery or compulsory servitude was more the rule than the exception, especially in the early period of colonization prior to the massive use of African slaves. The missionaries protested against this practice at various times and were sometimes able, through their pressure upon Crown magistrates, to change slavery laws, abolishing them or partially reducing their effects during some periods. The colonists availed themselves of every loophole in these laws to keep their slaves. As a last appeal for enslavement, there was always the excuse of the so-called "just wars" that could be perpetrated against Indian peoples who were menacing colonial expansion in certain areas. Out of these wars, colonists—and even the Crown and missionaries—would obtain labor for their domestic tasks and for work in the sugarcane and tobacco fields.

Father Antônio Vieira, who bravely fought against the interests that sought to enslave Indians, participated as the obligatory clergyman in one of the countless expeditions to bring down or "descend" (descimento) free Indians from their territories to the colonization centers on the coast. His was an expedition up the Tocantins River in 1654 that "descended" some 1,500 Tupi-speaking Indians, apparently not Tupinambá, to Belém. From there this human chattel was distributed to the newly created missions, royal administrative villages, and private plantations. After 1686 in the main administrative towns, councils were established as a type of court to settle all Indian issues. These councils (juntas de missões) were constituted by representatives of the clergy, the Crown, and the colonists, who judged on the justness and legitimacy of Indian descent expeditions, slave expeditions, and just wars. They also decided to whom the newly descended Indians should be allocated. Once a descent was made the councils usually accepted the justifications for the condition of Indian enslavement proposed by their captors.[45]

One of the articles that made up the so-called Directory of Pombal, a law promulgated in 1757, extinguished Indian slavery and decreed the unconditional freedom of all Indians. But in 1808 the regent Dom João reinstated slavery in the case of the Botocudo Indians and extended it for other Indians, until it was revoked by the so-called law of the orphans, in 1831.[46]

As far as the Indians of colonial times were concerned, servitude, rather than personal slavery, was the more common form of economic exploitation. It functioned in administrative villages where groups of Indians were allocated to serve the town chambers or the officials of the king in such tasks as road construction, production of food monopolized by the Crown, or even as warriors in campaigns against other Indian peoples or foreign invaders. One can also say that the form of socioeconomic relation that existed in the missions was, likewise, closer to servitude than to slavery or cash labor. Under this social regime the Indians lived as vassals in a feudal system: they had the right to cultivate their own farm plots, so long as they did not neglect the provision of services for their masters as needed.[47] Accordingly, many Indian villages were fixed in locations near Portuguese settlements and towns. Several survived for long periods of time, and a few lasted until the twentieth century, when they were engulfed by the country's demographic expansion. São Miguel Paulista and Pinheiros, which today are districts of the city of São Paulo, São Lourenço (in Niteroi), Vinhaes (in São Luís), Caucaia (in Fortaleza), and others were old Indian villages that maintained this form of relationship with the encroaching Luso-Brazilian towns.

From the Indian's point of view, servitude was a relationship imposed by the Portuguese as a form of domination over them collectively, as a people. Slavery, on the other hand, entails a one-to-one relationship, does not recognize a community as such, and simply reduces Indians to the condition of chattel labor. From the colonist's standpoint, servitude seemed to be an advantage for the Indians, a form of "civilizing" them. The obligation to perform certain tasks would impose on these servants the needed qualities of discipline, probity, and respect for order. This happens also to be the ideological root of paternalism, the subsequent form of interethnic relationship that was to prevail in the aftermath of the abolition of slavery and servitude.

A Different Religious Experience

The Indians of Brazil have neither faith, law, nor royalty, claimed the Portuguese of the sixteenth century, as indeed their language supposedly lacked the sounds corresponding to *f, l,* or *r.* As a matter of fact, while they certainly possessed no king, they abided by law, as do every people of the world. We have seen how their social system, where law is concerned, was disregarded by the Portuguese. Now we shall see how their religion and their faith appeared in the eyes of the invaders, and how it was later remolded by Christian beliefs over five centuries.

It did not go unnoticed by the missionaries that the Tupinambá had a reasonably cohesive religious system, although it lacked a supernatural figure with the majesty of the Christian God. In selecting the term "Tupã" to designate their own God, Jesuits, Franciscans, Carmelites, and Capuchins knew they were dealing with a conception that was only approximate. In fact, *tupã* was no more than the word for "thunder," a notion that included a mythical being who, as he wandered about the heavens, caused the characteristic roars that herald rains—nothing more. For the Portuguese, not believing in an all-powerful God was indicative of a people who had no faith. Father Manuel da Nóbrega's "Dialogue on the Conversion of the Heathen," the first writing with a genuinely Brazilian theme, substantiates the dubiety the Portuguese—in particular the clergy—concerning Indian religion.[48] Of course that dubiety still remains in the judgment of many people today.

What we do know about the religion of the Tupinambá, compiled in a book with that title by Alfred Métraux, makes it clear that their religious sentiments, and, by extension, those of the other Indian peoples of Brazil, were sociologically and technologically complete. They had beliefs, rituals, and, as in other religions, they sought special explanations for the uncontrollable phenomena of nature. They feared supernatural elements as well, and employed magic to intercede for help in their doubts and anxieties. Finally, they had a complex, anthropomorphic mythological system that sought to explain the world and their culture in a symbolic and pedagogical manner. Part of this religious system can still be found in the Brazilian culture in a syncretic form commingled with elements of folk Christianity and African religions. Its influence can be perceived, above all, in the figure of the shaman (*pajé*) and his characteristic liturgy of incense, possession, trances, plus the use of tobacco and herbal medicines.[49]

Anthropological research carried out by modern methodologies has cleared up some issues and corroborated many of the descriptions and analyses of the sixteenth-century chroniclers regarding Indian religion. All Indian peoples conceive of death as an abrupt cutting off of life and the beginning of another one, this time without physical pains and filled with serene joy. In other words, heaven is paradise. Many Indian cultures divide the soul into two forces, one of which remains on earth in a dangerous condition for the living, while the other is transposed to heaven. They understand that the living can be manipulated by magical powers, by the dead, or by the souls and spirits of other beings of nature, such as animals and plants, and through the intercession of shamans. Their mythical world of creation and existence passes within a dimension where humans and animals are integrated with specific and immutable characteristics, which are prototypical or paradigmatic. In this world live the cultural heroes and demiurges who give meaning to the universe and to their cultures in particular. They are not heroes capable of helping the day-to-day existence of the living, since upon concluding their superhuman labors they abandoned earthly life and withdrew to some distant, unreachable place. They nevertheless remain in the thought and the memory of the living. Nor can one consider them gods in the mythological sense of Homeric Greece, for here there is no longer any interaction between the living and the dead, a condition that likewise rules out any analogy to Christianity's pantheon of saints. There is a spiritual link remaining, however, and it serves to connect the Indians with the spirits of the animals and, in some cases, with the souls of the dead. It is in this environment that witchcraft and shamanism find their justification and guiding principles.[50]

Sixteenth-century Catholicism, monotheistic in doctrine and polytheistic in practice, met with enormous difficulties in converting Indians who had neither gods, hierarchies, nor liturgical discipline. The first commandment was thus almost impossible for them to comprehend. As one adds to these difficulties the sociological contingency that binds religion to society, one can come to appreciate the anguish of Father Manuel da Nóbrega and other such dedicated missionaries at their inability to maintain the faith of their new converts within the prevailing Catholic standards. Instant conversion seemed to be quite easy, especially in the period immediately after the Indians were vanquished in war or threatened with slavery and imprisonment. The word of God would sound then like their own myths in grand and fantastic reverberations, and was thus perfectly believable. They did not feel constrained to take it seriously all the time, however, an attitude that thoroughly exasperated the priests.[51]

The magnificent "Dialogue on the Conversion of the Heathen" sets forth the entire dilemma of the missionary project. It demonstrates the correlation of brute force with conversion, the need for ultimate disintegration of a social system to open the way for a new religious system, and the process of Christianity's total domination as the doctrine of the new era. Between the ideas of the priest Gonçalo Álvares and those of the lay brother and blacksmith Mateus Nogueira the major opposing opinions about the religious and human nature of the Indians are confronted. Notwithstanding his knowledge of the Indians and of their language, Álvares sees in the Indian no more than an animal in a human body, incapable of being converted, whereas Nogueira, through his close contact with the Indians gained from repairing their iron tools, sees in them the image and likeness of God. Nogueira, therefore, believes the Indians can be converted; however, this is a mighty task that can only be accomplished in working with their children. He gives examples of Indians who became Christian and compares them with the worldly philosophers. In the end he reaches the conclusion that the Indians may be more easily converted than said philosophers. However, the secret of the art of conversion can be found only in the justifications of faith and ultimately rests as one of God's mysteries and designs.

This predicament has come down to the present day. It is known, for example, how the Bororo Indians came to Catholicism through the offices of the mission of the Salesian Fathers. They were converted not because of an inspiring persuasion but as a subdued response to the changes purposefully made by the missionaries in their cultural system—the mission forced the Bororo to change the architectural design of their village from a circle of houses centered within a political and cultural arena to simple parallel rows of houses. This action put the Bororos' minds in disorder and opened a breach for the penetration of the new religious complex.[52] When exogenous sociocultural pressures are misjudged and misapplied, as was the case of the Capuchin mission among the Guajajara Indians, the result can be an explosive and extremely violent rebellion. In 1901, 13 Capuchin missionaries and more than 180 local Brazilians were killed by the Guajajara as they attacked the mission and ambushed anyone who passed by. In return, more than 400 Guajajara were hunted down by military forces sent out by the provincial government of Maranhão.[53] On the other hand, in the mission of the Dominican friars among the Kayapó on the Tocantins River, the result, by the end of some forty years of missionary work, was the demise of the entire group of the Pau d'Arco Kayapó.[54]

In all of these cases, the documentation reveals that religious sentimentalism prevailed over genuine Christian sentiment and over basic humanitarian concern for the fate of these peoples. There is an abundance of literature that depicts the missionaries' zeal in receiving confession from, and giving extreme unction to, dying Indians so that at least their souls might go straight to live "in the bosom of God." First things first.

There is no doubt, however, that many Indian peoples, survivors of years of indoctrination by Jesuits, Capuchins, Salesians, or even the secular clergy, acquired a religious sentiment that has much of a Christian framework, both in beliefs and rituals, as well as in the social motivations toward an ideological integration with the populations surrounding them. The belief in an all-powerful god penetrates these syncretistic religions not only as a symbol of their subordination to a system that centralizes power in another, unreachable place, but also as a new element of aid and comfort for the social and existential needs that these peoples are experiencing. In other cases, one notices the functioning of two parallel religious systems that fulfill diverse needs in the cultural and social realms. However, we know of *no* cases of Indian peoples retaining a high degree of political and ideological autonomy who have acquired significant Christian sentiments. Scientifically based, or at least methodically oriented techniques for learning Indian languages (used today with great dedication by fundamentalist missionaries to translate the Bible into the vernaculars in the hope that the divine word might suddenly illuminate the hearts of the Indians), were also known to the Jesuits. But they never proved to be sufficient in producing an integral and permanent conversion in anyone. As Nóbrega's "Dialogue" recognizes, "the art of converting souls is the greatest of all there be on the earth and thus requires a higher state of perfection than any other."

In truth, the greatest experience the Indians had with Catholicism was more of a social rather than religious nature. It was through religion that the Portuguese found themselves forced to respect the Indian's humanity and to suffer a few pangs of conscience over the violence and inhumanity they wreaked upon these peoples. It was through the social and economic experiments in Jesuit villages that many surviving Indians were incorporated into the Brazilian social system.

In the Amazon, the expulsion of the Jesuits in 1759 led to the collapse of a majority of the more than sixty villages that the Jesuits had established and managed for the glory of God and Caesar.[55] Many of these villages were transformed into townships that later became cities, such as Santarém, Bragança, Viana, Guimarães, and other such places with classical Portuguese names found throughout that region. In southern Brazil, the departure of the Jesuits was more dramatic. It put an end to the great experiment of the Missions of the Seven Peoples, which, upon passing from Spanish into Portuguese dominion (by the Treaty of Madrid of 1750), was completely demolished by Portuguese forces. The Portuguese were rather restrained in their view of Brazil and did not want a parallel power within their realm. At least 60,000 Indians were killed in a few years of warfare and the survivors were forced to migrate to Paraguay and the Argentine province of Missiones.

These missions had been established after the São Paulo slave hunters, the merciless *bandeirantes,* had destroyed the Guairá missions in Paraná and the Itatins missions in Mato Grosso during the first half of the seventeenth century. The new missions prospered through the next one hundred years to establish a social system that has often been called "primitive Christian communism" by their apologists, and "Jesuitical feudalism" by their detractors. They were organized townships of hundreds of Guarani Indians who somehow followed the strict command of the Jesuits, apparently with some religious motivation, to increase economic production. Given the Jesuits' competence in founding missions and in managing the Indians' labor power, the Missions of the Seven Peoples soon became centers of large-scale agricultural, cattle, and *yerba mate* production. That ended up drawing the envy of colonists and royal officials alike, who harbored the hostile impression that the Jesuits were involved in these activities for enrichment and power. In the missions, Indian economic output expanded with better organization and with the acquisition and improvement of techniques for making semi-industrialized craftwork, for example, in ceramics, architecture, and wood carving. The baroque grandeur of the ruined churches, such as those found in Santo Ângelo and São Miguel (in the state of Rio Grande do Sul), attests to the artistic skill and creative capacity of the Indians and the Jesuit experiment. The planned, deliberate destruction of these missions shows how serious was their perceived challenge to colonial powers, and how petty and vengeful those threatened colonial powers could be.[56]

THE INDIAN BECOMES A CABOCLO

Once the Cabanagem Rebellion was quelled, in 1841,[57] the Indian question effectively ceased to be a military issue and became one of administering disputes. In fact, apart from the Amazon and parts of the Brazilian plateau where there were still many tribes living autonomously, the Indian question had practically been settled. Peace had been enforced in the Northeast ever since the end of the War of the Barbarians, in the beginning of the eighteenth century; in the south, dating from the defeat of the resistance of the Missions of the Seven Peoples, in 1768.

From then on the Indian begins to be seen rather as a caboclo, a mixed breed, living in the gray zone between the Indian and Brazilian worlds. Whenever a new economic upsurge boomed in regions where Indians lived, their welfare was invariably ignored by the expansionist movements, particularly when the latter were backed by political interests. Their continued existence was, until recently, a motive more for an undisguised feeling of shame than anything else on the part of the ideologues of Brazil.

The great majority of Brazil's Indian peoples today do understand, with various degrees of precision, the main social, economic, and political mechanisms that move the country. This knowledge has been acquired through a record of close, but not cozy, experiences with the dominant Brazilian society. The transition from autonomy to stable cohabitation has been processed through a kind of tacit pact, in which the surviving Indians have had to accept the rules and norms of an interethnic relationship that originated in the period of servitude. Accordingly, they are permitted to maintain part of their historic heritage, to have a restrictive knowledge of the world that surrounds them, and to have a minimal experience of the development of modern Brazil.

That is the condition of being *caboclo*. The term originally meant "halfbreed," "mestizo," the child of an Indian with a white or black. In São Paulo the term *mameluco* was heard more often and had the same connotation. It was, and to some degree still is, a deprecatory term accepted by no one. In the mid-eighteenth century, its use was expressly prohibited by an article of the Directory of Pombal. The term caught on first as a label or designator for the Indians who, defeated in war, had survived to accept the imposed peace terms. Then it was extended to those who survived the years of coexistence with Luso-Brazilian settlements and towns. In the first years of colonization, Indian caboclos constituted the majority of the Brazilian rural population. Later, when the proportion of Indian caboclos to other non-Indians had greatly diminished, the use of this word was extended to the impoverished non-Indians living on plantations and ranches, or squatting on free land. Nonetheless, even today, in the regions of old colonization and low economic development, Indians are still referred to as *caboclos*, by which is meant "tame Indians."

To become *caboclo*, in the broadest sense of the term, was considered a most benevolent fate reserved for the Indian, according to the ideology of the Indian policy that began during the empire. It should be noted, however, that such was also the understanding and the evaluation of historians and anthropologists until quite recently. The idea survived in many cases as a rationale for the country to make use of easy, cheap labor in remote areas, which the caboclo would perforce provide. Several famous indigenists, from José Bonifácio to Rondon, used this type of argument to defend the permanence of Indians. Others thought that becoming caboclo was the only chance the Indians had to survive, at least physically. As it turned out, many Indian peoples became so integrated as caboclos that they ended up either disappearing as ethnic groups or sacrificing a major part of their cultural heritage, such as their language, religion, or rituals of social solidarity. Clearly, such a loss happened concomitantly with the plunder of their lands and with mounting pressure to conform with the social and economic laws of the surrounding social polity. Today many Indian groups are working to restore to an operational minimum their ancient cultural heritage that had previously been decreed—literally—to have vanished in the Brazilian melting pot. Several Indian groups were once considered extinct after losing their lands in the nineteenth century.[58] Others disappeared through a more constant, slow process of invasion of their lands, economic coercion, epidemics, mixed marriages, and forced migrations.

THE INDIAN CEASES TO BE A CABOCLO

Less by voluntary option, as the anthropologist Eduardo Galvão supposed in 1955,[59] and more as the result of the social process of the country's recent history, the Indians are ceasing to be caboclos, refusing to accept a position of social inferiority and marginalized ambiguity. Instead, they are beginning to seek, in a generalized and absorbing effort, to affirm their ethnic identity and to demand a new, active social position in the political realm. The determinant factor in this ethnic awakening comes as a reaction to the intensification of the expansion of Brazilian economy and society into their areas. This modern expansion tends to transform all previous social relations based on servitude and paternalism into less personalized, more capitalistic relations. Land becomes no longer a question of social prestige, but is now valued as merchandise and as a reserve of value for speculation.

Facing these new economic relations and incapable of adapting quickly enough, the Indians end up transforming themselves—together with the neighboring peasant components of precapitalist traditions—into pockets of resistance in a denial of the process of capitalization of land and of life. From the northeast to the south, regions of ancient colonization, to the west and north, whose pioneer fronts are subsidized by the Brazilian state, with an intensity almost unheard of in the history of interethnic relations in the country, several Indian peoples at different stages of acculturation or "caboclization" are reacting by defending their territorial and cultural legacies.[60] In some regions the reaction is to keep their economic sustainability and preserve land, as in the case of the Xavante, Tapirapé, Kayapó, and Tenetehara. Among others, such as many northeastern groups, but also the Kaingang and Guarani of the South, it is a struggle to recover lands that were taken from them, as well as to rescue items of their cultural heritage that were abandoned under pressure from the dominant society.[61]

Although they are not mere cogs of the wheel of history, the Indians, as is the case with all peoples and social realities, live in history and move through time in pace with the dominant current. This current is not absolutely inexorable and inescapable, but it cannot be regarded lightly. In Brazil it works as a kind of "savage" capitalism that uses all the traditional as well as the new devices to change everything into its own image. The Indians must learn the new ways in order to best set up their survival strategies. The refuge areas of Indian anticapitalism exist as oxbow lakes by the banks of an overflowing river. Perhaps to secure them as reserves for the future, perhaps because it needs to face its opposite, but above all because the Indians do not really challenge it, capitalism allows Indian peoples to continue with their existence, and by some unexpected means even promotes their survival. In what other way can one explain the actions of the World Bank in favor of the demarcation of Indian lands and the protection of their inhabitants, even as it finances capitalist development projects that are detrimental to the Indians in Brazil?[62]

That the Indians are conscious of the historic process through which they are passing can be demonstrated by their discourse and their actions.[63] They know that this is the moment for determined action to strengthen their ethnic bases and to seek a new position on the national scene. We shall see that there are stumbling blocks in the path of consciousness raising, and that the outburst of liberation from paternalism is painful and might cause the upsurge of an even worse form of relationship. The Indians know, by means of tradition, that the history imposed on them has reduced them to a position of demographic and social marginalization in the context in which they live. They know that they once had the continent all to themselves, and that they once lived more fulfilling experiences of coexistence. Yet they also know that they might one day be able to find new and more dignified forms of interethnic relations.

As we become conscious of these new possibilities we are called to join efforts with the Indians in developing better ways of living together. For therein lies our best chance of survival.

2

Indian Policies

REGIMENTS, LAWS, AND CHARTERS

It did not take very long for Portugal to set up a framework for understanding the Indian peoples of Brazil and to formulate a policy to deal with them. Its contemporary experiences in North Africa and Asia, aggressive and inclement as they had been, were passed straight on to Brazil without significant modifications, and often by means of the same officers. Indeed, many of the first captains-general and governors who arrived in Brazil had earlier been conquerors and administrators in Asia. Furthermore, the driving economic interests of the active Portuguese mercantile class, which bolstered commerce and colonization, could hardly have been different in Brazil from what they had been elsewhere.[1]

The colonial project would rarely permit any leeway within the parameters that established as a principle the position of Indian peoples as royal subjects, vassals in their own land of a faraway master. By the terms of the Treaty of Tordesilles, signed between Portugal and Spain on June 7, 1494, the newly discovered lands were divided between these two countries, the boundary being an imaginary line drawn 370 leagues west of the Cape Verde Islands, off the African coast. On its eastern half, which belonged to Portugal, lay a considerable portion of—but less than half the present territory of—Brazil. Although Portugal had no doubts concerning the legitimacy of its claims, it is worth noting that this treaty was contrived without the mediation of the Pope. This constituted a daring act of independence from papal sanction, which effectively set a precedent for other countries, such as France, to consider themselves entitled to conquer and colonize lands and peoples in the Americas.[2]

Earlier, however, Portugal had been mindful in obtaining papal sanction for conquest. In 1454 Pope Nicholas V, through the bull *Romanus Pontifex*, guaranteed the right to conquer new lands of "barbarians" and "infidels" and submit their peoples to servitude by the use of arms. Spain had also secured its Christian right of conquest by the bull *Inter Coetera,* issued by Pope Alexander VI in 1493.[3]

So as to leave no doubts, Catholic sanction was eventually reaffirmed for the Portuguese in 1529, when all over Europe the legitimacy and brutality of the conquest were in debate. The bull *Inter Arcana,* issued by Pope Clement VII on May 8 of that year, makes use of expressions that seem to totally ignore the arguments of Friar Bartolomé de las Casas in favor of the natural rights of the Indians.[4] It demonstrates an utter indifference toward the physical and spiritual integrity of the Indians, as it pontificates:

> that the barbarian nations come to the knowledge of God not by means of edicts and admonitions but also by force and by arms, if it should be necessary, that their souls may partake in the kingdom of heaven.[5]

Recognizing the difficulties of conversion, the Pope could not be more royalist than the king. The king, for his part, needed make no great effort to follow the papal words and remain a Christian. The justification for the use of arms to Christianize heathens was always one of the main reasons for ordering and executing "just wars" against the Indians throughout the entire period of Portuguese rule in Brazil.

To the Indians such reasoning did not seem legitimate. They did not passively accept the abrupt invasion of their territories and the persecution unleashed on them by the Portuguese in the early years. It became obvious that the Indian disposition was against accepting outside control over their lives, and that their ways of life and political systems did not favor blind obedience or a statutory hierarchy. The demands imposed upon them, even in peacetime, were excessive in the extreme, incomprehensible to peoples who had always lived in freedom.

Indian reaction came through wars, guerrilla activities, and escapes from slavery and forced labor. They suffered immensely from all sort of brutalities that the Portuguese inflicted in the years of conquest and in the business of colonization. In Brazil cruelty toward Indians went beyond justification, even in comparison with what the Portuguese had already done against the Saracens and Hindus. It was cause for thought and deliberation in the inner circle of the Crown, above all because the colonial discourse had been public and explicit in proclaiming that the purpose of the Portuguese presence in the New World was to propagate the Catholic faith among the heathen. Furthermore, there were legal questions to be settled regarding the doctrine of the natural rights of non-Christian peoples who were being conquered. Laws were prepared by court jurists who, for the most part, came from the ranks of the clergy and sought to follow the canons of the Christian doctrine of the day.

On various occasions rights of Indian sovereignty were explicitly acclaimed. For example, in the Royal Dispatch of March 9, 1718, the Indians were considered exempt from any sort of royal jurisdiction.[6] At the same time, however, Portugal maintained slavery as a norm that could theoretically be applied to any Indian people. In contrast to the Spanish, who were always more formal and legalistic, and who since 1542 had decreed the unconditional liberty of the Indians, Portugal would do likewise only in 1570, but not unconditionally. In 1578 it reinstated the terms of enslavement, and only in 1609 would it declare the unconditional freedom of Indians. A mere two years later, however, enslavement was made legal again. The Indians were next declared free of all forms of slavery in 1757, but beginning in 1801 exceptions were made. Portuguese standards toward Indian policies were devious, ambivalent, and casuistic, to say the very least. The logic of conquest, colonization, defense of territory, and the inexorable need for labor demanded, in the Crown's view, measures of extreme severity and inflexibility. At no time should any measures be considered separately from the overall purpose of total supremacy.

The first royal orders and recommendations on how to relate with the Indians are contained in charters known as "regulations" (*regimentos*), which the king bestowed upon the captains of ships bound for trade in the lands of Brazil. Although they regularly declared that the Indians should be treated well, there was a certain expectation of the possibility of capturing some of them to be brought back to Lisbon. Whenever such schemes met with success, Indians were shipped under the hypocritical expression "voluntary apprehension." Beginning with the Regulations of first governor-general Tomé de Souza in 1549, through the law of 1570 and up to the Directory of Pombal of 1757, all legal texts that set out to clarify the issue of freedom versus slavery consistently left loopholes for the persecution, captivity, dispossession, and reallocations of Indians, in short, any acts that might be found necessary to secure the colonial enterprise. It is relevant here to know some of the essential terms used in the colonial period with regard to the Indians:

heathen nation (*nação gentílica*)—a non-Christian nation or people.
village (*aldeia*)—an original Indian village or a grouping of Indians forced to live together by officials of the Crown or missionaries.
descent (*descimento*)—the search for, location, and transfer of Indians from their home lands to predetermined places near Portuguese settlements, usually downriver.

entry parties (*entradas*)—expeditions inland to contact and submit Indians. They could be private or official, with or without the presence of missionaries.

exploratory or slave parties (*bandeiras*)—private expeditions to hunt down and capture Indians as well as to search for precious minerals. Many were employed by Crown officials; some were operated without official permission. These expeditions were especially associated with slave hunters (*bandeirantes,* literally "flag bearers") from São Paulo, the so-called *Paulistas.*

ransom (*resgate*)—the act of obtaining an Indian prisoner from another Indian group by trade, supposedly to save him or her from certain death. Later, the pretext was the salvation of the Indians' souls from hell.

allocation villages (*aldeias de repartição*)—villages where Indians were settled to be available for distribution to colonists, town chambers, and missionaries.

administration villages (*aldeias de administração*)—villages of descended Indians under the exclusive jurisdiction of town chambers or governors or captains-general.

captivity (*cativeiro*)—slavery.

just war (*guerra justa*)—declaration of war against Indian groups. It was the prerogative of a ruling board—the council of missions—to decide on the justness of a war and the time for carrying it out against a specific Indian group. The principal criteria for this decision were: (1) that the Indians were setting up obstacles to the propagation of the Catholic faith; (2) that they were attacking or threatening to attack Portuguese settlements or rural properties; (3) that they were cannibals; (4) that they were allies of the enemies of the Portuguese.

council of missions (*junta de missões*)—a ruling board, made up of representatives of the missions, the bishop, and the king's officers. It determined the legitimacy of Indian issues, especially wars and the allocation of descended Indians.

Up to the independence of Brazil, some of the main Indian ordinances were:

1. *The Regulations of Governor-General Tomé de Souza,* of December 15, 1548.

    Recommends peace with the Indians in order that Christians may settle in their territory; orders wars on enemies; initiates policy of gathering Indian villages near Portuguese settlements so they may be better indoctrinated and their labor power made readily available.

2. *Law of March 20, 1570,* on the liberty of the Indians.

Reacting to the practices of indiscriminate enslavement, prohibits captivity of Indians, save those obtained in "just wars"
carried out with license from the king or governor; states the
criteria of just war and mentions the Aimoré, particularly, as
"uncivilizable people," and therefore the target of planned wars
of extermination.

3. *Law of February 24, 1587,* declaring which Indians may be made
captives and which may not.

Based on the Law of 1570, it prohibits incursions into the hinterland without the authorization of the governor and Jesuit
priests; regulates the allocation of Indians "persuaded" to descend to the coast to work in plantations and sugar mills.

4. *Law of November 11, 1595,* "on not allowing the capture of the
heathen of the parts of Brazil, and their living in liberty, save in
the case declared in this law."

Revokes the Law of 1570 and prohibits war and captivity, save
by express license of the king. "I desire that those against whom
I order no war to be made shall live in any of the said parts
where they may be in their present liberty, as the free men which
they are."

5. *License and Regulation of July 26, 1596.*

Regulates the role of the Jesuits in descents of Indians and in
the supervision of Indian labor on farms; Indians are to be
contracted for a maximum period of two months, to be followed by an equal period of leisure.

6. *Provision of June 5, 1605,* on the total liberty of the Indians.

Although recognizing that captivity is acceptable in some cases,
declares all Indians to be free, be they Christian or pagan; prohibits abuses of Indian labor, irregular descents, and requires
payment for services rendered.

7. *Law of July 30, 1609,* on the liberty of the heathen of the land.

Confirms the Provision of June 5, 1605, and the terms of the
License of 1596; prohibits captains-general from exercising any
greater power over the Indians than they hold over other free
men; reiterates the freedom of Indians including those previously captured.

8. *Law of September 10, 1611.*

Declares the liberty of the heathen of Brazil, save those taken
in just wars, and revokes the previous laws; renews the terms
of just wars: they must be declared in agreement with the gov-

ernor, the bishop, the judges, the chancellor, and the prelates of the religious orders, under the approval of the king, or, in case of urgency, with his subsequent approval; accepts the enslavement of captives and of Indians bought or ransomed who had been condemned to death; creates the office of *captain,* replacing that of the regular judge, to oversee Indian villages, which should have also a resident priest; establishes a number of three hundred couples per village of Indians descended from the hinterland.

9. *Laws of March 15, 1624, June 8, 1625, November 10, 1647, and September 5, 1649.*

Regulate the administration of villages, the time, and rates for services performed by the Indians in the manner of previous ordinances.

10. *Royal Charter of October 21, 1652.*

Authorizes Jesuit Father Antônio Vieira to command and supervise the descent of Indians in the state of Maranhão and Grão Pará.

11. *Provision of October 17, 1653.*

Reestablishes the terms of just wars, allows entry parties, and prohibits the presence of captains in Indian villages; creates the *council of missions.*

12. *Provision of September 12, 1663.*

Withdraws the powers of the Jesuits over Indians ruling in Maranhão and Grão Pará; allows entry parties and allocation of Indians.

13. *Provision of April 9, 1665.*

Restores commanding power to the Jesuits to carry out entry parties and manage the service of Indians; in turn, Indian slavery is maintained.

14. *Law of April 1, 1680.*

Declares freedom for the Indians, in conformity with the Law of 1609, maintaining, nonetheless, the status of existing slaves; continues to allow just wars and the imprisonment of Indians, with the restriction that prisoners be treated "as are persons who are taken in the wars of Europe"; grants full power to the Jesuits to establish exclusive missions in areas where there are Indians who do not wish to descend; in Christian villages Indians should be governed by their chiefs and the local parish priest; allocation of descended Indians is placed under the responsibility of the bishop, together with the Franciscan prelate and one representative of the town chamber.

15. *Law of September 2, 1684.*

    Concedes the administration of descended Indians to private parties, specifically in the state of Maranhão and Grão Pará; regulates the labor of Indians (one week for themselves, another for the masters).

16. *Royal Charter of December 21, 1686,* or *Regulation of the Missions.*

    Grants spiritual and temporal powers to Jesuits and Franciscans in the villages and missions created along the rivers and in the hinterland of the Amazon; regulates the administration of villages, prohibiting the presence of non-Indians; orders villages to have at least 150 couples, and, in the case of different ethnic groups descended to one location, that they should be situated separately from one another; regulates allocation of Indians among colonists and missions.

17. *Royal Charter of February 19, 1696.*

    Grants the inhabitants of São Paulo the administration of free Indians, who become obliged to work while receiving a salary; regulates mixed marriages between Indians and African slaves.

18. *Resolution of January 11, 1701.*

    Addressed to the governor of Pernambuco; permits the buying and selling of Indians only in public marketplaces; in the hinterland such sales should be performed in the presence of judges.

19. *Provision of October 12, 1727.*

    Prohibits the use of *língua geral,* the reduced form of Tupi-Guarani language that Jesuit missionaries disseminated throughout Brazil as a lingua franca; commands that Portuguese be taught in towns and villages.

20. *License of May 3, 1757,* also known as the *Directory of Pombal.*

    Collection of ninety-five articles that constitute the last major Portuguese ordinance on the Indians. Among the many rulings, it reiterates the withdrawal of temporal and spiritual powers of the Jesuits; grants freedom to all Indians; favors the entry of non-Indians in Indian villages; encourages mixed marriages; creates towns and districts of Indians and whites; nominates lay directors for the new towns; promotes agricultural production; creates new taxes; orders Indian lands to be demarcated; and makes the use of Portuguese language mandatory.

21. *Royal Charter of May 12, 1798.*

Abolishes the Directory of Pombal; institutes a paternalistic master-servant relationship between whites and the Indians in their service; reinstates the notion of defensive wars; promotes the Indian to the condition of orphan; allows free settlement of whites on Indian lands.

22. *Various royal charters of 1801, 1806, 1808, and 1809.*

Declare offensive wars against the Botocudo, Coroado, and Guerén Indians, granting concessions to those who organize their own armed parties, and include the rights to enslave prisoners for periods ranging from ten to fifteen years.

This brief compilation of Indian laws and ordinances does not exhaust Portuguese legislation on the subject. The number of licenses and royal charters addressed to governors and captains-general is much larger and more diversified. A great number of these documents were issued to deal with questions of local nature—specific to certain Indian groups only—and thus often had little or no consequence for the remaining Indian population. The laws presented here give an idea of what was involved in these more than three hundred years of official relationship between the Portuguese Crown and the Indians of Brazil.

In the first place, one must note the sheer persistence of laws that were extremely cruel to the Indians. Slavery was almost always a reality. Until the Directory of Pombal, only in 1605, 1609, and 1680 did legislation declare unequivocally against any form and justification of slavery. Considering that a law during that period could take from three months to a year to travel from Portugal to its destined address, one may conclude that they had very little effect except to provoke the ire of colonists, be they town dwellers or plantation owners, who made use of Indian labor. In contrast to the Spanish with their juridical formalism, whose very carefully drafted laws were not necessarily meant to be fulfilled, the Portuguese were quite lackadaisical in formulating laws and policies and even more half-hearted in carrying them out. This was the case above all when the laws were contrary to their economic interests. For no lesser reason did Father Antônio Vieira protest with characteristic righteousness against the perfidy and corruption of the king's officers and the colonists in general.

In the second place, it is appropriate to discuss the relationship between the Crown and the religious orders in the formulation and administration of Indian policies. It is necessary, at the outset, to acknowledge that the so-called secular power, the power of the king, and the spiritual power, the power of the religious orders, sometimes including the regular clergy, should not be taken as opposites of one another, as frequently happens in Brazilian historiography, but as a complementary set in the colonization process. There were indeed many moments in which these two parties of the colonial project contrived discord and opposition, but above all they were linked in both general purposes and economic interests as well as by legal means. The institution of the Padroado, a pact established between the Church and the Crown that lasted until the final years of the Brazilian imperial regime, represented an alliance of concrete, mutual interests. It functioned particularly in relation to their general view of heathen peoples, for the pact began prior to the discovery of the Americas. From the Indians' point of view, church and state appeared as members of the same body polity. If they sometimes acted distinctly from each other, most of the time their attitudes were of the same nature.

We have seen how Governor Mem de Sá and Father Manuel da Nóbrega in the early years of colonization got along well and shared ideas on how to persuade or otherwise subdue the Indians to the colonial system. This unity of tactics, based on an identity of general purposes, was in fact predominant in the relations between church and state during the colonial period. They disagreed mostly on the manner by which the Indians should be administered. Only in 1775, when Portugal was attempting to modernize its administration under the command of Minister Plenipotentiary Marquis of Pombal, does there seem to have occurred an abrupt but not definitive breach between Crown and church with regard to treatment of Indians. By then the Jesuit Order had been expelled from Brazil and the entire Portuguese kingdom, and for that matter from the Spanish kingdom. The other orders were also prohibited from administrating Indian villages on the grounds that they retarded their economic development and their social integration into the Portuguese realm.

Jesuit sympathizers contend that the Directory of Pombal, issued in 1757, meant to establish a new Indian policy, was actually specifically aimed at the Jesuits. Indeed a great many complains by the colonists against the Jesuits had accumulated over the years. They were accused of controlling Indian labor, hindering their integration, and enriching the order. Although the Jesuits were everywhere and were even responsible for the education of the children of the colonial elite, it was in the Amazon and in southern

Brazil that the order had amassed conspicuous power over the Indians. Although it is doubtful that the Society of Jesus had accumulated much wealth, the Marquis of Pombal certainly felt that the Jesuits were a hindrance to his new plans. In 1759 he issued a royal charter that expelled the order from the Brazilian territory and later from Portugal. It is worth noting, however, that the Society of Jesus also came to be expelled from the Spanish colonies and from France, and by 1782 Jesuitry was extinguished as a religious order by the Pope himself. What all of this suggests is that Jesuit controversies were not specific to the Portuguese state.[7]

At the local level, the relationship between church and state, that is, between the religious orders and the governors or captains-general, was more tense, and many times reached a state of conflict. Here the interests were more concrete and the disputes, as a consequence, more real and devoid of any aura of omniscience or omnipotence. Basically the dispute had to do with who had rights over the Indians and what the best way to civilize them might be. Crown officials thought the Indians should be civilized by means of their enforced individual labor on colonial projects. In opposition, the clergy thought that civilizing should be a matter of religious instruction together with the organization of collective labor. The officials wanted to control the administration villages from which they could pick Indians to work on both public projects and private plantations and in sugar mills. The clergy wanted the Indians in mission villages where they would retain exclusive rights over their labor. Another motive for disputes was the allocation of descended and ransomed Indians, for which it was necessary to define the condition of the Indian as free or legitimately enslaved.

In these disputes the Church was not always united. On the contrary, many times the secular clergy allied themselves with Crown officials against the Jesuits. On other occasions, there were enormous conflicts between the religious orders—Jesuits, Franciscans, and Carmelites. Abrupt changes of Portuguese laws often mirror these disputes, indicating shifts in the Crown's position: now in favor of the Jesuits, now in favor of the Franciscans or Carmelites, now in favor of the officials. In all likelihood this lack of coherence is an honest reflection of the differing perceptions of those who made up the Portuguese colonial power establishment, particularly with regard to the Indians. Although this turned the Indian question into a bone of contention, it was not, in the final analysis, a sufficient incentive to make the fate of the Indians more favorable.[8]

In the third place, the legislation also reflects the Crown's concern with the interests of the colonists, without whom there would be no colony. The colonists' persistent interests in relation to the Indians varied from their need for cheap labor—particularly before the onset of massive African slavery—to vacant, unimpeded lands.[9] The Crown itself made use of cheap Indian labor not only for public works but also as defense troops against foreign invaders. It knew that the Indians would be available and that the colonists as much as the religious orders were necessary to command them. Therefore it tried to promote peace and order between colonists and Indians for security reasons as well as for the health of the local economy. It did so with the power and the arms it could muster, and the hard part eventually fell upon the Indians. In regard to the colonists' greed for Indian labor, the Crown found itself divided between arguments against slavery, and arguments in favor of it, or of intermediary forms. In its ambiguity the Crown often ended up providing the grounds for the countless collisions between the colonists and the religious orders, the Jesuits above all.

Because of their sometimes unbending stand against Indian slavery (but not slavery of Africans), the Jesuits were forced out of several captaincies by determined opposition movements. From São Paulo they were expelled twice in the first half of the seventeenth century, at the height of the cycle of Indian enslavement campaigns that the Paulista Indian slavers, or *bandeirantes,* waged against the Missions of Guairá and Itatins, which were under the control of Spanish Jesuits. From these mission villages the slavers imprisoned several tens of thousand Guarani Indians and carried them off for sale to the sugarcane planters of Rio de Janeiro and Bahia. In these last two areas the Jesuits came close to being expelled two or three times. They managed to avoid this embarrassment through negotiations that ended up reducing their temporal power over the Indians and their moral force over the colonists. In Paraíba they were expelled and forbidden to return as missionaries, leaving the Crown no choice but to designate the Franciscans to administer the Indian villages of that captaincy.

In the Amazon, which began to be colonized in the second decade of the seventeenth century and had a separate government from the rest of Brazil called the State of Maranhão and Grão Pará, the Jesuits were expelled three times between 1625 and 1682. In all cases the motives rose from disputes over the use of Indian labor. The second time, in 1661, Father Antônio Vieira, who enjoyed high prestige in the Portuguese kingdom and throughout the European Catholic world for his oratorical gifts and his political influence, had to suffer this humiliation personally while in the company of his Jesuit brethren. The third time, in 1682, the Jesuits' expulsion occurred in the midst of a social and economic upheaval, a small revolution known as the Revolution of Bequimão (so named after the leader, who was eventually hanged), who with his followers had taken up arms to protest against a set of commercial monopolies established by the Crown. The Jesuits' return to Maranhão was assured by the Crown and imposed upon the rebellious colonists. The Provision of September 12, 1663, reflects the negotiated return of the Jesuits without the powers over the Indians they had obtained under the previous Provision of April 9, 1653, granted directly to Father Vieira. The Jesuits' return was followed by the Royal Charter of December 21, 1686, which created a new Indian policy, the Regiment of the Missions (which was to remain valid until 1757). It reflects the Crown's double purpose of uplifting the Jesuits in the face of the previous upheaval and, at the same time, assuring the colonists' fidelity through the legal means to descend Indians and make use of their labor.

A final word needs to be said about the Directory of Pombal and the laws against the Jesuits that immediately preceded them. The definitive expulsion of the Jesuits from Brazilian territory, the transformation of Jesuit Indian villages into towns and districts (*lugares*),[10] and the promotion of the physical and cultural miscegenation of Indians were parts not only of a policy of modernizing the Portuguese state and its sway over the colonies and eventually of defining its frontiers, but also of promoting, in a hypocritically peaceful way, the elimination of Indians as *nations* or autonomous ethnic groups. In enforcing this policy the Crown reckoned that an unshackled self-rule of former Jesuit mission villages would mean in effect the breakdown of Indian communities. Indeed, a short time thereafter many of those villages had their lands usurped and the Indians themselves became mere squatters on their own lands, or, at best, humble artisans in new Luso-Brazilian towns. Only in a few isolated areas were the new districts able to maintain themselves as Indian, and were, therefore, collectively poor but cohesive. There was, moreover, a financial benefit to the local colonial elites. A few years after the enactment of these laws, the real estate and the economic assets under the Jesuits were brought to public auction. The beneficiaries of these auctions became known as the "*contemplados*" or bequeathed ones, such was the ease with which they obtained control of these properties.

Several of the new Indian/Brazilian villages immediately attracted Brazilian and Portuguese immigrants and eventually prospered and turned into real towns—to the detriment of the Indians who lived there. In the Amazon alone, more than sixty Jesuit mission villages were transformed into towns and districts, some of which grew and became important cities. A great many of them, however, simply plodded along through the following decades mired in poverty and injustice, as the dominant Luso-Brazilians moved in and gained control of their economies and administrations. The majority of them ceased to exist altogether, and their lands were turned into private estates and ranches, as happened with the villages of the Xingu and Itapecuru rivers.[11] Forty years later, in 1798, a royal charter expressed concern over this state of affairs and abolished the Directory of Pombal. It merely made matters worse. Instead of improving the political conditions of the Indians in the new villages and towns, it conceded more benefits to colonists to recruit Indian labor. In addition, it instituted the paternalistic or patronage relationship by formally declaring that the Indians should be treated as orphans and should act as "servants to their masters." This charter was to become the basis for future Indian policies.[12]

All of the preceding was effective mostly in the Amazon and in the northeastern captaincies, where the Jesuits and the other orders had mission villages. In what was to become southern Brazil the so-called Mission of the Seven Peoples, a socially and economically well-structured system of mission villages, had a different outcome. These villages had been established with Guarani Indians by Spanish Jesuits and had flourished economically, socially, and artistically for approximately one hundred years. With the Treaty of Madrid (1750), which defined the borders between the Portuguese and Spanish colonies, they suddenly found themselves in Portuguese domain. Thus they were ordered to clear out, and when they offered resistance, they were attacked and their villages razed to the ground, while the surviving Indians dispersed.[13]

Near the end of Portuguese rule, perhaps as a result of the tensions and fear of losing its main colony (which was partly motivated by Napoleon's invasion of Portugal), the harshest, most inhumane royal charters were promulgated against specific Indian peoples in Brazil. They officially reinstated the legitimacy of wars of extermination, legalized private violence, and reenacted the right to enslave captives. It was, so to speak, an erstwhile restoration of *bandeirante* philosophy that set the tone and provided justification for what was to happen seven decades later when latter-day Indian killers, the *bugreiros,* were hired to clear the land for a new wave of European immigrant colonization in southern Brazil.[14]

In evaluating more than three centuries of Portuguese dominion one can come to the conclusion that such a course of policies was certainly more brutal than necessary for conquering the Indians who inhabited Brazil and for establishing colonial power. Not only were the periods of personal and collective freedom deceptively few and short, but entry parties and wars of extermination were virtually uninterrupted. If on occasion some law or royal charter bespeaks of the "natural freedom" of the Indians or treats them as "prime overlords" of their lands, this is always in specific circumstances and in the context of an act that is already discretionary, such as an order for removing Indians from a territory or for descending them near Portuguese settlements. In no known case can one conclude that the Crown intended to endorse, make legitimate, or enact any Indian claim to natural rights.[15]

By the end of the colonial period, of the original 5 million Indians, perhaps 800,000 remained either as caboclos, or half-breeds, still speaking an Indian language and thus being discriminated against, or as free and autonomous peoples. Of them, 200,000 were Amazonian caboclos, at that time called *tapuios,* who descended from the former mission villages; another 200,000 were the remnants of mission and administrative villages around the country; and perhaps 400,000 were autonomous ethnies.[16]

UNDER THE BRAZILIAN EMPIRE

The independence of Brazil from Portugal took place in 1822, when Portuguese prince Dom Pedro de Bragança sided with Brazilian patriots and announced his decision to proclaim the country free. He was then crowned Dom Pedro I, the first emperor of the Brazilian Empire. A Constituent Assembly was convened to institutionalize the new nation as a parliamentary monarchy. Among the many issues that were to be settled was the question of what to do about the Indians. In that regard, the Brazilian scientist, poet, and statesman José Bonifácio de Andrade e Silva sent a paper he had written a few years previously in which he proposed that the Indians, though brutish and inferior, were to be considered legitimate parts of the new nation and should be integrated into it by peaceful and Christian means. However, the assembly was dissolved by Dom Pedro I, and Bonifácio's proposal was disregarded. The first Brazilian Constitution was imposed by the emperor and promulgated the following year; it contained no mention of Indians. Dom Pedro I's reign lasted until 1831, when he was pressed by matters in Portugal to leave Brazil. He renounced his right to the throne but bequeathed it to his six-year-old son, who was later to become Dom Pedro II, the second and final emperor of Brazil.

During the early, confusing years of independence, the Indian question was legislated by the Royal Charter of 1798 and later royal charters, as well as through new decrees ordained by the new provincial governments and the recommendations issued by the central government to the provincial councils. They all seemed to be prompted by the exclusive and immediate interests of the elite of the new country. Nonetheless, the ideas of Bonifácio began to take root among a small but influential segment of the Brazilian political elite that thought it necessary and fit to create an ideology for the new nation. Although the new Brazilian elite did not differ much from the old Portuguese rulers, they had in mind that the Indians should be made a part of the commonwealth through peaceful and educational means, and especially through Christian indoctrination. Indeed, the idea that the Indians could achieve a certain level of civilization only through religion flourished once again, and it would last through the whole period of imperial rule. In the 1820s there was a vague proposal for calling back the Jesuits (whose order had been reconstituted in 1814), and, later on, for inviting Trappist monks. Ultimately the decision was made in favor of the order of Capuchins from Italy. The expression *"catequese e civilização,"* or "Christianization and civilization," became the motto and guiding principle of the Indian policy that was to prevail for the rest of the century.

Between 1831 and 1840 Brazil was governed by politicians in a regime of transition known as the Regency. During its first five years there was a triumvirate of regents appointed by a convened parliament, followed by a period in which a single regent ruled in lieu of the future emperor. During this brief period several major rebellions broke out in a number of Brazilian provinces, threatening the unity of the country. The Regency had difficulty suppressing them and finally hastened to declare the fifteen-year-old Dom Pedro de Alcântara a functioning adult and crowned him emperor. It was in the 1830s that the first laws of national scope were promulgated regarding the Indians.[17]

1. *Law of October 27, 1831.*
   Revokes the Royal Charters of 1808; reaffirms the status of orphans for the Indians and orders the justices of peace to act as their tutors; all Indians held in servitude are freed from any obligations previously incurred.

2. *Constitutional Amendment of August 12, 1834,* also known as the *Additional Act.*
   One of its articles determines that the provincial legislative assemblies and their executive governments should be responsible for the Indians.

The most important and basic Indian legislation of Dom Pedro II's reign was a royal decree issued in 1845. It is known as the Regiment of the Missions because it dealt substantially with the procedures of how Catholic missions, particularly Capuchin, should be installed on Indian lands and how relations with the Indians should proceed. It unified the formulation of Indian policy under a secretary of the imperial bureaucracy and provided that every province should have a central agency called the Directorate General for the Indians. The Directorate was to distribute instructions, personnel, and moneys to the local level of intervention, that is, villages or groups of villages, which were called "partial directorates."

> *Decree Number 426 of July 24, 1845,* or *Regiment of the Missions.* Creates the system of Directorate General for the Indians. The nomination of the director general is the emperor's prerogative. Provides for rules and norms on how to deal with Indians at the local level. Favors Catholic missionization and forbids any form of slavery, servitude, or ill treatment of Indians. Requires Indians to be enrolled for remunerated public and military service, but without coercion, and establishes corrective penalties, including incarceration for a maximum of six days for Indians guilty of crimes.

During the period of validity of this law, which lasted for a few years after the civil dethronement of Dom Pedro II in 1889, small additions were made in Indian legislation and administration. They came in the form of notices, precepts, and official letters to the provincial directors general, alerting them to certain aspects of their administration or about new issues and events. For example, in 1865 the right of habeas corpus was extended to the Indians and so was communicated to all provinces.

Working side by side with the directors general were the Capuchin missionaries. Guided by the motto "Christianization and civilization," they were eagerly sought and warmly welcomed by the provinces. Generally they received commissions to install their mission stations in the least difficult partial directorates to be reached. In many cases they were commissioned to the so-called colonies, which were special directorates that received more money to develop economically and hasten the process of integration.

It must be stressed, however, that in relation to the survival of many Indian ethnies, the most determinant component in the imperial Indian policy was the so-called Law of the Lands, issued in 1850 and regulated in 1854. This law is considered by historians, sociologists, and jurists to have been responsible for the establishment of the political and economic preponderance in Brazil of large estates and landowners in opposition to small land ownership. The law stated that every property claim had to be registered in public land registrar offices to be recognized as legal. Since only the elite had access to lawyers and knew the ways to register lands, this law effectively excluded most small independent farmers and many of the Indian villages that existed near towns and amid private estates. Although there were persons of good faith in the service of land registration who recognized the Indians' rights to the lands they inhabited, and who worked persistently to demarcate them on site and register them in the public offices, the prevailing attitude was one of negligence and indifference in upholding the rights of the Indians. To make matters worse, in 1860 all land issues came under the sphere of administration of the newly created Ministry of Agriculture, which was in the hands of former slave owners and big plantation proprietors.

The political scope of action of the provincial Indian directorates was also pulled into the orbit of that ministry. The upshot of this process was that dozens of Indian villages were formally extinguished, and their inhabitants condemned to become landless squatters and to lose their specific cultural characteristics. A documented example of this process occurred in Pinheiro, a small town in the interior of the province of Maranhão. In 1816 the Indians who lived near that town received by donation a tract of land of "three leagues in length by one in width," that is, approximately 10,800 hectares. In 1854 this donation was confirmed and registered in the local land registry office. Twenty years later, however, the registration was annulled with the allegation that there were no longer any Indians on the said tract of land. By default, as it was argued, the tract was to become the property of the town chamber, which could dispose of it as it pleased. Today there are no longer any Indians on the land in question nor in any area of the municipality. In the state of Ceará, with one stroke of the pen in 1860, the provincial president nullified all the existing Indian villages and made the lands public.[18]

The Brazilian Empire has been characterized by conservative apologists as a period of peace and slow progress.[19] In fact, it was the period that established the hegemonic power of the slave masters and landlords by the maintenance of slavery and the legitimization of large estate property. It closed the doors on a possible emergence of small property holders and consequently on a possible rise of a democratic spirit among the middle classes and the people in general. As far as the Indians were concerned, the main consequence of this period was a continued loss of their lands, a substantial portion of which were usurped by contrived legal means as well as by sheer political power. Even those lands that had been formally donated to the Indians as land grants were disregarded by the authorities and put up for grabs. As they were not registered after 1854, they lost validity in the judgment of the imperial government and the provinces.

The establishment of the statute whereby the Indian was defined as "an orphan and of relative capacity, both mentally and judicially," was the legal foundation for the prevailing paternalism, or rather, patronage, of the times. Even the liberal-minded friends of the Indians, such as general Couto de Magalhães, believed that the correct manner to relate to the Indians was to treat them as children, guiding their will, admonishing them, punishing them in their errors, and seeking the best for them by instilling the ideal of work, obedience, and religion. Such paternalism, however, did not exempt the state from applying less gentle forms of indoctrination, such as the use of provincial police and private militia to hunt down autonomous Indians under the pretext of defending settlements and farms from marauding.

Finally, it was during the nineteenth century that the opinion that the Indians were fated to extinction became entrenched in the public mind. Ironically, this notion arose not necessarily on account of the mistakes and faults of Indian policies, but rather from the opinion concerning the Indians' lack of adaptability to human evolution. Social Darwinism, even in the diluted form that reached Brazil, was invoked to ease the guilty consciences of the enlightened persons of the period. Moreover, it justified the lack of political action in defense of the Indians, their natural rights, and their landholdings, making it easy for usurpers to grab hold of their lands and resources. Wherever Indian lands became valuable, their immemorial or acquired rights were withdrawn. This was the worst imperial legacy that the Indians received.

At the end of the century we may calculate the number of surviving Indians at perhaps 400,000 (counting some 100,000 caboclos on the way to assimilation), a deficit of 400,000 in relation to the beginning of the century, which can only be imputed to the policy of the independent Brazilian nation. Except for a few Maué villages, almost all Indians on the lower Amazon were extinct, along with the *tapuio,* who had lived in the former mission villages. There was also a substantial drop in the overall population of all those peoples who, until the beginning of the nineteenth century, had been autonomous, but had subsequently been brought into the realm of influence of the new socioeconomic culture. Peoples such as the Munduruku, the Mura, the Karajá, the Timbira, the Bororo, and many others, whose numbers ranged in the tens of thousands, all lost considerable amounts of their populations.

THE REPUBLIC

Among the themes uniting the various social forces that called for the end of the empire and the establishment of a republican regime, the Indian question was absent. This is not to say that there were no defenders of the Indian cause among the political and intellectual forces in the country. In the last quarter of the nineteenth century, the positivists—a group of influential military leaders, scientists, and intellectuals who had founded a sort of religious sect called the Church of the Positivist Apostolate—and segments of the middle classes and the imperial bureaucracy who dealt in some way with Indians had come to recognize that the main problem the Indians faced was the security of their lands. Although the commissions charged with demarcating and registering lands of Indian villages had generally failed to fulfill their role, in a few cases they had acted positively for the Indians and against the interests of local landowners, as recent research in archives of land registry offices in Maranhão, Bahia, and other provinces demonstrates.[20]

Perhaps not surprisingly, the Constitution of 1891, which adapted the country to the republican regime, did not provide any article on the Indian question. The only such mention is in article 64. In conformity with the spirit of political decentralization and empowerment of the newly defined states, ownership of all untenanted lands, previously under the control of the Union, was passed to the jurisdiction of the states. Among these were certainly included Indian lands that had not yet been legally recognized, although those already demarcated and registered were not supposed to be classified as untenanted lands. At any rate, according to the analyses of several jurists and defenders of Indian rights, the lack of clarity in defining untenanted lands allowed the states and their municipalities to presuppose a legal capacity to control and make use of Indian lands that were within their territorial domains.[21]

During the debates of the constituent assembly in 1890, an extremely innovative and radical proposal was presented by the Positivist Apostolate as a contribution to the Indian question. It maintained that the Indians should be considered as free and sovereign *nations,* and that they should be organized as special kinds of *states* to be called "American Brazilian States," as opposed to the other states of the federation designated "Occidental Brazilian States." Such states would have cultural and political autonomy and control over their territories. Any outside intervention that might be deemed necessary, such as the construction of a road, could only be made with the explicit permission of the organized Indian peoples. Moreover, they would also be guaranteed the protection of the federal government against possible invaders. Interestingly enough, these ideas come close to the statements handed down by the venerable chief justice of the United States Supreme Court, Justice John Marshall, in the early days of the American republic, when he proposed for the Indians the status of "dependent domestic nations" with the right to be so recognized in treaties.[22] Of course both propositions were never enacted by either country.

As might be expected, the positivists' proposition was viewed with scant sympathy and considered eccentric. It sounded like a whimsical formula lacking in political realism. The new political trend was rather the opposite, in the direction of state autonomy in such matters. Indeed, Indian policy was passed by republican decree to the jurisdiction of the states, which had acquired the right to prepare their own constitutions and to hold control of untenanted lands. Some states actually came to issue legislation on Indians, notably Rio Grande do Sul, which created its own Indian service under the aegis of positivist guidelines. In the first three decades of this century it demarcated several Indian reservations, known regionally as "Indian refuges," for the Guarani and Kaingang, who lived within state boundaries. However, the majority of states maintained the legislation and the practices of imperial times. Some reinstated the policy of inviting religious orders to Christianize Indians, although such moves met with open and brash criticism from the part of positivists. Although their imaginative proposal had been dismissed, they and their supporters continued writing about the Indians in their journals and newspapers, considering them a national question and an issue of morality and self-respect for the country.[23]

From the last quarter of the nineteenth century to the first decades of the 1900s, there was a considerable inflow of rural European immigrants, especially German and Italian, into southern Brazil. Many of them had contracts with real-estate companies and were sent to settle in the Araucaria pine forest areas of the states of Paraná and Santa Catarina. A good portion of those promised lands belonged to Kaingang and Xokleng groups, who still lived secluded and in autonomous fashion. As could be expected, conflict flared between the prospective colonists and the Indians. By the 1890s colonists' newspapers were publishing articles defending the idea that progress in the region could not advance in the presence of Indians. To solve that problem the colony companies and their leaders took the course of hiring professional Indian killers, the previously mentioned *bugreiros,* to clear the way for new immigrants as well as land speculation.

While the *bugreiros* were busy massacring Indians, including poisoning their water sources, to the verge of genocide in the states of Paraná and Santa Catarina, a little to the north, in São Paulo state, feverish work was being carried out on the construction of the Northwest Brazil Railway to link that state with the up-and-coming agricultural state of Mato Grosso. The railroad was passing through the territory of several autonomous Kaingang bands, and the Indians reacted by attacking work teams and sometimes the moving train. In counteraction, the railroad company hired gunmen to protect their workers and even to hunt the Indians down.

The news of this uncivilized confrontation eventually reached the press and the general public. Voicing the sentiments of European immigrants, German-born scientist Hermann Von Ihering, director of the São Paulo's Paulista Natural Museum, published an article in the museum's journal in 1907, explicitly proposing the extermination of the Kaingang Indians, who dared oppose the railroad, the immigrants, and progress in general.[24] Shortly thereafter, at the sixteenth Congress of Americanists, held in Vienna in 1908, accusations were charged against not only the immigrants but also the Brazilian government, strongly suggesting that Indians were being massacred as part of a national policy of extermination. Thus began Brazil's bad reputation for anti-Indian activities, an ill fame that was reignited in the 1970s.

THE INDIAN PROTECTION SERVICE — SPI

An uproar of indignation was raised among educated Brazilians in the main cities of the country. Being accused of killing off Indians seemed intolerable for the humanitarian pride of the nation. The federal government was thus pressured to take action, and in September 1910, it solemnly created a new Indian agency, the *Serviço de Proteção aos Índios* (Indian Protection Service), known by the acronym SPI.[25] To organize and direct it, the minister of agriculture, under whose office the new agency was placed, appointed Colonel Cândido Mariano da Silva Rondon. A military man of positivist training and unwavering convictions, Rondon had become a national figure because of the job he had been doing for the previous fifteen years of installing telegraph networks across the most remote hinterlands of Brazil. In that activity he and his work teams of backwoodsmen, engineers, and military men had come to make contact with several Indian tribes that lived on those lands, and all of these contacts had been engaged peacefully.[26]

The SPI was the political product of the ideas proclaimed by the doctrine of positivism but was also supported by the liberal views on the Indians that prevailed in those years. The underlying motivation that united these two conflicting sets of ideas and ideologies came from a vague sympathy for the Indians that had been held by the middle classes since the long yesteryear of literary romanticism. However, at no point in its history did the SPI and its ideologues ever muster enough power to revive the aspirations of the Positivist Apostolate to regard the Indian peoples as autonomous members of the Brazilian polity. It is fair to say that in its political and administrative course of action the SPI consistently viewed the Indians as people worthy of being part of the national commonalty, but never in an autonomous way. It held the view that the state had the duty to provide every Indian group with the economic and social means conducive to a gradual evolution toward a superior level of culture, and from there to be fully integrated into the nation. The SPI worked on the expectation that the Indian would one day become a full-fledged Brazilian.

To accomplish this goal, the SPI set out to guarantee and demarcate all Indian lands; to protect them from potential invaders and usurpers; to defend the Indians from those considered to be cunning, dishonest, and brutal-minded, especially traders and peddlers who exploited them, but also landowners, miners, and even foreigners; to teach them new techniques for farming and for administering their property; and to succor them in their illness. The autonomous Indians were categorized as "people in isolation," or "evading," and should be "attracted" or "pacified." The word "savage" or "wild" was banished from the agency's vocabulary. Should any Indian people react in a hostile manner to other people entering their territories, a so-called pacification team formed by SPI personnel would be sent out to make contact and come to peaceful terms with them. These operations should always be done with extreme care so as not to harm any Indian. If the pacification team were attacked by an Indian party, they were expected to remain calm and not counterattack with firearms, but rather offer presents as a means of peaceful suasion. As for the Indian groups that had survived the long years of a close and unequal relationship with Brazilian society and were integrated into the socioeconomic world around them, the SPI's policy was to teach them new mechanical skills and provide formal education for a better integration. Religious instruction was excluded from SPI orientation, but Catholic and Protestant groups were tolerated and allowed to set up missions on their own responsibility.[27]

Rondon's determination and leadership, recognized by the government and the press, attracted many diligent and dedicated people to the Service. In 1912, when the minister of war requested the return to the army of those military personnel who were in the SPI, many preferred to abandon their military careers and remain in the Indian Service. In the first years of existence, a large proportion of SPI personnel consisted of military engineers, captains, colonels, generals, and former assistants of Rondon in the telegraphic service. Later they were joined by scientists, anthropologists, film makers, medical doctors, and engineers. With the Revolution of 1930, which flew in the face of the Rondon group's aims and principles, the SPI was degraded from the status of autarchy to a simple section of the frontier department of the Ministry of War, and it suffered through an irregular and obscure period. For close to ten years Rondon lost control of the Service. In 1935 he was appointed by President Getúlio Vargas to head the Brazilian diplomatic mission in charge of mediating a frontier conflict between Peru and Colombia, on the upper Amazon River. Three years later, having proved his ability in this mission, Rondon was rehabilitated with full honors.

By 1939 the SPI was again under his control, and he quickly made the moves to overhaul it. He created the National Council for the Protection of the Indian (CNPI) to serve as a consulting organ attached to, but with powers over, the SPI and invited a number of national intellectuals and military men to be part of it. He obtained a decent budget and with it began to restore the SPI to its original standards of action. This ascendant phase was to last until Rondon's death in 1957. In this period, throughout Latin America and the United States, a new surge of Indian sympathy had upgraded the national Indian agencies into better functioning systems. Mexico was in the forefront of this process because in that country the Indian issue had become a matter of national security and ideology, as well as of social development (as understood by the notion of *indigenismo*). Additionally, it profited from the political support of all Mexican federal administrations since Cárdenas in 1938. Brazil, with its smaller Indian population, earned the respect of its neighboring countries and of anthropologists as well because of the actions of the SPI and the prestigious name of Marshal Rondon.

Two outstanding actions were taken by SPI before it began to decline. First, there was the founding in 1953 of the Museum of the Indian in Rio de Janeiro. The museum was intended by its founders to show the general public what the Indians were really like so as to help fight racism and prejudice. Its permanent material culture exhibit was seen by many people, and its documentary and research activities were praised by various international museums as well as UNESCO. The other action was the proposal written by Darcy Ribeiro and Eduardo Galvão and taken by Rondon to President Vargas defining the terms of justification and reference for the demarcation of a large tract of land intended to hold the Xingu Indian Park, homeland of some twelve different Indian peoples who lived in harmony with one another.[28]

There is no doubt that the existence of an organ such as the SPI, with its programs of Indian assistance plus its unflagging efforts to dignify the Indian in the public mind, helped consolidate in the nation a sense of historic responsibility toward the Indians. When the third Brazilian Constituent Assembly was convened in 1934 to mold the country after the designs of the Revolution of 1930, the Indian question was taken into account and debated. The prevailing ideas were based on the ideals and goals of the SPI, as can be seen in article 129, which states:

> The ownership by forest peoples (silvícolas) of the lands in which they are permanently located shall be respected, they being, however, forbidden to transfer them.

Article 5, item XIX, makes Indian policy exclusively federal domain, finally doing away with the ambiguity regarding the role of the states, especially in relation to Indian lands. These were positivist ideas that had in the end gained constitutional legitimacy.[29]

The subsequent Brazilian Constitutions, the one conferred upon the nation by the dictatorial regime in 1937 and the liberal-democratic one of 1946, copied the same points—a clear demonstration that Indian rights had been consecrated before the host of different social and political forces of the nation. The Indian question had not until then been a point of disagreement between ideologies. The dispute had been rather between regional economic interests against humanitarian ideals of historical reparation. In this sense, conservative arguments could be put forth in defense of the Indians, and in many cases progressive arguments were employed to belittle the Indians or to reduce the size of Indian lands. In a rapid appraisal of history, we may conclude that the Indian question transcends the ideological dichotomy that prevailed in many other national issues. The basic argument that unites Brazilians in support of the Indian cause is to be found in the ideology of nationalism, which joins both leftist and rightist activists into the same equation.

The SPI's scope of action covered practically all parts of the national territory, from the Amazon to the extreme south. Except for the autonomous Indians, most Indian groups were recognized and assisted in some way, at least in the best years. By 1955 the SPI had 106 service posts located in Indian lands, many of which assisted two or more distinct Indian groups. Nevertheless, and to no one's surprise, the Indian population kept falling. It was at this time that the Indians reached their population nadir, with less than 130,00 persons, perhaps as low as 100,000 according to one well-known estimate.[30] From then on, however, there began a demographic turnaround, and their numbers began to rise, although in most cases slowly and almost imperceptibly. (Only at the end of the 1970s would this demographic turnaround come to be seen as significant and permanent.) Many of the autonomous peoples who were contacted after 1910 became extinct, such as the Xetá of Paraná State, the Oti-Xavante in São Paulo, the Botocudo in Minas Gerais, the Kepkiriwat of Rondônia, the Krẽjé of Maranhão, and dozens of others, sometimes subgroups and entire villages. Some suffered enormous population losses, reaching the bare minimum for physical survival and already with considerable loss of their cultural identity, as was the case with the Krenak, the Pataxó, and the Xokleng.[31]

The SPI was incapable of hindering the economic and demographic advance over Indian lands in regions undergoing development, such as the northwest of São Paulo and Paraná in the 1910s. In these cases it functioned rather as a "pacifier" of autonomous Indian bands, after which the lands they effectively occupied were divided and distributed among the interested parties. Nor was it able to avoid armed attacks against defenseless Indians by Brazil-nut gatherers and rubber tappers in the Amazon, and cattle owners in southern Maranhão and Goiás. Furthermore, it had to ally itself with a varied sort of new religious missions, such as the Salesian priests in the upper Rio Negro and in Mato Grosso, and British and North American Protestant churches, to attend to the minimal requirements of the Indians in those regions.

The SPI was responsible, however, for consolidating the sentiment that the Indians deserve to have a place of their own in the Brazilian nation, as one of its integral and severely penalized components. It instituted the concept of Indian parks, thus bringing two powerful ideas together: the defense of cultures and the defense of the environment. In concrete terms, the SPI demarcated around one-third of the known Indian reservations, totaling some 20 percent of the Indian national territories.

The major contributions of the SPI to a national commitment toward Indians and the notion of indigenism focused on the execution of a policy of respect for the Indian as a person, of establishing the historical responsibility of the Brazilian nation for the destiny of the Indian peoples inhabiting the national territory, and of instilling an altruistic attitude in its field personnel. That the results in Indian demography and in land guarantees fell far below expectations should not be counted against the people who staffed the SPI. That shortcoming is due rather to the deficiency of the Brazilian state and its administrators, as well as to the frailty of the political power of the Indians' historical allies as they had to contend with the dominant anti-Indian forces of the country.

THE NATIONAL INDIAN FOUNDATION—FUNAI

The leaders of Brazil's 1964 coup d'état did not hesitate to take control of the SPI by immediately removing public health physician Dr. Noel Nutels, who presided over the agency. He had been placed in that position in November 1963 by the João Goulart administration, in an attempt to revamp the agency to the standards it had held at the beginning of the 1950s. A few months previously news had flared up in the national press with accounts that some one hundred gunmen hired by cattle ranchers had invaded the lands of the Canela Indians of south-central Maranhão state. The Canela war leaders were able to trick the attackers into defensive traps and save the majority of their people from being hurt. Only six Indians were killed when the village was surrounded, but panic broke out and the Indians ran for help. They were hosted in the lands of the Tenetehara-Guajajara Indians (forest lands, not savanna), and there several children and old people eventually died of hunger and diseases such as typhoid fever and malaria.

The new lords of power viewed the Indian question, and the SPI in particular, with the disdain and righteousness of the avengers. They let matters go from bad to worse for two or three years, until news of fresh Indian massacres came to the attention of the press. Particularly scandalous because of a gruesome photo published in the newspapers (showing a man with a machete ready to cut in half a naked Indian girl hung upside down with legs spread apart) was the so-called Massacre of Parallel 11, which was directed against the Cintas-Largas Indians of northern Mato Grosso state. Their village had first been bombed by aerial raids, and a party of assassins finished the job on the ground. The scandal was greater still because the leader of the murdering party had been a former SPI member who knew the ways of the Indians. The massacre had happened in 1963, but it was only in 1965 that it came out in the press.

Other SPI employees were charged with participating in acts of corruption, land sales, and inhuman practices against the Indians. Forced finally into action by such appalling circumstances, an inquest was carried out by a Ministry of Agriculture's committee that produced a dossier of over one thousand pages of accusations of presumed administrative crimes liable for penal sanctions. The dossier was never published, but parts of it found their way into the press, and, just as in 1908, there was an international outcry calling for punishment and for reform, which forced the federal government to extinguish the SPI. Just prior to this action, a fire broke out in the SPI archives as they were removed from Rio de Janeiro to Brasilia. Thus a great deal of information was lost on Indians and Indian lands.[32]

The act of opening an official inquest and abolishing the SPI was an indication that the military wanted to change Indian policy, supposedly to redeem Brazilian history from its past errors. Thus, with great fanfare, the National Indian Foundation (FUNAI) was created by law in December 1967. As usually happens in those early moments, the first task to be carried out was a moralizing campaign. In military fashion, SPI personnel judged as "bad elements" were fired and replaced. A new kind of thinking and acting was enforced to forge a new esprit de corps among the new employees so as to place them apart from the old ones. The main purpose of the new agency was to settle the Indian question once and for all. That could only mean, in effect, enforcing new measures to transform the Indians into Brazilians, to integrate them into the nation, and to assimilate them culturally into the general Brazilian way of living, even if that meant skipping some stages of acculturation.

At any rate, in the beginning FUNAI was to follow the traditional ways and paths established by the SPI. It intended to intensify the procedures of contacting autonomous Indian groups and organize more efficiently the economy of others. The guiding principle was to link the purpose of this effort to the military doctrine of "economic development with national security." The steps to be taken included the demarcation of Indian lands, contacting autonomous ethnies, providing formal education and health care, and equipping Indian economies to viably enter the market economy. Surprisingly enough, the founders of FUNAI intended the agency to be self-sufficient, that is, to generate income to pay for its expenses. This income could only come as revenues from the sale of forest products from Indian lands. None of these goals was fully achieved, which in most cases was better for the Indians.

The military regime made itself legal by a new constitution that was promulgated by a submissive Congress in 1967, only to be toppled over by Institutional Act Number 1, which handed down a more fitting charter for the times, the Constitution of 1969. As far as the Indians were concerned, however, the new constitution followed those preceding it, with one important modification: Indian lands were to be considered inalienable Union lands, with the Indians retaining exclusive possession thereof. In a way, this represented a a grave judicial and political setback in the history of Brazilian concepts concerning Indian lands. On the other hand, the substance of the text of article 198 presented genuine advantages to those involved in the process of demarcating Indian lands, as it explicitly declared that the Indians had rights to lands they occupied for reasons of historic precedence or immemorial control, and these rights superseded any other alleged subsequent claims.

> Article 198—The lands inhabited by the forest peoples are inalienable in the terms which federal law shall determine, to these accruing permanent possession thereof, and with their right being recognized to exclusive use of the natural resources and all serviceable goods existing therein.

> §1—The judicial effects of any nature which have as their objective the domain, possession, or occupation of lands inhabited by forest peoples are hereby declared null and extinguished.

> § 2—The nullification and extinction dealt with in the previous paragraph do not give to the occupants the right to any action or indemnification against the Union and the National Indian Foundation.

In light of this article, the executive branch prepared and sent a bill of legislation to Congress and on December 19, 1973, the so-called Statute of the Indian was enacted as Law Number 6,001. The statute functions to this day, with all contradictions contained therein, as the legal charter regarding relations between Brazil and the Indians. It ordains the social and political condition of the Indian vis-à-vis the nation and stipulates measures of assistance and advancement for Indians, both as ethnic groups and as individuals. Following in line with the Civil Code of 1916, it decrees the Indian to be a legal minor in age and only "relatively capable" of his or her acts, thus needing to be under the guardianship of the state, as represented by FUNAI. The statute then establishes the conditions of emancipation from guardianship at both the individual and collective levels. Next, it delineates the procedures that justify and determine the terms for the demarcation of Indian lands, making FUNAI the sole agent responsible for defining Indian lands and how they should be demarcated. Once all the steps are taken, the final act of recognition of an Indian land remains a prerogative of the president of the republic.

Since the mid-1980s, however, the demarcation procedures have been changed three times, making it progressively more difficult to implement the demarcation process through to its conclusion. Recently the new administration of President Cardoso issued a decree that once again changed demarcation procedures, making the process slower and the size of the new lands smaller. In addition, it allowed third parties to contest in court the validity of the demarcation of any Indian land, including those already registered in the National Heritage Registry (SPU). This setback touched off protests across the whole range of the indigenist movement in Brazil and abroad because it had opened a new attack against Indian rights.

One of the most significant, most closely received articles of the Statute was that which set the deadline date for the completion of the demarcation of all Indian lands for the end of 1978. Unwilling to fulfill this legal determination, the third military government, led by President-General Ernesto Geisel, in a move that caused surprise and indignation nationwide and had international repercussions, decided in its closing days to hasten the process of emancipating the Indians from state guardianship. The Ministry of Interior, which controlled FUNAI, accordingly prepared legislation that stipulated the conditions and procedures for individual and collective emancipation. Its purported justification was that many Indian peoples were fully aware of their social position and were virtually integrated, lacking only the legal status. Although it is undeniable that being a ward of the state blemishes the status of Indians, what lay behind this move was actually the crass intention of paving the way for non-Indians to be able to deal directly and legally with Indians for the exploitation of their lands and perhaps to venture into outright purchase of lands that would otherwise remain inalienable.

This proposal, which became known as the Indian Emancipation Project, and which unfortunately was concocted with the accord of Brazilian anthropologists linked to the military government, seemed to many observers to be an act of unqualified despotism. The idea of transforming Indians into Brazilians who would inevitably end up in poverty no longer had supporters in the national political environment. Likewise, the undeniable swindle of dividing Indian lands into family or individual property so as to allow their sale did not inspire even the most radical defenders of economic liberalism and private property. Brazil was then going through the waning days of the military regime, and the defense of minorities and labor unions—not to mention the citizenry's basic political rights—was beginning to arouse the nation. Almost unanimously, the media came out against this proposal and in support of the Indian cause as defined by anthropologists and jurists. As a result, the next and final military administration, that of president-general João Figueiredo, filed away the emancipation project. Nonetheless, the twin ideas of Indian emancipation and liberalization of Indian lands for sale continue to circulate among those who view the Indians as obstacles and a challenge to national integrity and security.[33]

FUNAI's history is not exactly glorious, but it can be said to have had two or three periods of intense demarcation activities and favorable relations with the Indians. The first such period was from 1975 to 1979, when even the hard core of the military regime felt a certain pressure for democratization, and the young indigenists began to stand up to and influence the generals who controlled the agency. The second period was from 1984 to 1985, as the military regime was giving in to a civilian government, and the Indian agency's presiding colonels (no longer generals) had to accept the return of the indigenists they had expelled in 1980. Perhaps a third period was the first three years of the 1990s, when two indigenists were in charge of FUNAI, and the incumbent president seemed to believe that demarcating Indian lands would lend him international prestige.

The outcome of almost three decades of existence of FUNAI is that approximately 80 percent of the Indian lands have gone through some of the stages of the demarcation process, some 60 percent are fully recognized and registered, while 20 percent have scarcely received recognition as Indian lands. Of course, many of those lands have gone through a process of re-demarcation based on work previously accomplished by the SPI. The impulse for these spurts of activity came during times of outbursts of democratization and were carried out by the indefatigable dedication of field indigenists, practical action anthropologists, agricultural engineers, topographers, journalists, and attorneys who were imbued with sentiments of solidarity with and responsibility for the destiny of Indian peoples. On those few occasions FUNAI leadership was manifestly pro-Indian and sought to demonstrate that the Brazilian government shared their concern. In those moments there was a search for an honest dialogue between Indians and indigenists, and Brazilian society seemed to approve of it.

More often, however, a dismal climate of confrontation has prevailed between FUNAI leadership and the Indians and their allies. In May 1980, forty indigenists were summarily fired by FUNAI on the pretext that they had founded an association that was threatening the agency. They certainly were defying its leadership, which at the time was in the hands of colonels with close links to the National Security Council (CSN). These links eventually led to full control, especially after Decree Number 88,118 of February 23, 1983, withdrew from FUNAI its prerogative of defining and identifying Indian lands in accordance with anthropological criteria and of demarcating them by means of an internal administrative process. Instead, the process of land demarcation was transferred to a board made up of representatives of several ministries—such as agriculture, land reform, interior, planning—as well as the National Security Council. This board was authorized to call on any other federal agencies or state administrations to opine on the legitimacy or non-legitimacy of Indian rights over the lands in question. The demarcation processes henceforth began to move ever more slowly as obstructions were made by interested parties and anti-Indian lobbies, especially when merged with agrarian, political, and military interests.

Lacking autonomy to demarcate Indian lands, FUNAI inevitably lost power and a large measure of legitimacy in national and international public opinion, which by then was actively supporting the efforts of Indians and anthropologists dedicated to their defense. Indeed, ever since the federal government had threatened the Indians with a unilateral emancipation project, the Indian question had turned into an Indian cause. Its former analysts and sympathizers had become defenders and militants. Worse for FUNAI, it began to lose face before the Indians, who were mustering courage to relive the experiences of times long past when they had an active voice in their destinies. As they became fully conscious of their rights and of the truthfulness of their allies, they concentrated their drive on the struggle for the right to define and guarantee their lands.

In the last ten or so years FUNAI has been depleted to such a point that it retains very little of the spirit of loyalty and self-sacrifice that have characterized the work of action anthropologists and indigenists in general. Maybe it will not last for much longer, and it may be replaced by yet another Indian agency. At any rate, assuming that one day all Indian lands recognized by FUNAI will be demarcated, they will amount to some 890,000 square kilometers, or 10.5 percent of the national territory—no mean feat after all.

In regard to FUNAI and the autonomous Indian peoples, still referred to as "isolated," the same techniques established by the SPI are still being used for contact. The general mechanism is based on avoiding confronta-

tion and using the tactics of setting out "attraction fronts" to make contact. Generally, the Indian area is interdicted to strangers, so as to make
contact more easy. Once contact is established on a more or less permanent
basis, an Indian attraction post is set up. Though most often a territory is
rightfully presumed and a process of demarcation is initiated, in some cases
the contacted groups may be removed to other areas, particularly when
some portion of the territory is slated for other national interests. In essence, there is a power display on the part of FUNAI personnel to con-
strain the Indians within the paternalistic system of relations. Among the
more than twenty groups contacted in the 1970s and 1980s, all suffered
substantial population losses and loss of territory. The Kreenakarore (who
call themselves Panará), the Avá-Canoeiro, Waimiri-Atroari, Parakanã, Ara-
weté, Assurini, Guajá, Arara, Urueuauau, Cintas-Largas, Suruí, Zoró, Salumã,
Mynky, and others became well known in the process of being contacted
and in its aftermath. Films, news reports, and televised scenes—in some
cases overtly sensationalistic—were seen everywhere.

The Panará Indians, for example, were described as "giants" by FUNAI
personnel who wanted to call attention to them, and as "the people who
flee civilization" in a well-known British documentary film. Contact with
them was forced by the opening in 1973 of a highway that passed through
their lands. A high-level government decision was made to remove them
from the area and transport them to Xingu National Park. This relocation
was done in 1974 through the use of military helicopters. By the time the
Panará were transported to the park they had lost more than two-thirds of
their population, struck down by influenza and other infectious diseases.
After a decade or so they began to recover their population, and in recent
years they were enticed by a team of bold anthropologists to make a move
back to their old territory. That territory was demarcated in 1996.

The lands of several Indian peoples, such as the Waimiri-Atroari,
Parakanã, Guajá, Cintas-Largas, and Arara, were invaded by mining,
agribusiness, ranching, and timber companies. To everyone's surprise,
however, with the notable exception of the Guajá, most of these people
obtained reparations in the form of other tracts of nearby lands.

Autonomy and Integration

A best guess estimate made by FUNAI indicates that there are still some
thirty autonomous peoples in Brazil. The great majority of them live in the
Amazon, and many live in areas coveted by economic interests or government mining or hydroelectric projects. FUNAI is not only unequipped to
protect these peoples, but it also has been unable to change the approach

and outlook of making contact and establishing a decent relationship with autonomous Indians. This is certainly the main reason why Indians suffer such terrible health and emotional consequences in the first years of contact.

The majority of surviving Indian peoples have maintained some sort of relationship with the broader national society for years. Some have a very intense relationship, either because they live near towns and villages and their economies depend on regional markets, or because they share many cultural traits with the surrounding rural society. In the terminology of FUNAI, they are said to be "in the process of integration" or "integrated" to the national community. Indian peoples who maintain a less permanent form of contact with the regional society—who have self-sufficient economies with little need for extra goods and speak poor or inept Portuguese—are said to be in "intermittent contact." The autonomous groups are simply called "isolated." As a matter of fact, these notions have more to do with the wider political project of bringing Indian peoples and their cultures into the Brazilian social and ideological melting pot and assimilating them as Brazilians, than with anthropological reality. The remaining Indian peoples of Brazil have survived and are what they are precisely by virtue of the differences they have maintained in relation to the rest of the Brazilian population. In many cases such differentiation is observed not so much by distinguishable cultural traits as by the conservation of internal social mechanisms, such as the continuing regulation of endogenous marriages and of a cooperative economy. Many Indian peoples live as effectively integrated into Brazilian society as can be, but this does not mean that they are on the way to assimilation—unless they are coerced—since they persist in identifying themselves as Indian and in being identified as such by the local population.

FORMAL EDUCATION

Besides the obligation of guaranteeing lands to the Indians, FUNAI has the task of providing them with formal education as a means of their integration and assimilation. In the early 1970s FUNAI hired linguists and educators to define a strategy and develop the contents of educational programs for several Indian peoples. The new programs were based on more adequate presuppositions than those used in SPI times, when the educational content was formalistic and unreal. In his introduction to the 1961 edition of the book on the Tenetehara, Charles Wagley notes that the Portuguese primer used in the 1940s began with the unexpected phrase "the earth is a planet of the solar system." It is worth remembering that during the Jesuit period even Latin grammar was taught to the Indians. In contrast, FUNAI began with the idea that the Indians would learn better if taught in their own language and by Indian teachers. These programs were called bilingual educational programs, and several of them functioned relatively well for a few years.[34] The programs for the Guajajara, Kaingang, Karajá, and a few others reached a certain level of accomplishment up to the third or fourth grades, because the Indian teachers had been well trained. After a few years, however, the programs lost their original drive, salaries dropped, and teaching became repetitive and lacking in purpose. As students finished fourth grade they did not have any more to learn from their teachers. In some cases the more advanced and ambitious students were sent to nearby towns to continue their learning process in the cultural milieu of other Brazilians. Many Indians became literate, learned the ways of Brazilians, and began to demand new positions for themselves in terms of employment and social privileges. In some cases they went on to be leaders of their peoples, particularly in dealing with FUNAI and the surrounding official world. This development, in a sense, fulfilled some of the objectives of the educational process.

In the last ten years, however, most educational programs have shifted their pedagogy from native languages to Portuguese. It apparently became difficult to train new native teachers, and in some cases the Indian communities began to demand to learn correct Portuguese and follow the traditional model of Brazilian primary education. Many Indians today know that the earth is a planet in the solar system, but this learning process is more a reflex to the times than the result of a consistent educational policy on the part of FUNAI.

HEALTH POLICY

The health of the Indians has been a motive of concern since the Jesuits, who greatly prided themselves on their care for the sick and their knowledge of medicine, which in those days included herbs, bloodletting, and the application of the holy oils at the right moment. For many years massive deaths of Indians were attributed to their own frailty. It was only with the overhauling of the SPI in the 1940s that more effective measures were initiated to combat epidemics through vaccination programs and to control endemic diseases, such as typhoid fever, malaria, and tuberculosis, through modern and preventive medications. The pioneering work of public health doctor Noel Nutels from the late 1940s through the 1960s in combating tuberculosis and in installing mobile health teams became deservedly well known in the country because of media coverage, especially in popular magazines.[35] FUNAI, for its part, was to maintain the health programs that had succeeded in reaching to their target groups either by access roads to Indian areas or via the Brazilian air force.

To attend to some Indian ethnies, agreements were signed with health institutions in the country's main cities, the best known of which is with the Paulista School of Medicine in São Paulo, which for more than twenty years has been monitoring the health of the Indians of Xingu National Park. Some states, such as Paraná and Mato Grosso, launched programs for vaccination and set up outpatient clinics with some success. For their part, in recent years various nongovernmental organizations dedicated to the Indian cause have been able to finance public health programs that provide vaccines, an assortment of medicines, and paramedics. The continuity of such programs is frequently hindered, however, by difficulties in maintaining a financial influx, in dodging administrative obstacles, and with maintaining a good working relationship with the Indians. Interestingly enough, no health assistance program promoted by FUNAI or any other organizations has succeeded in preventing population decreases among recently contacted peoples, although many programs have contributed to the relief of stricken populations and in some cases have contributed to establishing equilibrium and even demographic growth in areas of long lasting contact.

In any case, it is not clear whether the turnaround in the Indian demographic curve—which began to occur at the end of the 1950s—is due to the active presence of health programs or to an immunological reversion endogenously obtained by the Indians after years of contact (and at the cost of many deaths). In some cases, as with the Urubu-Ka'apor, it was the intervention of physicians hired by FUNAI that, after detecting the extremely high incidence of syphilis in this population (in 1977 it was almost 95 percent), was able to eradicate that disease and reverse the declining population curve (in 1928 they were 1,200; in 1950, 630; in 1977, 460; but in 1998, 660). On the other hand, the growth of peoples such as the Kaingang, Guajajara, Tikuna, and Makuxi apparently began in the late 1950s and had little to do with medical intervention.

What is most evident is that the physical survival of the Indians is perfectly possible in our times. The medical experiences of FUNAI and various aid programs demonstrate that it is possible to stop the sacrifice of Indian lives blamed on "destiny" or caused by the lack of immunological resistance to the epidemics brought by Europeans. All the same, it is necessary to pursue an efficient, effective policy of medical assistance and equip the Indian agency with the necessary resources, especially in terms of medical personnel.[36]

ECONOMIC INCENTIVES

Another major task assigned to the Indian agency is to provide means to "develop" Indian economies. Nothing in FUNAI's daily routine is more enervating than having to attend to the complaints and requests of an endless number of Indians for manufactured goods, services, and even food. Following the example set by the SPI with its agenda of economic projects, FUNAI had a section charged with promoting Indian economies during the 1970s and 1980s. The basic idea was to introduce new agricultural techniques, new types of crops or varieties of cultigens, and domestic animals where possible. With these novelties it was hoped that the Indian natural economies would be better equipped to produce surpluses, or to take advantage of marketable natural resources, such as timber, *babaçu* palm nuts, Brazil nuts, cacao, rubber, and so on, so that the Indian societies might become self-sufficient, or at least not dependent on FUNAI to meet their new consumer demands.

Following SPI practices, FUNAI launched in the early 1970s several economic projects in areas that yielded softwood timber, such as those of the Kaingang and Guarani in the states of Paraná, Santa Catarina, and Rio Grande do Sul. Some areas received investments in the form of sawmills, tractors, and trucks, while other areas were leased to lumber companies with the goal of producing high dividends for the Indians and the agency. These projects were destined to failure and administrative corruption. Even worse, they led to deforestation in forest reserves of *araucaria* pine in southern Brazil, contributed to the extinction of wildlife species, and provoked land invasions coupled with allegations of property rights acquired by these companies. In the state of Paraná, FUNAI and the Kaingang are still fighting with the Slaviero e Irmãos company over ownership of an area of *araucaria* forest that the lumber company had been leasing continuously since the days of the SPI.

An even more scandalous use of Indian resources for the benefit of FUNAI personnel occurred in the 1980s with the Parakanã Indians. They had been contacted and transferred from their original territory in 1971 because of the TransAmazon Highway, whose route was projected to pass near one of their villages. Later, with the decision to build the Tucuruí Dam for hydroelectric energy, FUNAI found itself obligated to transfer the Parakanã yet again. At the same time it was charged with the task of removing the timber that would be flooded with the closing of the dam. To accomplish these goals, it hired an insurance firm, CAPEMI (linked to the military group then in power), which in its turn subcontracted other companies. At the end of this sorry affair almost no timber had been removed. Today these lands are inundated, the wood rots in the water, and the shores are plagued with the consequences of the ecological imbalance brought about by the artificial lake.

On a smaller scale and with the intention of making the Indians self-sufficient, FUNAI created "community projects" for many Indian peoples and villages. These also failed. The projects presupposed that the Indians had a collective mode of production and would share in common the goods produced. Therefore, the method imposed on them consisted in regimenting the labor power of the community to do collective tasks. Each man or head of family would be paid weekly or monthly a certain stipend in consumer goods, such as cooking oil, food, kerosene, or soap, which he or she would have to pay back with the product of the harvest, usually some commercial produce such as soybean, rice, or corn. In some cases, especially with the Xavante, a great deal of money was invested in infrastructure, with granaries and warehouses, trucks, jeeps, tractors, and harvester combines. In almost every Xavante village there was an economic project going on. As a result, large villages broke apart to form newer, smaller ones so that the leading headmen could have his own project. They would generally begin with plenty of resources, but around the middle of the timetable, in the second or third year, the Indians would lose their enthusiasm, stop working with the required assiduity, and the project would break down.[37]

Subsequent analyses have demonstrated that the problem could not be reduced to the presumed laziness of the Indians, as prejudice would have it, but was to be situated in a lack of understanding on the part of the Indians concerning how such productive activities should be linked with their sociocultural reality. In this sense, neither FUNAI nor even practical anthropologists, particularly those engaged in devising projects, obtaining funding from overseas NGOs, or working as advisers, were ever able to resolve the problem of Indian economic self-sufficiency. In fact, the crux of the problem may be found in the lack of definition of the sociopolitical position of Indian societies on the national scene. It is not a matter of economics, but rather a question that can only be answered in the context of a new Indian policy that should create the bases for a suitable and permanent relationship. In other words, once the Indians know the purpose behind their production, and if this purpose suits their cultural and political needs, they will certainly know what to produce and how to produce.

CONCLUSION

I have presented and discussed in some detail the several sets of official measures that have been imposed upon the Indians during five centuries of military, political, social, economic, and judicial control. That which makes up the historical Brazilian Indian policy can be typified as the legal accouterment of a colonial system. As has been repeatedly stressed, Brazil was a colony that grew and expanded over the bodies and resources of the Indians. Although it broke loose from external colonialism, in relation to the Indians it continued to maintain a relationship model of internal colonialism.[38] In Brazil, Indians continue to be seen as "relatively capable" persons, as inferior cultures, and as nonviable autonomous political systems.

Considering the way of life and thought transplanted by Western civilization to the Americas, there is no reason to imagine that things could have been different. To all intents and purposes, the Indian was no more than an obstacle to be overcome. At the end of half a millennium, however, the lifestyle of each of the neo-American nations has been molded in accordance with the historical circumstances of its formation—in many cases, with the distinct coloring of native cultures and as a result of the interplay of socioeconomic relations based on the socioeconomic level of the Indian peoples who inhabited the territories of these new nations.

In Brazil, where the great majority of Indian ethnies had cultures founded on a mode of production based on slash-and-burn agriculture and a social system of autonomous villages, which induced a high degree of political autarchy and individual liberties, the weight of colonialism fell with gratuitous force. Submission of Indian peoples predominated—at first, in both explicit and disguised forms of slavery, together with a more flexible form of servitude; later, with a peculiar mixture of patronage and paternalism. Only in rare moments did individual and ethnic liberty prevail. In practice, to be free an Indian people had to live outside of, or at best, on the margins of the colonial system.

During the colonial period the only alternative for this system was undertaken by the religious missions, principally those of the Jesuits. On one hand, their presence and activities slowed the destructive impulses of colonization, giving it a Christian coloring. On the other, they attempted to effectively create a different type of colonial system through a mode of production that could be seen as semifeudal or servile. Here the Indians were to live in communities organized by the priests, under the aegis of Christian morality, and had their labor power arranged collectively to work on either farm or craft tasks.

Undoubtedly, the undisguised ill-will of both the Portuguese Crown and the colonists towards the Jesuits led to the religious order's expulsion from Brazil in 1759. In consequence, there ensued a deliberate destruction of the Missions of the Seven Peoples and the transformation of other mission villages into Luso-Brazilian towns. These are concrete examples that demonstrate the cupidity of Portuguese colonialism and its internal and external insecurity.

The recognition of the sovereignty of Indian peoples and of their natural right over their lands and their ways of life was explicitly set forth several times in royal charters and ordinances. They attest to a judicial and legalistic concern on the part of the Portuguese Crown to morally justify the conquest. Such a concern, however, had very little practical and administrative significance. Not only were these royal pronouncements generally issued for the purpose of specifically admonishing some governor or captain-general concerning a select Indian people, but also because the orders contained therein were not expected to be followed with great diligence and precision. Certainly they rarely were. Nevertheless, it is on account of these legal instruments that jurists and legal anthropologists can today argue for an historical recognition of the rights of Indian peoples over their lands.[39]

Notwithstanding the permanence of an internalized colonialism and an undisguised streak of conservatism in its ontological aspect, Indian policy has undergone tangible changes since Brazil's independence. The Indian, who had been placed as the opposite of the Western being, began slowly to be brought closer to this model of humanity, albeit as an orphan and a ward, a type of bastard child of an anguished and guilt-ridden father. I believe this is the historical disposition most deeply ingrained among Brazilians in relation to the Indians who survived the programmed plunder of their lands.

On the political scene, the Indian has been gradually transformed into a client of the state, albeit a state with staggeringly inconsistent approaches to reparations and redress. This, it seems, would be the general trend that can be recognized ever since the Regency, going through the second half of the Empire, and throughout the old and modern republican periods.

To be sure, the Law of the Lands of 1850, more than any other since the

Directory of Pombal, directly caused the demise of dozens of Indian villages that were part of the Brazilian socioeconomic system, many of them with stable or growing populations. Their inhabitants began to live as caboclos and landless peasants and lost their earlier cultural characteristics, in many cases barely maintaining a mythological memory of their past. The fact that some of these ancient villages have actually survived to present times demonstrates that many more would have been able to do so. The indifference of the authorities entrusted with defending the Indians, and their ideological and economic alignment with regional and local elites, were responsible for this state of affairs.

The attempt to emancipate the Indians from state guardianship in the late 1970s could have resulted in a similar situation of territorial and cultural loss. It provides an example of the kind of dangers to watch out for. Returning subtly in the form of the liberal idea of self-control of lands (as happened in the early 1950s with the North American Indians), this "help" might be even more insidious. Since the early 1990s there have been in the Brazilian Congress several proposals that deal with opening Indian lands to mining, lumbering, and hydroelectric dams, and even with diminishing the size of previously demarcated lands.

The Positivist Apostolate was not able to make the Brazilian state recognize the Indian peoples as free and sovereign nations, but it did bequeath to the nation a tradition of respect for the Indian as a person, a recognition that these peoples are part of Brazilian history, and an attitude of dedication and love for their cause. This was, in a way, more than what liberal thought, through anthropology, left as an effective legacy to the Indians. However, this tradition always operated in subordination to the interests and styles of state administrations and the military. Whenever something deemed more important arose in Indian regions, such as programs of economic development, good intentions were left aside in favor of an overpowering reality. Thus, one cannot conclude with much conviction that the continuation of the positivist tradition would have been beneficial to the Indians.

The military regime, despite its efforts to destabilize pro-Indian sympathy, was not able to finish off with the Indians nor to transform them into common Brazilians within the period of twenty years beginning in 1976, as was then proposed by the Ministry of the Interior. On the contrary, it had to witness not only the rising curve of Indian demography, but also their concomitant cultural awakening and participation on the national political scene. An Indian was elected to the National Congress in 1982 and several times denounced violent acts committed against his people in hard and vehement tones. This came as an unexpected disturbance to the military regime.

With the official return of democracy in 1985 (but practically speaking since the previous year when political changes brought fresh air to FUNAI's leadership), it seemed that a new era was finally dawning for the Indians. The participation of anthropologists and Indians, and, more importantly, of new Indian leadership, in steering the direction of the agency was intense in the first months of that year. FUNAI quickly processed the demarcation of important lands, including the northern extension of Xingu Indian Park, and made legal the recognition for the Yanomami Indian lands. By October 1985, however, FUNAI had suffered another intervention, once more in the name of national security, of the military allied with anti-Indian politicians, whose goal was to purge the agency of any radical attitudes favoring FUNAI autonomy or greater participation by Indians, anthropologists, and other militants of the Indian cause. The projected Yanomami Indian Park, planned to have some 9.5 million hectares, was delimited into seven distinct and isolated areas, with less than 3 million hectares. There followed an invasion of thousands of gold and cassiterite-ore prospectors, who eventually came in close contact with the Yanomami, brought highly virulent diseases, and caused the contamination of their rivers.

Although in the early 1990s FUNAI has been led by personnel who are highly experienced and qualified to work with Indians, they have had their autonomy restricted and have been impotent in the face of governmental decisions emanating from national security guidelines and priorities. FUNAI thus has been losing the political substance that the Statute of the Indian had conferred upon it. At present the Indian agency is subordinated to the Ministry of Justice, but instead of gaining in administrative autonomy it is rather losing the prerogatives it once had in the matter of defining Indian lands and how to demarcate them. To be sure, the Yanomami Indian Park was demarcated with the originally planned area, but it has been constantly assailed by gold prospectors, who keep invading it in spite of governmental intervention. This important demarcation was processed by default and in spite of FUNAI. It was done exclusively on the autocratic will of the president of the Republic, Fernando Collor de Mello, who was in need of showing a positive image of the country at the World Conference on the Environment and Development in 1992. The agency's capacity to protect that enormous extension of land is so faltering that it cannot avoid the continuing presence of wayward gold prospectors and the consequent conflicts with the Indians.

In 1988 it was expected that the National Constituent Assembly and the National Congress would do no less than extinguish FUNAI and create a new agency, with moral foundations similar to the spirit of Rondonian indigenism. A new Indian agency would be based upon the knowledge acquired in the last thirty years concerning the causes of extinction and the chances of survival of Indian peoples. It should constitute itself to count on responsible, non-patronizing participation of the Indians on its staff, from the field stations to the top ranks of decision making.

This has not yet happened, although there is hope. Article 232 of the new constitution, which defines the position of the Indian in the Brazilian nation, was shaped with the participation of many anthropologists, jurists, and Indians, and is in the finest spirit of Brazilian indigenism. It reiterates the rights of the Indians over the lands they inhabit and the exclusive use of their goods and resources. It places the services of the Public Attorney's office at their disposal and grants them the right, individually or collectively, to bring suit against whomever offends them, including the federal government. In short, the constitution raises them to the status of citizens with full rights, without removing from them the security of state protection. Furthermore, it requires approval by the National Congress for any economic enterprise that intends to make use of the Indians' water and mineral resources, assuring them full participation in the form of royalties and dividends.

Despite its importance and novelty, this article has still not been implemented by statutory law. The National Congress vacillates between several proposals on the Indian question and is postponing its decision to an unspecified future date. On the other hand, the outdated Statute of the Indian continues to be in force, without in fact functioning. In the past few years FUNAI has been an agency on the verge of paralysis, barely meeting the interests of its own employees, and has been greatly incapacitated in concluding the demarcation of all remaining Indian lands. In fact, the deadline of five years for concluding this task, established by the Constitution of 1988, has already passed.

Despite the political advances achieved by many Indian leaders, foreseeing perhaps a new era, we can presume that the Indian question is in the final moments of a period still dominated by patronage and paternalism. This situation can be observed as the breakdown of an attitude and a form of political relationship that are based on a philosophical outlook in which the Indian is considered a primitive being, the equal of a child. It also comes from the general opinion that the Indians are condemned to extinction, to vanish from the face of the earth, or at best to be "white" or mestizo like everybody else. In this sense, it would be rash therefore to criticize the SPI and even FUNAI for having been paternalistic with the Indians, but now things have changed. The Indians have demonstrated a capacity for demographic recovery in the last forty years that forces us to reevaluate their supposedly inexorable social reality. They are not going to die out, nor must they necessarily vanish as peoples of the earth. Thus there is no reason to treat them piteously as bastard children with a terminal disease.

Equally important is to recognize that their alleged primitiveness is not an innate cultural fact, as has been well demonstrated by anthropological research for more than one hundred years, but a political interpretation on the part of a civilization that sets itself up as a standard for all other cultures and civilizations that have existed in the world. The theory of evolution gave it a scientific basis, a banner which it has ostentatiously and arrogantly unfurled, waving it over other great civilizations, such as those of China and India. One cannot help noting that this banner is now somewhat faded, and that to seek a new infusion of color it must open itself to the contributions of other cultures and other civilizations. Indian cultures may be seen as viable in this context—not simply as singular and incomparable cultures, as the cultural relativism of anthropology concedes to them.

Finally, for all these reasons I believe there are new objective conditions to end the long-lasting era of paternalism, both as an attitude and a principle. Moving beyond this mindset, we might be able to think seriously about creating a new Indian policy to open the path for cultural and ethnic survival, as well as for a respectful coexistence between Brazilians and Indians. What we are going through today represents a crisis of paternalism and the pangs of liberation made concrete by the demographic growth of Indian peoples and by their quest for political participation. Even the anti-Indian forces know that they can no longer treat the Indians as children, even though they may still try to fool them. We—civil society, Indians, anthropologists, lawyers, and journalists—must recognize our limited power to conduct the paths of this possible new era of interethnic relations, but that should not stop us from working toward such a goal.

What We Think about the Indians

First we should ask: what do the Indians think about us and about our world? To write about this with much conviction would be an act of audacity since, strictly speaking, such a task could only fully be accomplished by the Indians themselves. What we really know about what the Indians think of us comes from a heterogeneous collection of loose statements, short histories, anecdotes, and secondary interpretations of Indian depositions, collected by people with the most diverse interests and purposes: anthropologists, travelers, indigenists, missionaries, country and city dwellers, the curious, and the mendacious.

Let us start our perusal into this matter with the interesting account given by the French philosopher Michel de Montaigne in his much acclaimed essay "On Cannibals." He begins by saying that around 1565 he had had the opportunity of meeting with some Tupinambá Indians who had been residing in France for some time (one or two had even married French women). He asked them what they thought of this European world, so different from theirs in Brazil. They are reported to have answered with three main points, one of which Montaigne confesses to have forgotten. Of the other two, the first was that they had observed great inequality among the French, with some being very rich and powerful but the majority poor and needy, and they were surprised that these poor did not rebel against the rich. The other point was that they found it absurd that a mere child (the dauphin, Charles) should be the king of the French, when there were so many strong and willing men who looked as if they could better exercise that role.[1]

As much as these remarks might appear to be a case of literary embellishment, as are the majority of anecdotes about Indians, they sound perfectly plausible. Anthropologists and indigenists who maintain amicable

and close relations with Indians and have accompanied them on their sojourning around Brazilian cities have reported similar observations. The
themes of inequality and hierarchy seem to be common in the Indians' observations of our world and in their subsequent queries. The Indian sociological vision is demonstrably concrete and empirical, like that of a foreign
observer who is still ignorant of the history, structure, and symbols of the
society being observed—like an apprentice of anthropology.[2]

There are infrequent accounts from the sixteenth century on in which
the voice of the Indian is present—if not verbatim, at least in the closest
form that the literature of the period permitted, although rarely with the
tolerant reception of a Montaigne. Jean de Léry, a French Huguenot who
visited the Tupinambá in Rio de Janeiro around 1562, transcribed a rather
candid dialogue he had with an Indian in the Tupinambá language. He
reports that an old Tupinambá wondered why the French have traveled
from so far just to gather brazilwood and take it back home: were they
suffering from a lack of firewood with which to warm themselves? In 1614
on the isle of São Luís, the French Capuchin priest Yves d'Évreux also takes
notice of the political cogitations of several Tupinambá elders, alternating
Tupinambá phrases with the French translation. For their part, the Jesuits
initiated the study of Indian languages with the elaboration of a grammar
that Father José de Anchieta prepared on the Tupinambá language, which,
being so ubiquitous in Brazil, became the basis for the religious indoctrination of almost all Indian peoples who were brought together in missions.
This veritable lingua franca, known as *nheengatu,* was used among Indians and non-Indians until practically the middle of the eighteenth century.[3]

The philosophical interest of the Europeans concerning the Indians was
rather short-lived, rarely appearing after the sixteenth century, once the
early years of wonder and curiosity were over. Accordingly, except for
the Tupinambá and Guarani—of whom there are at least five or six very
good grammars as well as a great amount of information—few other Indian peoples had comprehensive descriptions of their cultures and languages. It seemed as if once political domination was established and the
economic foundations for colonization were solid, both Portuguese chroniclers and Jesuits put aside their initial concern for understanding the Indians and making them known to their contemporaries and began to concentrate on more important business. Certainly both Protestantism and
inquisitorial Catholicism did not favor naked heathens who seemed immune to religious indoctrination. The cultural and psychological stereotypes established by the middle of the sixteenth century began to domi-

nate the literature on Indians, with few modifications until the eighteenth century. There are exceptions, of course, such as the account of the Indians of the middle São Francisco River written by French Capuchin Martinho de Nantes, and a grammar of the Kariri Indians produced by Father Luis Mami-ani, both at the end of the seventeenth century.[4]

It is perhaps also surprising that the Dutch, who controlled the sugar-rich captaincy of Pernambuco for nearly three decades (1628–1654), also demonstrated little interest in the Indians. The accounts they left of their close contact with Indian peoples express an almost exclusive concern with seeking political alliances and have little ethnographic information of any significance.[5] During the long years of war between the Luso-Brazilians and the Dutch, the Tupinambá-Potiguar Indians (who numbered less than 4,000) found themselves in two confronting parties, one side rallying with the Dutch and the other with the Portuguese. The Dutch group was led by Pedro Poti, who had been educated for several years in Holland, while the other had Felipe Camarão as their captain, a man who eventually became celebrated in Brazilian history for his role in helping expel the Dutch. For a few months Pedro and Felipe exchanged a most interesting written correspondence, in which each side accuses the other of disloyalty and religious infidelity. This literary testimony, tragic in its consequences, displays the voice of the Indian engulfed by the surrounding historical contradictions.[6]

The historiography on Indians is full of the most variegated remarks, observations, and interpretations of who the Indians are and how they think and act. It has generally led to more confusion than clarity and has been responsible for the array of preconceptions that were imprinted in the Western imagination. For instance, it has been said and repeated—even been taught in universities—that the Aztecs and Incas were defeated and conquered by the numerically inferior Spaniards largely because of the paralyzing and disorienting panic they felt on seeing the horse, or more accurately, the horse-man combination. Not only the horse but also this "centaur" was supposedly unknown to the Indians, and the Spaniards deployed it on the battlefield with their characteristic dexterity. However much such a weapon may have been crucial to the conquest of those people, one cannot but sense the exotic purpose in that assertion. In fact, since the Indians are generally regarded as good observers, and the Aztecs and Incas could not have been exceptions to that rule, the strange new beast must have in a short time been correctly perceived in its true nature. All the same, mounted soldiers could still induce great awe and terror among the Indians, such was the power of their attack.[7] The anecdote, however, suggested by the accounts of the first conquistadors, has survived, and many enjoy repeating it as an example of all that is curious, exotic, and naive about the Indians.

Another similar example comes from the Indians of the island of Hispaniola, now the Dominican Republic, who are said to have had such doubts concerning the humanity of the Spaniards that they at one time drowned some of them and then kept their cadavers immersed to test if they were immune to putrefaction. Such a story, or more accurately its subsequent interpretation as a sign of the Indians' awe at the marvels they saw before them, their supposed belief that the newcomers were supernatural beings, is retold even by an anthropologist of great intellectual and humanist insight, Claude Lévi-Strauss.[8] Along the same lines, another anthropologist hurriedly analyzed the fact that the Tupinambá called the French *mair*, a "demiurge" or "enchanted one," as if they considered them godlike people. Why then did they call the Portuguese *peró*, a word whose meaning seems to have been lost and which may have been no more than a corruption of the word "Pedro," as some Brazilian historians suppose? Could it be that the gunpowder, ships, and steel of the Portuguese were not as magical as those of the French?[9]

For the civilized world, the reports that the Indians confused Europeans with gods could only be due to their naiveté and fuzzy awareness of the concrete reality of the world. As early as the sixteenth century Father José de Anchieta reported an incident in which a Tupinambá woman accused a Jesuit priest of having had sexual relations with her. With faith in the chastity of his colleague, Anchieta interrogated the woman more closely and discovered that the act had occurred only in dream. He thus drew the conclusion that the Tupinambá Indians could not distinguish between dream and reality. Centuries later, a variation on this story was evoked by French anthropologist Lucien Lévy-Bruhl as having happened with an Englishman among the Chaco Indians of South America. An Indian accused a surprised Mr. Grubb of having stolen vegetables from his garden. The Englishman retorted that he could not possibly have done the mischief since on that occasion he had been 150 miles from the scene of the theft. On further questioning it was discovered that the Indian had dreamed of this incident, but nevertheless continued to affirm it as fact. These two examples are used without any sense of critique by the same anthropologist and by other modern thinkers as examples of the way Indians are wont to think and how this kind of thinking is incapable of objectivity.[10]

Clearly, these interpretations do not help us appreciate what the Indians think of us and of the world in general. They rather represent what many, if not most, civilized people think about the Indians. Those who know them well, however, recognize that the Indians do not take Europeans to be godlike and are perfectly capable of understanding the process of gunpowder combustion, the making of steel, and other such things, even without seeing and understanding the theory behind them and their development. After all, few of us understand the theory of the atom and nuclear energy, but we know what these things stand for, at least to some degree.

Degrading, disparaging, and mystifying Indian thought has long been almost a requirement of the Western world, and this iniquity is still with us. This is so perhaps not always out of a sense of ill will, but because we still do not know how to situate ourselves and our ways of thinking in an appropriate relation to the Indian peoples.

In any case, it is likely that the Indians admire Western civilization for its accomplishments, its material production, its power, and its capacity for expansion. It is entirely unlikely that they admire the social inequalities, the poverty and misery, the explosive violence, the excessive disciplining of children, the unbridled egotism, and the disrespect for nature. They know perfectly well that they are the minority partners in this unforeseen union of civilizations, and that they live in danger.

The Humanity of the Indians

Throughout the Western history of the Americas, the Indians have been represented by an array of interpretations, images, and stigmas, many of which have become engraved in the depths of our hierarchical and bigoted minds. These images were nurtured in the prevailing ideologies and in the social and economic relations built to accommodate the Indians in the making of each of the neo-American nations. They were further colored by the roles the Indians played in the political formation of these nations, whether as slaves, as free, servile, patronized, or salaried labor, as allies in war, as fierce enemies, as obstacles to expansion, or as hindrances to economic development.

The impression of the novel and the unknown that the Indians immediately made upon the Europeans, beginning with the reports of the first voyage of Vespucci along the Brazilian coast, also fired their desire to form a clear idea regarding these peoples. Were they descendants of one of Noah's sons? Were they visited by one of the apostles? Considering their cruel, inhuman habits such as cannibalism, their indifference toward the material symbols of European power such as gold, their intemperance, and above all, their irrepressible desire to live in freedom and in nature, the Europeans asked themselves whether or not the Indians were really human beings. Did they possess the faculty of rationality and, if so, to what degree?

Although for some Europeans these questions carried a philosophical interest, for many they were formulated in a rhetorical manner and were intended for the sole purpose of reducing the Indians to the status of animallike creatures, thus justifying their exploitation. Few times in human history has a constituted power ever come to the point of questioning whether or not another people were human, although as a psychological attitude the debasing of others is quite common among peoples grappling in rivalry. But among the Portuguese and the Spaniards, among their jurists and clergy, and among the common people as well, a controversy arose over this issue and reached such a level that it required the intervention of the Vatican, the final court of appeal in the Western world up to that point. Through the bull *Veritas Ipsa,* issued on June 9, 1537, by Pope Paul III, a Renaissance man, the Indians were classed together with other humans, and their enslavement was prohibited on pain of excommunication. Such a seemingly radical decision (which did not include the black peoples) was deemed necessary in face of the high level of cruelty being practiced in the Spanish colonies against the Indians, a fact vehemently denounced by the Dominican friar Bartolomé de las Casas. As for Brazil, it should be noted that this bull was only made public a century later, by means of another bull, *Comissum Nobis,* which was issued by Pope Urban VIII, on April 22, 1639, reaffirming the terms of the previous bull and threatening anyone who enslaved Indians with the same penalty.

On the other hand, on the concrete level of person-to-person interaction, the corporeal humanity of the Indians was recognized by most people from the beginning. They were acknowledged to be of fine and proportionate shape, and of having a mind that was both practical and sagacious. However, doubts were raised concerning their spirituality, especially since they proved so disinclined to embrace Christianity, adore God, and venerate the saints, and to abandon their own religion, myths, and customs. (It should be noted that in the nineteenth century some racist theories would call into question even the physical humanity of the Indians.) The search for signs of cultural and spiritual inhumanity was so intense that merely because the Tupinambá language lacked the sounds *f, l,* and *r,* the Jesuits perversely deduced that the Indians had neither faith, nor law, nor king (*rei*). How could any people lack these attributes and still be human? This first linguistic-structuralist deduction was repeated practically until the nineteenth century.

Before becoming the "good or noble savages" through the far-reaching, albeit faltering, analyses of such Enlightenment philosophers as Rousseau and Diderot, the Indians remained for a long time on that dangerous threshold between nature and culture, between the animal kingdom and the realm of humanity. They were part of the most important debate between two opposing doctrines concerning nature and culture (or civilization). On one hand, there was the doctrine that nature was good and civilization bad, Rousseau's paradigm, so to speak, which was formulated in the mid-1700s; on the other, there was Hobbes's paradigm, expressed a century earlier, which stated that nature was bad and cruel, and that man could only live in peace by means of civilization.[11]

In a sense, the humanity of the Indians is conceived to this day according to whether one embraces one or the other of these paradigms. Through the late eighteenth and the whole of the nineteenth centuries it is probable that the Hobbes's notion was more prevalent and acceptable than Rousseau's vision. It was easier to consider the Indians, with their simple and unencumbered lifestyles, as "nasty, brutish, and short-lived" beings, to use the phrase from Hobbes, than as representatives of a pristine era of paradisiacal happiness. It was easier, anyway, to use this coarse image to justify the historical facts that were leading to the destruction of many Indian peoples.

The myth of the noble savage was and perhaps still is a powerful notion of Western civilization. However, in its first formulation by Rousseau it carried a certain ambiguity that captured the imagination of those times: noble but naïve; good but mindless. The Enlightenment philosophers who worked out the idea of human progress thought of the savage as the unfolding of a human potentiality found in nature. However, in practice, most of the philosophers did not look with favor on the state of being of the Indians. In large part they were considered degenerate states of a prior ideal that had not been able to evolve by virtue of the climate or catastrophic events. Buffon, in his *Natural History of the Peoples,* interpreted savage society as "a tumultuous gathering of barbarous and independent men who obey only their private passions." As in Hobbes's paradigm, it was necessary to have some ordering of this state of existence so that social living and reason might flourish together with happiness.[12] Even Rousseau considered that for humans to be happy their lives needed to be regulated, and that there should be private property and even a certain degree of social inequality. His concept of the noble savage is preceded by an earlier stage in which man is not quite human yet, but is rather like a lonesome animal living in nature. Here humans are guided exclusively by instinct, do not distinguish beauty from ugliness, are not curious, and do not even recognize their own children. Although this vision is not flattering, it contrasts with the idea of degeneration that was propounded by other philosophers. Rousseau believed that there were no living peoples at this early stage, but there were those at the next level, "between the indolence of the primitive state and the petulant activity of our self-love." This would be the ideal state for humanity, in his view, and it was there that he placed the contemporary savage peoples.[13]

The debate that ensued over the kind and quality of the past of humanity was fundamental for modern times. It opened new possibilities of thinking about Indian peoples and cultures and provoked a strong influence on utopian and revolutionary political philosophies. In the end, Hobbes's paradigm of the need for hierarchical command and the ideas of human degeneration lost, particularly regarding the development of the social sciences.

However, as far as the Indians were concerned, Hobbes's paradigm turned out to be stronger and more permanent in the political-administrative circles of the colonialist metropoles and colonial elites. By the early years of the nineteenth century, even such an enlightened statesman as José Bonifácio thought the Indians were indolent and feeble-minded. However, since one of the main causes of this state as well as the theory of degeneration depended upon the environment (America and especially the humid tropics were thought to corrupt and weaken people), it became a hard task to find a way to escape the idea that this would also eventually implicate the white people who had been living for long periods of time in those regions. The solution to this dilemma was found subsequently by the theory of evolution, which transfered the blame from the environment, or geographical determinism, to biology. By the middle of the nineteenth century, historians such as Adolpho de Varnhagen and politicians such as Senator Dantas de Barros Leite saw in the poor Indian remnants—lacking land and possibilities for living autonomously—signs of this irreversible natural state, and not the results of a social phenomenon.[14]

Actually, philosophic thinking concerning the Indian was not abundant in colonial Brazil. The Jesuits did not interest themselves in developing any profound reasoning in this regard, both because their intellectual foundation was Scholasticism and because their interests were mostly utilitarian and religious. They showed interest only in whether or not the Indians had the capacity to be converted to the Christian faith. In this endeavor they soon discovered that conversion would not come simply by the word of God, but would only follow physical and cultural subjugation. Only by the yoke of the sword and the rod of iron, in Anchieta's expression, could religious indoctrination be carried out with success. With this attitude the Jesuits also abandoned the curiosity for the specific cultural forms of the Indians that they had cultivated in the first period of missionary work. For all practical purposes, Father Fernão Cardim, at the end of the sixteenth century, was the last Jesuit to produce an original ethnographic description, and even this was on the Tupinambá, already widely known. Simão de Vasconcelos, the Jesuit chronicler who wrote during the middle of the seventeenth century, added no further ethnographic information on the Tupinambá or other Indian ethnies. Father Antônio Vieira, the great champion of the Indians and of the missionary work of his order against the fury of the colonists, never demonstrated the slightest cultural or intellectual interest toward the peoples he defended, whom he brought down to live near Portuguese settlements or whom he pacified.[15]

The Jesuits soon discovered that the best vehicles for indoctrination were Indian children, once the political domination of their parents had been established. They invested all their efforts in teaching them how to read and write, sacred music, theatrical pieces, arts and skills in ironwork, masonry, and woodworking, and developing their intellects in arithmetic and Latin. Obviously the Indians learned, which left no doubt as to their intellectual capacities. If the task was difficult at first, it became easier as Indian culture, now under harsh attack, rapidly lost its sociological reason for being. Although the majority of Indians brought to missions died there within a few years, those who survived paid the high price of their cultural transfiguration. They became mission Indians, and the Jesuits were not in the least interested in reflecting philosophically about them.

However, not all Indian peoples were subjugated and settled in missions or enslaved or engaged to live on Portuguese plantations and towns. There were many who remained as autonomous peoples living a pristine existence and refusing much contact with the Portuguese world. Their way of life seemed to express generosity, a collective spirit, and joy in living. At the same time, however, there was such sexual licentiousness, a deeply rooted sense of freedom, and cannibalism. Although in the beginning a few Jesuits tried to examine and resolve this predicament, they soon became immersed in the business of dealing with the mission and colonists and did not produce any meaningful discussion on the matter. It took someone from outside the Portuguese colonial regime—someone in a less stable position who could still keep the spirit of inquiry—to elaborate an argument on the Indian predicament. This person was Yves d'Évreux, a French Capuchin, a member of the religious mission sent to help establish the French colony in Maranhão at the beginning of the seventeenth century. In the year he spent among the Tupinambá (1614), d'Évreux spoke with dozens of them through the *turgimons,* the French interpreters who lived with the Indians and knew their culture and history. From this experience, he elaborated the following argument: nature is good; the Tupinambá are part of nature, with few rules, and therefore they are also intrinsically good. They have become evil and act imperfect because Satan is in their midst to inspire and corrupt them. It is thus necessary to extricate them from this cohabitation, and therein lies the function of religious indoctrination.[16]

This interesting syllogism can be seen as a forerunner both of the classical representation of the myth of the noble savage and the justification of all modern religious indoctrination. It is even more alluring than Rousseau's original construction, because whereas his is placed on an evolutionary and presumably scientific plane, d'Évreux places his own on an atemporal and therefore mythological plane. Indeed many of us today still think in similar terms: that the Indian is pure, free, and lacking in natural wickedness—but in contact with civilization (Satan) becomes corrupted and degenerate.

The myth of the noble savage, born of speculation on concepts such as nature, culture, progress, and degeneracy—although on the political level its arguments were based on the European problems of the eighteenth century—carries within itself a generous and idealistic vision of the Indians and implies a more humanitarian stance in relation to the Indian. However, its permanence on the intellectual scene and in the imagination of present times is due to other less positive factors. The myth places the Indians in the lowest position on the evolutionary scale and in doing so provides the main motive for their extinction, as it considers them a phase or a stage of human development already left behind, as bearers of a type of culture that is unviable in modern times. The myth accounts for both the goodness and the cruelty of the Indians, for their sense of liberty, for their purity of heart and sagacity, for their indolence and physical resistance, and finally, for their life and death. From the scientific point of view, the myth takes on varied evolutionist expressions in the writings of Charles Darwin and Herbert Spencer, Karl Marx, Lewis H. Morgan, V. Gordon Childe and Julian Steward, or rises up as a stage in the process of acculturation, which to the modern taste seems more acceptable and empirical. Together with other less rigorous views of the world, sentiments, and thoughts, it constitutes what I have called the paradigm of acculturation.[17] What is common in all these variations is an utter disbelief in the future survival of the Indians; at best they accede to the Indians' physical assimilation into the (Brazilian) mainstream population and perhaps the permanence of a few cultural items that were absorbed by that population. However much the Christian churches have entertained an interest in the Indians, Christianity does not have much faith in the survival of the Indian. The Indian is a lost cause for which, in the case of the Catholic Church until very recently, the Church was prepared to minister the last rites. The Indian's torment and plight have been compared with the passion of Christ (who, being God, rises again—but not the Indian).

It has been for some time a genuine surprise for everyone to discover that many Indian populations are recovering and that the Indian has therefore become historically viable. Not everyone is aware of this phenomenon, and many know only of its repercussions, such as changes in the political behavior of the Indians toward the nation, and particularly toward the Indian agency. Civil society observes these changes, sometimes suffers through them, more often is frightened of them, and without meaning to, withdraws in its solidarity. The Indians no longer seem to be noble savages, and society is at a loss as to how to interpret them. The myth of the noble savage seems to be exhausting itself as the Indian goes on living. If it is not subsumed by a new myth, based on new explanations of this changing reality, it is probable that the myth of the noble savage will find new ways to recycle itself.

The Integration of the Indian in the Brazilian Nation

Just before independence from Portugal, the Indian presence in Brazil was still quite massive, comprising between 500,000 and 800,000 (15–20 percent of the total population), according to the estimates of various imperial authorities. To their discomfort, the ideologists of the insurgent imperial nation could not avoid considering the Indians as part of the nation. The Indian menace to the colonial project had apparently been exhausted in most of the country, except in the most isolated and least populated regions, such as in the Amazon. There were still a few pockets of Indian resistance and political autonomy in such provinces as Goiás, Bahia, Minas Gerais, and in the southern end of the country. The surviving, autonomous

Indians of Minas Gerais and Bahia were being taken care of in those years and only much later would the southern Indians be cause for concern but never any great danger. What was really disturbing was the possibility that some Indians might ally with freed and escaped blacks, as happened in the Balaiada Rebellion (1838–41), and with greater intensity in the Cabanagem Rebellion (1835–41). These rebellions broke out with sentiments that were shared by the common folk and consequently brought together an enormous concourse of blacks and Indians: blacks who had been living either as slaves or as poor, free artisans, and Indians who were remnants of the former Jesuit villages and the old administrative villages, all of which had been changed into mixed settlements that essentially still functioned in a collective economic system. The Cabanagem Rebellion of the lower Amazon attracted a few autonomous Indian ethnies that could hardly speak a word of Portuguese, although they had been living under the yoke of periodic recruitment for labor and appropriation of their extractive products. The Mura and some of the Maué Indians, together with the generically named Tapuio, made up the major part of the rebel forces that succeeded in taking Belém. However, in the last months of the rebellion, they were abandoned by their white leaders and had to pull back to their villages, where they were mercilessly persecuted and massacred. This region, as has already been noted, is now as empty of Indians as the dry *caatinga* scrublands of Rio Grande do Norte, Paraíba, Ceará, and Piauí, the northeastern states that suffered the raging power of the War of the Barbarians (1654-1714).

The alarm caused by these rebellions precipitated the loudest anti-Indian clamor of the beginning of the Empire. In the course of the Balaiada Rebellion, for example, the future historian João Francisco Lisboa, then a radical journalist who had rallied in favor of change in Maranhão, renounced his engagement to the political arm of the rebellion and to the party that had supported it. He condemned it vehemently and deplored the untrustworthy, treacherous, dishonest, destructive, cowardly, intellectually inferior, and degenerate character of the Indians and the mixed people who participated in that rebellion. His arguments were based on episodes of the history of Brazil as well as on the reality he had come to know in the old and decaying Indian communities of Maranhão. He was not an exception in alluding to the theory of degeneracy to deplore the nature of the Brazilian Indians. Lisboa also derided the romantic and poetic raptures of his fellow Maranhão poet and man of letters Antônio Gonçalves Dias, a defender of the Indian cause, as being "phony *caboclo* [mixed-breed] patriotism." Oddly enough, the poet—who at the time (the 1850s) was a great success at court, being a friend to the young emperor—considered the current Indians to be decadent forms of their past splendor, and in a Rousseau-like manner blamed civilization and its agents for this state of things.[18]

Nevertheless, in the following years, as Lisboa moved to Rio de Janeiro and then to Lisbon, where he did archival research, he was to change his mind in a substantial way about the Indians. Whether because of newly acquired knowledge or because of a widening of his political and cultural vision, Lisboa addressed an ascerbic polemic to Adolpho de Varnhagen, the chief historian of the empire, over the character of the Indians, their origin, and their position on the national scene. Varnhagen had been championing the cause of the landholders and thought Brazil could only justify its existence as an extension of the Portuguese civilization. In several writings, including the *General History of Brazil*, his masterpiece on Brazilian history, and his "Organic Memorial," Varnhagen used moralistic, historic, biological, and philosophical arguments to discard the Indians as a fundamental component of the Brazilian nation. He had even considered them to be invaders of the Brazilian territory, in which sense the Portuguese were level with them. In his mind the final solution for the Indians could only be their extermination by force of arms, as seemed to be happening in North America at the time, or at least the enforcement of a rigid education of all Indians for a period of fifteen years, after which it was hoped that they would become well behaved and productive.[19]

Lisboa contested Varnhagen on historical grounds, attempting to demonstrate the violent character of Portuguese colonization and attributing the Indians' fierce reaction as the outcome of a legitimate instinct for survival. The proposals for the use of force against the Indians offended the liberal thinking that was being formed in the country. It led Manoel Antônio de Almeida, future author of the book *Memoirs of a Militia Sergeant*, to publish an article entitled "Civilization of the Indians," in which he condemned Varnhagen's analyses and proposals as inhuman, harmful to the country, and scientifically outdated. If Varnhagen made use of De Maistre and Vatel to justify the use of force and the biological inferiority of the Indians, Manoel Antônio de Almeida was to rely on the German naturalist Wilhelm von Humboldt. As an epigraph to his article he cited a paragraph taken from Humboldt's book *Cosmos*, which deserves to be reprinted here as an example of the quality of discussion during that period:

> By maintaining the unity of the human species, we reject, as a necessary consequence, the distressing distinction between superior races

and inferior races. Undoubtedly there are families that are more susceptible to culture, more civilized, more illuminated; but they are not nobler than the others. All are equally made for liberty.[20]

The late 1840s and the 1850s were a period of extreme importance for the future of the Indians because it was then that the imperial government defined in several measures the character of the regime as far as economic interests and politics were concerned. It is for no less reason that Varnhagen frequently made use of arguments publicized by powerful politicians, such as Senators Vergueiro and Dantas, to better characterize his anti-Indian arguments, displaying the horror that these peoples elicited among the dominant Brazilian elite and the challenge they apparently posed to the political and economic hegemony in their regions of influence. Varnhagen related that the origin of his ill will toward the Indians came from a personal experience in his native region of Sorocaba, in the interior of São Paulo state, where there were still autonomous Indians who from time to time attacked travelers encroaching upon their territories.

On the other hand, this anti-Indian radicalism was already an indicator that there existed contrary positions, that a wider critical consciousness of the Indian question was appearing on the scene. Gonçalves Dias became the main symbol of the Indianist literary movement that was to culminate in the works of novelist José de Alencar. The small, literate middle class read these novels and the articles in magazines and newspapers such as *Guanabara* and the *Revista do Instituto Histórico e Geográfico Brasileiro* and even encouraged the foundation of societies against the traffic of African slaves and in favor of the colonization and civilization of the Indians. One such society was created in 1850 by Dr. Nicolau França Leite and seems to have lasted for some time, since it is cited in Perdigão Malheiro's book, written in 1866.

The romantic Indianist movement was sparked off with the publication in 1845 of the epic poem *The Confederation of the Tamoios,* by Gonçalves de Magalhães, apparently by commission from the emperor. Notwithstanding its dubious literary quality and fanciful historical underpinnings, the poem served as a catalyst in the 1850s for a genuine sentiment of interest in the Indians and produced a long-lasting literary movement and a substantial polemic on the best ways to civilize the Indians. The literary high points of this movement can be found in the poems of Gonçalves Dias, while the works of greatest ideological influence are the novels of José de Alencar, beginning with *The Guarani* (1859). In this book, the Indians are idealized in their honor, dignity, and pride as a native American counterpart to the Portuguese medieval past. The joining of these two elements is what constituted the Brazilian nation. It is a book about the myth of creation of Brazil, and as with the myth of the noble savage the destiny of the Indian is extinction, at the same moment in which a new human and cultural epoch is brought into existence.

Without a shadow of a doubt, the greatest liberal work on the defense of the Indian is *Slavery in Brazil,* a book written by a jurist and member of the parliament, Perdigão Malheiro. It was published in two volumes in 1866-1867, the second one being dedicated to the historic situation of the Indian.[21] Besides the intrisic value of its research, the book unsparingly denounces the enslavement, cruelty, and inhumanity of most Indian policies practiced up to that time. As a good liberal, Perdigão Malheiro had hopes that the most recent law of 1845 would lead the Indians on the right track. He considered that the law defended the Indians from official and private attacks, prohibited slavery and obligatory service, provided for the demarcation of lands, and promoted education, all under the aegis of Christianizing the Indians, an absolute prerequisite for their coming into the fold of civilization. However, he realized that the Law of the Lands, enacted in 1850, would usher in the dissolution of many Indian villages that had survived until then, as had happened in such provinces as São Paulo, Rio de Janeiro, Ceará, and Sergipe during the 1860s. Perdigão Malheiro's vision of how Brazil should treat the Indians is opposite that of Varnhagen's: if choosing

> between persecuting the Indians, hunting them like ferocious animals, exterminating them or frightening them away—and leaving them free to wander the hinterland in their errant live as in primitive times,

he preferred the second option. Civilization cannot be imposed upon the Indian—such is his liberal conclusion. Nevertheless, he is under no illusions as to the future of the Indians:

> As the state grows in population, in ease of communications by land and by water, as the territory is covered with more settlements and the hinterland burgeons, the torch of civilization will light the path, thrashing the darkness of savagery, and, either they must necessarily lodge in the arms of civilized man and become indistinguishable among the general mass of the population, or they will be forced to leave the field in this unequal fight, in which victory, while uncertain at the time, is certain and infallible, for it is the decree of God

omnipotent in the providential order of the Nations, manifested throughout the history of the world.[22]

Beginning with the second half of the empire, one can say that the Indians finally became a part of the Brazilian nation. Their legal status was that of orphans, which meant that they were considered not fully capable and not responsible for their acts; thus they were socially and juridically dependent, in need of special protection from the state. This legal condition went side by side with the two conflicting visions that the Brazilian elite had formed for the Indians: the romantic vision of the Indians as a founding element of the new nation, as in José de Alencar's novel *The Guarani*; and the disparaging vision that they were nothing but savages and irreconcilable with civilization.

Either vision, however, took it for granted that the Indians were condemned to a sorry end. Their redemption could only be achieved by civilization, and the means to achieve that goal could only come through religious indoctrination. Very few people trusted that the government would be capable of efficiently civilizing the Indians. In previous times, it was thought, whenever Indian villages were placed under the yoke of public administrators, as in the times of the Directory of Pombal (1757–98), governmental neglect and the meddling of economic and political interests had destroyed them. The Law of 1845, which instituted the imperial system of directories for the Indians, had been preceded by Decree number 285, of June 21, 1843, which conferred upon the Capuchin order the administration of the partial Indian directories and colonies. This decree was not effectively carried out only because there were never enough Capuchins to fill the existing posts and because in many cases the friars did not adapt to the difficulties of missionary life in the most desolate backlands of the country.

However unevenly treated, the Indians were no longer forgotten. Journalists, men of letters, military men, and scientists began to write about Indians through various perspectives, mostly urging that they be respected and accepted by the nation, with their peculiarities and with the benevolence of the other citizens of the empire. This sentiment is expressed, for example, in the book *The Savage*, by General Couto de Magalhães, written in 1870.[23] The author was a competent administrator and a respected figure among the rising circle of middle-class intellectuals. The emperor had appointed him president of the provinces of Goiás and Pará, and in that capacity, like a few other presidents of the period, he had been concerned with enabling the Indians in his charge to advance economically, to make "progress" in their social reality and become full citizens. In this spirit, Couto de Magalhães founded the Santa Izabel School for Indians, on the banks of the Araguaia River. Here education in letters and crafts was dispensed in a boarding school environment to Indian children from the ages of five to twelve. The school also took in an occasional adult Indian and eventually young rural Brazilians whose parents lived near the school. The Santa Izabel School opened in 1864 and functioned well during the administration of its founder, but after that it went into decline, and a settlement grew around it, eventually giving way to what is today the town of Aruanã, in the state of Goiás. There are still some Karajá Indians living there, descendants of the old school's students.

There were a few other educational experiments for the Indians in the nineteenth century for which there is less information. The earliest may have been one created by a former French militaryman, Guido Marlière, for the Botocudos Indians of the upper Doce River valley, and another established by the Ottoni brothers for the Indians of the Mucuri River valley. Both were created in the 1830s and lasted for a few years. Both attracted immigrants from other areas—in the latter case, Germans—and eventually the Indians' lands were taken over. These educational experiments had many things in common. To begin with they adopted a pedagogy based on the old Jesuit method, which focused primarily on working with children, as adult Indians were considered resilient to any form of education. In response to the demands of the times they made considerable efforts to bring in the social and economic means for a fast integration of the Indian with members of the surrounding society.[24] In these cases, as with many partial directorates across the country, the settling of European immigrants and landless peasants in or near Indian settlements led to the loss of the Indians' ethnic identities and to their transformation into caboclos or generic Indians.

As new biological and social ideas began to make their way into Brazil, the time came for naturalists and multidisciplinary scientists to present their views on the Indians. The Indians began to be seen within the perspective of evolution, which meant as primitives, sometimes noble, other times wretched peoples, as remnants of a past that would certainly not survive the nation's development. João Barbosa Rodrigues, who was for many years the director of the National Museum and who may perhaps be called the first Brazilian (physical and cultural) anthropologist, did field research in the Amazon, visited Indian settlements, and reported firsthand on Indians. His most interesting book on this matter is *The Pacification of the Crishanás*,[25] which deals with the Crishaná, or the present-day Waimiri-Atroari, of the middle Amazon. He discusses the plight of those Indians and the methods the local Indian directorate was using to bring them into submission. Barbosa Rodrigues was responsible for the organization of the first Brazilian Exposition of Anthropology in 1883, for which he wrote descriptions of various Indian peoples of the Amazon. Another scientific-minded man of letters was José Veríssimo. In his *Amazonian Studies*[26] he described the old *tapuio* or caboclo villages that slumbered along the Amazon. Veríssimo is actually the first person to speak positively of the caboclo and to see him as not only the biological but also the cultural descendant of the Indian. In sum, by the end of the empire, many intellectuals had contributed to a national appraisal on the Indian by writing essays and historical chronologies of their provinces, as well as by translating works of foreign naturalists who had visited Brazil and written about Indians. Many of those works were published in the triannual volumes of the *Journal of the Brazilian Historical and Geographical Institute*.[27]

In short, one could conclude that the intellectuals of the empire who were inclined toward a liberal, romantic vision of the Indians had a sympathetic or commiserating attitude towards their condition. However, except for the general ideas of people such as Couto de Magalhães, and the Indian official policy itself, they had no proposal to offer as a solution for the problems they saw. On the other hand, those who considered the Indians to be an obstruction to national development and a symbol of things that should be eliminated for the "salvation" of the country, felt it was a waste of time to deal with them. In becoming a subject of the exclusive interest of the liberal-minded, the Indians began to be viewed as a lost cause—one for poets, idealists, or at best, a matter to be handled by the government.

THE REPUBLICAN INDIAN IS A CHILD

If the vague sort of liberalism and literary romanticism that characterized Indian sympathizers fed off the guilty conscience of the imperial elite, positivism, the new fashion in political philosophy that penetrated the country from France in the late 1870s, sought to find solutions because it felt itself capable of doing so, or at least it made a great effort to believe it could. As an ideology of basically insecure and dependent middle classes, positivism proposed a quite orthodox and inflexible vision of humanity, bringing together scientific dogma and moral belief. It worked in the late empire as a revolutionary ideology intended to rid the country of the yoke of slaveholders, monarchists, and the clergy—in other words, the dominant classes. To reach this goal, the self-appointed heralds of the positivist doctrine envisioned Brazilian society as an organic body to be ruled as a republic by means of a rigid intellectual and moral code. The arms of this republic would be formed by the workers; the women would be its moral force; and the patricians, that is, the moral and intellectual elite, would head the organization. Among the patricians the positivists counted themselves, as well as the new industrialists, intellectuals, lawyers, doctors, and the military. This philosophic doctrine produced a religious ideology, almost a theology, and an organization that was called the Church of the Positivist Apostolate, whose influence is recognized by historians for the period extending roughly from 1880 to 1930. The Church of the Positivist Apostolate had a sect, a theology without gods, but with great human heroes instead, and a determination to spread its doctrine across the country.[28]

Positivism is one of the main varieties of evolutionism elaborated in the second half of the nineteenth century by French philosopher Auguste Comte. As it was brought and adapted to the Brazilian situation, the Indians came to be viewed as living examples of the first stage of human evolution, the animist stage, in which one's vision of the world is based on the belief that any natural object can have a soul, a spirit, an *anima*. Persons and peoples in this stage would be incapable of rational and objective thought, because they would not comprehend the principle of causality. In the evolutionary scheme people evolve from one stage to the next according to competition, but through education and other means evolution could be accelerated, allowing people to skip steps and move to higher stages. Such was the argument that the Brazilian positivists used in regard to the Indians. Thus, the solution to quicken the pace of their full integration into the Brazilian nation as full-fledged citizens would be to furnish them with the proper economic, social, and pedagogical means to raise their standard of living, to enhance their understanding of the world, and thence to make progress to a new state of being.

In the Constituent Assembly convened in 1890 to determine the major laws of the Republic, the Positivist Apostolate presented its proposals to the Brazilian nation. The Indians were to be considered free and sovereign nations under the national confederacy and were to be organized as autonomous states. Such a high place in the confederacy was justified by their historical precedence in the formation of that nation. However, there was not much future for such Indian nations and states, as in the long run they were expected to be physically and culturally incorporated into the Brazilian nation, thus molding a special physiognomy onto the Brazilian people.

These ideas did not bear any fruit, but less radical versions thereof were eventually to take root in the years to come as part of a new mentality of republicanism. At first the new Brazilian states, this time with new constitutional powers that made them less dependent on the central government, continued to follow the terms of the imperial Indian policy, taking the view that the Indians should be civilized—which could only be accomplished by converting them to Christianity. The Church had been separated from the state, but its influence continued to be of great importance. Many states adopted a policy of inviting religious orders to organize missions for the Indians of their jurisdictions. The Positivist Apostolate, however, especially through its leader Raimundo Teixeira Mendes, would not relinquish its mission of spreading a laic, integrative, and rationalistic vision of the Indian and of the special role that the state should have. Its ideas were taught in the national Military College at Rio de Janeiro and were disseminated across the country by means of its official journal, in newspapers, profes sional journals, and through affiliated societies such as the Center of Sciences, Arts, and Letters, at Campinas in the state of São Paulo. Through these channels, the Positivist Apostolate called on the state to formulate and exercise a new Indian policy.

In 1906 the federal government recognized that it had to take responsibility in Indian matters and passed a decree stating that Indian problems should be dealt by the Ministry of Agriculture. But it was only in 1910, after a national campaign of wide repercussions, that the Indian Protection Service (SPI) was created, coming immediately under positivist control and inspiration. This movement, which brought together positivists, liberals, nationalists, part of the middle classes, the armed forces, and the state bureaucracy, represented a political consolidation of the national sentiment that considered the Indians an integral part of Brazilian nationality. To a certain degree it anticipated the nativist and nationalist aspects of the wide-ranging movement that began in 1922 with the Week of Modern Art, and which laid the basis for the modern version of Brazilian nationalism.

From the inception of the Indian agency until the late 1940s a kind of official positivist doctrine, represented by General Cândido Rondon and his companions, dominated the vision that most Brazilians had about the

Indian. Nevertheless, by the 1910s there were already a few intellectuals who had gone beyond positivism in their conception of the Indian, in his relation to history, and with regard to the scientific foundations of modern anthropology. The historian Capistrano de Abreu, whose vision of Brazil praised the hardworking and generous role of its people in opposition to the inertia and egotism of its elites, would naturally become politically and intellectually interested in the Indian. Although initially a positivist, Capistrano was later influenced by German cultural geographers such as Ratzel, leading him to elaborate a more dialectical vision of Brazilian history. He became especially interested in the history of what was then called the *hinterland,* the great interior, which, as opposed to coastline society, most organically represented Brazil. His interest in the Indians led him to undertake a copious correspondence with several naturalists and scientists who had visited the Brazilian hinterland, such as Karl von den Stein, Max Schmidt, Paul Ehrenreich, as well as with people who were writing about Indians, such as the young Franz Boas, who was then studying the peoples of northwestern Canada. In 1895 Capistrano published a book on the Bakairi Indians of Mato Grosso, and in 1912, another on the Caxináua, both studies focusing on their respective cultures and languages. Part of the data he obtained came from information brought to him by scientific and military personnel who were part of the Rondon Commission. Other data came from direct interviews with Indians who were brought to Rio de Janeiro for this task.[29] Such methods of doing anthropology, so to speak, were rather unusual for the times. The results elaborated by Capistrano are certainly to his credit as an excellent interviewer and observer, and to the credit and the good will of his informants.

In a country that still lacked universities, not to mention professional courses in anthropology, new knowledge of Indian peoples came in a great part from the elaboration of data obtained in the Indian posts established by the SPI. Another portion of this data was obtained from the accounts written in books and journals by missionaries and travelers. The SPI began to feel a need to systematize these accounts in some fashion so that they could be of help in their policies. At the same time the faculties of science and letters in some cities as well as the new universities of Rio de Janeiro and São Paulo also began to find it important to teach about Indians. By the 1930s we find a number of books that incorporate this corpus of divers material and especially the more recent anthropological theories. The intellectual caliber of many of Rondon's assistants resulted in a considerable production of articles and books on Indian societies, the description of many Indian cultures, and the production of recordings, photographs, and films of great ethnographic value. In subsequent years, their contributions continued to consolidate the image of the Indian as a being who deserved to live, who needed understanding and help.

The political ideology of the SPI was characterized by an attitude of anti-clericalism and scientificism. Throughtout its history the SPI displayed very little tolerance of missionaries, from the secular clergy to the traditional or the new orders, such as the Jesuits, the Salesians, and the Dominicans. The Protestants had begun to come to Brazil in the last years of the empire, and by the end of the century they were making plans to establish missions among several Indian tribes. By the 1920s they had indeed created their own Indian missions, although they were frequently badgered by SPI agents. For economic as well as ideological reasons, the SPI was not able to achieve hegemony over Indian affairs. The Catholic Church continued to have a great deal of influence over the state and the Indians had been part of their concern for many years—of course, in many Indian areas Catholic missions had long preceded the presence of the SPI. Thus the SPI had to forgo projects of establishing posts in some important Indian areas, such as the Upper Rio Negro, and with some Indian peoples, such as the Bororo Indians of the Meruri mission.[30]

Though scientific, as the years wore on the SPI became excessively rigid in its positivist principles, which made its intellectual efforts progressively cumbersome in the face of the theoretical advances in anthropology. For example, until the end of the 1940s Indian policy was guided by the idea that all Indian societies were matriarchical, because this cultural feature theoretically characterizes societies with small-scale agriculture. This assertion had been made more that a century earlier and had already undergone unquestionable empirical adjustments.[31]

From the beginning anthropologists participated or collaborated in one way or another with the SPI. Curt Nimuendaju, for example, visited the Tembé Indians in 1912 and participated in the pacification of the Parintintin in the mid-1920s at the invitation of the SPI. Academic-minded participants such as Edgar Roquette-Pinto, Herbert Baldus, and Heloísa Alberto-Torres eventually came to exert some influence over the agency's philosophical orientation—which helped give it a certain intellectual quality, particularly when compared with equivalent agencies in other countries. John Collier, who from 1933 to 1945 was director of the Bureau of Indian Affairs in the United States unreservedly praised the SPI, recognizing its dedication and its humanist philosophy with regard to the Indian.[32] In the postwar period, until the mid-1950s, the SPI experienced another great intellectual period, having anthropologists such as Darcy Ribeiro, Eduardo Galvão, and Carlos Moreira Neto on its staff. It had become the de facto spokesman for the positive indigenist sentiments. The founding in 1953 of the Museum of the Indian—dedicated to collecting material on Indian cultures, producing and transmitting knowledge to the Brazilian community with the intent of combatting atavistic anti-Indian prejudice—is an example of this scientific spirit.

In its best years (perhaps between 1940 and 1955) the SPI brought together many sorts of people. Besides anthropologists there were scientists from the National Museum and the Paulista School of Medicine, and the exceptional medical doctor Noel Nutels; military and positivist intellectuals such as Luís Bueno Horta Barbosa, Alípio Bandeira, José Maria de Paula, José Maria Estigarribia, Vicente de Paula Teixeira da Fonseca Vasconcelos, Manuel Rabelo, and Sebastião Xerez; and *sertanistas,* or "hinterland Indianists," such as Telésforo Fontes, Pimentel Barbosa, Eduardo Hoerhann, Francisco Meirelles, Cícero Cavalcanti, and the Villas-Boas brothers. The SPI seemed to have attracted these people not only because they were interested in Indians but also because the philosophy of the agency allowed them to put into practice what they thought should be done. Many soon found out that the difficulties were immense and gave up, but those who persevered were as capable of writing on what they experienced as they were of maintaining a dialogue with an Indian people, of setting up an assistance post as well as making a speech in defense of the Indian at an official gathering or in the National Congress. Joining the capabilities of intellectual and practical men was undoubtedly a key factor in the cohesion and quality the SPI enjoyed under the moral leadership of Marshall Rondon. The decadent years of the SPI and the philosophy of the new Indian agency, FUNAI, separated intellectual from practical work, thus placing anthropologists and indigenists against each other and causing considerable damage to the type of indigenist work that had been established in Brazil.

One of the most permanent characteristics of the SPI was its philosophy of "pacification" of the so-called isolated Indians. The notion of pacification appeared at the end of the nineteenth century, exemplified in Barbosa Rodrigues's book, and represents a further step from the notions of "domestication" and "taming." These terms are still used today to characterize the first contact made with an autonomous Indian people. In pacification the Indian is viewed as a wild and aggressive being; in the others, as an animal. The notion of pacification is biased because it denies the Indians their political characteristic of being a people with an autonomous socio-political unity, with whom one should seek friendly relations through frank and respectful dialogue. It implies a position of superiority on the part of the "pacifier." Pacification is always a political act of intervention and control, which changes a people from autonomous to heteronomous.

Nonetheless, "pacifying" was the most humane tactic possible at the time, certainly in contrast to former tactics of warfare. The method of pacification was developed in the years prior to the advent of the SPI by the Rondon Commission, in the process of making contact with the Indians of Mato Grosso. It was based on the principle that anyone who entered Indian lands was actually trespassing on sovereign territory, and consequently that the Indians had every right to defend themselves, including attacking the invaders. It was a moral duty for the pacification team to accept this reality. It should seek to demonstrate signs of good intentions and should never react with violence to an attack. From this attitude came the famous motto "die if need be; never kill," as a guide for the actions of all pacification teams. Many indigenists and teamworkers died upholding this principle, giving irrefutable proof of the dedication, moral force, and the esprit de corps that guided the SPI in its best moments.

The final result of the dozens of pacifications effected on peoples such as the Nambiquara, Kaingang and Xokleng at the beginning of the SPI, followed by the Botocudo, Gueren, Baenan, Umotina, Parintintin, Urubu-Kaapor, Kayapó, Xavante, Suruí, Xikrin, Gaviões, and Cintas-Largas, to the most recent efforts with the Kubenkrakem, Txikão, Suyá, Parakanã, Arara, Urueuauau, and others, did not conform to the best expectations. On the contrary, these efforts led to the extermination of several tribes in a few years and to the cultural submission of many others. All of them suffered distressing population losses and immense territorial deprivation.

Nevertheless, the philosophy of pacification can be considered as a contribution to Brazilian humanism. Even during authoritarian and anti-Indian periods of Brazilian politics, this self-sacrificing philosophy of pacification has imposed itself as a principle and ideal. Certainly there have always been perfidious and irresponsible people in pacification teams who have added distress to the Indians they contacted. By the mid-1970s pacification came to be seen as an improper concept to justify the advent of the contact relationship with autonomous Indians. Instead FUNAI and its authoritarian, military-minded staff introduced the notion of "attraction" as the process of contacting with Indians—a step backwards. In this approach, Indians were viewed as isolated, furtive, wandering peoples who needed to be attracted to our world, an attitude that reverberated with the vulgar sensationalism of those days.

In fact neither pacification nor attraction should characterize the Indian agency's approach to Indian peoples who choose to live autonomously. What must prevail is the idea that the Indians are in their territory, almost always peacefully, and it is only with the highest of motivations that one should seek a relationship with them. To achieve good relations by agreements with an Indian people only to later exploit their territory is the modern equivalent to declaring an offensive war in the manner of the seventeenth century.

Positivism and the SPI also have the merit of equating the Indian issue in Brazil, including their population decrease and their inadequate position in the nation's sociopolitical dynamic, as a historical problem with historical solutions. They definitively broke with the strategy of Christianization and civilization and focused the philosophy of indigenist work on modern sociology centered on human beings.

THE ANTHROPOLOGICAL TURN

Parallel to the positivistic and practical work carried out by SPI, the notions and concepts of modern anthropology were being formed. Here humans are seen as fundamentally cultural, that is, determined more by their social actions, their constituted past, and their interrelationships with other humans than by geographical determinants or biology. In this perspective, humans become responsible for themselves and are therefore capable of conscious action for change. Although anthropology arose from the same sources that gave rise to positivism, that is, enlightenment and evolutionism, it also developed a strong critique of the nineteenth-century evolutionary scheme of human development. Empirical studies, based on the anthropologist's presence in a particular Indian group, demonstrated that the variety of human societies was greater than the classical evolutionists and the positivists had supposed, and that their patterns of life and thought were likewise much more complex. It was proven and corroborated that the so-called primitive peoples possessed functional and complete cultures that owed nothing to those called civilized in the sophistication and subtlety of their thought. Therefore, the scale of cultural potential was not correlated with a putative scale of intelligence, nor with any ranking scale of moral values.

Through the notion of cultural relativism all human societies and cultures are seen as unique. They must be explained in their own terms and not in comparison with other cultures, thus there are no superior or inferior cultures. Indian cultures, then, were raised to equal standing with any other culture, including that of Brazil. Once this notion was put into practice, much was learned about the Indians as attention was given to discovering the smallest details of their lives and visions of the world, their cultural singularities, and finally, the integrated totality of their societies.

Just as with the liberal guilty conscience of the past, however, concrete, political reality had to be faced. The Indians might be seen as equal to us, but in fact there was no doubt they were losing ground. Their populations were constantly diminishing, their cultures being bastardized, their visions of the world were becoming more confused and inclined to follow the visions of the civilized. These phenomena came together in the notion of the "process of acculturation." In the history of humanity the Indian was indeed defeated; he was a being fated to extinction, a conclusion that was spread to the four winds. Why had this happened? Because of the overpowering influence of civilization, perhaps because of a certain lack of adaptability of Indian culture, and perhaps even because of his biological makeup. All things considered, perhaps it was because of a certain kind of inferiority, even if it were only relative or in specific areas. In facing this reality, cultural relativism lost its power of conviction and became at best a methodological principle and an ethical attitude with regard to human cultures, not a substitute for social evolutionism.

In fact, the conceptual advance of modern anthropology was not as revolutionary as one might suppose. The criticism applied to the evolutionary scheme did not overthrow the validity of the older empirical studies of Indian societies, nor the premises that organized the resulting analyses. Indeed the great thinkers of our century, such as Durkheim, Freud, Piaget, and Lévi-Strauss, who analyzed various aspects of Indian peoples and cultures, based their original findings on the scientific knowledge of their times, which, in many cases, still reflected the same sixteenth-century visions of the Indians.

To develop his ideas on the Oedipus complex, for example, Freud looked for raw material and ideas in books written by such anthropologists as R. R. Marret, James Frazer, Spencer and Guillen, Robertson, Smith, Durkheim, and Mauss, who ranged from traditional evolutionists and diffusionists to early critics thereof. With such data and partial analyses Freud came to the conclusion that so-called primitive peoples, the savages, have a mentality equivalent to that of a civilized child, and that their religions, animist in nature, are based on psychological sentiments corresponding to those of a neurotic. The primitives, in his understanding, go beyond the neurotic, for not only do they find it difficult to make a distinction between doing and thinking, they also have no inhibitions in trying to convert thought into action.[33] How is this different from Father Anchieta's anecdote about the Tupinambá Indian woman who believed she had had sexual relations with a priest because she had dreamed about it?

In his acclaimed books on the development of intelligence in children, Jean Piaget frequently suggests that the thinking of primitive peoples is on the same level of that of a seven- to eight-year-old child. It is characterized by an ingenuous realism, a vision that is egocentric, prelogical, precausal, based on transductive reasoning (as opposed to deduction and induction), "impermeable to experience," and dominated by the power of conviction (or what Freud called the "omnipotence of thought"). In short, primitive man is incapable of distinguishing the real exterior world from his or her subjectivity.[34] Piaget did most of his experiments with child psychology in the 1920s and 1930s and published his research up through the 1970s. He was acquainted with the anthropological literature that had criticized social evolutionism and the authors who had influenced Freud. He had certainly read or knew of the critical analyses of Marcel Mauss and others on the ideas of anthropologist Claude Lévy-Bruhl, especially his concept of *participation,* which posits that primitive thought cannot distinguish external reality from the internal reality of the individual, being therefore prelogical. Piaget attempts to redirect the concept of participation to signify a special kind of relation between an individual and an object—not as a mystical sentiment, as it had originally seemed to Levy-Bruhl, which was the major reason for its rejection by the majority of anthropologists. In this way, Piaget reaffirmed the correspondence of primitive thought to that of a child who is still living in the egocentric stage.[35]

It was not only the great psychologists who thought like this. The evolutionist heritage is present also in the anthropology of Franz Boas, when he says that primitive thought is characterized by "emotional associations" that obscure objectivity. It is found also in E. E. Evans-Pritchard, when he emphasizes the need of the primitive to seek explanations for everything and ignore chance. It is even found in the anthropology of Claude Lévi-Strauss, when he creates the notion of "pre-cept" to characterize the concrete thinking of the primitive classifications, as opposed to the "con-cept," which characterizes scientific thinking.[36] It is true that this so-called primitive thinking is defined as relative by Lévi-Strauss, who affirms that this type of thinking is also present in the civilized world, and that it therefore does not represent an exclusive attribute of the primitives. However, this concession seems undoubtedly gratuitous, since his analyses show the primitive as dominated by what he refers to as the logic of the concrete, while among the civilized this form of thought would be no more than a vestige of bygone eras, relegated to the thinking of common folk and set apart from the scientific mode of thinking that characterizes civilization.

The equation primitive = child is argued by these scientists on the basis of the ontogenetic/philogenetic correspondence, according to which human beings develop through forms identical to those through which humanity has passed as a species and a culture. Piaget states that if it is impossible to go back in time and study early man, he nevertheless finds him in the child and in the surviving primitive peoples. Freud—and Jung even more so—conceive of human psychology, especially group psychology, as containing prehistoric, atavistic, perhaps even prehuman, elements.[37] Primitive peoples of the present day would be examples corresponding to these various phases of development of the individual person.

It is worth noting, parenthetically, that none of these authors write in this fashion as a means of deprecating the primitive, their cultures, or their ways of thinking. Although Freud equates primitive thinking with neurotic thinking, he does not necessarily demean the former, since he considers it to generate the arts and religion, the foundations and mainstay of human culture. For his part, Piaget argues: "Logical activity is not all of intelligence. One can be intelligent without being very logical. The two essential functions of intelligence, that of inventing solutions and that of corroborating them, do not necessarily lead one to the other: the first participates in the imagination; only the second is properly logical."[38] As for the anthropologists in general, their books and theories clearly demonstrate their empathic vision and efforts on behalf of equality with regard to the primitive.

Although challenged by the elaborated results of empirical research carried out by anthropologists over the past one hundred years—in which, on one hand, the potential for scientific thought is recognized in the primitives, while on the other, magical thought or the denial of chance is found among the civilized—the theoretical vision that places primitive thought in opposition and subordinate to civilized thought fulfilled and justified a general sentiment that civilized people are essentially different from and superior to primitive people. The imputation of infantilism fit nicely with the theory of evolution, with the ontogenetic/philogenetic correspondence and with the idea that present-day primitive peoples represent survivals from our most remote past.

These ideas and sentiments weighed heavily on the liberal conscience of anthropologists who defended the notions of equality of peoples and cultural relativism. These anthropologists tried hard to fight against the ideas of inferiority, infantilism, and primitivism, sometimes ignoring their existence, but they could not avoid the perception of a real dilemma that influenced their relationship with their informants. However much one might see his or her informant as an equal, as one did research in Africa and Oceania the informant was invariably a servant or a temporary employee. In Brazil, he would be seen as a minor, or a ward in relation to a guardian. How then could an Indian be equal to a Brazilian when he was also a dependent? How to reconcile equality with servitude? It is extremely significant that, to escape this dilemma, North American anthropology ended up conceiving as a methodological principle the idea that an anthropologist, when studying a primitive people and practicing the method of participant observation, becomes as a child in the eyes of these people, and in a sense, to her or himself. The idea is that the anthropologist enters a new world as an innocent, and only little by little begins to understand it, and concomitantly experiences growth, until at the end of this period he or she becomes an adult in the eyes of the natives of the culture being studied. Taking this methodology for granted it was concluded that being a child was a temporary situation, one which depended on the point of view being adopted. Even a civilized person would be a child in certain contexts. Everything was relative after all. Many studies were carried out on the basis of this methodological principle. It seemed to soften the anthropological dilemma and the real political situation through a dissimulated psychological inversion.

The resolution to the dilemma came not from the efforts of anthropology, however, but as a result of political changes brought on by the end of traditional colonialism and the rise of modern African nations, and with the participation of the Indian, the aborigene, the native, the "primitive," on the wider political scene. By adopting, with identical verve and competence, a political discourse equivalent to that of the civilized peoples, native peoples began to change the idea that they were like children, or neurotics, or that they were incapable of distinguishing the objective from the subjective. For the Indians of Brazil, this only became truly possible when their populations stopped diminishing, reversing a process set in motion in

1500. They began to fight for their survival with the instruments they had available and with their own previously unknown strength.

It is obvious that anthropology, as a science, has still not formulated a new and integrating vision to embrace this fundamental change. It has so far only been able to express its self-criticism regarding its own political participation in colonialism and the consequences of speaking for, instead of speaking together with, its subject of study.[39] It is now necessary to consider human and cultural equality as potential and necessary realities and thus furnish the bases of argumentation to influence the reformulation of other related sciences, such as psychology and even philosophy, with regard to the ideas they have embraced of the primitive and of cultural differences.

In the new political processes we are witnessing, in the concrete behavior of interethnic relations in Brazil, there still remains a vision of the Indians as infants. The very maintenance of their legal condition as minors is a case in point. When challenged to justify this condition, most people, including anthropologists, rely on realistic political arguments, such as the allegation that only in this way can the state defend the Indians from social and economic injustices, as well as protect their lands from the permanent threat of plunder. (It seems rather hypocritical when the Brazilian state uses this argument at the same time that it bolsters economic interests in Indian lands.) Legal paternalism is thus justified as an historical requirement and as the result of a social pact created within the ensemble of forces that make up Brazilian nationality. All things considered, the Indian has become a kind of bastard child of our civilization—furthermore, an ill bastard child, for he is seen as suffering from a terminal disease, inexorably condemned to death. The state's social and humanist, if not Christian, duty, then, would be to ease the sufferings of these people and ensure that they meet death with dignity.

THE SEARCH FOR A HIGHER SOCIAL IDENTITY

Many people continue to think that the Indian is fated to extermination, be it physical, through cultural assimilation, in terms of Per-digão Malheiro's liberal lament or those of scientific positivism, or by anthropological acculturation. The statistics point to a new reality, however, and people have begun to perceive the demographic turnaround in many Indian peoples, especially if their time frame extends to more than thirty years ago. They are also sensing a change in the behavior of these Indians. The appearance of several Indian personalities on the national scene in the last twenty years or so, products of the Indian movements and the internal movements of Brazilian society, has caused astonishment and shaken the vision people had of the Indian, this noble savage, this child of ours. Why, they are so articulate and crafty! Why are they threatening the world with violence? How have they become able to manipulate public opinion? Are they being corrupted, selling out, betraying their values? Why are they getting into politics and wanting to elect their members to congress? Whither their ingenuousness and their purity?

Public opinion no longer understands the Indian, but then the state and even anthropologists are perplexed. It is becoming clear that the Indians are not like children, even if they laugh more than us, are self-indulgent, and yet generous in giving and receiving. They want the right to keep their cultural inheritance and to be treated as equals—chief to president, leader to leader, man and woman to man and woman. Clearly there are misunderstandings and incomprehension on their part, but basically they have a general notion of how our society functions and thus want a relationship of parity. Somewhat awkwardly, they seek their place in Brazilian society. However, we do not know what spaces to open for their advance, fundamentally because we do not know what type of society we are to build.

In the 1970s and 1980s, dozens of theses and books were written in an attempt to define what makes the Indian be and remain an Indian, above all those Indians who have lived for many years in permanent contact with Brazilian society. Unfortunately, most studies were done without an historical perspective, seeking only to delineate a conceptual framework that relied excessively on structuralist and interactionist concepts that take culture to be timeless structures or chance epiphenomena of social relations. The more radical structuralist studies even proposed that the Indians had lost their substantiality as cultures and were only the product of their relations with other societies. All the same, these studies can be taken as reflections of the changes that were going on in relation to the position of the Indians in Brazil and on how we ought to think of them. They also reflect a search on our part to re-create our national identity.

Anthropologists and other intellectuals have conjectured that the historic and continuous presence of the Indian peoples in Brazil can create new features for its society and culture. No longer taken to be the living dead, the Indians have assembled themselves to face our reality and to challenge it with new demands. It is up to us to define our view of this reality and to determine the acceptable parameters of Indian actions. It is to be hoped that these definitions will be established in an open dialogue with the Indians.

Some questions should be asked forthright. Do we want the Indians to control some 10 percent of the Brazilian territory? If so, what are the terms of this control? Is it understandable that the lands' resources be preserved for their own sake and as a collateral for our future, above all in the Amazon? Are Indian economic methods sustainable for the preservation of our forests? Should the Indians be encouraged through social projects to partake of the same economic incentives that are given to Brazilian peasants and farmers? Is the Indian a menace to the security of our national borders, or rather a bulwark for their defense? Does a specifically Indian identity threaten the integrity of our nationality, or does it complement, color, and enrich it?

These are the great questions that ought to be on the national agenda, and whose answers will direct our new attitudes and thoughts about the Indians. The petty and unjust opinions that have been tossed around concerning the Indians and their cultures will soon be nothing but senseless prejudice, for they will no longer be the markers of our new identity.

4

Who Are the Indians?

Browsing through the shelves of Brazilian bookstores specializing in secondhand, discarded books, one cannot help but be surprised at the quantity and diversified quality of books on Indians. Missionaries publish their memoirs, casual and professional travelers describe their encounters with real or imagined Indians, psychologists delve into the Indians' souls in search of the primitive, folklorists analyze Indian myths and rituals of the past, poets try their inspiration on the marvels of Indian sensitivity, local literati examine the influence of Indian societies in their towns, and military men after time spent in the jungle conclude something or other about Indian warfare or lack of development. Everything seems to be written with a conviction that astonishes the anthropologist. Of course, we anthropologists write about Indians in all manners and styles, and sometimes the subjects do not seem to like it. Sometimes we aspire to write about their minds and inner feelings, other times we describe them by their activities.

In this book equal importance is given both to what is analyzed and how it is analyzed. A view that tries to balance anthropological discourse and indigenist practice is perhaps best for placing the Indians in the political context in which they live and struggle to survive. Our main purpose, after all, is to reach out and connect as many people as possible with the Indians in order to further their cause in present times. To contribute to changing the relationship of Brazilian society and the state with the Indians is the ultimate goal of this book. The Indians themselves are most interested in seeing to it that a humanistic and democratic Indian policy becomes effective in Brazil. They express this purpose in many ways, sometimes with a clear notion of strategy and purpose, at other times rather aggressively. The majority of Brazilians are also struggling for similar objectives in a society that maintains a disturbing abyss between the rich and middle classes and the poor and that provides few opportunities for the majority to catch up with the privileged minority. In doing so, they inevitably take a stand side by side with the Indians in a common struggle against discrimination, injustice, and elitism.

Although most of the anti-Indian forces at play in Brazil are apparently driven by economic interests, prejudice and loathing (whose origins are more complex and develop through history) are motivations still found in Indian-Brazilian relations. Brazilians of all classes hold many biases and misconceptions on Indians as persons and on how their societies and cultures function. Much of this derives from the distortions found in the Brazilian educational system as well as from the country's own historiography. The Indians are still depicted as savages or at best as innocent primitives coming from a mysterious past, and in general they are looked upon as people destined for extinction. When real Indians are seen on television or reported in their day-to-day political transactions with Brazilians or the Indian agency, their image comes out blurred and erratic. In this chapter I shall try to clear the ground for a better understanding of the Indians by presenting a general picture of their diverse cultures, their social and political organizations, and how they position themselves to face up to the challenge of survival.

ETHNIC IDENTITY

For the general public the Indians constitute an aggregate population distinct from the mainstream population of the country. As individuals they are recognized for their physical characteristics, that is, their Asiatic phenotype, which sometimes leads to their being confused with Japanese or Chinese Brazilians. A case in point is that of a Terena leader who spent a good part of his urban life being called "Chinaman." Similarly, many Brazilians physically resemble the popularly held image of the Indian, which entails prominent cheekbones, slanted eyes, or straight black hair, and are by the same vein nicknamed "Injuns." This generic notion of the Indian is part of a folk classification that Brazilians, or for that matter many other people, devise for those who seem different. The Indians, for their part, also classify the non-Indian as "white," "black," "civilized," or formerly as "sailor man" or "Portuguese." In both cases, however, whenever close contact and personal relations are struck, a need arises for more refined distinctions regardless of the biases contained in the original classifications.

From the anthropological perspective, the Indian is defined and classified by means of a variety of sociocultural criteria, race or genetic makeup being the least pertinent. Some of these criteria seem to most people to be self-evident, although there is much controversy in the discipline about them. The very names by which many Indian peoples are known derive from sources other than their own self-designation, and a great number of them are plainly derogatory. The notions of ethnicity, mode of production, language, social organization, population size, and the level of intensity of contact with the national society are the most common criteria used in anthropological analyses of Indian societies.

Ethnicity is the basic anthropological notion that defines Indians as social groups. Actually, ethnicity defines any social group that is comprised of an integrated, self-reproducing population with common purposes. Ethnicity is a quality of being social that binds people together by virtue of mutual reliance, common sociability, and the sharing of social power—any self-defining social group constitutes an ethnic group or an *ethnie*. Thus when one speaks of the Xavante Indians, it is understood that one is referring to a population that shares a common life and common purposes, with cultural characteristics and self-interests that tie them together through feelings of personal loyalty and social constraints. It may or may not be implicit that such an ethnie speaks a distinct language or has a unique culture. The general public hardly recognizes this criterion in their view of the Indian. In fact, many people are surprised to find that every named ethnie might have distinct customs of their own. Brazilians keep in the back of their minds the idea that all Indians speak the same language—the Tupi language about which they have read in history books.

The Xavante ethnie, which speaks the Xavante language, "thinks Xavante," and lives in a territory it considers its own (even though this territory is divided into separate areas), is an indisputable social and political fact, but also a historical construct. That is, this ethnie has existed not since primeval times but by virtue of circumstances that have occurred through time and in a certain social, historical trajectory. Indeed, the Xavante as they are known today constituted themselves within the last two hundred years, as they migrated southward across the scrublands of Goiás to their present territory in Mato Grosso. In the process, as they moved into a rather isolated territory, they clung to a political stand that refused any form of relations with the expanding Brazilian population until the late 1940s. The Xavante are thus the product of this history. In divergence, some of the early bands that purposely straggled behind in their northern territories and in consequence lived through different historical circumstances, became another ethnie, today known as the Xerente. They live in one single territory in the state of Tocantins and speak a language that, though very similar to, is distinct from Xavante—unintelligible to speakers of the latter. They live hundreds of miles away from each other, and, although their cultures are very similar in many aspects, they are distinct. They thus constitute two separate ethnies in their own rights.

The feeling of ethnicity identifies and constitutes a people, but it does not determine their political unit. For most Indian ethnies every single village is economically self-sufficient and politically self-reliant. As autonomous villages, they relate with one another by means of the concrete social constraints of ethnicity, which operate as kinship loyalty, marital arrangements, and the consequent enforced preference for economic sharing and political alliances. Sharing cultural institutions and customs helps consolidate social bonds and ethnic integration. Although every village is autonomous, they often help one another when attacked by members of another ethnie. Most Indian ethnies conform to this model.

However, some ethnies maintain an intense level of mutual competition and animosity, even though their villages share the whole array of cultural traits. As a consequence, individuals who move to different villages become enemies of their original community. Such was the case with the sixteenth-century Tupinambá, and it is the state of the Yanomami today. They fight and kill one another more than they attack potential enemies of other ethnies. In these situations one might ask, Where is the feeling of ethnicity, let alone the workings of a political unit? Could they survive indefinitely in this way, or would they eventually lead their social organization to a point in which peaceful relations would be brought forth between the villages? These questions may be speculative, but we know that the Tupinambá lost out to the Portuguese partly because of their divisiveness. In the case of present-day Yanomami, the process of splitting into separate autonomous villages, each going their own way, has resulted also in the splitting of their original language into four distinct, possibly mutually unintelligible ones. One could talk about them as being four different ethnies, as the Yanomami, the Yanoam, the Sanumá, and the Yanomamo. Yet, given the many cultural characteristics they share, they still can be called Yanomami. Ethnic identity is as much an anthropological construct as an intangible feeling that may exist within a people. The maximum political unit found among the Yanomami consists of the fleeting political alliances that are sometimes built among a few villages living close to one another.

On the opposite end, there are Indian ethnies that are made up of one single population unit that constitutes both the ethnie itself as well as its maximum political unit. Here the village—or at most a parent village with village offsprings—is by itself the whole ethnie and corresponds to a full-fledged sociopolitical-economic unit. Such occurrences can be found even among ethnies that share a similar culture, the same language, and the same general repertoire of mythology and history. This is the case with the various ethnies generically known as Timbira, who live on the scrublands just to the east of the Amazon rain forest. Timbira they are, much as the peoples of northern Europe are Scandinavian, yet each self-identifying ethnie-village considers itself as a full-fledged autonomous political unit. Such groups include the Canela-Ramkokamekra, Canela Apanyekra, Krikati, Pukobye, Krepumkateyé, Krahô, and Parkateyé, and in the past there were many more.[1] The mythological stories each of these peoples tell about themselves can be traced back to a single point of origin. Almost all of their cultural traits and institutions, such as language, social structure, mythology, religion, mode of production, and worldview seem to be shared by all, with very few differences among them to justify such formal political divisions. They each constitute distinct political units, and in the past they have often fought against one another. But on various occasions they have been known to merge, especially when the autonomous survival of one group or other becomes untenable due to severe population losses or expulsion from one's lands.

Living among the Canela-Ramkokamekra, for example, are descendants of Txakamekrã survivors, and among the Apanyekra, remnants of the Kenkateye. Both Txakamekrã and Kenkateye individuals have over the years commingled socially and politically with their hosts. They have intermarried and begotten progeny who identify as belonging to the host ethnie. Yet, whenever any of them is involved in an altercation, their historical past is quickly brought up as a pretense for reproof or distrust.

The case of the Indian ethnies that live on the lands drained by the upper Xingu river—a southern tributary of the Amazon—the so-called Xinguanos, is an exceptional example of the range of possibilities that can be found in the equation involving ethnicity, political unit, linguistic affiliation, and cultural identity. In this region there are currently nine Indian peoples speaking languages that belong to five different linguistic stocks (some as mutually unintelligible as English and Arabic). The Kamayurá and Aweti speak Tupi languages; the Kuikuro, Mehinaku, and Kalapalo speak Carib; the Waurá, Yawalapiti, and Nahukua speak Aruak; the Trumái speak a language as yet unaffiliated within any linguistic stock. Their original cultural traditions were similarly distinct, but in the course of an unknown number of years they developed together, by a process of egalitarian cultural compression,[2] a highly homogenous culture in both material and spiritual aspects. Nevertheless, each ethnie preserved its own identity and continued to be organized autonomously as a distinct political unit. Among them there is no scale of ethnic prestige or pecking order. What prevails is a cultural understanding, a kind of sociopolitical pact that unites them. The Brazilian anthropologist Eduardo Galvão called this cultural assemblage the "Uluri culture area" (*uluri* being the tiny bikini-like garment used by Xinguana women), following the anthropological tradition that classifies people according to the sharing of cultural items. In addition to the original Xinguano Indian ethnies, there are other Indian ethnies such as the Juruna, Kajabi, Txukarramãe, and Suyá, who migrated into this area after it became officially recognized as the Xingu National Park. Although they still maintain much of their original cultural makeup, they are socially pressed to become part of the Xinguano cultural-political unit.[3]

The Xinguano case goes far beyond the mere notion of a culture area; it stands out as a singular political experiment involving the coexistence of distinct ethnies who live in peace with one another and without the need for a hegemonic force to control them and give them the import of a political unit. It is indeed a very rare social phenomenon, which—although much thought has been given to describing the ethnies themselves and their overall interethnic organization—remains rather poorly understood. Nothing better than intelligent guesses have been made concerning the time and circumstances in which this phenomenon developed. That they organized themselves in such a fashion for self-preservation is obvious, but why they did so remains in the realm of speculation. From the traditional evolutionary perspective, the evolvement of peaceful, egalitarian relations among competing ethnic groups as a distinct stage or as a possible course seems far-fetched for the establishment of a model. Political, interethnic egalitarianism seems fragile, unusual, and transitory in the face of the hierarchical forces that dominate the scenario of social evolution. Yet the Xinguano case is there to be accounted for.

ETHNICITY, SOCIAL STATUS, AND MODE OF PRODUCTION

In contrast to the Xinguano case is the example of the Tukanoan ethnies of the Brazilian Northwest Amazon. There, on the poor oxysol lands enclosing the basin of the Negro River, a northern tributary of the Amazon, a

number of ethnies speaking different languages belonging to the same linguistic stock live in similar kinds of cultures that can be traced back to one
single pattern. However, they relate to one another in a politically hierarchical fashion. The ethnies that inhabit the middle reaches of the Negro
River have certain economic advantages (more fish and better soils) over
those living on the upper reaches, and consequently they have acquired a
position of higher social prestige. A person from the Tukano ethnie or the
Baré, for example, is viewed with more distinction than a Wanano or Tari-
ana. This distinction does not entail political power as such, but translates
into more respect and social prestige and consequently a certain social hierarchy. To counteract the tendency toward a permanent inegalitarianism,
each and every ethnie is organized in exogamous patriclans, thus forcing
intermarriage and recycling group membership.[4]

This status hierarchy does not conform to the model of class society,
although one can say that it is but one step behind in a line of political
development or in a scale of social evolution. Indeed, in the archaeological
records of the Amazon there are examples of societies that were presumably divided into hierarchical groups of prestige and power. The Marajoara
societies, whose exquisite pottery has been found in the lower Amazon,
particularly on the Marajó island, seem to have functioned with class divisions or at least differentiated prestige groups.[5]

Presently, however, it can be established that there are no surviving Indian ethnies maintaining a social structure that divides its members according to socioeconomic criteria and a hierarchized distribution of political power. In short, there are no social classes among the Indian ethnies of
Brazil.

It could be no other way, since, to begin with, the great majority of the
Indian ethnies practice a mode of production that is not designed to produce an economic surplus for trade or stocking. It is based on a simple
model of agriculture, or horticulture, as some people prefer, known in Portuguese as *coivara* and in English as slash-and-burn, or swidden, agriculture. Slash-and-burn has been considered by many ecologists as the most
environmentally feasible and sustainable form of agriculture for rainforest and other equivalent environments. It consists of a set of practices
beginning with the choice of a forest patch and ending with the harvesting
of crops for a period of one to five years. In the first year, the underbrush
and trees are cut down in the middle of the dry season (which in the southern hemisphere ranges from June to November, and north of the equator

between October and March) and are left to dry in the sun for two to three months until they are ready to be burned, which should be done just before the first rains begin to fall. Then corn, beans, squashes, yams, tobacco, cotton, and other cultigens, especially manioc seedlings, are planted in this area, which was naturally fertilized by the ashes of the burned vegetation. After a few months of rain, the corn and squash ripen and are harvested mostly by women and children, while the other plants come to maturation in the following months. After a productive first harvest, one or two more crops can be planted in the same site, after which planting becomes difficult due to the invasion of weeds and rather unproductive because of the leaching of the top layer of fertile soil. The land is therefore left fallow for as many as seven to fifteen years or until the forest vegetation takes over and reconstitutes itself as secondary forest. If left in this state for thirty or more years, the vegetation eventually grows back to primary forest, with all its original luxuriance of trees and brushes, and its soil once again obtains the conditions to reconstitute itself in its prevalent, short-termed fertility.

Slash-and-burn agriculture has been analyzed and tested experimentally by ecologists and anthropologists in various areas of the Amazon. It is regarded as a method that allows the Indian population to perpetuate itself for many years, if a balanced proportion is maintained between population density and proper land accessibility. Indeed, this method has been in use for at least five millennia without substantially affecting the equilibrium of Amazonian ecology. In some areas along tributaries of the Amazon, some researchers think that, using this method, the Indians have even created a new, enriched type of soil, called *terra preta*, or "Indian black soil," as the result of a continuing packing of ashes that have been deposited over many years.[6]

In addition to horticulture the Indian mode of production includes hunting many species of mammals, marsupials, birds, and turtles, fishing a plethora of sea and river fishes, and gathering wild fruits, nuts, honey, insects and grubs, wild tubers, tortoises, and mussels. The rain forests, savannas, and scrublands of Brazil hold a great variety of animal and plant species, many of which are utilized for purposes other than eating. Tobacco, which was domesticated by South American Indians for religious purposes, has become—for worse, one might say at this point in history—the greatest and most widely used nonedible cultigen in the world. Of course, corn, peanuts, cocoa, avocado, potato, long-fiber cotton, beans, tomatoes, and other cultigens were domesticated in the Americas, and they revolutionized the world once they were spread to Europe, Africa, and Asia.[7]

The Indians in Brazil never came to domesticate any kind of animal, however. They immensely enjoy having all kinds of pets, particularly the many species of monkeys, parrots, macaws, curassows, and even wild boars and tortoises. Pets are obtained while at the suckling or immature stage, after their mothers are killed in hunting. Baby mammals are breast fed by the women until they can eat whatever food people are eating. Only tortoises, after they grow to large, cumbersome sizes, may eventually find their way to a cooking fire. All other pets are strictly taboo for eating and are considered members of the family to which they belong. However, very rarely do they reproduce in captivity, thus cutting off the possibility of full domestication.

The adaptive capacity of Indian cultures allowed them to know and explore almost all ecological niches found in Brazil, from the banks of the great rivers to the arid lands, from the savannas to the forests, from the grassy pampas to the wetlands. Their greatest population concentrations occurred on the floodplains of the great rivers and on the Atlantic coast, but the ecozones where savanna intersperses with gallery forests also permitted the highly localized concentrations of the Jê peoples. The northeastern *caatinga* scrub was inhabited by the Kariri, Tarairiu, Janduí and other ethnies with cultures similar to those of the Jê. In the Amazon and Atlantic forest, the cultural variations were greater, as was the number of different languages. Groups as varied as the Tupinambá and the small bands of Puri and Coroado could be found in the Serra Geral range from the sixteenth to the nineteenth centuries.

CULTURAL ECOLOGY

One of the most attractive theoretical models used by anthropologists to account for culture differences among Indian ethnies is cultural ecology, or its offshoot, human ecology. Defining ecology as the study of the interrelatedness of all beings—including humans taken as populations or cultures—within a distinct area, this model assumes culture to be a derivative of processes of adaptation to the environment. Thus, living in a blackwater river environment as the Tukanoan peoples have done for many centuries has entailed the rise of an economy focused on fishing and manioc and on a social pattern characterized by the stratification of the existing ethnies in accordance with their relative proximity to the more fruitful sites for fishing and farming resources. The picture is completed with the symbiotic, but unequal, relationship the Tukanoan ethnies carry on with the hunting-and-gathering Maku Indians, who live on the uplands away from river resources, and with whom they exchange manioc and fish for game meat. One may say that this Tukanoan culture pattern comes from a need to adapt to an environment with poor soils and varied density of fish and game populations.[8]

However, there are many cases of culture variations that one cannot explain by considering only ecological adaptation, unless it be in a simplistic and rather tautological way, as some anthropologists have been inclined to present. One such instance is provided by the Xinguano Indians and their preference for eating fish rather than game. Although the rivers that drain their territory are indeed quite abundant in fish, their terrain is also well populated by deer, peccary, monkeys, tapirs, and other edible animals. Yet the Xinguano eat only a few birds, such as one species of the curassow, and a couple of species of monkeys, while they reject all other terrestrial animals, considering them taboo. These same taboo animals are the most desirable and savory foods of their neighbors, such as the Txukarramãe, the Suyá, and others. The logic that ordains these different emphases in food preferences cannot easily be traced to some sort of ecological bottom line but derives rather from cultural choice, whose raison d'être seems indecipherable and unpredictable and whose origins are lost in the past.[9] It is rather curious that many Indian ethnies from many different areas reject the flesh of the capybara and the anteater, while they savor frogs, marsupials, and snakes. The Avá-Canoeiro, for one, love all species of rodents, including field and house mice. The Nambiquara in particular relish toasting and eating grasshoppers and certain types of frogs. The Canela are ashamed of the teasing they get from the Guajajara, but that does not stop them from eating bats whenever they have a chance. For their part, they make fun of the Guajajara for eating frogs.

A small number of current Indian ethnies do not practice agriculture and live exclusively by hunting and gathering, as if they were in the Stone Age. Interestingly enough, almost all of these groups are Tupi speakers, such as the Guajá, who live on the eastern fringes of the Amazon forest, the Aché or Guayaki in the forests of eastern Paraguay, and the Yuqui and Sirionó in the Bolivian Amazon. An exception seems to be the Maku, who speak a language related to the Tukanoan family and live in northwest Amazon.[10] In all of these cases the lack of agriculture does not appear to be a tradition going back to the first wave of peopling the South American continent, nor is it a form of permanent ecological adaptation. Rather, it is the result of deculturation, that is, of cultural loss, or culture retrogression, something that probably took place as a response to the onset of Portuguese and Spanish political and demographic pressure upon them. One may analyze their changing as a form of adaptation, but one that occurs more in response to social than ecological pressure, unless one uses ecology in a much broader sense of the word. This can be seen in the fact that at least the Guajá and the other Tupi speakers seem to have preserved a fairly good comprehension of the agricultural methods as practiced by their neighboring, rival Indian ethnies, and their languages contain most of the names of the Indian cultigens as linguistic cognates, not as borrowed words. This linguistic memory of agricultural names and concepts, however, is not accompanied by historical or mythological memory. Guajá and Yuqui elders, for instance, do not recall their grandparents talking about farming, and their myths do not include the revealing of agriculture by a civilizing hero. A few other ethnies, such as the Avá-Canoeiro and the Xetá, also Tupi speakers, are known to have reverted to intense nomadism, but they maintained the practice of planting small crops of corn, squash, and other cultigens whenever and wherever they had a chance. They represent the middle point between full-fledged agriculturists and exclusive hunting and gathering.

The absence or loss of agriculture does not represent a barrier to survival, as these ethnies demonstrate. Rather, it clearly demonstrates the capacity of human culture to adapt to social circumstances as well as to the environment in order to obtain all of its basic needs. One can not reduce culture to being an obligatory mechanism responding to the environment, as cultural ecology proposes. The case of the Guajá people, with whom I have been associated for many years as an anthropologist, shows that they became hunters and gatherers as a result of the political and economic pressures they suffered in the beginning of Portuguese colonization of their territory, which was then probably on the lower Tocantins River in present-day Pará state. They, along with other Indian ethnies, were pursued and hunted down by slave expeditions coming from the colonists' township of Belém, and they found their means of survival by adopting a more flexible and agile mode of production. At the same time, other ethnies of the same region either ran away, like the Urubu-Kaapor, Waiampi, or Parakanã, or were extinguished, like the seventeenth-century Tupinambá and other ethnies in the beginning of the twentieth century. The Guajá survived and migrated eastward to Maranhão state during the second half of the nineteenth century.

Cultural flexibility and group nimbleness constitute the very essence and raison d'être of a nomadic way of life. However, this nomadism should not be interpreted as a disorderly and random pattern of population movements over a boundless territory but rather as a culturally rationalized pattern ordained to maximize the procurement of food resources and other goods existent in a given environment. The recurrent migratory pattern from one location to another is carried out according to commonly shared and in some cases minutely detailed knowledge of the seasons for every forest product. Furthermore, for each band of hunters and their families there is a distinct, recognizable territory upon which another band can not trespass without the "owners'" consent. This rule binds people to band identification, which not infrequently gives rise to rivalry and to fighting that occasionally results in deaths, or else in peaceful arrangements and group coalitions. Migration out of one's territory to new, unknown lands is motivated either by a quest for better resources or for a place of refuge from more powerful enemies. If neighboring territories are emptied of people for one reason or another, nomadic ethnies usually take advantage of the situation and end up controlling large stretches of land and eventually spreading themselves thin. In such cases the bands tend to lose contact, and subgroups become isolated from one another, making it harder for their physical and cultural survival. For the survival of a nomadic ethnie this centrifugal propensity must be counterbalanced by the centripetal institutions that derive from the need for marriage partners and for partaking of rituals, religion, and knowledge.

The dynamics of group fission and fusion is a social characteristic not only of hunters and gatherers but also of agriculturists. Some cultural traditions, such as the Jê, have fairly large permanent villages, with as many as 700 to 1,500 people, which break up into smaller groups in the dry season to exploit and roam over their territory. The Tupi tradition, however, hardly ever sustains villages larger than 500 people for any lengthy period of time. They prefer to divide into two or more smaller villages when too many people concentrate in one area. We may recall, however, that the sixteenth-century Tupinambá had villages of 800 or more people. The largest Tupi village I have heard of in this century was the Tenetehara village of Canabrava, which in 1998 had about 540 people living in it. Other Tenetehara villages that came close to 400 people eventually broke up into smaller villages, each one with its own leadership. The Carib and Aruak traditions also keep numbers below the 500 level, unless they are situated on the margins of rivers or near Brazilian settlements where a trade economy has developed. That is the case of the large Tikuna villages found on the Solimões river, or the overcrowded, impoverished Guarani villages in Southern Mato Grosso state, or the equally destitute villages of the Fulniô, Xukuru, Kariri, and other ethnies of northeast Brazil. They concentrate population not as a normal development of their mode of production, but as a political means to impel the Indian agency to invest in services they need, such as education and health.

Village fissioning and population dispersal require an abundant supply of land as ethnic territory and a certain environmental uniformity so that every village should produce as much as, but never much more than, any other village of that ethnie. These socio-environmental factors are part of the so-called lowland South American Indian mode of production, and they make up what is perhaps the root cause behind the lack of hierarchical structures among Brazilian Indian ethnies. Socio-environmental constraints and this mode of production prohibit the development of storable economic surpluses, which could stimulate the creation of social classes through the appearance of an elite with differentiated activities. An environmental uniformity means a general uniformity of soil quality and consequently of crop quality. This in turn holds back a possible diversification of agricultural products and higher productivity, which discourages the appearance of differentiated economic functions, specialized producers, and more economically dynamic villages or settlements. All of these factors together could eventually lead to the formation of greater political power. One could speculate whether or not the presence in a certain ethnic territory of relatively less fertile land would force the Indian mode of production to change in order to secure new production methods, new technologies, and new crops to be more efficient. Such a change could eventually result in the transformation of the social structure into more hierarchical forms. Social change would also come about if in an ethnic territory there were better, more productive, or strategically advantageous lands where one village or group could secure more cultural and economic resources and thus stake a claim for more power and social differentiation.

Only on the banks of the great rivers such as the Amazon, the Tapajós, the Tocantins, the Xingu, the Madeira, and the Solimões and on Marajó island did economic production attain great sustainable intensity. The economic situation arose because of the presence of richly fertile, renewable farm lands on the floodplains, the larger yields of fish, and the hoarding of turtles in pens. Here we find large population densities and the beginnings of hierarchical societies. The coastline also allowed large Tupinambá concentrations, but they did not develop any permanent institution conducive to class formation. The majority of Indian ethnies lived in comparably productive environments over the Brazilian territory where no insurmountable barriers, such as mountains or deserts, could hamper migrations, flights, and human dispersal. The influence of Andean peoples and hierarchical cultures never advanced beyond the foothills of the Andean range, and although it seems to have played a role in the development of some Amazonian chiefdoms, it was not long-lasting and powerful enough to force radical changes on Amazonian traditions.

POPULATION AND SOCIAL HIERARCHY

Demography, or actually the fluctuations thereof, is a most important factor in a mode of production and in social and economic change. Before the arrival of Europeans, several Indian ethnies had attained quite high population levels, numbering perhaps in the hundreds of thousands. The Tupinambá are the best known of them, but Francisco de Carvajal, reporting on the first voyage down the Amazon in 1541, speaks of large concentrations of villages along the banks of the mighty river. The early Jesuits also marveled at the number of Nheengaíbas on Marajó island and at the number of Tapajós. According to Jesuit João Daniel, who spent many years with the Tapajós in the early eighteenth century (when their numbers had dwindled considerably), they are said to have possessed a religion that preserved the bodies of their prominent dead, an institution that certainly represents privilege and possibly an incipient stage of social differentiation.[11] Some Tupinambá and Guarani groups presented similar evidence in that certain of their religious leaders—the *caraíba*—were acclaimed by villages as special people with higher status.[12]

On a smaller scale, several historical ethnies attained populations in the tens of thousands. The Bororo, Munduruku, Pareci, and Maué had populations of between 30,000 and 50,000. They have survived to the present, but with much smaller numbers. Except perhaps for the Pareci, none came to display any institutions of status differentiation. The Pareci, an Aruakspeaking ethnie living in the savanna plateaus of Central West Brazil, are reported to have had large villages in the early seventeenth century, when Spanish Jesuits established missions among them. They are thought to have been organized in local chiefdoms, although the evidence is not very reliable. They had the oblique function of spreading some Andean culture traits to other ethnies in the lowlands.[13] The Bororo and Munduruku became known for their prowess in warfare, one ethnie in the savannas of central Brazil, where they controlled a vast territory in the beginning of the eighteenth century, the other on the Tapajós River valley, where they fought back all Portuguese attempts to invade their territory until the mid-eighteenth century, when for unknown reasons they offered peace, were settled near a Portuguese town, and began to die as a consequence of epidemics.[14] The Maué are inhabitants of the middle Amazon River and were missionized by the Jesuits in the eighteenth century. They were organized in clans and their villages were led by hereditary chiefs. During the great rebellion known as Cabanagem (1838–41), they were among the last to keep on fighting against the Portuguese forces. They paid a high price in lives, and it has taken them more than a century to restore their population to the tens of thousands.[15]

The Kadiwéu, the horse-riding Indians of Southern Mato Grosso and Paraguay, who may have numbered from 15,000 to 20,000 people, present an interesting and unusual form of political differentiation. Although they were known for being an energetic, dominating ethnie, it was with the domestication of wild horses brought by the Spaniards to the savannas of Paraguay that they gained a powerful edge over their enemies. By the late seventeenth century they had subjugated and held some neighboring ethnies under the condition of vassalage or clientage. They offered them their protection from common enemies and in turn received tribute in the form of labor power or agricultural produce. Internally, they constituted themselves in ranks of nobles, commoners, and servants, marked by privileges, duties, and formal subordination. These distinctions, however, were founded not on a special mode of economic production but on the war-making ability of the Kadiwéu noble class. Oddly enough, at the highest position of this social pyramid the Kadiwéu women were conditioned not to bear their own children but instead to adopt them from families of inferior rank! At the height of their power, around 1730, a noble Kadiwéu woman rejected an invitation from a Portuguese man of arms to go to Cuiabá because she felt she might be asked in marriage, and it would be embarrassing to turn the would-be fiancé down. By 1790 Kadiwéu hegemony over their vast territory was on a downward slope as their population, and consequently their striking power, had diminished considerably. They were persuaded to sign an alliance treaty with the Viceroyalty of Brazil relinquishing dominion over a large tract of land that was incorporated into Brazil. All the same, this was the only treaty that the Portuguese ever signed with an Indian ethnie, a clear demonstration of the respect they had for the Kadiwéu. In the War of Paraguay (1865–70) fought between Paraguay and Brazil in alliance with Argentina and Uruguay, the Kadiwéu were asked by the Brazilians to fight in their ranks in exchange for official guarantee of their lands. Indeed, Emperor Dom Pedro II issued a mandate that recognized the debt of Brazil to the Kadiwéu and registered a significant area of land to them.

The Kadiwéu settled down on their lands as poor cattle ranchers and diminished in numbers until the 1960s, when the population tide began to rise. Today there are some 1,100 Kadiwéu living on a 530,000-hectare territory in the Pantanal, or wetlands of west-central Brazil. Some portion of this territory was for many years rented out by the Indian agency to Brazilian cattle ranchers, who at one point claimed right to the lots they were using. The Brazilian Supreme Court rejected these claims and ordered them and their belongings removed. Although no longer ranked in classes and without the political prestige they once held, the Kadiwéu still command the attention and respect of neighboring ethnies and of visiting anthropologists.[16]

It seems self-evident that a small political unit composed of up to a few thousand people cannot possibly create formal and hereditary social differences. But even much larger ethnies are not foreordained to give rise to classes with rank and prestige. The large expanse of South America east of the Andes was not home to any significant, stable hierarchical society beyond the chiefdom level. The ecological and geographical constraints weighed most heavily in favor of population dispersal and self-sustaining economies. Working with these factors were the ideological factors of social egalitarianism and village autonomy, which in a philosophical vocabulary we may translate as the predilection for freedom and autonomous power. Whenever there appeared an occasion for the rise of social hierarchy, the egalitarian ideology surged upwards to impede the stabilization of rank privileges and to disperse the bases of hierarchical power. Such was certainly the case of the Tupinambá, where the power drive of the war leaders conflicted with the anarchical movement of the religious leaders.[17] All things considered, we may propound that, in the case of non-Andean South America, only through the active pressure of a great exogenous power could there arise the opportunity for the development of hierarchy and socioeconomic stratification. The Incas were not able or did not have the time to make a full-fledged attempt at such a culture, and hierarchy came as an imposition from outside with the arrival of the Portuguese.

The Indian ethnies with the largest populations today are the Guarani, Tikuna, Makuxi, the Tukanoan ethnies, Guajajara, Maué, Kaingang, and Terena, who all count more than 10,000 members each. The Amazon forest Tukano, Guajajara, and Maué—and for that matter the great majority of ethnies—live in small- to medium-sized villages ranging from a few dozens up to 500 people. They are found spread out over large tracts of land, some at great distances from one another, some in areas which are not contiguous. Consequently, many Indian villagers have never met but have only heard of one another. The Tikuna, who live on small tributaries of the Amazon in lands that border with Colombia, have villages that number as many as 3,000 people. The Guarani, Terena, and Kaingang are concentrated in a few crowded villages in small parcels of land scattered over several states in south-central and southern Brazil. The Terena are probably the most concentrated of all, living in some four or five Indian lands of Southern Mato Grosso and São Paulo, some of which are shared with other Indian ethnies, notably the Guarani. The Kaingang live in small Indian lands from Rio Grande do Sul up to São Paulo, and the Guarani are found in all these states, in most cases living in the same areas together with Kaingang and Terena. The Guarani's social pattern of migrating in small family groups from one village to another and even to new areas has taken them northeastward to Espírito Santo, and as far north as Maranhão.

None of these ethnies have created any social institution conducive to social hierarchy. Population is dispersed, and village concentrations are a function of a trade economy in which the greatest commodity the Indians have is their labor power. In all cases the political emphasis is placed on individual freedom and autonomy of social units.

Lack of social hierarchy does not necessarily mean a kind of social uniformity without any internal social differentiation. Indeed, there are a few good examples of Indian ethnies that have been able to aggregate relatively high populations in villages and develop cultural structures characterized by divisions and subdivisions of people into social groupings with differentiation in social and ritual functions, yet functioning within the ideology of egalitarianism. The best known of these are the cultures associated with Jê speakers, such as the Canela, the Kayapó, and the Bororo. The Canela-Ramkokamekra, whose territory is located in the savanna of south-central Maranhão, live in a single village with a population of around 1,500 people at present. Their culture encompasses the notions of division, segmentation, and hierarchization of social groups. Membership in these social groups is obtained according to the interplay of kinship lines, age cohort association, and traditional lore. The distinct groups serve social and economic functions, some being permanent, others organized in accordance with the demands of the culture's annual calendar of economic production and ritual-ization. They can play one against the other as if with the purpose of one outdoing the other. In the end, however, it becomes clear that these roles are played in order to maintain internal social harmony. It should be noted that the present-day Canela population is the largest known since at least 1830, but we know of even larger concentrations among other Jê peoples, such as the Apinayé, Krahô, and Kayapó, who have had villages with as many as 3,000 members before population losses or splitting themselves up into two or more villages. The Bororo today have small villages of less than 300 people, but they had larger ones in the past.[18]

THE DIVERSITY OF LANGUAGES

The potential for dispersion, autonomy, and adaptability of the Indian cul-tures in lowland South America resulted in the emergence of the largest quantity of distinct languages in the world. It is estimated that in 1500 half of the languages existing in the world were to be found in this region, perhaps some 5,000 languages and dialect variations. To establish how many of these were spoken by Indians in Brazilian territory is quite a diffi-cult task, but if in general terms we correlate one language for each ethnie, we would have perhaps 1,000 to 1,200 languages spoken in Brazil.[19] Cur-rently, this number has dropped to 170, although there may be some 10 to 20 more unknown distinct languages.

The correlation of language with culture is not perfect because both are historically determined entities, each in its own right and with respective rates of change. Given a certain kind of external influence, the intensity of cultural change might be deeper than the changes a language might un-dergo in the same period. On the other hand, the scientific definition of where to locate the boundaries that divide a language from one of its dia-lects or from a similar language is not as absolute as might be supposed. It is said that a dialect becomes a specific language when its speakers are not understood by the speakers of the original language or dialect. It remains a dialect when the two are mutually intelligible. By this criterion, Portuguese is distinguished from Italian or French, but with regard to certain dialects in Spanish the distinction is not so clear. In another example, if one should take some of the spoken dialects of English, such as those of African-Ameri-cans in the southern United States, and confront it with London Cockney, one could hardly expect mutual intelligibility. In this case, the criterion that defines these two forms of speech as belonging to the same language is more politically oriented than genuinely linguistic.

Accordingly, there are several cases of Indian language affiliations that are still controversial. It is still not clear, for instance, if the various groups that make up the Yanomami people speak distinct languages or dialects, or if the dialects spoken by certain of the Eastern Timbira can be distinguished as separate languages, or how much of the Pano languages are indeed languages or dialects of one another. Thus estimating the number of languages spoken by Indian ethnies in Brazil is more difficult than establishing the number of the ethnies themselves.

The main linguistic stocks that have representatives in Brazil are the Tupi, Jê, Carib, Aruak, and Pano. The eminent American linguist Joseph Greenberg postulated that some of these stocks could be considered related to one another and to other stocks of languages spoken elsewhere in South and Central America.[20] In the end, of course, they must be related to one another if we accept the theory that they all come from a single source of population migrating from East Asia. Theoretically, every language derives or stems from an earlier one, which for its part was derived from another, which is even more remote in time, until, following this chain of regression, we would reach the first mother tongue spoken by our primeval ancestors. One can thus conclude that all present-day languages have developed through time and cannot in any way be considered primitive, but rather the temporal outcome of a natural history of languages.

Each linguistic stock is represented by a certain number of families of languages, and each family is made up of at least one, but often two or more languages. In the past there were many more language families than today, as many have disappeared with the extinction of their speakers. The Kariri language, for instance, was once widely spoken in northeast Brazil and was recorded by Franciscan friars in the early eighteenth century. Today there are Kariri Indians but no living Kariri language. There are a few linguistic families that have only one language within them and are classified as isolated because they are, as far as present-day linguistic knowledge is concerned, seemingly unrelated to other languages. Such seems to be the case of the language spoken by the Trumái, a small group living on the upper Xingu river, and of the Tikuna language, which is spoken by some 20,000 Indians of the Solimões, or upper Amazon River.

The Tupi-Guarani family is one of the most widespread in South America, particularly in Brazil. It belongs to what is sometimes called the macro-Tupi stock, which encompasses an expressive number of other linguistic families and languages, the majority of which are found south of the Amazon River. One of the best known representatives is the language spoken by the Tupinambá, who lived on the Brazilian coast. The early sixteenth-century Portuguese-Brazilian settlements, particularly the missionaries, learned how to speak it and reduced its grammar and vocabulary to a simpler form, which was adopted as a lingua franca to help bring together the many different peoples in the same missionary reduction. This lingua franca, also known as *Nheengatu*, or "good language," is still spoken in some isolated areas of the Amazon. It was widely spoken in Brazil until the middle of the eighteenth century and left its marks in many Brazilian toponymical features. One of its dialectical variants, spoken by the Guarani Indians, who lived in Paraguay and southern Brazil, led to modern Guarani, a language currently spoken by the majority of the Paraguayan people.

Ethnies that speak Tupi languages are generally characterized as holding cultures that are sociologically flexible, whose religions are based on a mythological complex centered on the figure of the twin hero, the strong role of shamans (*pajés*), the use of tobacco in ceremonies, as well as other accouterments found among other ethnies, such as rattles and collective dances. This correlation is accurate especially for ethnies who speak languages of the Tupi-Guarani family, but the exceptions indicate that this cultural pattern was formed in relatively recent times, apparently resulting from adaptations to recent historical circumstances. The Guajá and Ka'apor, for example, do not have *pajés*, whereas the Tapirapé have adopted institutions of social segmentation supposedly through the tangential influence of Jê speaking peoples such as the Kayapó and Karajá. It should also be noted that the tendency to social flexibility can also be found among other non-Tupi peoples, especially the Aruak and Carib of the Amazon.

The great majority of ethnies that speak languages of the Jê family, part of the macro-Jê stock, live in mixed ecozones with *cerrado* and *caatinga* scrub vegetation interspersed with gallery forests, found mostly on the Central Brazilian plateau. Although displaying several degrees of variation, they are renowned for a cultural pattern of internal divisions and segmentation, circular or semicircular villages, and a pronounced emphasis on the ritualization of their daily lives. They are sometimes contrasted with the Tupi as if they were opposites, but this argument has rather restrictive methodological value and no historical or philosophical bases.[21] The genesis of their cultural formation may be in part the result of their initial adaptation to the *cerrado* and *caatinga* ecozones, but many of them live and depend on forest environments for their livelihood. Perhaps one can postulate that they moved to forest environments after they had already adapted to scrubland and have not since then felt the need for radical changes in their social structure.[22] One can think of the nineteenth-century Timbira ethnies that lived either on forest or scrub lands, such as the Txakamekrã and the Canela, and yet had very similar social institutions.

The Carib and Aruak stocks are made up of languages and linguistic families that are widely scattered throughout South America and the Caribbean. Aruak and Carib speakers were among the first Indians encountered by Columbus, and it is from a Carib language that we derive the corresponding words for Caribbean as well as for cannibal. The Ciboney, an Indian people who lived on the Florida peninsula, probably spoke an Aruak language. In Brazil these languages are spoken by ethnies adapted to the Amazon rain forest (the Palikur [Aruak] and Atroari [Carib]) to the scrublands of central-west Brazil (the Pareci [Aruak] and Bakairi [Carib]) and the natural grasslands of the Guyana Plateau (the Wapixana [Aruak] and Makuxi [Carib]).

The Aruak are regarded as peoples who have more complex cultures than the Carib and Tupi, and as having been in earlier times the intermediaries between the Andean civilizations and the lowland tropical cultures. The Pareci of central-west Brazil and the Campa of lowland eastern Peru were among those ethnies that served as culture brokers in the past. Their material cultures were more elaborate and supported denser populations and political organizations at the chiefdom level.[23] The Tapajós and Aruans of the lower Amazon were probably Aruak speakers. They suffered irreparable population losses in the seventeenth century and did not survive to present times as ethnic groups. Only those groups that remained—or fled to—the upper reaches of Amazonian tributaries survived in small numbers to present times.

Carib-speaking peoples are also found in tropical forests. To the north they inhabited the smaller islands of the Caribbean Sea, but they are all extinct. The Bakairi are probably their southernmost representatives together with the Kalapalo and Yawalapiti, who belong to the Xinguano culture complex. The Makuxi, a Carib people who live on the grasslands of the Guyana Plateau in the present-day state of Roraima, are one of the three largest Indian population groups in Brazil.

The Pano linguistic stock is made up of several languages that are quite similar and whose ethnic speakers live in a more restricted geographical region, mostly in the basins of the Purus and Acre rivers and adjacent areas. It includes portions of Peru and Bolivia. In Brazil this area encompasses the state of Acre and the western portions of the states of Rondônia and Amazonas. This whole region is drained by rivers that plunge downward from the Andes forming large beach areas in the dry season. It is also the richest region in rubber trees, because of which it suffered a violent influx of Brazilians who were brought in to work as tappers during the rubber boom that occurred between 1870 and 1912. Many Indian ethnies were massacred in those years and practically until the 1930s, and they lost large portions of their territories. Some of them were completely wiped out, and survivors remained scattered for many years in the midst of the rubber tappers. They were entrapped in the patron-client system of debt peonage and barely survived as autonomous ethnies. The Kaxinawa, Kulina, and Jamamadi are survivors of the rubber boom days, whereas the Matis and Marubo, both Pano speakers, survived by running away from the region and migrating into areas where there was no economic interest until recent times.[24]

INDIAN RESPONSES TO NEW SOCIAL REALITIES

The Indian cultures and ethnies of today do not live the same way as they did five hundred years ago. For one thing, the surviving populations are smaller and have begun to experience growth only in the last forty or so years. They live differently mainly because the world around them has changed, and the original intercultural dynamic that supported them in the past has lost its vigor due to the extinction of dozens, even hundreds, of other ethnies. Nowadays Indian ethnies are like islands in a sea of Brazilians. It was not until a few decades ago that most of them began to have contact with and knowledge of one another, in a sort of *pax brasiliense*. The opening of new highways, the expansion of modern means of communications, and the centralization of political power in Brasília, the capital of Brazil since 1960, brought them together to share their experiences with one another. They have become accustomed to the fact that they are a minority in Brazil. In many ways they have adapted to this social and political reality, although they are not satisfied with it and continue fighting to obtain a better position. It seems that many of them long for a more self-sufficient existence, if not a return to the past. There are indeed a number of ethnies—perhaps twenty or thirty—who live on their own, with little or no social contact with other ethnies or mainstream Brazilian society. They know little of the world outside and when faced with abrupt contact with Brazilian frontiersmen or representatives of the Indian agency, they suffer terrible population losses and cultural anomie from diseases and exogenous cultural-political constraints. It is as if they were living through the same historical processes of contact and colonization that had previously been imposed on other ethnies. One can say, therefore, that Indian ethnies change nowadays less because of environmental constraints than in response to new, compelling social realities different from all that they had previously experienced.

One of the most noteworthy aspects of Brazilian anthropology is the contribution it has made to the sociological understanding of how the Indians were decimated and how they struggled to survive through the cultural and military pressures characteristic of Brazilian history. From the archival and field studies of Curt Nimuendaju and Herbert Baldus in the 1920s and 1930s to the studies of cultural resistance and ethnic identification in the 1970s and 1980s, Brazilians of all types and classes have acquired the sense that Indian ethnies are not only different peoples in themselves but political beings inserted into a wider, more powerful world. We know that, from the outset, the economic development of Brazil was carried out over the broken and dead bodies of the original inhabitants of this country.

Brazilian historiography teaches that the country was colonized and developed in economic cycles that came and went according to the market value of their export commodities. These economic cycles affected different ethnies in different ways. The first cycle of sugar production (which peaked from 1560 to about 1660)—just as every other economic cycle based on an agricultural commodity—was characterized by the need for good lands and intensive labor to sustain itself. Sugar production was thus the reason why the Tupinambá were first used for labor and then wiped out on the Brazilian coast, where the best lands are found. The next important cycle was the expansion of cattle throughout the *sertão* lands of the northeast. A cattle frontier needs land above all and little labor power. Thus, most of the Indian ethnies that lived in the path of this expansion were wiped out between 1660 and 1850. The colonization of the Amazon was originally made possible by a forest extractive economy that needed little land but intensive labor power. This labor was obtained first in the throngs of native populations and later by importing people from elsewhere. Each specific economic cycle and its frontiers developed its own modus operandi and modus vivendi with the Indians whose territories were being taken over. In general, the extinction of ethnies, the degree of population losses of others, and the possibility of escaping of yet others depended on the type of economy prevailing in a certain historical period.

The fact that very few Indian ethnies survived the cattle expansion of late seventeenth century in the Brazilian northeast, including later south-central Maranhão and northern Tocantins, is explained by the concerted action of violence of that expanding ranching economy and the official war expeditions chartered by the Portuguese Crown to destroy the Indian ethnies to prevent their allying themselves with the recently expelled Dutch forces. The few Indian villages that survived this double onslaught were forced to live in missions assigned to the Jesuit and Franciscan orders or else to administration villages ruled by local potentates. In both places they suffered the heavy burden of serfdom and forced labor, and by the middle of the nineteenth century the majority of those villages had either perished, disbanded, or become incorporated as undifferentiated Brazilian mestizo settlements.

In the mining districts of the states of Minas Gerais and Goiás, where gold and diamonds were found in the eighteenth century, most Indian ethnies were completely wiped out in the first years of exploitation as a result of an explicit policy of genocide practiced by both prospectors and official parties. It was feared that the existence of Indians would hamper business and could set a bad example to the concentrations of black slaves that were imported to work the mines. Only in areas where gold was quickly depleted and the prospectors had to move off for better sites did some Indian ethnies, such as the Avá-Canoeiro, manage to survive the onslaught by acquiring a cultural strategy of roaming over a vast territory and being less dependent on farming for a living. Others, such as the Xavante and Panará (formerly the southern Kayapó), fled westward to the less-popu-lated Mato Grosso.

Along the lower Amazon the great number of Indians—perhaps 200,000— who had survived being mission Indians until the outbreak of the Cabanagem Rebellion, was to lend their labor power to the collecting of forest products such as cacao, sarsaparilla, cinnamon, turtle eggs, and timber, products that constituted the main export commodities in a rather inelastic economy. They lived in villages along the mighty river and its tributaries together with a small number of Luso-Brazilians, who kept trickling in over the years in search of a better livelihood. A modus vivendi was established in which the Indians were on the bottom of the social scale and had to work practically under the conditions of serfdom they had experienced as mission Indians, but it was a serfdom inflicted with less piety than in Jesuit times. Some of these villages turned into townships and developed the caboclo lifestyle that can still be found in rural and semirural areas of the Amazon to this day. The independence of Brazil from Portugal and the economic changes introduced to incorporate the Amazon into the new nation also brought to the surface the socioeconomic contradictions of this unequal relationship. Eventually these inequalities led to the Cabanagem Rebellion in 1835 and the subsequent destruction of most villages and the semi-autonomous cultural condition they had had.

Focusing on these social realities and their small but significant variations led many anthropologists to propose that the interethnic situation of Indian ethnies is as significant to determine their cultural conditions and their possibilities of survival as their original types of culture and language. As an offshoot of acculturation studies the Indians came to be classified according to the degree and level of contact they maintained with the surrounding Brazilian society. The formulation presented by anthropologist Darcy Ribeiro in the 1960s, which he called "stages of integration," was actually adopted by the 1973 Statute of the Indian. Thus, Indian ethnies were classified and dealt with politically as "isolated," which could also be phrased as "resistant to contact," if they kept themselves away from contact with Brazilians or other ethnies who had contact with Brazilians. It was felt that these Indians should one day be contacted by the Indian agency, for otherwise they would certainly be contacted by one of the economic frontiers invading their territory and would suffer a worse fate. There were specific regulations and policies concerning these ethnies; Indian agents who dealt with them were called *sertanistas,* or backwoodsmen, and had a higher status within the FUNAI bureaucracy. A second group under this classification was constituted by those ethnies who had been contacted in recent times but were still living autonomously without much regard for the influence of the Indian agency or the surrounding Brazilian society. They were classified as ethnies "in intermittent contact." A third group included those ethnies that had "permanent contact" with both the Indian agency and members of the Brazilian society but still kept a distinct culture functioning. Finally, a fourth group was formed by the ethnies who had a long history of contact with Brazilian society and were thus "integrated" or undergoing "integration" with Brazilian society and polity.

Throughout the 1970s and 1980s the Indian agency tried to develop different policies according to this scheme of classification. There was much concern and some confusion among indigenists and anthropologists as to which category a certain Indian ethnie should belong. In the mid-1980s the

Indian agency, still under the influence of the military, tried to introduce the administrative concept of "colony" to categorize those ethnies that were undergoing integration and could accelerate their pace of assimilation by having their lands open to non-Indians who wished to live with them. We may recall that this was precisely the policy introduced by the Marquis of Pombal in 1757, which destroyed the autonomy of the great majority of Indian villages in the Amazon. This concept was vehemently criticized by both Indians and anthropologists and was dropped by the subsequent administration.

The economic policy of the Indian agency excluded the ethnies that had recently been contacted and were still going through the hard process of changing their society and economy. It was taken for granted that certain types of economic incentives could be appropriate for any ethnie according to its received level of integration. For instance, cattle could be introduced as an economic project to Indian ethnies in permanent contact or undergoing integration, but of course such a project would be out of the question for Indians in intermittent contact. For the latter, one could induce them to produce artifacts that would be bought by the Indian agency or exchanged for manufactured items of interest to them. It was acceptable that paternalistic methods of gift-giving be used, but not for the integrated ethnies.

The idea behind the classification scheme of levels of integration was that it constituted an historical progression through which all Indian ethnies would undergo. The last level to be reached was full integration, which would ultimately represent the ethnie's cultural demise and physical assimilation into the Brazilian mainstream society. In many aspects the purpose of every Indian policy ever conceived by the Brazilian state has been precisely that, and perhaps it still is.

Although the question as to whether an Indian ethnie integrates or assimilates into the mainstream of a modern society is no longer discussed by anthropologists, the fact is that most people still think that the final destiny of the Indians is their assimilation into the national mainstream. The theoretical solution most anthropologists propose to this quandary is that these ethnies can change their cultures to adapt to new social, economic, and political circumstances, and in a sense they can integrate themselves into a larger sociopolitical entity. However, through the maintenance of the social institutions that give support to the feeling of ethnic identification they can, or have the potential to, always remain who they are no matter how economically or politically integrated they may be.

On the other hand, the notion of levels of integration seems no longer applicable when we try to put into the picture the perspective of the Indian ethnies. Is isolation a significant concept for those ethnies who live fully by themselves? Does a permanent contact relationship entail the loss or weakening of ethnic identification? Overall it seems that the crucial distinction in the relationship between Indian ethnies and the Brazilian society may not be the time or intensity of contact but whether or not there is the possibility of maintaining some kind of cultural and therefore political autonomy in their lives. In this sense, the scale of differentiation goes from complete autonomy to complete heteronomy. Although this scale may coincide with the scheme of levels of integration, it has the advantage of taking into due consideration the perspective of the Indian ethnies. It is a proposition that takes into account the understanding that Indian ethnies live according to a measure of political consciousness of the world. The exogenous character, particularly the economic makeup, of the contact is of course important, but so is the capacity of the ethnie to react to and impose its own terms on this relationship. In this way we can have an analytical framework that can better explain why the Xavante, who are easily acknowledged to be in a situation of permanent contact, have in no way been moving in the direction of assimilation because of their ability to maintain a high degree of self-identification and cultural autonomy. It can also account for the fact that the Guarani, who have been in permanent, compulsory contact with Brazilian society for two centuries or more can hardly be said to be integrated or assimilated. In short, what is important to make a better appraisal of the survival conditions of an ethnie is to set up a model to take into account the ethnie's own culture and history, the way it has inserted itself into the Brazilian socioeconomic context, and to follow up the results of this political interplay through time.

POPULATION AND CULTURAL DYNAMICS

The most reliable estimates we have about the number of Indians in Brazil give figures that range between 330,000 and 350,000, as of May 1999. In 1987 I had estimated them to be around 230,000 and to be growing at an average yearly rate of 3.5 percent. That rate is probably still valid. The Indian agency itself has numbers for many ethnies and for different years, but has not made a full census of all the Indian ethnies since 1985. The present numbers are thus estimates gathered within FUNAI and nongovernmental organizations that have a good deal of contact with the agency. It is also estimated that there are presently around 220 ethnies, speaking some 170 known languages. The difficulty in obtaining precise numbers stems from a rather incomplete assessment of the number of autonomous ethnies. The majority of these are found in the far reaches of the Brazilian economic frontiers, in the heartland of the Amazon, although there are some groups found in more accessible regions, such as the Guajá in the west of Maranhão state, and the Avá-Canoeiro on the headwaters of the Tocantins River in Goiás state, and the Xetá in the state of Paraná, who became extinct as late as the 1960s. In regions such as the Javari Indian Park in western Amazon, and the Trombetas River basin in the lower Amazon, there are signs of the existence of a few yet uncontacted Indian ethnies.[25] Their numbers are appraised in the few hundreds, according to the sites of villages that have been spotted from the air and by the accounts of other Indians who occasionally come across these elusive autonomous ethnies. In addition, there is also very imprecise information about the number of Indians who live in large cities such as Manaus, Boa Vista, Rio Branco, Campo Grande, and even São Paulo. Sometimes their ethnic origin is unknown or disregarded, and they become known generically as Indians from the Rio Negro, or the Solimões River, or the northeast. There are also a certain number of old Indian villages, some of which had been officially "extinguished" in the past, which continue to be recognized as *aldeias de caboclos*, or villages of Indian mestizos, both by their surrounding neighbors and by the villagers themselves, but are not officially recognized as Indian by the federal government. There are examples of these cases in Maranhão, Piauí, Ceará, Goiás, and in many places in the Amazon. Some of them have requisitioned the Indian agency to recognize them as Indians, whereas others prefer to keep themselves in this ambiguous position for fear of suffering harsher discrimination in the remote areas where they live.

Even though official recognition by the government is not indispensable for an Indian ethnie's sense of self-identification, it does play an important factor in the chances of survival of a specific Indian population. It is only after official acknowledgment is made that an Indian ethnie begins to enjoy the specific rights conferred upon Indians by the Brazilian Constitution of 1988 (as well as the previous ones), the Statute of the Indian of 1973, and whichever statute is passed as law by the National Congress. These sets of laws provide guarantees for Indian lands, which are considered property of the Union, where the Indians have inalienable rights of possession and exclusive use to be exercised as they see fit. Other than through this provision, there are very rare cases in which an Indian ethnie has been granted rights to lands purported to belong to them by virtue of having been part of a former village of theirs in the past. In general, lands belonging to Indian communities that lost their ethnic status have been seized by local land grabbers, either by force or by buying out individualized plots of lands. At one point in the preparation of the 1988 Constitution, the concept of collective property was presented and discussed in assembly but was not favorably received by the authors. Should collective property have been acclaimed as a type of property, those old Indian lands that had been extinguished but were still in the hands of self-proclaimed communities would have had a chance to be guaranteed as such if the descendants of the Indians so wished. Furthermore, present-day Indian lands could be passed over directly to the hands and responsibility of the Indians themselves, without the intermediary role of the Union, and they still could not be disposed of. Finally, many traditional groups—who claim to be descendants of Indians or of former black slaves, have survived through decades, mostly due to their isolation from economic centers of development, and have preserved a sense of community—would have had a better chance of surviving simply because their members would not have felt enticed to sell individual portions of their lands.

The great majority of Indian ethnies in Brazil are found in the Amazon, the states of Amazonas and Roraima having the largest percentages in relation to total population. Roraima has some 35,000 Indians, who comprise about 20 percent of the state population. Among them, the Makuxi comprise the second largest population, with about 20,000 individuals. The Yanomami, who add up to 20,000 if we count those living in Venezuela, comprise some 9,000 in Brazil, mostly living in upper Roraima with a few villages spilling over to northern Amazonas. In Amazonas state there are such large ethnies as the Tikuna, with some 20,000 on the upper Solimões River, the Tukanoan ethnies of the Rio Negro, who number some 15,000, and the dispersed Maué and Sateré, who add up to 20,000 people in all.

The state of Pará comprises the lower basin of the Amazon, where most of the colonization as well as the Cabanagem Rebellion took place. The caboclo life style is most vivid along the mighty river and its tributaries, and the former Jesuit mission villages are now Brazilian towns and cities such as Gurupá, Santarém, and Óbidos. The current Indian populations are to be found away from the Amazon River in areas where economic development has arrived rather recently. The arrival of the cattle frontier on the grasslands of southern Pará in the beginning of the nineteenth century decimated some of the Timbira tribes that lived in the lower Tocantins and Araguaia river basin. The commercialization of Brazil nuts and tree rubber, which were found in southern and central Pará, caused a minor economic boom at the end of the century, and the incoming population brought violence and destruction upon some Kayapó bands and several Tupi ethnies such as the Suruí, Parakanã, and Assurini. The Catholic order of the Dominicans found a mission for Indians near the present town of Conceição do Araguaia and caused the total demise of the Pau d'Arco band of the Kayapó in a matter of some thirty years. Today the remaining Indian ethnies have populations in the hundreds, with the exception of the Kayapó, who, counting all the subgroups, number some 3,000 to 4,000 individuals.

Several rain forest ethnies have rich mineral deposits of casseterite, diamonds, and gold within their territories, as is the case with the Waimiri-Atroari, Yanomami, and Kayapó. Petroleum and gas are found in the Javari River valley, inhabited by Marubo, Matsé, and other autonomous tribes, and in the Madeira River basin, where there are territories of the Munduruku and Maué. Unquestionably this fact has been one of the main reasons why in many instances the state has stalled in recognizing the boundaries of Indian territories and in taking measures to demarcate them. In the specific case of the territory of the Waimiri-Atroari, the Indian agency reached the apex of irresponsibility and corruption when it demarcated that territory in 1971 only to annul it a few years later after pressure by the Paranapanema Mining Company, whose owners and most important stockholders were closely linked to high-level members of the military regime. However, by the late 1980s it had corrected its early mistake and demarcated an area around 1,800,000 hectares for the Waimiri-Atroari.

In some regions of the Amazon time seems to have stopped, and many social situations resemble those that were common in the past. Many Indian ethnies live in a social pattern of dispersed settlements within vast areas where only a few settlements or townships of Brazilian peasants live by extracting forest products. They relate to one another in a milieu of mutual acceptance but continuous suspicion. Such situations can be found particularly on the upper Madeira and Tapajós rivers, where scattered Brazilian settlements endure side by side with Munduruku, Parintintin, Pirahã, and remnants of once larger populations, such as the Tupi-Kawahib, who are now reduced to the bare surviving minimum, as small ethnies known as Diore, Juma, and Jaboti.

On the other hand, in the westernmost state of the Brazilian Amazon, Acre, where the rubber boom had been a veritable scourge to the Indian who lived there in the early twentieth century, the Indian agency until the early 1970s considered there to be no Indians left. They had either been wiped out or miscegenated with the rubber tappers. Suddenly Indians began to show up around the towns, and incoming Indian agents and missionaries began to map their locations on the upper reaches of several rivers of that state and on the border with Peru and Bolivia. Today there are some twenty Indian ethnies, with more than 13,000 Indians in that state. Their style of living still reflects the long years of rubber tapping, when many Indian villages were dispersed in small groups to exploit rubber for an absentee boss. With the help of a few dedicated anthropologists and Indian agents some of these Indians have been able to organize themselves into cooperatives that help them sell their rubber and Brazil nuts at reasonable prices, and whose needs for industrialized merchandise are met without the exploitation so characteristic of the old system of debt peonage.[26]

Because Brazil is a country that borders with most South American countries, there are several cases of Indian ethnies that have territories and villages in another country. A few of them, such as the Yanomami on the northern frontier with Venezuela and a few Sirionó bands on the western frontier with Bolivia, are not affected by the notion of national frontiers and move back and forth between the two countries unawares and unperturbedly. On the borders with Colombia, Peru, and French Guyana, the Tukanoan ethnies of the Tikuna, the Campa, and the Galibi are quite aware of this duality and have taken advantage of this fact by adopting when possible both nationalities. In some aspects there is an advantage in living in Brazil, as the Brazilian Indian agency offers occasional economic advantages and gives guarantees to lands, which oftentimes is not the case in Peru and Colombia. On the other hand, the latter countries offer better educational and health services than can be found in Brazil. The Tikuna are most capable of taking advantage of what Brazil, Peru, and Colombia offer them. Most of these ethnies are bilingual or multilingual as they may speak both Portuguese and Spanish or French besides their own languages.

The widely proclaimed antagonism among Indian ethnies cannot be taken as an intrinsic, predestined characteristic of Indian societies, no matter how frequently it shows up in their interethnic relations. Competition and antagonism are indeed conditions of being human, but they surface only in specific situations and for historical reasons. Competition for territory and resources are two motives that lead to antagonism and ethnic rivalry, sometimes lasting for generations, particularly when an ethnie is undergoing a process of demographic expansion and needs more than they culturally have. However, ethnic enmity also breaks loose for endogenous reasons, such as when a culture requires warlike behavior of its members to maintain social cohesion. One may suppose that this requirement has its roots in competition for resources, but it often happens that the aggressive behavior is maintained even after the original demands are fulfilled.

The opposite of ethnic aggression is ethnic tolerance and mutual acceptance. There are but rare occasions in the ethnographic records in which several ethnies come together and agree to establish a modus vivendi of cultural and economic exchange. The best known case is that found within the Xingu National Park. There twelve or more Indian ethnies speaking languages that are mutually unintelligible developed a common culture that transcended their previous traditions and society, constituting an interdependence of discrete social and political units. Today nine ethnies survive and each has remained politically, but not economically and socially, independent. Their common culture developed a need for economic exchange and symbolic amalgamation, which are fulfilled by means of ceremonial trade and intertribal rituals. In this way one ethnie becomes specialized in manufacturing large clay pots, as do the Waurá, while others, such as the Kamayurá and Aweti, specialize in making bows; the Kuikuro make snail shell necklaces, and in the past, the Trumái specialized in stone axes. The exchange of these goods takes place in a ceremonial fashion according to preestablished values that are known and shared by everyone. A certain amount of value fluctuation and bargaining may be allowed, according to the quality of the product, or sometimes for reasons outside the purely economic sphere, such as marriage alliance or the redressing of wrongdoing. All of these activities go on without the use of a lingua franca, except for Portuguese, and are guided by the respect for traditional practices and the help of bilingual or multilingual persons who can be found in most villages.

It seems evident that this cultural complex has developed during a certain period of time as the outcome of a fortuitous convergence of several ethnies, including some that have become extinct in this century. They have consciously set up a modus vivendi that is capable of balancing the principles of autonomy and egalitarianism, and which can certainly be emulated as framework for an imaginable and workable pan-indigenism.

In other regions, such as the upper Rio Negro with the Tukanoan ethnies, or the Mato Grosso Pantanal wetlands with the former Guaikuru and Guaná, there also developed similar situations of close interethnic relations. In both cases ethnic autonomy was preserved but not ethnic egalitarianism. On the contrary, in both regions there appeared signs of a hierarchization of ethnies, some playing the dominant part and holding symbols of power, while others were held down as subordinate. On the upper Rio Negro, a lingua franca was adopted from one of the dominant ethnies and disseminated among the other ethnies involved in the system. This lingua franca is spoken by virtually every person as a second and even third language. Here, then, is a situation that may have been common in other regions in pre-Columbian times, particularly along the Amazon river, when there was more steady pressure for the formation of federations of Indian ethnies under the command of a more populated, bellicose, or better situated ethnie.

LAND AND ECONOMIC POWER

Although most of the better lands were taken from the Indians throughout the history of Brazil, there are many Indian territories that have abundant extractive resources such as gold, petroleum, tin, and timber. Local, national, and international economic interests are eagerly examining the possibility of exploiting those resources for as low a price as possible. Over the years the Indians have acquired a sense of the importance of their natural resources and cultural products. They have also come to share with one another the knowledge each ethnie has acquired of the ways and means of exploitation they have suffered under the dominant society. They have begun to demand that their resources be exploited exclusively by them or for their own interests. The Sateré, for example, were rather firm in 1986 in demanding indemnities and reparations for the environmental damage that the French company Elf-Aquitaine caused in their territory as it set off explosions in its search for petroleum. The Gaviões of Pará state, whose lands were first crossed by the power transmission lines of the Tucuruí Hydroelectric Power Plant and then crossed again by the Carajás Railroad, obtained quite reasonable financial indemnities on both counts. The Vale do Rio Doce Company, the big mineral and railroad conglomerate responsible for the Carajás Railroad, settled the case in 1984 with a payment of about one million dollars, which was deposited in a savings account in the name of the Gaviões as a community. In the following decade of high inflation that scourged Brazil the Gaviões made good use of that money by cashing in only on the interest that it produced. However, in the last four or five years of low inflation they began to cash in on the principal, and the money began to dissipate. As it seemed to many who knew of the agreement at the time, it has become clear that it would have been better for the future of the Gaviões had they decided on land compensation instead of money. The Kayapó and Munduruku, both also of Pará state, in whose lands gold is found in placer mines that have attracted a great number of prospectors, have made exploitation possible by taking in a percentage of the results. However much they may be deceived by the declarations of the mining results, they have been considerable enough to make Kayapó leaders opulent and wasteful.

Timber is the most abundant natural resource in the Amazon. However, only a small number of species are harvested and marketed in Brazil and for export. Mahogany, two varieties of tropical cedar, *virola, ipê, maçaranduba,* and *cumaru* are some of the most sought after, but they are not found everywhere. Mahogany, the most valuable of all, is found scattered in groves of low density across some regions of the Amazon. In Pará state it has been found mostly on the lands of the Kayapó, Xikrin, and Parakanã. Since the mid-1980s it has been so intensely exploited that it has become scarce. In 1996 the Brazilian environmental agency declared a moratorium on harvesting mahogany for two years, but in 1997 it opposed a United Nations attempt to pass a resolution placing mahogany on a list of endangered species. Timber is harvested by big companies, usually with the permission of the Indians, either for a fee for every tree cut or a price that covers the exploitation of a certain area regardless of how many trees are cut. Some contracts are made with the agreement, albeit illegal, of the Indian agency. In the late 1980s a president of FUNAI contracted directly with logging companies for the harvesting of several Indian areas of the states of Rondônia and Mato Grosso and was paid off handsomely. He was denounced by the Public Attorney for corruption and embezzlement of national resources.[27] The Kayapó have had their lands logged for over ten years and received a considerable amount of money, most of which has been spent on the purchase of superfluous goods and some rather expensive items, such as airplanes. The Guajajara of Maranhão state had three of their forested territories cleared of every valuable hardwood tree in some ten years of intense logging. Continuous logging has also taken place in the state of Rondônia, where the Cintas-Largas and Suruí Indians have opened their lands for the same logging companies that had exploited the Pará lands. All of these activities have been done illegally, since the Brazilian constitution prohibits the exploitation of natural resources that belong to the Union, as is the case with Indian lands.[28]

FIGHTING AGAINST A DEVASTATING PAST

Although several Indian territories in the Amazon are large and coveted for their resources, elsewhere most of them are small and devoid of commercial products—although this has not stopped ranchers from wanting them for themselves. They belong to those ethnies whose initial contact with Brazilian society was characterized by intense processes of violence and land usurpation. Such is the case with the Kaingang, Xokleng, and Guarani ethnies, who live in the southern states of Rio Grande do Sul, Paraná, and Santa Catarina, and who were submitted to the control of the new European immigrants in the last quarter of the nineteenth and early decades of the twentieth century.[29]

It is also the case with the Guarani and Terena of Southern Mato Grosso state, whose lands were opened up for Brazilian colonization at about the same time. In both cases the Indians were dispossessed of most of their territories, their lands having been reduced to minimal sizes, and the remainder allotted among new colonists and ranchers. An example is the Panambi Indian Land, most of which the Guarani lost to a federally funded economic project that allotted it to farmers immigrating from other states. The Guarani were left with only two of the divided thirty parcels, as if they were landless colonists themselves, perhaps the worst situation that an Indian ethnie can undergo in present-day Brazil.[30] In the northwestern region of the highly industrialized state of São Paulo this process took place as late as the 1910s and resulted in the confinement of the last autonomous Kaingang bands in small reservations and the utter destruction of the Oti-Xavante ethnie.[31] In the 1930s the Indian agency brought in a number of Terena Indians from Southern Mato Grosso with the idea that they would help the Kaingang become better farmers. The Kaingang territories of Icatu and Araribá have become even smaller.[32]

In the northeast, the Indian ethnies that survived the many long years of brutal colonization had their lands reduced by the encroachment of cattle ranchers and landless peasants, who in some cases ended up founding villages and towns next to and around Indian villages. The Tuxá, descendants of various ethnies who lived along the middle São Francisco River and had been brought together in a mission established in the seventeenth century by French Capuchin friars, had their village encircled and almost taken over by migrants in the nineteenth century. This village became the town of Rodelas, which slumbered through this century until it was displaced by the inundating waters of the Itaparica hydroelectric dam and transferred to a nearby area. Rodelas was a town inhabited by the Tuxá as well as blacks and whites, all living in a social symbiosis that was probably not uncommon during the last century, obviously under the political command of the dominant white population. To survive in this arrangement the Tuxá had control of a small island on the São Francisco River, where they practiced floodplain agriculture. They also worked in the town as water suppliers, street cleaners, and so on. By the 1960s the Indian agency had helped them obtain some formal education. Their lot began to improve, and they began to be more respected by the other townspeople. They are a rather rare case of Indians who have preserved their self-identification while living in an urban environment and despite constant pressure from the surrounding population. They were able to do so by maintaining ties of social solidarity woven into networks of marriage, ritual parenthood, and mutual aid in work. They maintained a few old religious rituals, including the drinking of a hallucinogenic beverage, and adapted some of their dances and festivities to the urban milieu and integrated them into the calendar of religious observances of the other two ethnic groups.[33]

With the destruction of Rodelas, a new town was built a few miles away. The Tuxá were allotted an equivalent portion of land to compensate for the loss of their island and were grouped to live in a district of the new town in houses that were built by the hydroelectric plant company. However, the Tuxá had split into two groups, and one of them decided to live far upstream under conditions similar to those they were accustomed to. The chances for their continuing survival as one ethnie are dimmer than ever, but they may also keep on being Indians and in the future constitute two separate ethnies. For the time being there is much suffering and complaining against the new conditions under which they have been forced to live.[34]

However small in comparison with the past and with the increase in population in recent years, the territory of an Indian ethnie is fundamental to its survival. Indeed, all the ethnies that lived through colonial times have survived precisely because they have been able to retain at least a part of their ancient territory. In the past these lands were acknowledged as Indian lands in the form of state donations, such as those that were granted by Emperor Pedro II or much earlier by the kings of Portugal. Many of these donations were ratified by the Indian agency, both during SPI times and by FUNAI. A few examples suffice to illustrate this process.

The seventeenth-century Tupinambá subgroup, the Potiguara, who fought alongside Portuguese colonists and black freedmen and slaves to expel the Dutch from the northeast, received titles to land located in the famous and beautiful Baía da Traição, or Treason Bay, on the coast of Paraíba state. Their descendants, today called Potiguara, have kept a good portion of that land grant as immemorial possession. However, it has taken considerable effort and determination on the part of the Potiguara to retain full control of those lands, for there have been many attempts to dispossess them. In the 1930s the SPI made the first move to demarcate a portion of those lands, but it was not until the late 1980s that the Potiguara felt safe with the conclusion of the whole process of land guarantee. Together with the Tremembé and Jenipapo-Canindé of Ceará state, the Guarani of Rio de Janeiro state, the Tupininkim of Espírito Santo state, and the Pataxó of southern Bahia state, the Potiguara are among the last Indians to keep a portion of the Brazilian coast.[35]

The Pataxó Indians live on a strip of land on the balmy coast of southern Bahia, at the exact point where Brazil was first sighted in 1500 by the ships commanded by Pedro Álvares Cabral. At that time the land was inhabited by a sub-group of the Tupinambá, who had expelled other tribes living there previously. In contrast to the Potiguara, the Pataxó only appeared on the national scene at the beginning of this century, when southern Bahia was opened for immigration and became a new economic frontier with the cultivation of cacao. The Pataxó were part of a number of ethnies—Kamakã, Maluli, Gueren, Baenan, all generally known as Botocudos—who in the early nineteenth century lived in the valleys of the rivers Doce, Jequitinhonha, Prado, Contas, and others, a large territorial part of eastern Brazil that had been kept isolated by the Portuguese for fear of it being used as a route by gold smugglers. The Portuguese king-regent Dom João opened the area for immigrants who came in with the legal sanction to kill Indians if needed, and Capuchin friars were officially favored in their intentions to build missions and towns. Many of the Botocudo ethnies died out, but not the Pataxó, who kept to themselves and avoided any permanent contact. But a new wave of immigrants that arrived in the early 1900s was much more powerful. Their territory was invaded, parceled out, and turned into cacao farms. Massacres, bloody skirmishes, deliberate contamination of clothes left on their forest paths, and even the poisoning of their water springs were methods used to destroy the Pataxó.

In the early 1920s the SPI made contact with all the surviving Pataxó and Baenan bands and gathered them together in an area where they could be protected. In 1928 this area of some 50,000 hectares was officially mandated for the Pataxó, but seven years later, under the pretext that a communist guerrilla movement was in the making in the area and that the Pataxó themselves were involved with it, the local police forces attacked the Indians and expelled them. The area was divided up for leasing and sale to cacao planters. The Pataxó dispersed and seemed on the verge of extinction. Years later a few Pataxó families began to trickle back to this area, build small, peasantlike houses, and plant for subsistence. By the 1970s some 2,000 Pataxó descendants, many of whom had intermarried with Brazilian peasants and no longer spoke an Indian language, had settled back in a portion of their old territory that had become part of the Monte Pasqual National Park, under the jurisdiction of the Brazilian environmental agency, IBAMA. They have since been struggling adamantly to recover at least a decent portion of their lands, which can only be done with the eviction of the people who now claim to be the owners. Living on national park lands, they are not allowed to hunt wild animals or collect forest products, which makes life yet more difficult. In the end, however, they do hunt and collect and are courted by timber companies and local economic interests to allow them into the park to log the remaining spots of forest for a small price. In such circumstances to be and to live as an Indian becomes a convoluted, ambiguous possibility in which the rules of coexistence with the dominant society are inconsistent and haphazard. Yet they live by the sea.[36]

In the Brazilian northeast life is a constant struggle for survival due to the harshness of the climate, which periodically subjects the region to times of extreme drought, and the traditional economic disparities between the landowners and the destitute peasantry. The Indian ethnies remaining there have managed to survive by accepting their lot at the very bottom rung of the social ladder. They have sometimes aligned themselves with the poor Brazilian peasantry in their search for fairer conditions of life. The Kiriri Indians, whose lands are located in the municipality of Mirandela in central Bahia state, have the interesting story of joining the hosts of peasants who made up the so-called Canudos Rebellion. Led by the millenarian prophet Antônio Conselheiro, it burst out in the backlands of Bahia in 1896, aimed against the social and political conditions that were prevalent at the end of last century. In reaction, the township of Canudos was razed to the ground, and most of its members were killed in the massacres perpetrated by the Brazilian army. The Kiriri who had joined in were also killed, and those who had stayed on their lands suffered the consequences imposed upon the sympathizers of the dead messiah. Fortunately for the Kiriri their lands had been donated previously by Emperor Dom Pedro II, and they held on to that grant as proof of their rights.

In the 1950s these lands began to be invaded by small farmers and cattle ranchers on the pretext that the boundaries claimed by the Kiriri exceeded those recorded in the terms of the donation. The debate was seemingly focused on the notion of "square league," a measure of area often used in the nineteenth century that varied according to the point from which it should begin.[37] However, the fact was that the Kiriri were right in that they and the traditional townspeople knew exactly where the boundaries were supposed to be, whereas the new invaders wanted to find a rationale for their intents. The Indian agency finally demarcated the lands of the Kiriri, but not before a number of them had been killed in fights with the peasant invaders. Today the Kiriri are split up between two contending groups, and there is frequent infighting between them.

ETHNICITY REBORN

The case of the Kiriri is emblematic of other Indian ethnies in the northeast, such as the Xocó of Sergipe state, the Tingui-Botó of Alagoas state, the Pankararu and the Truká of Pernambuco state, and even the Xacriabá of Minas Gerais state. It is in the backlands of the northeast, including northern Minas Gerais state, where one finds the greatest number of surviving ethnies at a high stage of culture change and socioeconomic integration to the surrounding Brazilian society. Looking at them with a sociologist's eye, they indeed look like peasants who live communally. Only one of the more than twenty ethnies in that region has maintained an original language, the Fulniô of Pernambuco state.[38] However, since the 1980s, several of them have been making an enormous effort to keep up their collective memory, to recall and use original words and expressions from their languages, and even to learn another Indian language so as to reaffirm the sentiment of ethnic identity that is so important for them and that they feel commands some respect from present-day Brazilians.

For these ethnies what settles the question of being or not being an Indian is not the presence or absence of more visible and easily recognized pre-Columbian symbols of Indianness, such as rituals, hunting practices, tools, forms of dress, religion, and language. Many anthropologists argue that it is simply the contrast with which each ethnie operates in relation to others—in this case, the larger Brazilian commonalty—that maintains them as separate and distinct. Being Indian would no longer mean a traditional form of being, but a specific way of being, a self-imposing difference or contrast with the other, even if this is realized exclusively through discourse and self-affirmation and mirrored in the recognition imparted by others.

Indeed, the very act of self-affirmation triggers the development of substantial forms of being, which in turn establish the specificity of a way of being. In other words, it is enough for a community to want to be and to declare itself Indian in order for it to develop institutions that become Indian or contrastive to non-Indian institutions. The basic institution of an ethnie is the recognition of a rule of filiation and descent that enculturates the young and incorporates the outsider through marriage. The very acts of enculturation and incorporation develop institutions and forms of being, a sense of community and purpose, which become specific, if not unique, and contrastive to others. As it so happens in Brazil, what ensures the maintenance of such a group is the possession of a territory of its own. That is why the struggle for land is paramount for the survival of an Indian ethnie. With a territory, a social group easily produces a culture of its own.

With those considerations in mind, in recent years the Indian agency has begun to grant full recognition as Indian to those self-enclosed communities that claim to be descendants of Indian ethnies, even though they had relinquished almost all of their traditional characteristics and their members were highly miscegenated with blacks and whites. Such was the case of the Xocó, Tingui-Botó, and Tapeba, all of whom used to live as caboclo communities ancillary to Brazilian towns and villages without any assistance on the part of the state, and who were in danger of losing their lands. Anthropological and historical studies have demonstrated that almost all of these communities are indeed descendants of historic ethnies that had been extinguished by the provincial presidents in the nineteenth century, but which for various motives had been able to maintain the minimal ties of social solidarity and their rules of descent and incorporation.[39]

State recognition vested them with legal and concrete conditions to keep the lands they had retained and to defend their established social and economic heritage against all possible adversities. The Indian leaders know this and are conscious that to be an Indian ethnic is of greater human advantage than to be just a group of poor peasants at the mercy of the economic and political interests that oppress them locally.

However, there are a few cases of similar communities that refuse to accept the status of Indian and would rather be known as caboclo than be under the tutelage or protection of the Indian agency. It seems that the idea of being considered Indian would entail the assumption of a number of locally vented stereotypes, and this may be a high price to pay for the intangible or unknown advantages and rights enshrined in law. What they would rather have, as can be ascertained in the case of the caboclo communities of Taquaritiua and São Miguel, both in Maranhão state, or those of Canto in Piauí state, is the plain, irrevocable right to keep the lands they possess as indivisible collective property to be used and enjoyed in accordance with customary rules and practices and eschewing the legality of parceling the land into individual private lots.[40] Should such an agreement be reached, many other similarly constituted communities, not only of descendants of Indians but of former black slaves or mestizo groups as well, may be able to endure without the need of appealing to other legal means.

Conclusion

The spectrum of situations faced by the current Indian ethnies in Brazil ranges from the most isolated and autonomous groups to those who do not know they are Indians or do not want to be considered Indians. In all of Brazil only in the state of Rio Grande do Norte, on the easternmost corner of the northeast region, are there no surviving Indian ethnies or self-enclosed communities. In Piauí the caboclos of Canto refuse to be taken for Indians, but there is information of other surviving communities that may one day reconsider their present status. In Ceará state, the Tapeba, the Tremembé, and other descendants of former missionized Indians have been officially recognized as Indians. In Rio de Janeiro and São Paulo, the most densely populated and industrialized states, several Guarani families have banded together and settled on lands that they now claim to be their own, and the Indian agency has granted them full right of possession. Several Indian villages are located near towns and cities. A Guarani village is on the outskirts of São Paulo; the Tapeba are just outside Fortaleza; a few thousand Indians from the Rio Negro, the middle Amazon, and the Solimões have established permanent residence in Manaus, although they maintain close ties to their relatives back home; in Campo Grande, Dourados, and Aquidauana, cities of Southern Mato Grosso state there live Terena and Guarani; and in Brasília there are a few hundred Indians from the central-west, such as Xavante, Bororo, Xinguano, Karajá, Pareci, and Terena, who reside in town and work for the Indian agency or other federal offices.

There are also an unascertained number of Indians who temporarily leave their villages and work in nearby towns or even in big cities, where they sometimes acquire a trade. A few of them, perhaps twenty or thirty, have been able to graduate from college. One has been elected to the National Congress, and a few others have been elected to local, municipal legislatures. Those who acquire the urban experience and later decide to return to their lands come with a deeper knowledge of the society that oppresses them and pressures them to live constantly in search of cultural defenses for their survival.

Being Indian and living an Indian life in Brazil do not constitute immutable historical realities from a pre-Columbian past. Even the autonomous ethnies in the most isolated and unexplored reaches of the country have changed culturally and have acquired an awareness of the world that surrounds them. Keeping to themselves is indeed an act based upon this knowledge and is meant to enhance their chances of survival. The heteronomous ethnies, those that have lost much of their autonomy and have learned to coexist with a dominating world, have changed the most and have thus become much more different entities than in the past. Each one is the product of its struggle for survival, treading a historical path that has left many behind. They continue to struggle in a socioeconomic and political context that leaves very little room for social maneuvering and few existential options. They must trudge on and do whatever is possible to further their cause. Hence, we cannot ask of them any more than they can give in practice. We cannot demand of them cultural coherence or a sweeping, comprehensive view of their lives, or a strategically disciplined course of political action. Theirs is a narrow road with limited possibilities of action. The rather scanty resources they can muster are thwarted and undermined by the many obstacles set up both by the Brazilian state and the Brazilian society at large. The state, and particularly the Indian agency, FUNAI, is not a monolithic institution against the Indians, but it is often managed by people who would most probably take sides in any contention, particularly land disputes, with the anti-Indian forces. The Brazilian public, though sympathetic to the plight of the Indian, is most often moved by economic interests that are clearly against the best interests of the Indians.

History seems to conspire against the Indians. Most of them were wiped out, and the surviving ones still struggle for peace and for a dignified place to live their lives as they see fit. Even those who seem to be on the way to a better life, with lands demarcated and guaranteed, now feel the need for money and in consequence open up their lands for gold and timber exploitation. As we compare these acts with what happened to the Indians in southern Brazil, whose pine forests were cleared out in the past, we can be sure that the same thing will happen to the rain forests of the Kayapó, Guajajara, Parakanã, Cintas-Largas, and many more. As for gold mining, let us not forget that no Indian ethnies survived in the mining districts of Goiás and Minas Gerais. However, even as we speak of conspiracy as if there were teleological, historical movements arrayed against the Indians, we refuse to go further and think of historical condemnation. We cannot tell what is going to happen in the future, of course. Our best guesses can only be based on our present knowledge of the relations between the Indians and Brazil and on the assurance that the Indians are becoming quite conscious of their position and their possibilities of continuing existence. Their political and cultural activities as a self-conscious collective will be the new factor in the unfair political equation in which they are involved.

5

The Indians Today

In the history of humankind, the Indian question is no more than an episode in the expansion of Western civilization and its clash with New World civilization. In the future, the outcome of this clash may be comparable to the results of the outgrowth and expansion of Indo-European tribes as they moved in conquering migrations from the Baltic lands down and across prehistoric Europe and Asia: in some places, decimation of the original populations and scorched earth were all that was left; in other regions, the result was physical miscegenation and social amalgamation; and in still others, there remained pockets of ethnic survival and cultural resistance.

For Brazil, the consummation of the fifteenth-century clash came to pass along the timeline of its historical formation and its sociocultural makeup, but it is clearly still in the making. In an historical span of 500 years, much of the process has run its course, and perhaps no more than 100 or 150 years may be left until its conclusion. In making an historical valuation of this process one can certainly discern an unequivocal tendency for the preponderance and continuation of the same social forces and the same problems that constituted the Indian question from the very beginning, although today the problems seem more overwhelming due to the nation's population growth and economic development. Moreover, a certain ambiguity continues to prevail in these forces, as if the process were still simmering.

If one were to equate the Indian question to a geometrical model, it would probably appear in the form of an irregular triangle whose sides were formed by the state, the church, and society, all constraining the Indians inside. This model is not really so different from what happened in the sixteenth century; all one needs to do is change "colonists" for society. During these five centuries the sides of the triangle have altered greatly in terms of size and thickness. On some occasions they have squeezed in the Indian center and made it occupy an ever smaller space. Over the years the side of society has thickened and currently encompasses the dominant economic forces, the landowning elite, the industrial and service businesses, and their opposing social product: landless rural workers, the urban working and middle classes, all with their own views of reality and of the Indian question. The side of the church is no longer as robust, but it has been consolidated by the presence since the beginning of this century of Protestant churches and missions, particularly North American and British. For some elements of these sides there is quite a bit of inconsistency. Where shall we place the military, for example, as an element of the state or of society? Is public opinion the product of the middle classes and a self-imposing force, or is it now a resonance of more modern economic forces, including the globalization of culture and the internationalization of postindustrial capital? How does international public opinion relate to Brazilian public opinion, and how much of it is motivated by a universalist view of the world or enjoined by national and economic interests? Since these elements operate within historical contexts, their relative positions depend upon an unstable and temporary balance of forces to which the Indians by themselves currently contribute but little. That is why it seems easy to say that the Indians are at the mercy of social forces to which they are hardly ever able to respond adequately, let alone control. As a matter of fact, even for the social scientist the dynamism and trajectory of these social forces can rarely be perceived beforehand and with clarity.

In the brief historical appreciation presented in previous chapters, it was observed that the church, represented by the missionary orders, above all the Jesuits until 1759, had a compelling role in imprinting upon at least a part of the Brazilian consciousness the notion of defending and protecting Indian ethnies as a national responsibility. Nonetheless, one must not forget that at certain moments the missionaries sided with the economic and political forces acting against the Indians, especially during the empire. At the other end, it was the state, supported by specific segments of the society, that promoted the creation of the bases of modern Brazilian Indian policy, independently of and deliberately against the church, which, at the beginning of the twentieth century stubbornly insisted on continuing with the same methods of indoctrination that had prevailed in the previous four centuries. On that occasion, an important segment of the military sector was tuned in to the dispositions of society, as if it were a part of it and not of the state, and it played a substantial role in creating the new indigenist ideology. Today one can no longer say that the military continues to feel any special sympathy toward the Indians, as the ideological concepts that influenced and motivated them in 1910 no longer hold sway and today bring together no more than a small minority of its personnel. However, this may yet change.

At any rate, we take it for granted that the Indian question is today essentially the same as it was in the past. It also continues to be based on a degree of historical instability. This chapter will present a comprehensible analysis of the principal social factors that currently determine the sense and character of the Indian question. These factors are the most important in pressuring the Indians themselves into taking the political stances they have been taking in the last twenty or thirty years.

ECONOMIC INTERESTS

Mining

There is little doubt that the economic interests and their agents, who covet lands and natural riches, are the worst enemies of the Indians. For the most part they originate in Brazilian society, but they also come as foreign capital and even through the action of the Brazilian state. It is the state that, in the final analysis, gives support to these interests in Indian areas. Indian labor is no longer relevant except in new frontiers and in very localized situations. But it has become important for economic interests to have the permission, acceptance, or at least the indifference of the Indians to operate on their lands. One of the most common examples is that of the companies mining for gold, diamonds, or cassiterite on Indian lands. They operate in general with the tacit, sometimes covert, support of FUNAI—even if illegally—but they also count on the Indians' agreement.

Mining activities on Indian lands are done in different ways by various methods. Perhaps the most common is that in which the gold miners (*garimpeiros*) relate directly with the Indians. Among the best known cases is that of the northern Kayapó, where gold placer mines (*garimpos*) are found on several spots of their 3.5 million hectare territory. Here, a few thousand gold miners pan for gold found on three or four riverine sites, and they pay the Indians a percentage in cash of the gold that is extracted and registered. They have established a relationship in which representatives of the Indians and representatives of the *garimpeiros* meet every week to receive payment and sort through problems that arise out of the inner tensions of this arrangement. A second method of mining on Indian lands is that in which a big mining company establishes itself and operates a mine site. A good example of this has been occurring on the Waimiri-Atroari Indian land in the state of Amazonas. There, since the early 1980s, the Paranapanema Mining Company has been exploiting by concession of the federal government one of the largest cassiterite mines in the world, without paying a penny to the Indians. They claim that the mining areas they exploit do not belong to the Waimiri-Atroari Indians, although there is plenty of ethno-historical evidence that they were there in the recent past and were forced to migrate several years ago. A third method is actually a possibility of mining. Since a great deal of Brazilian territory has been mapped, knowledge of gold sites is public. Usually a mining company applies for the right to explore a certain area for minerals and to mine it within a certain period of time. The Vale do Rio Doce Company, a huge state-owned mining conglomerate that was recently sold to private interests, is the owner of the gigantic Carajás mining district and possesses research licenses and warrants of concession for a large bauxite mine in the Serra do Tiracambu mountain range in Maranhão state, on the eastern fringes of the Amazon forest. Since they are busy exploring other such mines, they are biding their time with this territory. However, this bauxite mine is located in the traditional territory of several Guajá bands, some of whom have fled in recent years, escaping from loggers and land speculators.[1]

These three examples cover some of the possibilities for mining on Indian lands. All of them present grounds for concern on the part of both the Indians involved and the defenders of the Indian cause. The ethnographic records show that close contact with people who extract minerals has always resulted in fatal damages to the Indians. Miners are usually people who come from impoverished social conditions, and their aggressive behavior and rough lifestyle take no account of and show no respect for Indians. The history of mining in the state of Minas Gerais illustrates this process.[2] In our times, the relationship between mineral prospectors and Indians involves not only the use of violence and the practice of discriminatory attitudes, but also the transmission of highly contagious and dangerous diseases, such as STDs, tuberculosis, influenza, and malaria, the latter in strains extremely resistant to medicines. Mining also entails the destruction of the environment through the pollution of creeks and rivers with mercury and other chemical products. The main Kayapó village on the Fresco River needs to find a new source of drinking water elsewhere, since that important river drains the waters of other creeks polluted by placer mines. In the Waimiri-Atroari territory the debris of extracted cassiterite, which is retained in man-made ponds, is often washed away by flood rains and by leakages and ends up polluting the tributaries of the Abonari River, which runs through several Waimiri villages.[3]

The presence of mining, whether by companies or by individual prospectors, attracts the Indians in a very beguiling way, which is certainly almost as dangerous as the consequences already mentioned. There is danger in the excitement with which the Indians see the possibility of money, industrialized goods, and services that come along with it. In the past, the story ran that the Indians were totally naïve and that they would let themselves be fooled by and contented with any trinket or gift, such as tobacco, salt, old clothes, a pot, a straw hat. Today one can no longer say that they are contented by little. They want videocassettes, shotguns, bicycles, sound systems, freezers, booze, easy life, prostitutes, and in extreme cases, airplanes. Among the Kayapó and the Gaviões most of these goods are now found in many houses. In fact, the houses themselves are made of brick, with water supply systems, built by architects from São Paulo, advised by people who believe that the Indians should participate in the same type of progress that exists among the privileged levels of the Brazilian population.

With the small but significant percentage of gold extracted from their lands, the Kayapó have already bought two airplanes to fly in and out of the small landing strips built in the clearings that have been opened everywhere in the Amazon forest. With these planes the Kayapó, or rather, their young leaders, have acquired quite a bit of mobility and spend part of their time shopping in nearby towns or *garimpo* settlements, or visiting with their Indian cousins, the Xikrin and Txukarramãe, or traveling to cities such as Belém and Brasília. It has been argued that this mobility has brought about a greater consciousness among the various Kayapó bands who live very far apart and who were great rivals in the past. In this case, *garimpo* money is considered to have been a new and positive factor. By using videocassettes, for example, they have achieved electronic communication in a speedy, highly visible, synthesized language among bands or villages, whereas previously this was only possible by personal contact on rare occasions through rituals of social solidarity, or even through sorties by warring parties. What this may mean for the growth of a pan-Kayapó solidarity is yet to be seen, although they have recently banded together in many political activities in defense of their interests.[4]

This case is presumably a strong argument for accepting mining on one's lands, both for the Indians, who feel that they have benefitted and for the promoters of these lucrative activities. But the social consequences of such

exploitation are still unknown in Brazil. In the United States, such practices have been quite common. In the past they have resulted in the sale or
loss of territories and in the impoverishment of many Indian ethnies. In
recent times many North American Indian ethnies have been able to obtain
some economic advantage through the indemnities they have been entitled
to receive, but at a high cost to their environment and a deterioration in
tribal life. The process is completed by cultural and social assimilation within
the broader society, in other words, the passage from an autonomous society to a dependent minority.[5]

Timber

With logging and timber companies, this type of trade relationship is repeated more frequently and in many varieties. One of the earliest and long-
lasting ones is the case of the Kaingang of southern Brazil, holders of the
last reserves of araucaria pine forests. One may say that their lands have
been by now almost totally cleared of timber by loggers and timber companies, a process that began in the 1930s. In fact, it all started under the
auspices of the SPI, which, in that mixed attitude of business-minded orientation and paternalism that characterized its relationship with the Indians, invited timber companies and facilitated their establishment on Indian
lands, granting them rights not only to log trees but also to install sawing
machines in Indian areas, almost always without consulting the Indians
themselves. The idea behind this action was that, with the money obtained
from such leases, the Indian post in the area could sustain itself, that is, its
staff and incurring expenses, and could buy machinery, better seeds, cattle,
and other goods that would eventually stimulate the Indians to better farming. Over time the Indians would learn new skills, which would bring them
permanent dividends, including their emancipation by acquiring their own
industrial assets.[6]

The results of this policy are less comforting. The majority of these Indian lands today is made up of secondary growths and grass fields, not
araucaria pine forests. The foremost consequence has been a deterioration
in the diet of the Kaingang and Guarani Indians because of the lack of
nutritious pine nuts, which fed them during a good part of the year; as a
consequence they have become dependent on imported foods. In some areas, the lease was transformed into an acquisition, a sale not only of logging rights but of land as well, leading many sawmill companies to assume
they had obtained property rights over the lands they used. The Slaviero
and Brothers Company, for example, took a stubborn stance to remain

and was removed from the Mangueirinha Indian land only a few years ago, leaving a trail of irrecoverable losses to Indian forests and lives. All in all, leasing Indian forest lands for logging was but a wasteful process that can be perceived as useless and irrational, a typical result of a lack of historical vision and administrative neglect.[7]

Worse yet: the example set by the SPI, and later FUNAI, of allowing economic interests on Indian lands influenced Indian communities to maintain previous concessions on their lands to loggers and sawmills as well as to landless farmers who had entered their areas or even been moved there by government programs. Such was the case of the land reform that the state of Rio Grande do Sul made over the Kaingang lands in Nonoai in 1962. The cash income, even if small in comparison with the percentages obtained from the gold mines, has induced the Indians to accept the presence of whites and the exploitation of their lands and riches. Reversing this process comes about only through an obstinate fight against the surrounding, alluring reality, against government pressures for conciliation and compromise, and against regulations and court injunctions that enforce the principle of the continuation of consummated facts.[8]

Timber exploitation has moved completely to the Amazon after the devastation of the southern araucaria pine forests and the Atlantic rain forests of southern Bahia and Espírito Santo. One cannot but be amazed at the capacity for devastation of these timber companies. It has been estimated that more than 90 percent of these latter forests were felled in twenty to thirty years' time. By the mid-1980s they had done their job and began to move en masse to the Amazon region. Their know-how and human power is now being applied without restrictions in the Amazon and on Indian lands.[9]

In Maranhão state, whose western side is part of the already-weakened fringes of the Amazon forest, the process of devastation is proceeding rapidly, roughly, and, as far as we can tell, irreversibly. Around the areas of the Guajajara, Ka'apor, and Guajá lands the forest has already been cleared out, and the installed timber companies now press for rights to enter new forests. With the Guajajara, they seek to make personal arrangements in which the Indians are paid for the timber removed; with the Guajá, who do not participate in economic relations with Brazilian society, the companies simply invade their lands, frighten the Indians into fleeing, and cut what they want.[10] In the Serra do Tiracambu, one of the traditional areas of the Guajá, there are now countless access roads to areas with the finest hardwoods. From the air, one can see reddish-colored, meandering clearings everywhere, signs of this senselessness. As is the case with almost every Amazon mountain range, the Tiracambu is the source of innumerable creeks and rivers and serves as a watershed divide for the Pindaré, Gurupi, and Turiaçu river systems. The clearing of its slopes will endanger the basin of those rivers as far down as where there are villages and towns, because of the danger of floods and water shortages in the future. Aggravating things still further is the existence of a bauxite mine in this mountain range and the plans of the Vale do Rio Doce Company to exploit it in the future. There is more: so far, three ironwork mills have been installed—a half-dozen more are planned for the future—along the Carajás Railroad, which is located a few kilometers away from this area and only a few hundred meters from the Caru Indian land. These mills will rely on the use of vegetal charcoal for their functioning, despite recommendations to the contrary.[11] If these plans are carried out they will lead to the definitive and irremediable destruction of these forests and of the Indians who inhabit them. Needless to say, they are under the control of the federal government.

In the denser areas of the Amazon, timber companies are more selective in their choice of tree species. No more than two dozen types are exploited among more than one hundred with possibilities for industrial use. The wealth seems to be so abundant that choices are not based on criteria of rationality or productivity. Devastation proceeds apace, despite all the warnings of Brazilian and foreign scientists regarding the ecological fragility of the Amazon. Cutting down forest trees should be done only under the supervision of viable programs of reforestation, such as the one the environmental agency IBAMA requires for the areas opened to timber companies. But such requirements have served simply as another incentive for forest felling, since the reforestation goals are never met.[12]

Deforestation is proceeding most swiftly in the states of Pará and Rondônia. In the areas of the Xikrin, Tembé, and Parakanã Indians in Pará, the timber companies approach the Indians individually and try to convince them to lease portions of their lands for timber cutting in exchange for a price of less than 10 percent of the market value of the coveted hardwoods. Nevertheless, the money sounds good enough to the Indians. To remove 8,000 cubic meters of mahogany in February of 1984, a company offered the Xikrin some two million cruzeiros (about US$140,000).[13] With this money the Xikrin could buy many things and thus achieve an equal footing with their Kayapó cousins, a few hundred kilometers to the south. This was undoubtedly one of the motivations that convinced FUNAI to allow and even promote the operation. Another argument behind this change was that the Indians have full rights over their natural resources, including the right to sell them, so as to be able to experience, through money, the natural benefits of civilization. Taking advantage of the anthropological notion that the Indians have the right to self-determination, FUNAI often extrapolates it to the sphere of economic decisions. Disregarding the sociocultural context in which the Indians are embedded, FUNAI has propounded the judgment that timber cutting in Indian lands can become rational if the Indians themselves participate in it. It capitalizes on the supposition—attributed to anthropologists who have worked with the Kayapó—that the utilization of the ecological knowledge the Indians have of the forest would induce the companies to cut only those trees that the Indians marked out as exploitable. This further presupposes an unexpected good faith on the part of timber business, on the one hand, and a permanent ecological dedication from the Indians, on the other.

In the state of Rondônia, the clearing of forests started with the arrival of hundreds of thousands of landless peasants, farmers, and cattle ranchers. Rondônia is a state in the far west of the Amazon and it had remained practically untouched until the 1960s. With the help of a US$300 million loan from the World Bank, Rondônia had become one of the most dynamic economic frontiers of the country. Timber companies followed with their enormous trucks in the wake of the construction of a highway reaching the city of Cuiabá, from whence timber could be taken to São Paulo and other markets. They lost no time in setting up sawmills and contracting with farmers and ranchers to sell the trees they would fell. In the last decade dozens of timber companies have firmly established themselves in Rondônia and have taken advantage of both Indian and non-Indian forest lands. As in the 1970s there remained some ambiguity as to the correct boundaries of some Indian lands, and the state, the federal government, the colonization companies, and the big landowners took advantage of this temporary lack of definition to invade Indian lands. Even the Aripuanã Indian Park, which had been officially established by edict since 1966, suffered invasions and threats of redivision and reduction. For many years the Indians defended their land rights by attacking invaders and refusing any sort of compromise. They were helped by FUNAI inasmuch as it justified these actions to public opinion. However, by the mid-1980s, with the connivance of a president of FUNAI, the tactic of offering Indian leaders cash payments and goods began to weaken the Indians' spirit of autonomy and intransigence, and they opened their lands to timber exploitation at an unprecedented level of intensity.[14]

Land Owners and Squatters

The Indian issue in Rondônia has become further complicated because of the many government colonization projects that were established near and sometimes on Indian lands. Migrants from several states moved to this new frontier, and the government placed them in areas for colonization that increasingly tightened the noose around Indian lands in the region. For several reasons many immigrants were not able to succeed at farming and ended up giving up on their allotted plots, opening the way for the more capitalized farmers and ranchers to buy out the "improved" land—that is, the deforested land—to create pastures and release cattle on it, thus forming large land properties. In doing so, ranchers calculated to stake out a claim and rights of ownership to lands that belonged either to peasants or to Indians. In this manner the Nambiquara Indians lost much of their territory and now live in land areas separated from each other, with ranches and roads strewn all around them.[15]

To be a *fazendeiro,* that is, a plantation or cattle owner, in the Amazon region today does not mean simply to have a bit of land with coffee or cacao planted, a few hundred head of cattle, and the help of two or three dozen farmhands and their families. It means, in the first place, to be part of a political-economic system that encourages one to invest some initial capital, which can be immediately multiplied several times through government fiscal incentives and the ease of low interest credit obtained through political patronage. One does not need to live on the ranch or farm; in fact, there is almost always more than one farm for the same person. One merely needs a foreman, radio communication, and a quick means of travel, preferably an airplane. Without cultural roots on the land, without interests other than economic ones, linked to an unfair and unequal political system, hemmed in by social demands, and vilified nationwide, the *fazen-deiro* does not have sympathies or feelings of responsibility toward the Indians, let alone any awareness of their rights. These ranchers enjoy a lifestyle based on the exploitation of others and hold an attitude of aggressiveness towards visible and invisible foes. Even when this mode of production shows signs of weakness because of its inability to generate profits without government aid, the rancher does not give up. On the contrary, he or she rages with all the fury of one unjustly treated, with the arrogance of a centuries-old elite, and thus drags along the support of those who think they share the same status and of those who live in their shadow.

Traditionally *fazendeiros*—including modern large-scale planters of export crops such as soybeans, corn, rice, and, in earlier times, coffee, cacao, and sugarcane—and cattle ranchers have been the most violent enemies of the Indians. It was their class that decimated the Indians of the northeast after the expulsion of the Dutch, the Indians of southern Bahia and the Rio Doce Valley, and reduced the Indians of southern Brazil and of Southern Mato Grosso to the condition of enclave minorities with so little land that, to obtain the bare minimum of their needs, they must hire themselves out as farm workers or ranch hands. The manner and process in which these ranchers and farmers are being allowed to expand into the Amazon at present leads us to conclude that, left to their own devices, they will do the same there as they did with Indians in other times.

The plantation owner or the rancher, as the master to the slave, Hegel would say, exists as a socioeconomic category only as a result of his or her counterpart, the peasant—today the landless peasant, the land squatter. It is not in a relationship with the peon, the cowboy, the hand laborer, the foreman—who partially deny and partially affirm the large landholder as a social being—but it is rather in relation to the waves of miserable and dispossessed families who live as destitute people that the landholder, the *fazendeiro,* becomes a total socioeconomic category. At least this is the case in the Amazon. Those who possess lands do so because there are those without land. The incentives the *fazendeiro* class receives from the government are justified, first, by the assumption that they produce the food that feeds the nation, including the poor; and second, that they produce export crops that produce revenues, whereas the dispossessed do not. This ideology is what allows ranchers and plantation owners to maintain their posture of being simultaneously the elite and victims, and thus to manipulate their image before public opinion at will.

The most ironic and ominous consequence, with regard to the Indians, is that the landless squatters, the dispossessed of the earth, appear on the political scene on the same footing with the plantation owners and ranchers. It is as if they also want to expel the Indians from their lands and are equal participants in the historical process of spoliation of the Indian. Whether one analyzes the so-called agrarian question in the simplest or in the most complex way, one can perceive that the plantation and ranching class would lose its raison d'être and its power once the dispossessed obtained the lands to which they have rights. Certainly there would still be an abundance of lands for the Indians, and much more would be left for the future as well.

Landless squatters function also as spearheads for ranchers and plantation owners of present-day agrarian capitalism. They move into the new frontiers ahead of everyone else, dispossessed of capital and expelled from lands where they had lived and labored for many generations. They clear the forest for planting, and after one or two harvests they move on, leaving behind land for the rancher to plant grass for cattle. This style of life produces fearless and rootless men and women, ready to fight for some concrete dream—such as gold in the *garimpos*, where they often go—but at the mercy of both the unknown and the powerful known: the rancher, the politician, or the government. Their contact with Indians is marked by this condition, which leads them to attitudes both of expectation and of aggressiveness and contempt. In any case, it is unfair to ascribe to the poor squatters an intrinsic animosity or a structurally determined opposition to the Indian. Their genesis is to a large extent Indian, both genetically and culturally, but at present they are no longer the counterpart of the Indian, as they were in the first three centuries of colonization. Squatters and Indians, each in their own corner, live together well in various parts of Brazil and only come into conflict when the mechanisms of pressure from above are brought to bear upon the squatters.

Some examples may be seen in Maranhão and Pará. In the most isolated regions of those states, Indians and peasants had been living for many years in a kind of balanced relationship. Land disputes between them were sparked off in the 1960s, when a new wave of medium and large-scale ranchers from Goiás, Minas Gerais, and São Paulo—many supplied with faked land titles—began to settle there and buy up the traditional land claims of the peasants.[16] In a short time the peasants found themselves without land and were thus incited to invade Indian lands, especially those that were still not officially demarcated. In Maranhão this happened, for example, with the Canabrava and Araribóia Indian lands of the Guajajara Indians. To remove the invading squatters the Guajajara Indians had to mobilize their people, together with the aid of some dedicated FUNAI indigenists, anthropologists, and journalists, with Brazilian public opinion also on their side. After many years of tension, which resulted in the death of several Indians and squatters, these lands were cleared of intruders. On the Canabrava Indian land an old settlement called São Pedro dos Cacetes came to have as many as 2,000 people and lasted through the 1980s and mid-1990s. This settlement was mostly made up of peasants who needed land to make a living, but it grew to have shopkeepers and merchants, and a road connected it to the town of Grajaú. Politicians wanted it to become a municipality, and for a while it seemed that the Indians were going to lose it for good. But a few Indian leaders did not give up on the issue, bringing pressure on the authorities and mobilizing public opinion in their favor. On one occasion they destroyed power lines; on another, they kidnapped passengers of buses that were passing through; and on still yet another occasion, the Guajajara held as prisoners officers of the Federal Police who had entered their villages in search of marijuana dealers. The minister of justice, under whom FUNAI operates, was forced to go to the area and negotiate with the Guajajara for the release of hostages. In the end, the World Bank, which was arranging a loan with the state government, brought pressure upon it to find new lands for the invaders. In February 1996, the invaders packed their belongings, destroyed their houses, and left. The Indians had won back the full rights to their lands.[17]

Still in Maranhão, in the region that later became the municipalities of Santa Luzia and Bom Jardim, the expansion frontier was made up exclusively of landless peasants, particularly from other regions, such as the northeast. In the 1970s they ran up against the boundaries previously established by FUNAI and stopped there. It seems that the landless peasants had a cultural feeling that Indian lands should be respected. Thus today there are four demarcated Indian lands in the pre-Amazon region of Maranhão comprising around 1.1 million hectares. Land invasions have been achieved in the past by small groups of squatters, but the great majority of cases constitute sporadic entries to hunt and collect *babaçu* palm nuts, the extractive sources of a low-productivity economy. However, on two occasions organized parties of invaders entered the Turiaçu Indian land, cleared large areas of land, and tried to settle there forcefully. On both occasions the Indians and FUNAI agents, together with the Federal Police, were able to push them out, at the cost of some deforestation and a few deaths. On the Caru Indian land there are a few farm invaders who have staked out some land for themselves. They are protected by state politicians and have refused to leave. It will take vigorous effort to move them out.[18]

Elsewhere in Maranhão, in the municipality of Montes Altos, a major problem of land invasion tormented the Krikati Indians for many long years. A part of the territory claimed by those Indians had been invaded and occupied by local potentates for some seventy years. Beginning in the 1950s, landless peasants were also encouraged to stake out claims for themselves. The local elite of ranchers were able to retain the support of lawyers and politicians to contest the Indians' rights to those lands, and even argued that the Indians were not the traditional owners of those lands, but mere invaders, in a surprising inversion in Brazilian history. In the 1970s, when most Indian lands in Maranhão were being demarcated, the ranchers did not allow the Indian agency to demarcate the Krikati land. In 1982 lawyers were able, through the negligence and connivance of FUNAI in São Luís, to ensure that the ranchers had the legal right to demarcate the lands as their own in defiance of Indian rights. FUNAI reacted against this development in 1985 by trying to block the mandate, but in 1986 the ranchers proposed a demarcation line that would leave the Krikati with no more than 12,000 hectares of their lands, which had been calculated at around 146,000 hectares. The Indians did not allow this to take place, but they were willing to demarcate an area of 86,000 hectares. The ranchers did not accept, and the Krikati continued to pressure FUNAI and court public opinion. By 1994 the ranchers had lost their cause in all appeals, but they would not budge from their previous stance. By late 1996 the situation had become extremely tense, and the Krikati were about to enter into open conflict with the ranchers and their henchmen. In February 1997, the Krikati set fire to two power-line towers that crossed their territory, causing blackouts in nearly every city of Maranhão, including São Luís. In the wake of negotiations between FUNAI and the state, once again with some pressure from the World Bank, a group of courageous indigenists and the Krikati, with the help of some 160 Indians from other areas, demarcated an area of 140,000 hectares, much to the chagrin of ranchers and recent land invaders. In comparing this case with others one can see the difference between the power of the squatter and that of the rancher in relation to the Indians,[19] but the Indians won in the end.

In Pará, other cases of disputes between Indians and squatters and ranchers corroborate the examples from Maranhão. Comparing the demarcations of the Apinayé Indians, where there were concrete interests of ranchers and politicians, with that of the Parakanã, where there were squatters, one sees the use of violence and protracted resolution in the first case, contrasting with agreements and a speedy solution in the second.[20]

In the Gavião Indian land, which had already suffered ecological and social distress caused by putting up the Eletronorte Company power lines and building the Carajás Railroad, the difficulties increased after squatters were settled in part of the area, the result of an understanding between a regional colonizing agency—now defunct and absorbed by Incra, the Instituto Nacional de Reforma Agrária—and local ranches where those squatters were living. This happened as late as in 1981, and the Indians protested and demanded the removal of the intruders. They were expelled, but in the end the episode left an atmosphere of mutual hostility that would have been avoidable if there had been more clarity and responsibility on the part of the authorities who direct the agrarian question in the country.[21]

The countless invasions of the Guamá reserve of the Tembé Indians are due almost exclusively to the expulsion of squatters from lands on which they used to live and which were occupied through legal ruses by large companies of national and international capital, such as CODEPAR, Swift, and Volkswagen. In this region of Pará state, a scenario of regional land disputes created a type of Robin Hood bandit of the squatters, known as Quirino, who with a band of former squatters fought the hirelings of the companies and the municipal and state police, until he was killed in January 1985.[22]

MAJOR ECONOMIC PROJECTS

These projects are distinguished from the influence of ranchers and squatters and of mining and timber companies, because of the kind of political support they receive. They are all backed, and almost all financed, by the federal government or international lending institutions, such as the World Bank, and are part of national development programs.

As government programs, the projects are planned with the responsibility to fulfill the laws and norms of the Brazilian state. Officially they should be imbued with the obligation of defending the Indians' interests, that is, of protecting their lands and giving due assistance so that their populations do not suffer the direct and indirect impacts these projects tend to cause.

The largest and most far-reaching development projects carried out so far that have had a major impact on Indians are the TransAmazon highway, the Carajás mining and railroad project, the Polonoroeste highway and settlement project, and the construction of several hydroelectric plants. The Calha Norte and Tabatinga projects, which are of a military nature, have affected Indians of the frontiers of the Amazon.

Highways

The TransAmazon highway is the greatest uncompleted project of the most authoritarian period of recent Brazilian history. It was presented to the

Brazilian public as one of the major tools for the integration of the nation, one that would bring the most remote corners of the country close to their center of propulsion. Without having fulfilled its goals, it did nonetheless bring about various disasters with regard to Indian populations. In the first place, due to the simple fact that roads were supposed to be opened in Indian territories, there arose an immediate need to contact the Indian ethnies who lived there but were not in touch with Brazilian society, such as the Parakanã and Assurini. In some cases, there arose the need to transfer Indian bands and villages from their original lands to other areas. In this rather irresponsible and haphazard process, many Indians died a short time after contact and later in their new areas. The culture shock felt by the Assurini Indians reached the point at which they abhorred the idea of taking care of children and thus spent more than ten years without bearing any children at all, frequently inducing their women to abort.[23]

The highway known as BR-80, connecting Cuiabá to Santarém, cut the Xingu Indian Park in half and led to an urgent need to contact the Krenhacarore (now known as Panará) Indians who had until then been living autonomously. Of some 230 Indians initially contacted in 1973, only 70 reached their new location two years later in the Xingu park. They were called "giant Indians" by the sensational publicity created by FUNAI authorities during that period and by photographic magazines in the country. A film produced in English was made to show how mysterious contact is made with a "primitive" people who "hide from the [white] man." The subsequent results have been forgotten or suppressed.[24]

In the wake of the roads came the settlement projects, which brought in thousands of landless peasants from the northeast and the south, the eager garimpeiros, and large-scale agribusiness. Land conflicts continue to be part of the political situation of these regions today. For the recently contacted Indians, or even those with longer experience such as the Kayapó, the world of the white people seems to be a whirlpool of novelties and violence in which the price of progress is connivance with or acceptance of aggressive manners, venality, trickery, and an utter lack of meaning. What gives significance to all of this?

The Carajás project involved the building of an 890-kilometer railroad linking the great mineral complex of Carajás, which has an estimated duration of almost 500 years of continuous exportation of iron, copper, gold, manganese, and other ores to the port of Itaqui, near São Luís, the capital of Maranhão state. The Indians most impacted by this project were the Xikrin, a Kayapó subgroup whose lands, also rich in minerals, border on the Serra dos Carajás; the Gavião Parkateyé, through whose lands the railroad passes; the Guajá, whose lands have not yet been demarcated but which are coveted by the Vale do Rio Doce Company and by the iron mills installed in the municipalities of Açailândia and Santa Luzia; and the Guajajara, whose lands are coveted and besieged by some 40,000 landless and destitute peasants, pressured by the arrival of new agribusiness companies attracted by the advantages of the railroad.

Between 1983 and 1987 the Vale do Rio Doce Company, in accordance with the terms of a loan received from the World Bank, had to invest nearly US$11 million to protect the Indian lands and improve the lot of the impacted Indian ethnies. Since most of the lands were already demarcated, the money was squandered in all kinds of unnecessary consumption. The money helped expel intruders from the Xikrin Indian land, but the areas of the Krikati and Guajá continued to be in dispute. One may conclude that the measures taken were not capable of guaranteeing the integrity of the Indians' territories, nor to enhance the conditions of their ethnic survival and growth.[25]

The lands of the Guajá Indians were obviously not demarcated because the economic interests of prospective miners and cattle ranchers were too powerful to be dissuaded. Part of the Guajá territory was requisitioned by the environment agency—IBAMA—since it belonged officially to the Gurupi Forest Reserve. In this process, since IBAMA has always had less clout than FUNAI, the reserve was invaded by medium-size ranchers from other states, with such political support that demarcation has become extremely difficult. Meanwhile, several Guajá bands, because they are a nomadic people who regularly move through and out of the boundaries of the territories allotted to them, are becoming encircled by ranchers, colonization projects, timber companies, and mining prospectors. As they are forced into contact they end up being transferred elsewhere, thus losing their lands and diminishing in numbers.[26] Here the role of the World Bank has been almost nil.

The case of the Parkateyé or Gavião Indians deserves a more detailed explanation. They were first contacted by SPI contact expeditions in the 1950s. By the 1960s their population had decreased to less than fifty, and they were on the verge of extinction. In the early 1970s they began to increase in numbers and became wiser in trading an important cash crop found on their lands, Brazil nuts. By the time the power lines coming from the Tucuruí Hydroelectric Plant crossed their land, they knew how, with help from anthropologists and indigenists, to negotiate a decent compensation. In 1980 work began for the passage of the Carajás Railroad through their lands. Hundreds of Brazil-nut trees were destroyed, which caused a major depletion in the Gaviões' economic surplus income. A few thousand families of squatters were then brought in to occupy the lower part of their lands. As indemnity to the passage of the railroad, the Carajás Railroad compensated the Gaviões in 1983 with a sum equivalent to US$1 million. Although the Gaviões Indians at first accepted these changes, soon they began to protest and demand the withdrawal of the squatters. For many years, particularly during the decades of high inflation, the Gaviões lived off of the monthly interest on this money. They began to cash in on it, however, and now they are fast running out of funds. They are viewed by the poor people of the region with enormous envy and a great deal of animosity. For the Vale do Rio Doce Company, the arrangement seemed an acceptable solution and became part of the company's advertising campaign stressing its social responsibility in the Amazon. For those who know how Indian peoples can lose themselves with the entry of large quantities of money, as has happened with various North American peoples, this solution points to a perverse and subtle determination to undermine and destroy a way of life without the wounds becoming visible to the naked eye.

As a whole, the impact of the Carajás project upon Indian ethnies, including those whose lands were not crossed or closely impacted by the railroad, has been more vigorous and permanent than the TransAmazon highway. The railroad attracted new investments in agriculture and ranching, iron mills, and the utilization of vegetal charcoal, all of which has brought about more land conflicts, distorted economic expectations and dissatisfaction, increases in land prices, and uncontrolled urbanization of rural districts—who knows what will come next? The Indians are pushed into a world of continuous and unpredictable change, where money buys everything, from gewgaws to prostitution. It seems unjust to them that they must work so much to acquire so little from the sale of their agricultural produce. As a consequence, once the money they received as compensation was gone, they began demanding favors from FUNAI in the form of more cash or stable employment with adequate pay. Moving along with the current of the times in the late 1980s, they began to feel that they had acquired certain rights and privileges in view of the changes around them. They began to claim that the state had a responsibility for their well-being, including that of providing them with employment and payment to their chief. They justified their requests and monetary demands with the argument that if previously they had lived without industrial goods because they were autonomous, now, since they had been forced to live surrounded by a multitude of people, the state, through FUNAI, should be obliged to supply their new needs. This argument for compensation seemed strong but naïve, yet the Indian agency, so inefficient in fulfilling the Indians' minimal real needs, was unable to respond with its own arguments. It let the Indians down, as they were well aware. As a consequence they pushed their demands as hard as they could, and much confusion was brought up in the latter half of the 1980s. This exacerbation of misunderstandings between the Indians and FUNAI was another sinister consequence of the economic projects and their reckless ways of reaching compensation and agreements. It was also a sign of more generalized misunderstandings and dissatisfaction.

Furthermore, although the Carajás project hired anthropologists as consultants to identify the Indian ethnies' problems and make suggestions to ameliorate the expected consequences, this action did not bring positive results. Most of the anthropologists' recommendations concentrated on the problems of land and health. While the project lasted, however, the most urgent areas to be demarcated, those of the Krikati and Guajá, were left untouched. For a long time the attention of the consultants was diverted to meeting some of the Indians' most personal claims: to solving problems of invasions in other areas, to making spurious suggestions to increase Indian lands that had already been demarcated, and to take action on smaller, localized projects. After five years of consulting work, the final appraisal cannot be considered very encouraging. This should alert one to the fact that the role of the anthropologist in these enterprises cannot escape being linked to the overall interests of the projects. Under a mantle of good intentions, the presence of anthropologists can be manipulated, and, in the end, what is accomplished is pretty much what was intended from the beginning. The confrontations that anthropologists eventually take on within a project to gain the sympathy of the technical staff and politicians involved and against the declared enemies of the Indians serve mostly to pacify their consciences, because their efficacy in having their suggestions carried out is generally circumscribed by the greater economic interests involved in the project, by FUNAI's inaction, and by the disregard of the national authorities.[27]

Another huge project financed by the World Bank that affected many Indian ethnies and lands was the so-called Polonoroeste project, the backbone of which was the construction of the BR-364 highway linking Cuiabá in Mato Grosso state to Porto Velho, the capital of the state of Rondônia, with a future extension to Rio Branco, the capital of the state of Acre. Once again the World Bank gave its support and demanded investments seeking to protect the Indian populations in the affected areas. Once again anthropologists were hired as consultants, and their recommendations concentrated on demarcating the Indian lands in the area of the project. On paper, since this was an extremely vast region with a sparse population, there should have been no great problems with the task. But the project began late when the highway was already under construction and could not cope with the uncontrolled and irresponsible migration process that ensued in the late 1970s. When it began to operate it found several Indian lands already invaded and in open conflict.

The Guaporé Valley, the traditional territory of many Nambiquara bands, was rapidly taken by ranchers in the late 1960s and 1970s. The Nambiquara ended up having their territory cut up, and the boundaries of the newly established Indian lands were drawn according to the presence of existent Nambiquara villages, not to the Nambiquaras' concepts of territory and land. There rose the argument that Indian lands are those where there are villages or those that are currently used by the Indians. In the case of the Urueuauau Indians, a Tupi-speaking ethnie still living autonomously and aggressively with regard to invaders, it was possible to demarcate an area of 1.7 million hectares, considering that part of the area has been designated as a national park, under the supervision of the environment agency.

The Aripuanã Indian Park, which had been established with fixed boundaries in the mid-1960s, as well as the Indian lands of the Zoró and Suruí, neighbors of the better-known Cintas-Largas, suffered invasions by both timber companies and ranchers. At one point, during a very short period of time, a settlement of some 3,000 peasants was established in the middle of the Aripuanã park, with the support of the federal and state governments, through various colonization projects. The Indians from time to time killed the more distracted hunters who wandered off from their points of reference. On one or two occasions the Cintas-Largas Indians came to the point of attacking squatter families, causing a generalized panic in the region.[28]

Throughout the 1980s most of the interethnic problems in the Polonoroeste project arose from the fact that of the sixty-two Indian lands identified in the area, close to half had not been fully demarcated. By the mid-1990s there were still some twenty Indian lands to be fully guaranteed, including most of the lands of the autonomous Indian ethnies. Several of these ethnies are remnants of previously large populations who were decimated by rubber tappers and Brazil-nut gatherers or by epidemics. In the early 1990s the Diahoi numbered eighteen people; the Juma, nine; the Katawixi, ten; the Himarimã, twelve; the Torá, seventeen; the Kanoé, twenty-three; and more than twenty of these ethnies had populations of less than one hundred people. The recently contacted Omoré are but fourteen people, and they run the risk of being further reduced. Without demarcation of their lands and the clear definition of a policy for their survival, these Indians run the risk of being extinguished. They and many others are in the same situation, which ensures that an Indian policy lacking a government agency with the legitimacy and competence to carry it out is fated to be useless. The anthropologist and the good intentions of the World Bank, when they coincide ideologically—at least for this specific purpose—will not be able to promote the necessary actions, if the state is not sensitive to the issue.

Hydroelectric Dams

Among the most ecologically devastating and socially distressing development projects is the construction of hydroelectric dams, be they in the Amazon or in other regions of the country. As far as Indians are concerned there are some twenty hydroelectric plants that impact directly on more than thirty different ethnies. Most of these dams have been built on large rivers, and with few exceptions they inundated large areas, many of them in populated rural and semi-urban areas, others in forests and savanna country. Until recently most of these projects mixed state and private capital, and almost all are financed by foreign capital, especially the World Bank and the Interamerican Bank.

Hydroelectricity constitutes a cheaper and safer form of energy than nuclear energy, but the production thereof raises many objections, above all those of an ecological and social nature. The most visible and nationally known hydroelectric plants are Itaipu, on the Paraguay River in Paraná state, and Tucuruí, on the Tocantins River in Pará. They are the biggest plants in the country, each with the potential for more than 12GW of energy. Much of the electricity that serves the southern states comes from Itaipu, whereas Tucuruí feeds the states of Pará and Maranhão, including the large aluminum-processing plants.

The construction of Itaipu led to the transference of a group of Guarani, and Tucuruí caused the removal of the Parakanã Indians, both with loss of territory, lives, and above all, drastic changes in their ways of life. The Guarani received individual plots of land, outside the margins of the new dam lake, causing internal conflicts previously nonexistent among a people who viewed land as collective property. The Parakanã saw their lands invaded by landless squatters, loggers, a logging company called CAPEMI, and the contractors who built the dam. A few months after they were first contacted by a FUNAI team in 1972, they were transferred to an area near the future lake and then three years later to another. In the end, they saw their lakeside territories granted to squatters and farmers. It was a useless and wearisome experience for the Parakanã and a corrupt and demoralizing one for Brazil and its government.[29]

Other dams completed in the late 1970s and 1980s, such as Rio Itajaí do Norte in Santa Catarina state, and Itaparica, on the São Francisco River in Bahia, impacted respectively the Xokleng and the Tuxá Indians, with damages that went beyond the partial or total flooding of their lands, causing problems of social reconstruction and adaptation to the new socioeconomic challenges.[30] The Balbina Dam, on the Uatumã River, a northern tributary of the Amazon river, in the heart of the forest, is probably the most abject example of the incompetence generated by the years of military regime and authoritarianism in Brazil. Projected in the early 1970s to supply Manaus with electric energy, its production capacity in the end did not reach one-fourth of the current needs of that city. Nonetheless, the Balbina Dam flooded an area almost equal to that of the lake formed by Tucuruí, but with one-thirtieth of the latter's capacity. With regard to the Indians, the Balbina lake affected several Waimiri-Atroari villages on the Abonari and Taquari rivers and significantly diminished the speed of water flow in these rivers and their tributaries. The state company that built the Balbina Dam, Eletronorte, carried out a program of compensation that helped the Waimiri-Atroari cope with the early difficulties of adaptation,[31] but ecological consequences will tend to make things worse in the near future.

An interesting case of a hydroelectric plant affecting an Indian ethnie is that of the Serra da Mesa plant, on the upper Tocantins River, some 120 miles north of Brasília. When it was first projected in the mid-1970s, it was simply taken for granted that there were no Indians around its area of impact. In 1983, however, as the dam was being built, a group of four Avá-Canoeiro Indians was discovered by a peasant, who then contacted FUNAI. An Indian post was set up to assist these Indians and others who might be roaming around the area. FUNAI and later the public attorney's office demanded that the state company, Furnas, in charge of the future power plant should assume responsibility to recompense the loss of territory of the Avá-

Canoeiro. Though stalling for a few years, Furnas finally realized that it had to include that small group and the unknown ones as part of the people being impacted by the project. Furthermore, since the 1988 Constitution declared that the use of rivers on Indian lands for purposes of producing hydroelectricity needed the approval of the National Congress, Furnas was pressured to hire a group of anthropologists to study the conditions of the Avá-Canoeiro and write up an agreement to compensate the Indians. Though the dam was practically finished, the public attorney's office and the National Congress hesitated in allowing its operation. Finally, the agreement was presented to the congress in July, and in October 1996, Furnas was licensed to build the dam. The agreement provided for the demarcation of an area of some 48,000 hectares, including a great part of the margins of the lake, and for the financing of a long-term program to contact the remaining Avá-Canoeiro with the purpose of joining together all their wandering bands, a sine qua non condition for their possible survival as an ethnie. It was the first time that a power company met the demands of article 233 of the 1988 Constitution, setting a precedent that hopefully will be followed in the future.[32]

The most potentially devastating development, if carried out to the full, is yet to come. It is the so-called National Plan for Electric Energy 1987-2010, drawn up by Eletrobrás Company to secure Brazil's energy demands by the use of hydroelectricity. This plan foresees the construction of almost a hundred dams, the majority of them on rivers of the Amazon basin. Some seventeen of them will directly impact sixty Indian ethnies in more than eighty Indian lands, the majority of which have not yet been demarcated.[33] The dams will flood enormous areas of forest land, most of which are still not calculated or at least not publicly known. The impact on the environment is not yet predictable, although the consequences for the populations living along the rivers are easily foreseen. If one takes as models what happened in the aftermath of the Tucuruí and the Balbina dams, one may expect various types of well-known disastrous environmental results and social and political abuses. However, since Brazil is no longer under a military regime but rather under a democratic one with better accountability to the people—at least that is what the nation expects—we might have a less pessimistic vision and hope that the same strategic errors and blunders will not be repeated. It is expected that these construction projects will be preceded by exhaustive studies and responsible policies, not only to lessen the social and environmental impacts but also to create new conditions of survival with dignity for the Indians.

Large dams are planned for the main tributaries of the Amazon River, such as the Tocantins, the Araguaia, the Xingu, the Tapajós, the Madeira, the Purus, the Negro, the Jari, and dozens of smaller rivers. Some of these dams will flood enormous areas, such as the one named Babaquara on the Xingu River, the plans for which motivated many protests by national and international ecological groups and defenders of the Indian cause. It seems that the planned locations for some dams are inadequate to achieve the goals of aggregating the greatest hydroelectric potential with the smallest economic and social costs possible. One expects that these plans, whenever they become economically viable, will be examined by all interested parties in order to absorb suggestions for change so as not to jeopardize the greater interests of the nation—the Indians, the riverside populations, and the environment itself.

Among the sixty or more Indian ethnies to be affected by the possible flooding of their lands are once again the Gaviões Indians of Pará. It is hard to think of another Indian ethnie that has suffered through as many changes in their natural and social environment. The Xavante who live in the Indian lands of São Marcos and Sangradouro, the Bakairi, the Karajá, the Kayapó, the Apinayé, and the Makuxi are other ethnies who have undergone terrible social pressures in the last fifty years, and who once again are in the way of Brazilian progress. There are also some twenty autonomous ethnies, known only by names or nicknames given to them by other Indian ethnies, and about whom we have only a vague idea of their lifestyle and of how they would react to abrupt changes in their way of life.

A Brief Appraisal of Socioeconomic Impacts

It might be worthwhile to make a general comparison of the social and environmental impacts caused by a dam, a highway or railroad, an agricultural frontier, and other economic projects. It might seem reasonable to suppose that of all these the dam has the worst consequences in the short run but the least destructive characteristics in the medium and long run. In the short run its construction involves the destruction of an area for the installation of the project, the temporary diversion of the river, and so on. After the construction of the dam there comes the formation of an artificial lake, including the flooding of the banks of the main river and its near tributaries, and the reduction in speed of water flow. Deforestation and the presence of an artificial lake have a direct, immediate, devastating, and irreversible impact. A new ecological niche is created with little-known environmental, social, and economic consequences. The economic costs generally go beyond the original budgets, as can be seen in the cases already known.

In Tucuruí there was outright inefficiency and corruption in the process of clearing the forest. Chemical defoliants that had been banned in other parts of the world were used secretly, causing the poisoning of rivers and water sources. Even so, when the lake was formed most of the forest still existed, although it was flooded. In the years since 1982 these trees have been decomposing and releasing sulfur, methane, and other gases and minerals, which in the future will cause damage to the turbines by rusting them. In comparison, Balbina Hydroelectric Plant, located far away from town and roads, did not even pretend to have a plan to clear out the area to be flooded; they simply left the trees to decay and run the risk of water sulfurization.

It is still early to forecast the full and permanent ecological consequences of the Tucuruí Hydroelectric Plant. What we have now is a multiplication of the insect population around the lake area making life unbearable to humans and animals alike, and a substantial increase in the population of certain species of fish, particularly those more adapted to still waters and flooded forests, to the disadvantage of fishes adapted to running water. The edges of the artificial lake continue to be deforested illegally and with impunity, which is causing the progressive erosion of the soil, with the consequence of an unexpected increase of silt accumulation in the lake, thus enlarging its area and slowly diminishing the water pressure on the turbines. Besides the Parakanã Indians, who lost their original lands and were transferred, many of the traditional riverine inhabitants of the Tocantins River suffered irreparable losses of their lands and way of life. Relocation programs do not generally compensate for these losses.

These are the principal short-term impacts. In the medium to long run, however, if the ecological consequences do not prove to be absolutely negative, one might expect to see a social and environmental stabilization of the hydroelectric complex, perhaps without further modifications or damage. The presence of Indian ethnies around the lake area would make necessary the preservation of forest lands not only as Indian territory in and of itself, but also as inviolable ecological reserves, all of which would help to improve the security and longevity of the hydroelectric plant itself. Thus, the presence of Indians could be an advantage to the hydroelectric plants. Since hydroelectricity can be transported through power lines, there is no need for industry to be installed nearby; therefore preservation would be a must for both parties. There would be changes, of course, but those might produce satisfactory and positive conditions for the permanent survival of the Indian ethnies in question.

In contrast, a highway or railroad causes immediate and continuous impact, if it fulfills its function of serving as an economic stimulus to a given region. We have already seen the examples of the TransAmazon, the BR-80, and the Carajás Railroad. An agricultural frontier in Brazil resembles an army of leaf-cutter ants, which eats everything that is in front of it. Settlement projects and tax incentives for agricultural and ranching projects bring with them a socioeconomic way of life that can hardly be considered stable and productive, let alone sustainable in the long run. They appear to be just more examples of the many economic cycles through which the country has passed. In all these cases, the Indians are always seen as undesirable and dispensable partners. To be sure, they would have continued to be so if it were not for their rise in the national political scene through their ethnic affirmation and the voicing of their demands in recent times. To help them in their cause there rose also a growing awareness on the part of the Brazilian public toward the environmental problems of the Amazon and the country as a whole, as well as an increase in the concern for the fate of the Indian peoples.

THE MILITARY

The military regime that ran Brazil from 1964 to 1985 also determined the course of its Indian policy and its administrative agencies, the SPI and later FUNAI. Only in 1985 did direct military influence withdraw from FUNAI, in response to pressure from the Indian movement, public opinion, and the hopeful onset of the political transition from dictatorship to democracy. However, segments of the military entrenched themselves in the security and information sectors of the government, from which they continued to hold the strategic command of FUNAI until the early 1990s. One can no longer state that the armed forces have a say in the Indian question, but since they have the responsibility for the national frontiers, they still have an important role to play.

One can recognize four phases of the military control of the Indian question. The first phase goes from 1964 to November 1967, when they took power and purged the principal leaders from the SPI. In this period Noel Nutels, the last civil director of the SPI, was fired, as were Carlos Moreira Neto, José da Gama Malcher, and several other indigenists who were linked to the previous democratic regime. Many anthropologists and linguists were considered undesirable persons to undertake research or participate in the national Indian protection council. The SPI seat was moved from Rio de Janeiro to Brasília in 1966 and went through a rapid decline, culminating in a series of accusations that some of its personnel had been involved not only in corruption and land sales, but also in such unimaginable acts as the massacre of the Cintas-Largas Indians at Parallel 11 in Mato Grosso state. In its final months the agency's archives caught fire, destroying administrative documents and a great part of the ethnographic films and anthropological and indigenist reports accumulated during more than fifty years of existence. It has not been possible to date to comprehensively reconstruct the history of this period due to lack of documented data.

The second phase began with the creation of FUNAI on December 5, 1967. Although its first president was a civilian, who served for two years, the tendency was for direct control by the military, specifically by generals. This phase lasted through the Medici and Geisel governments (1968–78). During this period, the government enacted with the National Congress the Statute of the Indian, Law 6.001 of December 19, 1973. Through this legislation FUNAI not only became responsible for all acts pertaining to Indian matters, but also found the means to create its own esprit de corps. In 1971 it had begun to promote the professional training of a new crop of indigenist agents, through courses taught by anthropology professors from the University of Brasília, albeit military orientation. The Statute of the Indian established that all Indian lands should be demarcated within a period of five years, that is, by 1978. Although some efforts were made to demarcate lands, by the end of the Geisel presidency this goal was far from being reached. Instead, the Ministry of Interior, which controlled FUNAI, proposed a new policy to hasten the integration of Indians individually or as communities, without so much as providing for the integrity of their lands. The juridical figure to achieve this goal was to "emancipate" Indians from the state's tutelage. It was expected that by the year 2000 all Indians should be emancipated and fully integrated in Brazil. In that context, "fully integrated" meant having no claim to a different cultural orientation or protection from the state. Anthropologists, journalists, lawyers, scientists, and much of the public (those who understood the proposition) opposed this plan. Finally, with the inauguration of General Figueiredo as the new president in March 1979, the emancipation project was filed away.[34]

The third phase coincides with the first five years of the Figueiredo administration, from 1979 to 1984. No longer were generals the presidents of FUNAI, but the office was usually filled by colonels. The first president of this period, however, was a civilian with new ideas to revamp the Indian agency and conclude the demarcation of Indian lands. Seven months later he was out, and the time of the colonels began. It was a period that brought about the administrative demoralization of the agency. Few Indian lands were demarcated, the indigenist training courses were discontinued, and a period of personal corruption and disregard for the Indian cause began. In contrast, it was during this period that the Indians themselves began to demand participation in the agency. Worst of all, by the end of this period FUNAI had lost its autonomy and power in the process of recognition of Indian lands and administrative demarcation. Decree Number 88,118 of February 22, 1983, created an interministerial board made up of representatives of the ministries of Agrarian Reform, Interior, Agriculture, and the National Security Council, with the power to evaluate the claims of Indians and to judge upon the validity of demarcating Indian lands. In those years FUNAI became a smoke screen for camouflaged action by the military, as they foresaw the political changes that were to come.

The fourth phase began in 1984, when the Txukarramãe (Kayapó) Indians managed to avoid the dividing of the Xingu Indian Park and actually forced FUNAI and the Ministry of Interior to add an area next to the park. To reach this goal the Indians, led by Chief Raoni, went as far as to kidnap several FUNAI staff who had been sent to convince the Indians to accept the government's plan. During the signing of the agreement, which conceded to the Txukarramãe new lands to the north of the Xingu park, Chief Raoni slyly pulled Minister Andreazza's ears in front of the television cameras, as if to show him that he should have better judgment. Later on, in January 1985, militant anthropologists and indigenists who had rejoined FUNAI, together with a new president (albeit still military) of the agency, set up a strong resistance movement within the agency against president Figueiredo's just-released decree, which intended to allow and regulate mining and gold prospecting on Indian lands. The decree was, surprisingly, revoked, if only to be condoned in practice by the incoming presidency of the first civilian since 1964.

These two fearless and audacious acts created a feeling that the new civilian government, which took office in March 1985, would look upon the Indian cause with a better disposition than had the military regime. As far as the Indians were concerned, however, the presidency of José Sarney proved to be unfortunate. In the ensuing years, FUNAI had a number of presidents who were unable to do the agency any good, while some of them did the Indians and the Indian cause quite a bit of harm. One of them, a lawyer of some reknown, was nominated and did not even take office. Another, who was known for having been an indigenist agent in the heyday of the period of the colonels, was all fanfare but little action.

The most harmful of all, one who later became a politician and is now a senator from one of the Amazonian states, had never seen an Indian before. He was appointed with the task of shattering the indigenist movement, diverting the Indians' struggles from collective interests toward personal gains, paralyzing the process of land demarcation that had ensued in 1984–85, and, finally, of weakening public interest in the Indian cause. He had the support of the civilian president and thus was successful in some of these aims. He made internal changes in the Indian agency, hired a considerable number of staff who had never seen Indians, and fired several anthropologists and indigenists who condemned his actions and denounced his deals with loggers and gold prospectors. FUNAI, for better or worse, was never the same after this administration. During the public debates held at the subcommittee on blacks, Indian populations, handicapped persons, and other minorities, which helped in the writing of the Constitution of 1988, FUNAI did not even send representatives to debate or make propositions. For a while, it seemed that the agency was just waiting to be abolished.

Responsibility for this state of affairs is no longer in the hands of the military. With the onset of democracy, the military have positioned themselves on the defensive with regard to Brazilian society and its desires for political participation and structural change. During the Sarney administration, FUNAI still represented a small trench in a fight of skirmishes, advances, and retreats, but finally the military retreated to their constitutional obligations and, as far as the Indians are concerned, focused their interests on the Amazon. In March 1986, the government announced the so-called Calha Norte project. This project, which was drawn up at the National Security Council and directed by the military cabinet of the presidency, sought originally to open twenty medium-sized airports and create eight military bases in a stretch of some 6,000 kilometers along the northern frontier of the country by 1990. It also proposed to establish a 160-kilometer-wide band along the Amazonian frontier as a national security zone. Indian lands located on this zone would be deregulated and considered non-Indian. For what purpose? The most often-used argument was to protect this frontier from foreign invasions and drug smuggling. The majority of these airports as well as the military bases would be built on Indian lands.

National defense is certainly the main function of the armed forces, and they are supposed to know how best to take care of it. The drug problem is real, as are smuggling activities on the frontier, although how the army—instead of a special corps of the federal police—can help combat them is hard to understand. But why use Indian lands for their bases and why remove Indians from the international frontier? Do the military think that the Indians are an encumbrance to their possible maneuvers, or that they might align themselves with an improbable invader of the Brazilian territory? It is not entirely impossible that there are base intentions with regard to the control of Indian lands, and it is completely improbable that this frontier rule will make any sense to the Indians or to public opinion. In the end, there lingers a certain suspicion that this attitude on the part of the military represents a continuation of their former role in the Indian agency.

The Calha Norte project began its operation in June 1987, when President Sarney paid a visit to the town of São Gabriel da Cachoeira on the upper Rio Negro, where whites and Tukano Indians live together. The project has expanded to other areas, such as the frontier with Venezuela and Colombia, and plans to extend its activities to other parts of the Amazon so as to encompass the frontiers with Bolivia, Peru, and Guyana.[35] As of 1998, however, except for a program to install radar at several posts on the Amazonian frontier—a project budgeted at an amazing US$1.2 billion—it was mostly still a question of intentions and plans.

With regard to the Indians, the Brazilian armed forces, especially the army and the air force, have rendered incomparable service and aid in the past. The fact that the SPI was created and led by Rondon, who later became marshal of the army, was the fundamental factor that led Brazil to have a humanist-oriented Indian policy that was respected worldwide until the 1960s. The Indians came to be perceived and treated as a segment of the Brazilian nationality, and their survival was seen as essential for the general well-being of the nation. Many dedicated military men remained in the SPI in 1912, when the minister of war forced them to choose between either returning to the barracks or remaining in the Indian service. Many of them had a generous and integrative vision of the Brazilian people, and in their pronouncements they held that the survival of Indian ethnies presented a real possibility for the formation of a plural society in Brazil. They believed that the army was a national and democratic institution, both in its social composition and in its internal purposes.[36]

It is not altogether improbable that this vision might once again achieve a general acceptance in the army ranks, and in this sense one may not discard the role the army still has to carry out regarding the Indians. Whenever called, even during the military regime, it proved a valuable and worthy instrument in the work of demarcating and defending Indian territories. In some sectors of the armed forces where Rondon's image remains heroic and exemplary, there is a continuing determination to follow his trail and adapt his teachings to current times. How can one re-create the practice of dialoguing with the Indians without using paternalism? In what form can the state and Brazilian society come to terms with the Indians' new needs? How can one help to find a definitive solution for the demarcation of Indian lands in a way that will guarantee their security and inviolability for ever? These questions are consistent with the search for a longlasting role for the armed forces in relation to the Indians. They are also applicable to other sectors of the state and are raised in the broader context of a democratic Brazil.

THE CHURCH

The church—the Catholic Church, in particular—is a universal institution with varied national incarnations both in its form and its content. Its organic composition is quite heterogeneous, and its styles are adapted to the times and spaces in which it acts. Its genesis is dogmatic and indisputable, which provides it with a solid base of formation, with an almost uninterrupted 2,000-year history, and with few moments of defection. It carries within itself a hegemonic purpose, with minimal and acceptable variances that can be absorbed by its centralized organization and discipline. Bringing together a fair mixture of firmness and flexibility, it maintains itself as viable and acceptable to most people who belong to it.

As far as the Indians are concerned, the church's current attitudes and views do not depart substantially from its previous history, both in regard to its relationship with other surrounding social forces, and to the meaning and purposes of its action. It may be arguably said that the present is relatively equivalent to the past. In colonial times, there were the Jesuits, who at moments were radical defenders of the Indians; Carmelites, seeking to reconcile divergent interests; Benedictines and Franciscans, who pursued policies of noncommitment; and bishops and priests, whose attitudes varied from the inglorious Bishop Sardinha, defender of the agrarian interests of Portuguese colonists, to the priests who participated in the Cabanagem

Rebellion with the Indians. Today we have a corps of priests and lay brothers who are committed to liberation theology and to the ideals of ethnic incarnation. They are steadfast defenders of the Indian cause and the majority of them are engaged in the Indigenist Missionary Council (CIMI). On the other hand, there remain a number of Catholic missions whose views and methods do not differ much from those established one hundred years ago (which means, practically, the same as four centuries ago). By and large the church is still governed by conservative theologies that look upon the Indians as pagans, condemned to hell unless they are converted to Christianity. In such internal variation, although pulled together in a mystic body of doctrines, lies the social and institutional power of the Catholic Church. There is no reason to underestimate its capacity to adapt to the demands of modern and postmodern times.

In the dawning of the nineteenth century, the Brazilian church suffered the first strong political and social opposition to its secular mission of catechizing the Indians. The positivists and antimonarchists who helped install the republic, and even the incoming Protestants, contested its power and its doctrines everywhere in the cities and in most faraway towns throughout the country. They argued that the church's methods of indoctrination were backward, retrograde, and antihumanistic. The SPI rejected religious indoctrination altogether and was hostile to the church for almost as long as Rondon lived. The positivist military believed that the conversion of Indians to Christianity was forced and hypocritical, and that being Christian should not be a condition for the Indians to become Brazilian citizens. Since the SPI was not able to convince the government to expel the missions from Indian lands, there remained an awkward, at times tense, relationship between them. In the early 1950s, anthropologist Darcy Ribeiro, then director of the Museum of the Indian, took the initiative of starting a dialogue with Dom Helder Câmara, then auxiliary bishop of Rio de Janeiro, calling on the modern church to work in favor of the Indians and to create new methods to help them in their struggle for physical and cultural survival.[37]

The Catholic Church, up to then, had not been very active with regard to the Indians, at least not directly. The Salesian order had established a mission among the Bororo at the beginning of the century and had carried out a work of catechesis that involved learning the language and culture of these Indians. The SPI accused them of having appropriated lands that by right belonged to the Bororo. The Salesians were also on the upper Rio Negro, where they had created an institutional complex of boarding schools for Tukano girls and boys, which many critics have considered almost feudalistic in organization. In the 1880s the Dominicans set up a mission in the backlands of the Araguaia and Tocantins rivers and attracted many migrants to live near them. In the end, a new town, Conceição do Araguaia, was founded, but the Kayapó band known as Pau d'Arco was completely wiped out in the process, perhaps the most disastrous mission ever attempted in Brazil.[38] The Franciscans established a small mission among the Munduruku Indians, and the Jesuits, back in Brazil after almost two centuries of absence, opened a school in the town of Diamantino, in the state of Mato Grosso, which housed for indoctrination some Nambiquara and Pareci youths.

In parallel developments, Protestant missionaries had begun to come to Brazil and set up missions among both the general population and the Indians. By the 1950s there were twenty Protestant missions, mostly English and North American, such as the Unevangelized Fields, the World Evangelical Church, and the New Tribes Mission, among such Indian ethnies as the Krikati, Canela, Guajajara, Karajá, Guarani, and Terena. In contrast to the Catholic missions, Protestants did not receive subsidies from the federal government and frequently suffered disquieting embarrassments from indigenist agents who occasionally accused them of working as spies of the U.S. government, especially during World War II. In the case of the Summer Institute of Linguistics, a branch of the Wycliffe Bible organization, such accusations have recently been proven to be warranted.[39]

All in all, the SPI tolerated only the missions that did not establish residence on Indian lands. The occasional presence of missionaries, particularly Catholic ones, was accepted when it was part of the extension of the pastoral work of dioceses and prelacies in whose districts Indians lived. The religious obligations of priests and friars in these regions consisted mostly of baptizing, marrying, and teaching recited prayers, and regularly included the Indians. Often they served as paramedics, administering vaccines and pills for malaria and other maladies. For those Indians who effectively participated in the regional sociocultural system, these visits were a consolation and an affirmation of their place in the world. To be a Christian in these regions amounts to being human, and for this the occasional presence of a priest or friar is necessary. The anticlerical attitudes of the indigenist agents only confused the Indians, dividing their loyalty between the cross and the regional culture and the command of the government.

The rapprochement between the SPI and the church implied a recognition, on the part of the Indian agency, of the dimensions of the Indian problem and the agency's incapacity to take care of the matter singlehandedly. The truce was extended to the Protestant missions, especially those that could bring some contribution to the agency's action, such as the Summer Institute of Linguistics.

It would be rather fastidious to try to interpret this rapprochement as a political alliance or as a convergence of ideologies with regard to the Indians and their position in the national political scenario or inWestern Christian civilization. Certainly it did not amount to anything like a return to the nineteenth-century formula of "Christianization and civilization." On the contrary, the ideological gulf that was established between the SPI and the church since the beginning of the century widened with time. The incoming influence of the anthropological doctrine of relativism, on one hand, and the theological immobility of the church, on the other, at least until the first breezes of liberalization began to shake the clergy after the Vatican II Council (1962–65), also contributed to this gap. The old rivalry between church and state with regard to the Indians reflected on Brazilian society and politics. As late as 1954, for example, a representative in congress drafted a law proposing that the SPI be extinguished and its main functions passed over to the church.

The new period of liberalization of the church came to coincide both with the onset of the military regime and with the beginning of a process of self-reflection and critique regarding the way Brazil and its society had treated the Indians. This process entailed a radical critique of all situations of internal colonialism, of which the Indians were considered a more permanent example. The church and the missionary orders also participated in this process and positioned themselves to construct a new vision of their role with regard to the Indians. This was the beginning of their new phase as defenders of the Indian cause.

The new role of the church began to be constructed both intellectually and in practice. The Jesuits in the Diamantino mission presented the first results of their mission by publishing books and articles making strong criticisms of the past and proposing alternatives to the process of Christianization. They stressed that the state had a greater weight of responsibility for the destiny of the Indians but did not forget to acknowledge their own historical errors. Their major document of that time was a booklet called *Indian Directory*, in which Father Adalberto Holanda Pereira, S.J., introduced to his public new notions of anthropology, new interpretation about the so-called character of the Indians, and new recommendations concerning the objectives of missionary action.

At about that time—the late 1960s and early 1970s—a time of economic expansion in Brazil, a new crop of young priests and lay brothers came on the scene with adamant determination to become personally involved in the struggle to defend Indian ethnies, then conceived as victims of government development plans. In 1972 a varied group of these young priests joined to found the Indigenist Missionary Council (CIMI), whose role was to coordinate their actions nationwide and to promote the Indian cause within the church. Upon becoming an agency of the National Conference of Brazilian Bishops (CNBB) three years later, CIMI gained official recognition and legitimacy to deal with FUNAI and to represent the church in the Indian cause before the rest of the nation.[40]

In the last twenty-seven years CIMI's activities have developed within the general context of the doctrines established by the Vatican II Council, in which Christian indoctrination is supposed to be practiced together with the feeling of responsibility toward the survival of the Indians themselves. Religious teaching ceased to be the main instrument of indoctrination and was replaced by a new practice known as "incarnation," in which the missionary is to share in the life and suffering of the Indians. A theology was developed in which the imitation of Christ should be sought by direct and daily living with the Indians, so that in this way the cultural and spiritual lives of the Indians would be experienced in the person of the missionary. The collective and egalitarian society of the Indians was compared with the pure and communitarian spirit of primitive Christianity. The church began to recognize intrinsic values in Indian cultures, values which should be imitated, emulated, and adapted to modern life, such as the communitarian spirit, non-accumulation of wealth, child rearing, democratic practices in political life, and finally, living in harmony with and respecting nature. In its seminal and most complete document, written at the end of 1973, Y-juca pirama, a Tupi expression meaning "the Indian, the one who must die," CIMI, and by extension the liberalizing side of the church, proclaimed its new conception of the Indian, integrating anthropological knowledge with its theology of liberation, and politicizing its pastoral action through the inclusion of its members in the Brazilian social and political context of the 1970s.

Little by little, the new discourse began to trigger actions that produced immediate effect. The missionaries began to travel the country in search of Indians who could become leaders and representatives of their own peoples. In 1975 they convened the first assembly of Indian leaders, and since then they have had assemblies almost every year. In each one, a new crop of Indian leaders would be invited, and new sets of resolutions would be drawn up. Without wavering in its support of every legitimate Indian demand,

CIMI has become one of the most important and effective organizations in combating FUNAI's retrograde policies. It has advocated the participation of Indians in the Indian agency and in every issue that relates to them, particularly land demarcation, regional development projects, mineral and timber exploitation, and so on.

Together with other pro-Indian nongovernmental organizations (NGOs) that also rose in the 1970s and 1980s, CIMI has sought to interpret the fight for survival of Indian peoples as part of the general struggle against the military regime, the new flourishing of democratic rights in Brazilian society, and the recognition of the cultural and ethnic diversity of Brazil. The notion of self-determination and the acknowledgment of Indian ethnies as constituting nations within a larger nation were the principal political and intellectual contributions that arose from this movement. The first came directly from the founding charter of the United Nations and is the political basis for the independence and autonomy of a people, a precondition for their being recognized as nations.[41]

The practical application of these concepts, in the face of Brazilian political reality and the small demographic factor represented by the surviving Indian ethnies in Brazil, has a long way to go before becoming viable. The Brazilian state—its military sector in particular—does not view with favor the idea of setting up a plurinational state, perhaps not so much from fear of the Indians as from fear of more demographically significant immigrant ethnic groups. The term "nation" is indeed applicable to the Indians, but not to immigrant groups, because within the former are included the notions of culture and territoriality. During the colonial period the Indians were called *nations*, and it was only in the second half of the nineteenth century, with the establishment of evolutionist theories, that this term ceased to be applied and was replaced by other, less distinct terms, ranging from *horde, group, band*, and *clans* to *society, community, ethnic group* or *ethnie*, and *people*. The term *nation* certainly distinguishes an Indian people and would be completely appropriate if we excluded from it the notion of *state*, which the term seems to include nowadays. As for self-determination, the acceptance thereof by the Brazilian state is conditioned both by the broadening of democratic practices and freedom and by the capacity of the Indian ethnies to face the constant difficulties and economic restrictions that the other sectors of Brazilian society impose on them. For this to happen one day, time and determination are necessary, not simply aspiration.[42]

The church, finally, has contributed decisively in the preparation of the 1988 Constitution through its strong lobbying and its capacity for bringing together the other pro-Indian social forces. Bishop Erwin Kreutler, the president of CIMI at the time, was invited to speak before the subcommittee in charge of drawing up the articles pertinent to the Indian ethnies and issues.

The church is not exclusively made up of CIMI, however. It maintains within its ranks religious orders that still persevere in their antiquated methods, holding on to the idea that their mission in the world is to prepare all people for the kingdom of God. Being universalistic, this doctrine necessarily has a homogenizing effect. Of course this dilemma also acts upon other social doctrines. Nonetheless, in the case of the church, the fundamental perspective starts from the idea of a supreme being upon whom humans are dependent. If God and Christ are in people, the more peculiar forms of this manifestation must be disciplined. When the Brazilian state, through the SPI, established an Indian policy in which the Indian was conceived of in terms of his humanity and cultural evolution and not in relation to a trans-human spirituality, the church manifested much disquiet and rejected that presumption. No matter how much it has advanced in the direction of a Copernican worldview in recent years, one cannot expect the church to leave behind its history and its determination.

Furthermore, the political and global nature of the church conditions it to seek more conciliatory forms of relationships with both the state and society. Its doctrinal stance with regard to the Indians fundamentally depends on the balance it seeks to strike between society and state. If the Brazilian state should reach a point of developing more democratic means of functioning, and if Brazilian civil society continues its historic tendency toward secularization, it is possible that the indigenist vision of the church might become different from what it is today. At any rate, the role that belongs to the church in the continuing struggle for the preservation of Indian peoples in Brazil is far from over. The purported social and spiritual identification of primitive Christian communities with Indian communities is a permanent incentive for the internal strengthening of this role. It remains to be seen how this identification can be reconciled with a humanist vision of society and with the Indian peoples' aspirations for autonomy.

Civil Society

One may define civil society as the movement of a self-identifying population that defines its aspirations collectively in relation to the state. It is the active counterpart of the notion of public opinion, and it is distinct from other notions such as middle class, mass culture, and political or economic forces. Obviously one cannot attribute an ideological autonomy of civil society with regard to these other social sets, since there is an interface of economic interests and mutuality among their members. One must recognize, however, a certain modality of thinking and of political intentionality in this social set that justifies the idea of a distinct identity.

Brazilian civil society is mostly urban or urbanocentric, sharing a general identification with modernity and its often disparate and contradictory characteristics. Normally its members are recognized as being students, professors, white-collar workers, civil servants, artists, and intellectuals. But surprisingly, one can also include the anonymous masses of voters, who by their ballots express collective dreams and choices unconnected to immediate economic interests. These voters, for example, elected in the state of Rio de Janeiro the Xavante leader Mário Juruna as their representative to the National Congress.

Civil society forges its ideas and convictions in relation not only to the relative socioeconomic position of its members in the polity but also sometimes in accordance with new ideas and sentiments rising out of social and political movements. The power of an idea, such as the conviction that the environment is in danger, is an example of how it can produce a social movement and influence civil society. The Indian question became such an idea during the last years of the Geisel presidency (1974–78), when the military regime began to relax its iron rule against its political and social opponents. Not only the Indians, but other social minorities became objects and motives of political interest and social reflection, and this led to the formation of groups to defend them and disseminate information about their most serious problems. This movement has lasted until now, albeit with considerably less dynamism.

In the past there were two occasions—in the 1840s and 1850s and in the years between 1907 and 1912—when Brazilian civil society was stirred up and rose in defense of or in sympathy to the Indian cause. The first movement occurred within a small but significant part of the Brazilian political and intellectual elite that was eager to create a feeling of nationality, of what Brazil should be, and this goal involved the recognition of the Indian as part of the Brazilian heritage. The protagonists were romantic Indianist poets and writers such as Manoel Antônio de Almeida, Antônio Gonçalves Dias, Domingos José Gonçalves de Magalhães, and José de Alencar, and historians such as Adolpho de Varnhagen, João Francisco Lisboa, and Perdigão Malheiro. The concrete results of this movement seem rather intangible, but I believe that they were fundamental in forming a pro-Indian mentality in the country, without which the fate of the surviving Indian populations might have been much worse.

In the period between 1907 and 1912, Brazilian scientists, journalists, philosophers, and political authorities came forward to defend the Indians and force the Brazilian government to develop a new Indian policy. It was originally provoked by a denunciation, made by a scientist at the Vienna Congress of Americanists in 1907, of Brazil's condoning the massacres perpetrated in the states of Paraná and Santa Catarina by immigrants against the Indians. These actions of genocide had been justified by the German-Brazilian scientist Hermann Von Ihering in a much publicized article as the only viable solution for the development of Brazil. After a few years of dispute, the government yielded to the demands of the nationalist Brazilians and created the SPI in 1910.

As far as the Indians are concerned, anthropologists are one of the most important categories of Brazilian civil society. They have been, since at least the 1950s and perhaps since 1930, with Curt Nimuendaju, Herbert Baldus, Arthur Ramos, Edgar Roquette-Pinto, and others, the fundamental ideologues and proponents of current national indigenist thinking. Together with other scientific research, the main arguments in favor of the Indian cause in Brazil come from ideas developed in the field of anthropology, either as a result or adaptation of anthropological notions from foreign intellectual centers or as native notions. For example, the notion of cultural relativism contests arguments for cultural inferiority imputed to the Indians. Modern genetics, with its new emphasis pointing to the value of human variability as a factor of survival of the human species, places the Indians side by side with other populations in the maintenance of the biological potential of *Homo sapiens*. Thus social Darwinism, which values the idea of the strong as the survivor and sole agent of human reproduction, falls to the ground. Ecology, particularly human ecology, emphasizes the potential role of Indian ethnies in the maintenance of relatively fragile ecological niches, such as tropical forests, and stimulates their cultural practices for the preservation and optimization of the environment.

Brazilian anthropology has demonstrated that the disappearance of so many Indian peoples did not happen through assimilation or acculturation, but, in the great majority of cases, through direct extermination by violence and the plundering of their sources of survival, especially their lands. The miscegenation process, which had been previously viewed as the main cause of the disappearance of the Indians from the Brazilian coast,

today is seen as a lesser cause, although, on the other hand, it was fundamental to the physical constitution of the Brazilian people, at least up
through the eighteenth century. Indians have been considered one of the
pillars of the formation of the Brazilian people—together with blacks and
whites—since the last century. Many anthropologists today believe that
the Indian is essential to the sentiment of what it is to be a Brazilian, the
basis of our differentiation with regard to the other American nations.
This idea was set forth by the present author at a public audience of the
mentioned subcommittee on blacks, Indian populations, handicapped persons, and minorities, of the National Constitutional Assembly on April
29, 1987.[43]

Anthropologists, together with indigenists, are the people who have the
most contact with Indians in their daily life. They thus experience and live
cultural practices that are totally different from the life they live in the
cities. In many cases, they learn to speak the language of the Indian peoples
who receive them; they feel their joy, understand their projects, and many
times obtain from the experience an immense and permanent personal and
intellectual satisfaction. Anthropologists see ways of life that express a social generosity, leaving them envious of something that their own society is
missing. This understanding, in my opinion, is not exclusive to the anthropologist but represents a collective and atavistic curiosity of our society
toward a way of life it imagines to be more communitarian and interper-
sonal, a way of life perceived as something positive and that existed once
in our society and may yet come to be. In the history of Western civilization this longing can be recognized in the millenarian movements, in utopian projects, and even occasionally in political, social, and religious movements.

Indigenists are people who act as the immediate agents of Indian policy.
Therefore, the term includes everyone from the humblest manual laborer
at an Indian post to the chief of an "attraction front for isolated Indians";
from a nurse's assistant to the telegraph operator of a regional FUNAI office. But, by right, indigenists are those people who have closer contact
with Indians, and who seek to carry out their actions in the light of an
understanding that is close to the Indians' own interests. They are people
who try to reconcile these interests, even the most banal ones, with the
country's Indian policy, or what they feel this policy should be. Indigenists
are the heirs of the old-time backwoodsmen or *sertanistas,* who were the
organizers of Indian "pacification" expeditions in SPI times. In fact, they
are heirs to the whole Brazilian tradition of official relations with the In-

dian populations, since the days of the "fathers of the Indians," the "protectors of the Indians," the "directors of the Indians," and including the old missionaries.

The fundamental difference between indigenists and anthropologists is originally one of academic training and administrative action. Over the years, however, the characteristics have blended a bit, and the theoretical and practical knowledge now tend to be complementary. If an anthropologist by training dedicates his or her time to practical work with the Indians and to support their political interests, he or she begins to act like an indigenist; and if an indigenist decides to analyze his or her actions in terms of a broader conception of who the Indians are or what their practical work is in the social universe, he or she becomes an anthropologist.

Therefore, there is no fair way to distinguish these two categories as if they had antagonistic interests. Yet such an artificial division occurred during the years of the military regime and in the first years of civilian democracy. The situation was clearly due to manipulation on the part of the FUNAI authorities to reduce the impact of criticism by anthropologists during the Medici and Geisel years. They tried—successfully in many cases—to pit anthropologists against indigenists by saying that the former were less committed to the Indians' interests. Many young indigenists, recently graduated from universities, practical nursing programs, or from courses on anthropology and Brazilian ethnology, were influenced to behave as if they were the heirs of all the practical experience and truth regarding the Indians and of what should be done for them in the light of the development policies being implanted in their territories. On the other side, many anthropologists positioned themselves as guardians of the history and knowledge of the Indian question and focused all their mistrust on indigenist agents and their methods of work. This contrived disagreement persisted for many years among individuals, and it began to disappear simply because the number of indigenists has decreased over the years and has not been replenished at the Indian agency.

During the most disquieting periods of FUNAI, those times when there was total incompatibility between the direction of the agency and the indigenist staff, and no worthwhile work could possibly be done, the outcome was most often against the indigenists. In May 1980, forty-three of them were fired outright, allegedly because they had illegally constituted an association. Most of them were amnestied in 1984 and accepted the offer to return. But, once again, in September 1985, many of them, actually the most-experienced staff that FUNAI had ever trained, were fired as the anti-Indian forces in the government took control of the agency after an interregnum of a year and a half of a pro-Indian administration. On many other occasions various indigenists were fired, almost always for disagreeing with and contesting certain anti-Indian actions taken by FUNAI.

However, these people did not cease working with and on behalf of the Indians. They continued helping Indians to go to Brasília and submit their demands to FUNAI; they kept in touch with the media and denounced any action taken against the Indians; and they created nongovernmental organizations that financed economic projects directly applied to Indian lands. People began to talk of an "alternative indigenism," that is, the practice of working for the Indian cause apart from or parallel to the state and the church. As the Indian agency lost power in the state bureaucracy, several participants of this alternative indigenism felt they could eventually fulfill that role. Indeed, the late 1980s and early 1990s were the time when NGOs all over the world acquired a great reputation for doing work that the state could not longer do. It was thought, at any rate, that the state should not have a monopoly on indigenist action and that the current Indian policy should not be accepted as inevitable. Most of the alternative projects did not achieve the goals they set, because in general they lacked perseverance and continuity, and they suffered official opposition and disenfranchisement, as well.

What gave rise to alternative indigenism was obviously the feeling of despair over the prevailing official policy, but what motivated it at the personal level was, as it continues to be, the longing that indigenists and anthropologists feel to be around and work with Indians, to share at least partially in the pleasures offered by Indian cultures and the natural environment. Anyone who has lived in Indian villages and has carried out indigenist work knows how frustrating it is to be unable to continue with it, even as one takes into account all the unpleasantness and frustrations that come with such work. In this, both indigenists and anthropologists find a mutual identification of sentiments and purposes.

Daily Indian life contains joys and fulfillment but also suffering and frustrations. The high rates of infant mortality, calculated in the 1980s at around two hundred per thousand live births, and the destructive power of epidemics and other disasters violently affect the Indians in their daily existence. Furthermore, as one realizes that it is his or her own society that poses the most harmful threats to Indians, the anthropologist cannot avoid experiencing the terrible dilemma of being a broker in a situation in which she seeks comparative knowledge about a people who are massacred by her own people.

In the history of anthropology—which is a body of accumulating knowledge that has gained academic status since the creation of the first natural museums—many kinds of attitudes, theories, and opinions have been proposed to transcend these moral dilemmas. The most important one was the theory of evolution, which in its social and ethical development justified the disappearance of thousands of ethnies and millions of individuals in the name of the "struggle for survival." In the 1930s theories of social change and acculturation arose which also tried to placate the guilty conscience of anthropology and of our civilization regarding the continuing decrease in the population of the aboriginal peoples of the Americas and the Pacific Islands.

From the 1950s on, anthropology in Brazil and elsewhere began to look into this question and produced a clear argument about the political nature of the extermination of Indian peoples. Consequently, it developed an ideal of political engagement of this science and its practitioners with the destiny of the peoples who had been serving until then exclusively as objects of study. This ideal had, up to a point, a certain element of bad conscience: from the beginning it recognized its own uselessness, as the destiny of the Indians was seen in the most dismal of terms. The general understanding was that the Indians were condemned by the "inexorable march of civilization" sweeping across the globe, an inevitable phenomenon that was destroying and homogenizing all peoples and cultures. How could one fight such a force, and in Brazil, how could one fight the expansion of agrarian capitalism, mining companies, gold prospectors, and logging interests?

The most recent popular wave of sympathy and defense of Indians in Brazil began in the 1970s with this somewhat voluntary and unrealistic attitude. It grew with the support of other segments of civil society that were in opposition to the Medici presidency. As the military regime began to show signs of weakness—even as it adopted a policy of doing away with the Indian peoples by emancipating them from state tutelage and leaving them at the mercy of economic interests—the defense of the Indian won over a broad range of civil society, going beyond colleges and newspapers and reaching a surprisingly wide public. Between 1978 and 1982 people in Brazil became interested in what was going on with the Indians. I myself was once invited to speak about them to an audience of participants in a patron saint's feast in a small town in the interior of São Paulo state. Most people seemed to understand that the Indians' permanence in Brazil was a positive factor for the nation, no longer a cause for national shame or an example of social backwardness. They also understood that the incipient and fragile Brazilian democracy would only gain permanent roots if it were extended to all minorities, especially one that had irrefutable original, prehistoric rights to the land.

Associations and committees for the Indian cause began to sprout in almost all Brazilian capitals, from São Paulo to Rio Branco in the remote state of Acre. Anthropologists and indigenists were joined by journalists, lawyers, artists, and finally, politicians.

The new agenda of defense of Indian rights focused on the urgency for demarcation of Indian lands, which should, by law, have been concluded in November 1978. It had not been accomplished, obviously, and the wave of protest continued. The agenda also tried, although without much conviction, to include the points of self-determination, guided by the terms of the United Nations charter, and the concept of nation for the Indian ethnies. These points, however, never went beyond journalistic discourse and thus never received a more solid anthropological foundation. What was most successful in the anthropological agenda of those years was a concentration in historical studies on the reasons and causes of either the disappearance or the ethnic survival of Indian peoples. In these studies emphasis was placed on evaluating the economic factors and the political adjustments of the Indian ethnies vis-à-vis the encroaching society. Aspects such as change in religion or cultural adaptation, which had been previously considered more relevant in the studies of acculturation, were left aside.

Two other segments of civil society have also distinguished themselves in the defense of Indian rights in Brazil: journalists and lawyers. Many of the most relevant events in recent history, if they did not happen because of, at least achieved political significance due to the personal interventions of journalists and their coverage in the media. From the exotic image of the naked Indian—holding a bow and arrow, painted black, and looking cruel— Brazil began to hear of the Indian struggling for his/her rights, as the wise dweller of nature, the possessor of a vast body of knowledge about the environment, the bearer of an intricate and profound spiritual culture, the gentle educator of children, and so on. Many of the Indian leaders who have transcended their culture and have gained the respect of public opinion are the product not only of their individual iron wills but also of the good name journalists have established for them.

Much of what was done up until the 1990s in terms of demarcation of Indian lands has had the support of the press, its publicity, and its demands. When FUNAI and the civilian government of President Sarney set out their strategy to lessen the momentum of Indian support, one of the first areas to be targeted was journalism. The Indian agency made it a point in various ways to turn public events involving Indians into unflattering news, to implant false information in the media, and to divert public attention to curious and irrelevant topics. By the mid-1990s the Indian issue no longer held the attention of the public as it had in the early 1980s. The Indian agency certainly contributed to this turn of events, but Brazilians in general have lost interest in parallel issues, including the ecological one, due to frustration at not having had many of their aspirations and demands met as promised by the democratic regime.

Similar to journalists, who have a historical tradition of interest in the Indian issue at least since João Francisco Lisboa in the 1850s, Brazilian lawyers, including Perdigão Malheiro, for example, have also been interested in the issue for an equal length of time. In the most recent wave of sympathy and support for the Indian cause, they were responsible for the judicial defense of many individual Indians as well as Indian ethnies. They prepared the legal cases that argued for the unconstitutionality of the government emancipation project, defended the original rights of the Indians to their lands, and above all, accompanied step by step all the proceedings of dozens of suits brought against FUNAI in recent years: for negligence, bad faith, or inattention in its obligation to protect the Indians. Many distinguished lawyers publicly committed themselves to working with difficult and sensitive Indian lawsuits, in the certainty that they were contributing to the broadening of the rights of minorities and of citizens. Dozens of young lawyers threw themselves into the Indian struggle by becoming associated with civil and religious organizations. Many remain in this work, and one may say that at present they make up a more formal and juridically vital branch of the Brazilian style of indigenism. Together with anthropologists, indigenists, and Indian leaders, they may be able to propound new concepts and practices for a future Indian policy to come out of the articles of the 1988 Brazilian Constitution as ordinary legislation.

No one has any doubts today that without the full, legal, and concrete guarantee of their territory, there is no survival for the Indian. But no one is sure that this guarantee is enough. Health problems continue to be alarming, especially for the autonomous ethnies that are suddenly contacted either by economic frontiers or in a planned fashion by FUNAI. Moreover, the present form of relationship that the state maintains with the Indians, which can be designated as a kind of perverse paternalism, continues to inspire Indians with feelings of cultural frustration and social insecurity. The understanding that anthropology had gained concerning the Indians' situation and their chances for survival has begun to lose its perspicuity as new variables have gained greater weight in the interethnic equation. For example, timber exploitation and gold prospecting in some Indian areas indicate the possibility of a flow of cash that would have been unimaginable some years ago. What will happen when these Indians begin to enjoy the accumulation of wealth and acquire the insatiable consumer tastes of other peoples? Will they be able to keep their land resources out of the trade market?

These are new questions and new challenges posed by the present times, both to our anthropological science and to the Indians and their leaders who are rising up out of these new socioeconomic situations. The Indian movement, properly speaking, which also arose in the wake of the events that generated the indigenist movement, is the legitimate heir to the best consciousness that the Brazilian people might have toward them. This movement has already produced some important social and political effects on the Brazilian polity, of which the best known was undoubtedly the election of a Xavante Indian, Mário Juruna, to the National Congress. The founding of several Indian associations in the Amazon and nationwide, such as the Union of Indian Nations (UNI), was also a landmark of this movement. In the final chapter we shall discuss its political and anthropological relevance to the future of the Indians.

The Future of the Indians

If for many people the current situation of the Indians seems rather hopeless, what can we say about the future? As we look into the history of Brazil and propose to project it into the future, using as a point of reference a middle-of-the-road attitude of Brazilians and their political elites in relation to the Indians, we will certainly not arrive at an optimistic outlook about the Indians' destiny. If we wish to be optimistic with regard to a purported tendency that humanity is progressing and that the Brazilian people are becoming more tolerant, we can but consider ourselves naïve if we think that this will bring benefits to ethnic minorities. History does not march on account of these causes. Nonetheless, there are real motives for us to have some hopes for the Indians.

THE REVERSION OF THE HISTORICAL PROCESS

With amazement we have been witnessing and are hereby attempting to demonstrate that many Indian ethnies are beginning to see their populations grow after many years of constant decline. In some cases one can pinpoint the hand of the white people through the application of modern medicine, above all in the prevention of the most virulent and deadly epidemics that in the past swiftly took so many lives. No one dies anymore of smallpox, relatively few die of measles, tuberculosis and syphilis are curable, and leeches and bleeding are no longer applied to stop fevers and alleviate pains. It is true that malaria has been on the loose in the last thirty years, especially in the Amazon, and is causing a very high number of victims, some fatal, including many Indians. To take one example, among the 170 Xikrin of the Bacajá Indian land in Pará, there were more than 310 cases of malaria during a period of eight months in 1984, with at least ten deaths as a result. Many of the deaths among the Yanomami in the late 1980s and early 1990s were caused by malaria as well.[1] It also seems that the rates of malnutrition and infant mortality have risen among several Indian ethnies, particularly those that depend on hiring out their labor power to obtain money to buy food, since the lands left to them are not enough to support them. Flu epidemics are also increasingly potent among the recently contacted Indians, weakening them and sometimes causing considerable losses.[2] All the same, the difference is that today almost all of these health problems can be diagnosed and solved, which was not the case some years ago. The fear and terror that used to assail anthropologists and indigenists when they visited Indians in an early stage of contact—that they might be vectors of devastating epidemics, as had happened before—has ended. Today we know that when this happens it is not the fault of one individual, but of a policy of neglect in attending to these populations with simple medications, some teaching about prevention, and some nutritional assistance. In other words, we should know what to do when an Indian becomes ill, and if we do not always act in time it is for other reasons.

Medical progress, however, does not totally explain the reversion of the historical process of the disappearance of Indian ethnies. In fact, in the last fifty years, there have been several cases of ethnic survival that occurred without concurrent or previous medical attention. The Guató Indians of the upper Paraguay River and the Ofayé-Xavante of the Paranapanema plateau, both in Mato Grosso state, and several ethnies of Acre and Rondônia have survived after going through heavy reduction in their populations, without help from anyone. Moreover, for the great majority of surviving Indian ethnies, the quality of the medical assistance they receive cannot be classified as anything but precarious.

The general explanation for the phenomenon of survival may be related to three distinct but interconnected events. The first is the biological acquisition of antigens against diseases brought over from the Old World during five centuries of coexistence. Even among Indian ethnies who currently have no contact with persons integrated into Brazilian society, these antigens may be present, since these Indians are not isolated biological populations but have or have had contact with potential transmitters, generally neighboring Indian ethnies.

The second reason, also essentially biological in nature, has to do with the fact that many epidemics are now more or less under control and therefore appear less frequently in the Brazilian population, thus reducing the risk of contamination—or else, when an epidemic occurs, it strikes in a less potent way. This factor is due both to the expansion of mass vaccinations and to the general improvement in the conditions of hygiene and prevention all over the country.

The third factor is less concrete and somewhat conjectural. The phenomenon of ethnic historical reversion is taking place on a worldwide scale. It is happening to autochthonous and aboriginal populations in the Americas and the South Pacific, as well as in Africa, Asia, and Europe. The phenomenon, therefore, is of a transbiological character and has to do with a rearrangement of the cultural values of humanity as a whole. The political and military power of a few nations since the expansion of Western civilization, which spread its cultural values over the dominated nations and tended to create a homogenized culture everywhere, seems to be suffering a regression, for reasons as yet unclear. In China, Vietnam, the countries of the former Soviet Union, Italy, Spain, Sweden, Canada, and the United States—countries that encompass a significant diversity of political regimes and harbor many different cultural traditions, being composed of a dominant culture and dominated minorities—minorities have been holding firm and seem determined to preserve their values. They have waged a continuous fight to obtain more legal rights and social and political franchise within the social and political universe that encompasses them.

Although they are quite small in Brazil, Indian ethnies are also part of this phenomenon. Their demographic turnaround began in the mid-1950s, when this reversal had already happened to the Indians in the United States, but coincided with the demographic turnaround of the Australian Aborigines and other ethnic minorities in the Pacific Islands. It seems that we are beginning to witness a new period of ethnic affirmation and culture heterogenization. This phenomenon calls to mind what happened to the Roman Empire as it disintegrated into self-enclosed states and feudal communities; or one of the many periods of anarchy that have occurred during the cycles of centralization and decentralization in Chinese history. It may even be related to a human collective premonition concerning the difficulties through which humanity is passing because of problems it has itself engendered. In this case, humanity's diversification of cultural forms can be understood not only as an ethnic value in itself but also as a new factor to enhance its chance of survival. Whatever the case may be, Indian and aboriginal peoples all over the world are benefitting from these new times.

THE INDIAN MOVEMENT

As a consequence of their demographic turnaround and the new ways in which they have entered the consciousness of the Brazilian nation, since the late 1970s the Indians have been organizing themselves in political movements that have had some consequence in the Brazilian political arena. The political presence of Indians in Brazilian history is not exactly a novelty. It has occurred at various moments in the past, in alliance with other national forces, such as during the expulsion of the Dutch from the northeast, in the battles between the French and Portuguese for the conquest of Rio de Janeiro and São Luís do Maranhão, and during the war against Paraguay. This presence can also be noticed as a result of their own struggle against the Brazilian forces that oppressed them, such as in the Cabanagem Rebellion, the War of the Barbarians, the Canudos Rebellion, and thousands of other more restricted occasions. Indian heroes range from Araribóia and Felipe Camarão to Ajuricaba, Janduí, and Crespim Leão. During the Dutch period Indians participated in a parliament that the Dutch ruler Mauricius of Nassau convened to better administer Pernambuco and the other conquered provinces.

However, beginning with the empire and during the republic, a mode of relationship was established between the Brazilian state and the Indians that reduced the latter to the condition of legal minors, which meant they were conceived of and treated as children. With this farcical form of paternalism, the Indians were heard only with condescension and arrogance; their thinking came to be understood as unimportant, and the understanding of their reality was transferred to others, to the authorities, the indigenists, and anthropologists. Thus the current appearance of Indians on the national public scene has meant a great victory for the Indians in general—personal victories indeed, but also conceptual and political advances in national interethnic relations.

It has become clear that the Indians do not need spokespeople or intermediaries to communicate with authorities and the public. The physical presence of Indian leaders and their understanding and acquiescence to certain issues have become sine qua nons of any agreement that FUNAI strikes with other government agencies or with private parties. Their folkloric manners, in which difficulties with the Portuguese language and uniqueness of attitudes are characteristic marks, have come to be perceived as the accouterments of a different but real people, of political beings integrated in their own cultures, although not completely with ours. It is fair to say that in the minds of average Brazilians the Indians have become real thinking persons. Their social and political problems, particularly the need to have their lands secured and to have their health covered in some way, have become the most important items in the Indian issue.

The ongoing relationship between Indian leaders exposed to public scrutiny and their people back home confers on them an ethnic and a moral legitimacy to become their representatives before the political arena. It also gives them an unmatched clearheadedness about the political nature of the problems they face. On the other hand, it may be fair to say that the press, organized civil society, and Brazilians of all regions have come to grasp this new interethnic situation and the Indians' political advance. Furthermore, it seems that they are in favor of it. Such was the case at least in the early 1980s, when the process of redemocratization was taking place in the country. In Rio de Janeiro state this new view of the Indians was expressed in the voting in of Chief Mário Juruna as a representative to the National Congress.

The Indian movement rose in response to the same issues that were being trumpeted by the indigenist movement, that is, the defense of Indian lands, concern with health assistance and education, and the proposition of self-determination for Indian ethnies. Its most ambitious political achievement was the creation of the Union of Indigenous Nations (UNI). In 1979 a group of Indians from several ethnies, but mainly Terena, Tukano, Bakairi, and Xinguano, met at Aquidauana, in Mato Grosso do Sul state, to found a pan-Indian organization for the defense of their rights. It immediately gained the support of all the civil associations defending Indian rights and other NGOs with similar goals in Brazil and in other countries. Its program tried to bring together all Indian ethnies to a common front for self-defense and affirmation before the Brazilian state and nation. However, less than a year later UNI was facing internal problems and dissension, as it attempted to keep a balance of power and a genuine union of interests among its members. Dialogue among such varied types of Indian ethnies was difficult, particularly when economic interests were at play. Cultural diversity implies other forms of diversity, which hampers the chances for bringing together specific interests that require short-term solution.[3] In response to this diversity UNI divided itself according to the main five regions of the country. In the last few years only the southern branch and the Acre branch (not the whole northern Amazon) have been able to maintain a minimum of organization and political activity.

From the beginning FUNAI reacted rather negatively to UNI and made it clear that it opposed the idea that the Indians have a right to organize themselves. On various occasions it prohibited the Indians from promoting meetings of leaders, and at no time did it have a positive dialogue with UNI and its leadership. FUNAI hoped that by not treating UNI with respect, it would keep UNI from solidifying its position as a legitimate vehicle for Indian demands. UNI's isolation from the public arena is real only in the sense that it lacks concrete economic and strategic means for carrying out political action to promote a pan-Indian ideology in Brazil. Several of its leaders and founders ended up returning to their personal affairs, taking care to maintain their leadership among their peoples and waiting for a better time to position themselves in the broader political scenario. This option preserves the sentiment that an Indian leadership only makes sense if the leader keeps in direct and constant contact with his people, a kind of connection that very few members of congress keep with his or her constituents.

In the 1990s new Indian organizations were formed everywhere. Practically every Indian ethnie now has its own NGO. Several of them have been set up with the help of anthropologists and indigenists working for NGOs, in some cases for the purposes of obtaining economic help from foreign NGOs and even the World Bank. A few have been able to aggregate regionally, such as the associations of ethnies of the Rio Negro region and Roraima state. One or two have been able to follow the example of UNI and take in members from different ethnies and different regions. The most successful of them as of 1999 was CAPOIB, a group of ethnies from the Amazonian states that had the support of the Catholic Council of Indigenist Missionaries (CIMI).

The Juruna Phenomenon

Mário Juruna is a Xavante Indian who as a child had never seen a white man. His fearless and autonomous people had maintained themselves against the advance of Brazilian civilization until the mid-1940s, when an SPI pacification team made the first friendly contact with one of the Xavante bands. Before that meeting, the Xavante attacked any expedition that entered their territory and had in fact massacred an SPI team under the command of Lieutenant Pimentel Barbosa, killing all but one of its participants. The SPI spirit of "die if need be, never kill" was working. The "pacification" of the Xavante resulted in a relatively small drop of 10 percent in their population, decreasing from an estimated 2,000 in 1946 to 1,750 in 1955. From then on, their population began to rise, even among those who had been transferred from their original territory to more distant lands. The overall purpose of this pacification was to open an entire pristine region of savannas and brush forests to new settlers, including ranchers and land speculators. As the Xavante began to recover from the cultural and biological shock resulting from this sort of confrontation between cultures, they began to realize that they were surrounded by new ranches and roads and the sudden rise of villages and towns. Without feeling defeated—in fact quite the contrary, since the terms implied in the pacification accord stipulated that there should be material aid in the form of donations of manufactured goods—the Xavante in the early 1970s rose up to demand the demarcation of their lands.

Mário Juruna then appeared on the scene. Since the late 1950s he had been leaving his village and wandering off to work as a peon on the neighboring ranches, experiencing the life of a poor Brazilian peasant. He began to make longer trips to other parts of the country, with a characteristic drive and disposition that soon distinguished him among other Indians who were doing the same. He began to be noticed by anthropologists and by indigenists. He discovered the good use he could make of the tape recorder and began to record the talks and the promises that Brazilian authorities would make to him. Later he would confront them for what they had promised but not done. Eventually the press discovered him, and Juruna rose to the level of a celebrity, raising the expectations of those who sympathized with the Indian cause.[4]

His great step forward occurred when the PDT (Democratic Labor Party) in the state of Rio de Janeiro accepted his candidacy for the National Congress and promoted him as legitimate representative of all oppressed people. In an historic campaign, Juruna was elected with 31,000 votes in 1982. He obtained votes from many districts of Rio de Janeiro, both rich and poor. Half of them came from people from the lower-income Baixada and western part of Rio de Janeiro, who saw in him a kind of personification of down-to-earth bravery and determination. His presence in the National Congress had enormous repercussions in the country. He was responsible for the creation of a Permanent Commission on the Indian, one of the few commissions in the house of representatives, which meant the elevation of the Indian issue to formal recognition by the Brazilian congress. However, by the end of his second year in congress, Juruna began to lose prestige among his peers and to get bad publicity for inappropriate behavior, such as borrowing money, not paying restaurant bills, and taking advantage of his position to harass people. He disastrously and against the advice of his close friends and staff committed himself to the presidential campaign of the candidate of the PDS (Democratic Social Party), which had provided political support for the military regime. He recanted, called a press conference, and returned to a PDS supporter the money he had received from the group. It was a national scandal that helped turn people against the PDS and its candidate, but it did not help Juruna when he tried for a second term in the 1986 election. He lost, winning only a little more than 10,000 votes.

During the period in which his prestige was high, Mário Juruna was seen as a legitimate representative of his people, and by extension of all the Indians of Brazil. He was esteemed and respected by many people, as could be seen in the enthusiasm he generated when he spoke in the nationwide 1985 campaign for the reinstitutionalization of direct elections for the presidency of the Republic (which had been abolished during the military regime). He was often invited to give speeches to all sorts of associations as well as at anthropological meetings. He represented to many a voice that came from a place of sincerity and generosity, a voice the country needed badly in the final years of the military regime. For others, however, Juruna was an oddity and posed a challenge to the nation's establishment. He was considered an unwanted person, even a political liability, and they would not pardon him for having reached such a high political position.

At any rate, it was not exclusively due to personal faux pas that Juruna lost the position he had won, nor can it be said that he will not someday be recognized as a hero of our times. In moving from the position of leader of his people, a defender of concrete causes, to a generic leader of a heterogeneous collection of peoples—as he intended—and of less tangible causes, Juruna's sense of self-worth and self-service rose above what is allowed for an Indian leader. He became somewhat arrogant, a behavior never condoned in popular leaders anywhere in the world. At the same time, by the mid-1980s the Indian cause had begun to lose credibility with public opinion, both because of people's general frustration that their social problems were not being resolved (as still happens with many social issues, such as education, health care, and agrarian reform) and because of the harsh campaign raised by the right-wing media to demoralize Indian leaders in Brazil. This kind of campaign has been endorsed by many of FUNAI's staff, as it seeks to reduce the political impact of the legitimate claims of the Indians by transforming them into demands and requests for personal favors. In this treacherous context, Juruna was overcome.[5]

In several capitals around the country other Indian leaders arose in the wake of these events. Most of them are known only in their states, and their political activities are restricted to the concrete causes of their peoples. Several have appeared with such personal force that, in the battles they fought with opposing forces—absentee landowners, timber interests, and mining prospectors—they have ended by sacrificing their own lives. Ângelo Cretã, the Kaingang chief from Mangueirinha in Paraná; Marçal Tupã-i, a Guarani leader from Mato Grosso do Sul; Simão, a Bororo of Meruri Indian Land in Mato Grosso; Mateus and Alcides Lopes, both Guajajara from Maranhão, and many others were assassinated for political motives and today are on the roll of heroes of the Indian cause. None of these crimes has been solved, a surprise to no one in Brazil.

In the last ten years or so a new crop of young Indian leaders has arisen, and many have decided to live in the cities, where they think they can best develop political activities. In the elections of 1990, 1994, 1996, and 1998 a number of Indian candidates appeared in the cities of Manaus, Boa Vista, Rio Branco, Campo Grande, Goiânia, and even Brasília, but none were able to repeat Juruna's feat. The Terena Indians of Mato Grosso do Sul, who have a long, intense experience in urban living, since several of their villages are located on the outskirts of the towns of Dourados, Aquidauana, and other smaller towns, have elected city council members and state legislature members from among their peers. This situation has conferred on them a new kind of bargaining power in the political arena of those towns, as well as in relation to FUNAI. Together with the Xavante, the Kayapó, the Xinguano, and some Amazonian ethnies, they exert, together or separately, an ever-growing political influence. It remains to be seen how much they can impel the formation of a pan-Indian conscience in the future, either in a general association or by action within the Indian agency.

Many Indians who live in cities do so temporarily as part of their formal upbringing, which may include a period of studies outside of their villages. They learn the white people's ways and discourses and sometimes take upon themselves the task of being spokespersons for their people. But they can have the legitimacy to do so only when representation is granted by their own people, not by the level of coverage they temporarily achieve in the media. Indians with no formal education have achieved notoriety by their firm position in defense of concrete demands, always founded on the support of their people back home. This combination has happened with Txukarramãe chief Raoni, whose power of influence already transcends the limits of his people and is beginning to gain command over other Xinguano ethnies, such as the Tkikão, the Kubenkrakem, the Suyá, and even the

Xinguano ethnies of the upper Xingu river, such as the Kamayurá and Yawalapiti. Raoni has been working to become closer to his Kayapó relatives to the north, in an attempt to create a Kayapó nation, uniting all their areas into one sole territory—a new Indian area connecting the Upper Xingu Park with the lands already demarcated for the Gorotire and other Kayapó bands to the north. This area of land is presently the largest of all Indian lands, comprising some 11 million hectares. This is also the dream of other peoples, such as the Xavante, the Nambiquara, the Munduruku, the Timbira, the Tikuna and so on, but the difficulties are immense and other steps impose themselves as priorities.

The personal sagas of Indian leaders deserve special attention. Sheer will has been in many cases the drive that made them rise above their peers, but we must place them in the wider Indian movement and seek to understand them in terms of what they can add to the consolidation of a pan-Indian vision and a true integration of interests and union of ethnic polities. In this respect we should not lose sight of the social contexts out of which the urgency of their demands arises, such as the demarcation of lands, medical assistance, education and its bicultural purposes, and the increase in productivity of their economies. In the midst of these legitimate collective claims there are also the very personal demands that each leader inevitably makes and that sometimes take precedence over the collective claims. Many people are taken aback when they see Indian leaders making petty demands for themselves, as if they should be unpolluted by personal needs.

The activities of Indians in the Brazilian political arena in recent years has already generated positive results, despite their short history. They are heard by congress and by the media, and generally people feel that they can articulate their needs themselves. One cannot suppose, however, that these advances will easily become permanent. The diversity of Indian situations and their needs can be manipulated by the state, if it so wishes, to fragment the Indian movement and dilute its collective claims into personal wishes, favoring specific groups and even pitting one group against another. In fact, this has been happening since the late 1980s and has brought about considerable damage to the Indian cause in the public opinion.

It would be naïve to suppose that the Indian movement, in the political context of present-day Brazil, could simply take off and exist on its own. It is part of the broader movement of Brazilian society in its struggle to consolidate and expand political and social democracy, and in that it is but a minor partner. The other segments of our society that identify with these purposes have the duty to continue helping the Indian movement—understanding it better, dialoguing with it at both the individual and collective levels, and bringing it closer to the complexity in which the Brazilian political life is experienced. The Indian movement will have a chance to grow as it progressively increases its knowledge of the reality outside, and finds allies there.

THE REACTION TO CAPITALIST EXPANSION

The Indians will probably not be the power that will slow down the hegemonic advance of capitalism *urbi et orbi,* but it is precisely in the Amazon that the greatest challenge to the capitalist mode of production is taking place, hitting hard at its main engine: profitmaking. In-depth studies are lacking, but there are strong indications in scattered ecological, sociological, and economic analyses, partial though they may be, that agricultural production in the Amazon does not generate the rates of profits needed to repay the capital invested. This becomes most evident in the middle stages of the establishment of an agribusiness, since at first everything seems to produce a fantastic return.[6]

The Brazilian economic model has increased its level of concentration of capital in all sectors, especially in agricultural production, during the last forty years. Cattle ranches and plantations have been established in many regions of the Amazon, and the model used has been one of large-scale production. A Brazilian company, C. R. Almeida, claims to own more than 4 million hectares of land in the state of Pará alone. Another, owned by a former U.S. millionaire, Daniel Ludwig, with titles claiming over 3 million hectares, became in the 1970s and 1980s the paradigmatic example of the effort to concentrate capital in the Amazon, and at the same time, of the failure of that effort.[7] The myriad projects tried out by the Ludwig enterprise include the adaptation of new strands of rice, experimenting with an Asian softwood tree, the building of a cellulose factory, timber harvesting, and the mining of kaolin. Over more than twenty years of exploitation, only mining activities have yielded a profit. The extensive cattle ranches, sugar mills, and the gigantic plantations of rice, coffee, cacao, manioc, and corn in the majority of cases did not return the invested capital after two or three years. Other such huge investments in the Amazon have proven to be equally unprofitable in the medium run and totally unsustainable in the long run.

Therefore, it has been only at the cost of huge public investments that in the end bring no return and by means of fiscal incentives that capitalism has been able to set itself up in the Amazon. What is maintained there is a hybrid and perverse form of oligarchic capitalism, if I may use the expression, in which its agents sustain themselves through the continuous ingestion of public resources, and dominate, with their political power—like the landlords of yesteryear—the masses of the destitute who make up the population, as if they were servants of the manor.

Capitalism and the application of modern science and technology have conquered and dominated almost all the environments of planet Earth: from the fertile plains of Europe to the American deserts, the Canadian tundra, the mountains and the seas, and even up to the frozen poles. In the Amazonian tropical forests, its mode of production runs up against the fragility and interrelatedness of the ecological system, which reject the usual production techniques. This is true for agriculture and ranching. In mining, minerals being abundant and dispersed, the modes of production in the region—ranging from the use of gigantic machinery to antiquated forms of panning, and with the production force diversified among businesses and autonomous workers—investments bring ample returns. But this happens because mining production is based on a very low cost of labor power. Miners, particularly of gold found on river beds, in general work under extremely bad conditions in isolated and unhealthy places, under irregular and unstable contracts. Their style of work, driven by the illusion of striking it rich, seems to be based on a pact of life or death, depending on whether they have good or bad luck. If there were towns around, some kind of organized urban life, could there be the *garimpos* in the form in which they exist today? Certainly not, because then costs would rise, the profit rate would substantially diminish, and the system could only be maintained through enormous pressure. Therefore, even mining, which brings such high yields to its investors, if it were used to develop the region, would have problems in sustaining a capitalistic social formation in the Amazon.

Given these considerations, we should not have high hopes that mining or even agriculture and ranching ventures will leave the Amazon in the future and that the capital behind them will be withdrawn—that would be expecting too much of the low political rationality on which lie policies of development in Brazil. Nonetheless, we may affirm that the situation of the Indian and the Amazon is not as hopeless as some people believe, for several reasons. In the first place, the impetus and motivation that have driven this mode of production for forty years have diminished in potency and in will—not only because they have worn out politically, but mainly because they do not bring the expected returns, no matter how favorable the political conditions of their application have been. The Amazon is, in fact, an irremovable, solid obstacle to the expansion of capitalism, both in its geography and ecology and in its socioeconomic system. In the second place, we can see everywhere in the Amazon the signs of the useless devastation that these investments have caused. Immense areas have been cleared of forest, and what is left is the ugly emptiness of a new environment that is unsustainable. Much of the original investments made from the 1960s through the 1980s have withdrawn, and those that remain slumber over their poor results as if awaiting the arrival of new fiscal incentives and the possibility of future speculation. In the third place, which particularly interests us here, the invasion and despoiling of Indian lands in the Amazon have decreased considerably since the late 1980s, both for economic reasons and because of resistance by the Indians.

As illustration we may use the example of the Pindaré Valley, an Amazonian region in the state of Maranhão that was opened up for colonization and exploitation practically only in the late 1950s. In the following forty years this region was inundated by both poor landless peasants and cattle ranchers. The latter came with titles to huge lots of land and with capital from fiscal incentives to set up farms and ranches and in the process to displace those already installed there.[8] The colonization included no less than the lands of Guajajara and Guajá Indians, and in consequence many villages were abandoned and the lands taken over by these invading migrants.

The surviving Indians took refuge in other Indian areas. By the late 1960s it seemed that the Indians would be left landless. After a few years, however, the ranches were faring poorly, and the wealth of the region did not increase proportionally to the number of people. In the mid-1980s the Carajás Railroad crossed the Pindaré Valley and produced relief from the dire situation in which most people were living, but it was not enough to establish productive activities and real economic development. This was bad for the poor settlers, but it was good for the Indians. A sizable portion of the territories of the Guajajara and Guajá were demarcated and protected, and since then they have not been substantially affected by new developments.[9]

The same may be said for other regions, such as the middle Xingu, the Tapajós, the regions encompassed by the stillborn northern Amazon highway, and others. However, in Rondônia, where the soil is richer, and in the areas of *cerrado*, instead of forests (whose soils can be improved by chemical applications and techniques), agricultural and ranching ventures seem to be advancing and taking root. It seems that in these regions the capitalist mode of production may have indeed overcome the difficulties imposed by the ecosystem.

In contrast to the capitalist mode of production we may posit the Indian mode of production as a factor that will enhance the chances of survival of these populations in the future. It is characterized by the collective use of the land and its resources, the application of a system of rotation and spacing of crops, and it is motivated by principles of self-sustainability instead of profit. Variations and innovations on this system may be arranged to help guarantee the sustainability of many non-Indian peoples in the future, without destroying the Amazon in the process. The Indian can in this way become a partner in a process of an integrated and permanent, sustained development.

The Ecological Rationale

What is most ambitious in the ecological rationale is the hypothesis that biological evolution and, by extension, human evolution are enhanced by the richness and variability of existing forms and their potential for adapting to all sorts of ecological niches, including those that are or will be undergoing change. What is most interesting to note in this new way of seeing the evolutionary process is its emphasis not on the intensity of specialization of a species but on the potential for generalization. With regard to human populations and their cultures, the capacity for diversification is what would count most. The paradigmatic example of evolution is thus no longer a mammal (such as the horse, so often used in textbooks) or the ubiquitous cockroach (that unanimously regarded success in evolution), but instead the flowering plants, with their myriad species filling specific as well as undifferentiated niches in an apparent redundancy of forms, an apotheosis of the baroque in nature. These plants have in themselves the potential for change according to changes in their ecosystems.[10]

The scientific bases of the ecological or environmentalist movement are founded on this reasoning. It is ironic that the parts of the world where the movement has greatest political clout, Europe and the United States, are precisely where there is a high concentration of human specialization. The environmentalist movement arises from and grows through the dialectic of the social process in which it is inserted. Its sympathy for the needs of minorities in undeveloped countries, the Indian ethnies, for example, is motivated as much by this desire for human diversification, which is felt to be lacking in the developed countries, as by ethical reasons and internal political purposes.

In Brazil, the ecological movement came out of the same general ethical concerns that are dominant elsewhere. But its raison d'être is based on internal politics, particularly on the rise of a new middle class that craves a new ideology. To establish organic roots in the country, the movement will have to face the social and cultural problems of the present times and bring new propositions to integrate them. Its principal test has been the elaboration of a model for the integrated development of the Amazon and the Brazilian regions with endemic poverty, where the various models that have been applied have not worked. This is not a task for one movement alone, but for a generation, and that is how this movement should be understood.

Although the Indians do not deliberately participate in the ecological movement, they are not simply one of its goals or objects of reflection. In fact, they constitute one of its basic foundations, as living examples of the human generalist potential, as tested experiments of cultures that exist in some kind of balance with the environment. They can be considered the main partners in the possible integrated development of the Amazon region, for two basic reasons. The first is that they offer the example of being the most experienced managers of the tropical ecological complex and the most trusted guardians of that natural heritage. In this sense, we know that many areas of the Amazon have not been destroyed in the last few years because the varied economic attempts to do so ran up against the Indians. The second reason is that the living Indian societies and cultures constitute the basic potential for the appearance of new social forms of living in the Amazon. For four hundred years the adaptation of European civilization to the tropics has been guided by Indian cultural items and social institutions, through techniques of production, forms of socialization of production and distribution of goods, and the subtle capacity for balancing the level of production with social satisfaction. The hundreds of small Amazonian communities, made up mostly of descendants of Indians, *tapuios,* and freed blacks, are the outcome of this original Indian potential, and their social satisfaction would be more complete if these communities were understood as viable models and not as relics of past eras.

The ecological movement was responsible for the establishment among many people of a new way of thinking as well as of feeling, a new sense of reality. Business, the state, and of course the World Bank are outwardly convinced that the ecological principles are correct and that what is needed is to determine the proper means to develop and apply them to concrete reality. This new sense of reality may appear to be a wave or fashion, but it is not and must not be temporary. The Indians, in their own way, are also part of this sense of reality, although it is not entirely clear how they can help consolidate it in the spheres of government and private investment.

BRAZILIAN NATIONALISM

In the defense of Indians, Brazilians and foreigners come together as one, mobilized by common interests and ideals. One should therefore not identify a nationalistic pro-Indian ideology in opposition to a foreign one, but as a specific variety of the general Western view of the Indian. Nationalism in Brazil, as indeed in any other country, means the political upshot of the sentiment of nationality. It entails the set of ideas, ideals, biases, and aspirations that have been building through history and are shared by the great majority of the population. This great majority is not homogenous in any way, nor even coherent, but divided and many times in confrontation. Nevertheless they bring to an arena of dispute and conciliation whatever opposing attitudes and ideas that exist. For this very reason, the sentiment of nationality is not a static reality, not a consensus of opinions, but a field of battle in a constant quest for balance.[11] Things that were understood in one way in the past may today be understood differently. Properly speaking, there is not a progressive evolution of positive factors in this sentiment, but instead a construction and adaptation through historical events and new historic syntheses.

The sentimental and conceptual integration of the Indian into Brazilian nationality, as we have seen in previous chapters, is an exemplary case of the constitution of Brazilian nationalist thinking. The Indian first appeared as part of the nation through the intellectual and political works of José Bonifácio de Andrade e Silva around 1819, and later on at the onset of the second imperial regime in the 1840s. The idea was contested by the conservatives of the times and defended by liberal and romantic writers of the mid-nineteenth century. By the end of that century the idea that the Indians were part of the formation of the Brazilian nation had been incorporated through the adamant insistence of the positivists. Whether as minors or as full citizens, the Indians' ethnic continuity or extinction continues to be a question in the minds of most Brazilians. Many doubts still linger about whether or not they can achieve self-determination or social assimilation, and whether or not they are economically and culturally viable in modern times.

In a general appraisal, however, we may safely conclude that the idea that the Indian is Brazilian—is part of and has rights to the democratic franchises forming the Brazilian nation-state—is an indisputable aspect of the modern-day sentiment of Brazilian nationalism. There are exceptions to this, but we may affirm that Brazil as a whole no longer is ashamed of including Indians in its self-conception, of being, in fact, part Indian. This is a real advance and the real meaning of the integration of the Indian into the greater nation. Nonetheless, the survival of the Indian is a question that is not yet totally resolved. There is still much prejudice and many opposing ideas in a major portion of the Brazilian dominating elites, sentiments that are motivated fundamentally by immediate economic interests, but also by mistaken notions and elitist beliefs about who the Brazilian people are. People who share and express these feelings are the Indians' declared enemies, and they are being fought on all battlefronts.

A RUGGED ROAD TO SURVIVAL

The 1988 Brazilian Constitution recognized the Indians both as individuals and social groups, with full rights of citizenship as well as special rights as a minority. The main debates waged by the various political factions and parties to define the position of the Indian in the nation had to do with what the Indians constituted socially and what specific rights they could enjoy. From behind the scenes the military vetoed the possibility of Indian ethnies being considered either as nations or distinct peoples. In the end, the best consensual term found among congressmen was "society," still far from a fair acknowledgment of what Indians are socially. Article 322 defines who the Indians are, the role of the state in regard to them, and their special position juridically. Section 2 states that natural resources found on their lands, particularly mineral and hydroelectric potential, can be used only after permission is granted by the National Congress. The executive branch of the state continues to have the responsibility for the well-being of Indian societies and the protection of their lands (which remain as inalienable lands of the union with exclusive use by the Indians). Article 323 states that the Public Ministry, a fourth power in the Brazilian power system, has the obligation of representing the Indians, upon request by any Indian individual or society, before the judicial system. In the transitory provisions of that constitution, it was established that the state had five years to conclude the demarcation of all Indian lands. The deadline came and went in October 1993, and there are still some 20 to 30 percent of Indian lands not provided for legally through the guarantee of the state. It is not surprising that this problem lingers, but responsibility for it must be heavily charged to every federal administration in the past fifty years, including in a very disappointing fashion the last democratic ones.

All things considered, neither the Indians nor the rest of the Brazilian people should count on the good intentions of any government toward the defense of the Indians. This is true not only because there is undoubtedly an immense gulf between what is legal and what is real in Brazil, but also because the social and economic factors that we have identified throughout this book as either the positive or negative causes of the Indians' extermination or survival are neither exhausted nor stationary in time. They are quite alive, although not always clearly discernible, and should rather be subjected to continuing evaluations. In addition, the current makeup of the Indian question, though seemingly positive for the Indians in many aspects, contains the seeds for potentially dangerous turns of events.

The most ominous of these pressing factors is mining on Indian lands, particularly on those that remain to be demarcated. After considerable debate, the 1988 Constitution allowed mining on Indian lands subject to the approval of both the Indian ethnies and the National Congress. However, gold prospecting continues to take place on several Indian lands without so much as the acknowledgment of the congress. Should these wayward and indiscriminate practices continue, one may foresee the rapid depletion of these resources, the devastation of the environment, alterations in the sizes of Indian areas, forced transference of Indians, dissemination of new diseases and epidemics, delay in demarcating recognized Indian lands, physical violence against the Indians and vice versa, and finally all kinds of attempts to corrupt and bribe Indian leaders and communities.

The corruption of Indians and Indian leaders is a practice that points to a much broader social phenomenon that includes other forms of social co-optation and domination of one society over another. Money has the notorious capacity of changing the behavior of most individuals who are not under an explicit discipline to the contrary. The Indians are in this sense regular folks who follow the general guidelines of their culture, while at the same time seeking to affirm themselves as singular individuals. They only start to covet goods obtainable with money when their culture becomes enveloped by the influence of these goods, and, in the final analysis, when they become politically dependent on the dominant society. Therefore one cannot simply attribute to the conscience of the individual whether he or she can be corrupted by money, as is normally supposed, but to the conditions in which his or her society is coopted by a more powerful society.

The examples we have today of this phenomenon, above all in areas of placer mining or timber exploitation, indicate that this coopting is very intense and embraces broad segments of these Indian societies, not merely their leaders. The collective anxiety for affirmation of these ethnies in the Brazilian regional world is more easily filled by imitating and absorbing values of consumption than by reaffirming traditional values of the Indian societies. Some think it ridiculous when an Indian wears jeans and flaunts a wristwatch and dark glasses, but this is not much different from a Brazilian who plays rock, eats hamburgers, and wears tennis shoes in the Rio de Janeiro summer. We may interpret the two events as simple examples of the phenomenon of cultural diffusion, or of a dialogue between cultures, or as a form of participating in the development of a global culture—even as cultural alienation. The difference lies only in the way these cultural loans are absorbed by the other culture, with what intensity, in what historical and psychosocial moment, and finally, to what political end. The major difference between the Brazilian example compared with the Indian case is that one is a society with 160 million people and the other is made up of societies with populations of no more than a few thousand individuals, in some cases, of a few hundred, which gives them an enormous disadvantage and fragility.

In no other moment of Brazilian history has an Indian society seen such a chance of obtaining so much money as now, in areas where mineral deposits are found. It is rather tempting to enjoy the allurements of civilization without making any great effort, by simply living off the royalties from minerals found on one's lands. How will the Brazilian congress legislate this matter so that the Indians do not give themselves totally over to this distortion? For many Indian ethnies it would certainly be a most irresponsible and pointless risk to allow mining operations on their lands, not only for ecological reasons but for economic ones, as well. In most cases, Indian lands should rather be considered *strategic reserves,* and should be left untouched for a certain number of years until deemed feasible and culturally useful in the future. The scattered deposits of minerals in the Amazon region allow us to suppose that, through rational and non-devastating planning, the country should be well served with minerals for the next hundred years without having to exhaust all of its mineral sources. By combining this principle with the intention of recognizing the cultural value of Indian ethnies for the future of Brazil, perhaps the state would realize the importance of maintaining these mineral deposits untouched.

There is very little chance that such a suggestion will ever be taken seriously. What we can more realistically hope for is that many of these mineral reserves—except gold and diamonds—will have less importance in the future and that their exploitation might not be profitable under present conditions of technology and social expectations.

Another factor that might bring potential complications to the Indians is the difficulty in procuring for them a commensurate political participation in Brazil. At first sight it would seem that the Indians could have two entries into political participation. One is through their specific institutions, that is, their ethnic or pan-ethnic political organizations; the other through the state apparatus, that is, by representation within the Indian agency. In both cases the Indians still need the help of the state in advancing their positions within the Brazilian commonality. One cannot think about casting off the responsibility of the state, especially because of the autonomous ethnies. As a third entry one might think that it would be advantageous for the Indians to have a presence in the National Congress, as occurred in the 1980s. Since we do not live in a corporativist state, this possibility is reduced, and will probably occur only sporadically. It is therefore necessary to have official mechanisms within congress for hearing the Indians, not only because of the nature of their claims, but also because of what they may be able to contribute to the nation. The house of representatives' Chamber of Deputy Committee on the Environment, Consumer Protection, and Minorities is the present forum that hears Indians out and attempts to take measures on their behalf, although the executive branch does not necessarily follow through on their recommendations.

All the same, even if these channels become available, there will still be considerable difficulty in making viable in the Brazilian political arena a pan-Indian *representation*. The Indians themselves, perhaps with some help from anthropologists, should make their sense of representation effective in order to work out the meaning of what would be a fair balance of interests for all Indian ethnies. This is indeed a hard task, given the cultural and economic diversity present among the 220 Indian ethnies of today. This problem makes it difficult to create a pan-Indian political mentality and generate authentic forms of political organization. As it is, with the fierce competition for the scanty resources that the state bestows upon them, it is rather easy for the anti-Indian forces to manipulate opposing interests, exacerbate enmities, and use certain ethnies or individual leaders to further anti-Indian sentiments. This problem has been the most pervasive of all and is by far the hardest one to fight. It was the reason that the Indian peoples historically lost the war of defense against the Portuguese invasion. It is thus a real tragedy that, besides their traditional enemies, the Indians have within their ranks equally strong enemies whenever they are incapable of joining forces—but in this they are not unique.

Conclusion: The Tensions in a Possibility

If it is true that each era asks itself the questions it can answer, ours, with regard to the Indians, is not very sure about the true question it must ask itself. During the last three decades it regretted, but considered as certain, that the Indians would not survive the expansion of Western civilization, the hegemony of capitalism, and the development of the country, as if these were three stumbling blocks in the Indians' path. Anthropologists tried to explain this phenomenon, which had been unfolding for the past five hundred years, by comparing it with other examples found in history and by reducing it to the level of an episode, albeit regrettable, in the evolution of humanity. They produced a varied set of interpretations and explanations all going back to the Enlightenment, which constitute what I have called the *paradigm of acculturation.* Its underlying logic rests on the premise that human cultures and societies change and evolve in the same way as other species in nature. The struggle for survival is the constant dispute between peoples who are different or unequal, the victory of one over the defeat of the other. By this logic there is no escape for the weaker, the less militarized societies, and that is why so many historians and anthropologists have decreed—too quickly—the end of so many Indian ethnies that are now surviving.

The Indian ethnies have survived, but clearly not in definitive terms. No one may be so enthusiastic as to think that the tripling of the populations of dozens of Indian ethnies in the past forty years is the sign of permanent success. There have been occasions in Brazilian history when such a phenomenon occurred, only to revert some years later to a previous situation or to an even worse one. Such happened, for example, with the *tapuio* communities of the lower Amazon, which increased their numbers between 1760 and 1836 only to be destroyed by the Cabanagem Rebellion. Such was also the case of the acculturated Indian villages that were extinguished in the middle of last century, a time when many had reached a reasonable level of demographic and social stability. Many other Indian ethnies that had grown and expanded into the demographic vacuums left by the extinction of other ethnies also experienced losses in population and in social autonomy, such as the Guajajara, between 1880 and 1950, and many Carib peoples of the Jauaperi Valley around the same time.

Population increases provoke new needs and bring about new demands, sometimes of different natures. The need for more lands, as is the case with all Indian ethnies in the northeast, Minas Gerais, Mato Grosso do Sul, and the southern states of Brazil, fits in with the traditional culture and social organization of these expanding ethnies. The need for more land arises as a natural consequence of a traditional mode of production. But the need for money and manufactured goods is a sign of a structural change, or, in the most favorable hypothesis, of difficulties with economic adaptation to the demands imposed by the etiquette of interethnic relations. Wearing shoes in towns, for example, is required by this etiquette in no uncertain terms.

When this need occurs in the Amazon region, among other demands for survival and adaptation to exogenous pressures, one has to be cautious about what is on the horizon for these peoples. Whether we call it an acculturation factor, a process of producing a mixed racial grouping (*caboclização*), a demand of the prevailing form of interethnic relations, the integration into the national economic system, a dialogue between peoples and cultures, or the human need to know and share the goods of global humanity, we must recognize that what is at work is the political-cultural influence that henceforth will be exerted over these peoples, with the consequent loss of their cultural and political autonomy.

What is most fatal in the desire for money and external goods is that it can be easily attended to. Sell your resources and you will fulfill the desire. In this way the cultural integrity of Indian ethnies is threatened by the craving for consumption, a fatal attraction of modern society. It constitutes a rather cruel trap for the Indian ethnies who are experiencing population growth and political maturation: the more people, the more consumption; for more consumption, more disbursement of resources. By a perverse dialectic movement, the greatly desired population growth of the Indians can become a menace to their cultural identity. The appropriation of industrialized goods gives the Indians a temporary self-confidence that they are on the right road to power and respect. However, if they forget to balance it with the demands of their traditional culture, they will begin to disregard their ways of thinking and their particular forms of social life. This may lead to a continuous and passive acceptance, which will in turn lead to the cultural and political transition to Western civilization. The example of the North American Indian ethnies, with their problems of adaptation after a first phase of identification with the modern world, must be carefully analyzed and compared with the Brazilian case.

To survive only to see one's children without social perspectives and without a cultural direction—some of them despairing to the point of attempting to take their own lives—is a tragedy that does not need to be repeated with the Brazilian Indian ethnies. An important ethnie, the Guarani of Southern Mato Grosso state, seem to have succumbed to that despair,[12] but one hopes there is still time to avoid it for the majority of other ethnies across the country.

The question that we should ask ourselves, therefore, comes only as an expectation, a possibility. It should be phrased with sentiments of indignation, suffering, and desperation—but also of hope. We do not know if the world will move toward a genuine, enriching dialogue among all cultures, as we were sure in the nineteenth century that economic and technological progress was going to continue and that one could think seriously about social utopias. We cannot be sure that Brazil will be an openly and proudly acknowledged mixed-race nation, blended by the diversity of cultures and societies that have constituted it. That is the reason we cannot yet formulate a new paradigm, one that could be called a *paradigm of cultural diversity,* to help us explain our times. We have only the first signs, clouded as they may be by disbelief, and a few premonitions that might help establish a new standard of thinking, of explanations and sentiments about the Indian and the Indian question in Brazil. Concepts such as ethnic transfiguration, self-determination, autonomy, affirmation of ethnic identity, cultural resistance, and ethnic survival, as well as an analytical shift toward the study of the history of Indians, are initial attempts that represent the threshold of a new conceptualization. These notions rise out of the refusal to accept the paradigm of acculturation, which we believe is showing signs of empirical and theoretical exhaustion. They are signs of the new events that are sweeping across the world, although these notions still lack the conviction of truth that is necessary to change scientific proposals into political action.

One must not undermine the primacy of economic influence upon the world, particularly in regard to Indian survival. Perhaps the fate of the Indians is more in the hands of the boards and CEOs of industry and business, of mining, logging, and the agricultural and ranching ventures, than in the reins of politics, religion, the military, or civil society. However, it is in the fighting, the confrontation of forces, and the dialogue of ideas that economic primacy gains meaning and direction. Let us, then, place our best bets on this dialogue-struggle, on the knowledge of what can be made practical to enhance the survival and permanence of Indian ethnies of Brazil.

If I may allow myself to make a profession of faith, it is that the survival of the Brazilian Indians is a goal that is perfectly within reach, both politically and culturally, both for Brazil and for humanity. This task belongs to the world and is in the hands of our generation. In projecting our future we must do so with the Indians by our side, not as orphans or as children, nor as innocents to be exploited, but as partners in a common destiny. Given all the perils that menace humanity, it will not be surprising if our survival shall be linked to the survival of the Indians.

In a world that is still expanding culturally, although with clear signs of a decelerating dynamism, will the permanence of Indian cultures and societies not be conditioned to internal changes that could lead to their virtual disappearance as specific cultures and societies? If so, why bother?

We should bother, at the very least, because the destiny of a part of humanity is at stake. The aspiration of this book has been to show that the process of destruction of the Indians is historically neither necessary nor inexorable, despite the harsh picture we have painted with as much objectivity as possible. Regarding the destiny of humanity, no matter how much we probe its structure in history, we cannot project it in the same way into the future. If there is a teleology in humanity, it has not yet been given us to know. But we have enough knowledge to evaluate the cultural dynamics within certain periods of human history and can from this make projections, facing the risk of either exaggerating or undermining what we know.

In the case of Brazil, we must take into account that over the years it has made considerable headway into modern times and even in a direction from which it has to reverse itself if it wants to survive as an autonomous nation. Furthermore, given the unjust nature of its class system, the incapacity for tolerance and equanimity, and the desire for immediate gains that moves a large part of its political and economic elites, one can see why the nation is reaching its furthest limits of sustainability. Brazil has to change in order to project a future with more responsibility and serenity, and in this project the Indians must be included—no longer as symbols of what is backward, but of the cultural and ecological balance that is indispensable for a stable country and for superior moral bases.

All things considered, and with a small grain of salt, we may think about the possibility that, say, a hundred years from now, there will still be in our midst a veritable Tower of Babel, with more than 170 distinct languages being spoken and a variable set of 200 ethnic groups living different cultural forms, not necessarily equal to those of today, but based upon them. We may imagine that there will still be pristine forests and rivers unspoiled by human activity, where one can still walk naked if one wishes, where one can "hunt in the morning, fish in the afternoon, rear cattle in the evening, and criticize after dinner,"[13] and share in a generous life of solidarity. All of us.

Appendix A

INDIAN LANDS

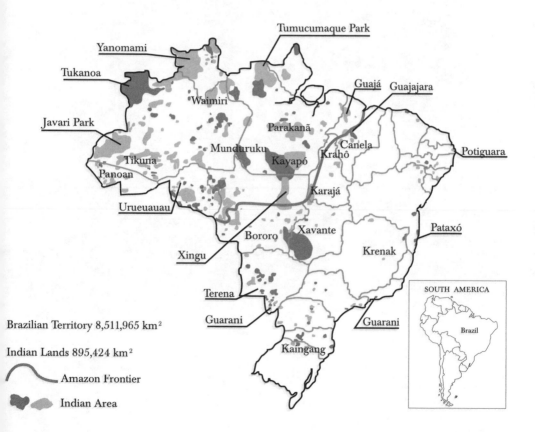

Brazilian Territory 8,511,965 km²

Indian Lands 895,424 km²

Amazon Frontier

Indian Area

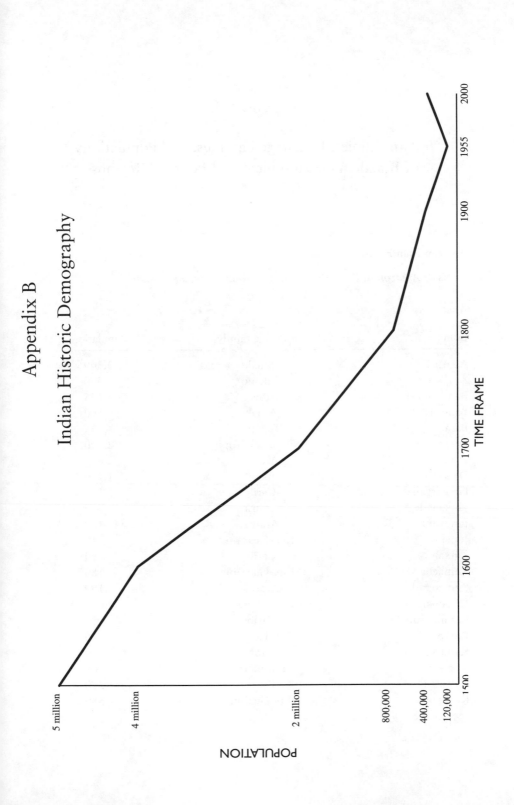

Appendix B

Indian Historic Demography

Appendix C

Indian Ethnies, Language Families, and Populations of Brazilian Geographical and Political Regions

Amazon Rain Forest

States of Amazonas, Pará, Roraima, Rondônia, Acre, and Amapá

Amazonas

Ethnie	Language family	Population
Apurinã	Aruak	3,300
Arapaço	Tukano	350
Banawa Yafi	Arawá	145
Baniwa	Aruak	3,500
Bará	Tukano	55
Baré	Nheengatu/Tupi	2,500
Deni	Arawá	620
Dessano	Tukano	1,730
Hixkaryana	Carib	120
Jamamadi	Arawá	340
Jarawara	Arawá	180
Juma	Tupi-Guarani	10
Kaixana	Carib	90
Kambeba	Tupi-Guarani	180
Kanamanti	Arawá	190
Kanamari	Katukina	1,600
Karafawyana	Carib	80
Karapanã	Tukano	60
Katuena	Carib	60
Katukina	Katukina	300
Kaxarari	Pano	280
Kokama	Tupi-Guarani	380

Kubeo	Tukano	240
Kulina	Pano	70
Kuripako	Aruak	920
Maku	Maku	2,400
Makuna	Tukano	50
Marubo	Pano	1,000
Matis	Pano	190
Matsé	Pano	660
Mawayana	Carib	80
Miranha	Bora	470
Miriti Tapuia	Tukano	140
Mura	Mura	1,800
Parintintin	Tupi-Guarani	150
Paumari	Arawá	600
Pirahã	Tupi	190
Piratapuia	Tukano	1,000
Sateré-Mawé	Tupi	7,000
Tariano	Aruak	2,000
Tenharim	Tupi-Guarani	400
Tikuna	Tikuna	24,000
Torá	Txapakura	30
Tsohom Djapá	Katukina	150
Tukano	Tukano	3,100
Tuyuka	Tukano	580
Wai Wai	Carib	1,450
Waimiri Atroari	Carib	800
Wanano	Tukano	530
Warekena	Aruak	500
Witoto	Witoto	40
Xereu	Carib	60
Yanomami	Yanomami	1,200
Zuruahã	Arawá	160
SUBTOTAL		68,030

Pará

Ethnie	Language family	Population
Amanayé	Tupi-Guarani	80
Anambé	Tupi-Guarani	120
Aparai	Carib	50
Araweté	Tupi-Guarani	270
Assurini do Tocantins	Tupi-Guarani	270

Assurini do Xingu	Tupi-Guarani	90
Gavião (Parkateyé)	Timbira/Jê	370
Juruna	Tupi	230
Kaxuyana	Carib	70
Kayapó (Gorotire)	Kayapó/Jê	3,400
Kayapó (Xikrin)	Kayapó/Jê	600
Krẽje	Timbira/Jê	30
Kuruaia	Tupi	30
Parakanã	Tupi-Guarani	700
Munduruku	Tupi	3,600
Suruí	Tupi-Guarani	200
Tembé	Tupi-Guarani	800
Tiriyó	Carib	430
Turiwara	Tupi-Guarani	50
Wayana	Carib	50
Xipaya	Tupi	30
Zo'é	Tupi-Guarani	140
SUBTOTAL		11,610

Rondônia

Ethnie	Language family	Population
Aikanã	Aikanã	190
Ajuru	Tupi	50
Arara	Tupi	160
Aricapu (Jaboti)	Tupi-Guarani	10
Arikem	Tupi	30
Aruá	Tupi-Mondé	50
Cintas-Largas	Tupi-Mondé	700
Columbiara	Isolated	30
Gavião	Tupi-Mondé	480
Kanoé	Kanoé	80
Karipuna	Tupi-Guarani	10
Karitiana	Tupi	190
Kwazá	Isolated Language	20
Kujubim	Txapakura	20
Macurap	Tupari/Tupi	150
Mequém	Tupari/Tupi	30
Nambiquara	Nambiquara	600
Pakaa Nova	Txapakura	1,400
Paumelenho	Unknown	80

Sakirabiap	Tupari/Tupi	70
Suruí	Mondé/Tupi	650
Tupari	Tupari/Tupi	240
Urueuauau	Tupi-Guarani	120
SUBTOTAL		5,360

Roraima

Ethnie	Language family	Population
Ingarikó	Carib	1,200
Makuxi	Carib	16,000
Wapixana	Aruak	5,500
Yanomami	Yanomami	8,800
Yekuana	Carib	230
SUBTOTAL		31,730

Acre

Ethnie	Language family	Population
Arara	Pano	350
Jaminawa	Pano	530
Campa	Aruak	830
Katukina	Pano	500
Kaxinawá	Pano	4,000
Machineri	Aruak	400
Nukini	Pano	450
Poyanawa	Pano	410
Yawanawá	Pano	310
SUBTOTAL		7,780

Amapá

Ethnie	Language family	Population
Galibi Marworno	Carib	1,400
Galibi	Carib	50
Karipuna do Amapá	French Creole	4,000
Palikur	Aruak	750
Waiãpi	Tupi-Guarani	530
SUBTOTAL		6,730

Central West Region

States of Tocantins, Mato Grosso, Mato Grosso do Sul, and Goiás

Tocantins

Ethnie	Language family	Population
Apinayé	Western Timbira/Jê	780
Karajá/Javaé	Jê	900
Karajá/Xambioá	Jê	300
Krahô	Timbira/Jê	1,400
Xerente	Central Jê	1,800
SUBTOTAL		5,180

Mato Grosso

Ethnie	Language family	Population
Apiaká	Tupi	50
Arara do Aripuanã	Unknown	160
Aweti	Tupi-Guarani	100
Bakairi	Carib	700
Bororo	Bororo	980
Cinta Larga	Tupi-Mondé	700
Enawenê-Nawê	Aruak	290
Iranxe	Aruak	280
Kalapalo	Carib	350
Kamayurá	Tupi-Guarani	320
Karajá	Macro-Jê	2,000
Kayabi	Tupi	1,300
Kayapó (Txukarramãe)	Kayapó/Jê	800
Kuikuro	Carib	380
Matipu	Carib	70
Mehinako	Aruak	170
Menky	Carib	70
Nahukwá	Carib	70
Nambikwara	Nambikwara	320
Panará	Kayapó/Jê	170
Pareci	Aruak	1,400
Rikbaktsa	Aruak	710
Suyá	Kayapó/Jê	230
Tapayuna	Kayapó/Jê	60
Tapirapé	Tupi-Guarani	430
Trumái	Isolated	100

Txikão	Carib	230
Umotina	Bororo/Jê	110
Waurá	Aruak	240
Xavante	Central Jê	10,000
Yawalapiti	Aruak	210
Zoró	Tupi-Mondé	280
SUBTOTAL		23,280

Mato Grosso do Sul

Ethnie	Language family	Population
Chamacoco	Samuko	40
Guarani	Tupi-Guarani	32,000
Guató	Guató	700
Kamba	Unknown	60
Ofaié-Xavante	Ofaié-Xavante	90
Terena	Aruak	18,000
SUBTOTAL		50,890

Goiás

Ethnie	Language family	Population
Avá-Canoeiro	Tupi-Guarani	14
Tapuia	Portuguese	140
SUBTOTAL		154

Northeast Region

States of Maranhão, Ceará, Paraíba, Pernambuco, Alagoas, Sergipe, and Bahia.

Maranhão

Ethnie	Language family	Population
Canela Apanyekra	Timbira/Jê	350
Canela Ramkokamekra	Timbira/Jê	1,500
Gavião (Pukobye)	Timbira/Jê	210
Guajá	Tupi-Guarani	370
Guajajara	Tupi-Guarani	13,200
Ka'apor	Tupi-Guarani	620
Krikati	Timbira/Jê	450
Krepumkateyé	Timbira/Jê	60
SUBTOTAL		16,760

Ceará

Ethnie	Language family	Population
Jenipapo-Kanindé	Portuguese	134
Kariri	Portuguese	456
Paiaku	Portuguese	235
Pitaguari	Portuguese	127
Tapeba	Portuguese	1,143
Tremembé	Portuguese	2,247
SUBTOTAL		4,342

Paraíba

Ethnie	Language family	Population
Potiguara	Portuguese	7,600
SUBTOTAL		7,600

Pernambuco

Ethnie	Language family	Population
Atikum	Portuguese	2,900
Fulniô	Yatê/Jê	5,000
Kambiwá	Portuguese	1,400
Kapinawá	Portuguese	450
Pankararu	Portuguese	4,100
Truká	Portuguese	1,100
Xukuru	Portuguese	3,500
SUBTOTAL		18,450

Alagoas

Ethnie	Language family	Population
Jeripancó	Portuguese	910
Karapotó	Portuguese	1,200
Kariri-Xocó	Portuguese	1,600
Tingui-Botó	Portuguese	190
Wassu	Portuguese	1,320
Xukuru Kariri	Portuguese	1,620
SUBTOTAL		6,840

Sergipe

Ethnie	Language family	Population
Xocó	Portuguese	270
SUBTOTAL		270

Bahia

Ethnie	Language family	Population
Kaimbé	Portuguese	1,300
Kiriri	Portuguese	1,700
Pankararé	Portuguese	810
Pankaru	Portuguese	90
Pataxó	Portuguese	1,900
Pataxó Hã-Hã-Hãe	Portuguese	1,850
Tuxá	Portuguese	1,100
SUBTOTAL		8,750

Southeast Region

States of Minas Gerais, Espírito Santo, Rio de Janeiro, and São Paulo

Minas Gerais

Ethnie	Language family	Population
Guarani	Tupi-Guarani	250
Krenak	Krenak/Jê	150
Maxakali	Maxakali/Jê	900
Pankararu	Portuguese	20
Xakriabá	Portuguese	5,500
SUBTOTAL		6,820

Espírito Santo

Ethnie	Language family	Population
Guarani-Kaiowá	Tupi-Guarani	330
Tupiniquim (Puri)	Portuguese	1,400
SUBTOTAL		1,730

São Paulo

Ethnie	Language family	Population
Guarani-Ñandeva	Tupi-Guarani	1,200
Kaingang	Jê	800
Terena	Aruak	1,000
SUBTOTAL		3,000

Rio de Janeiro

Ethnie	Language family	Population
Guarani	Tupi-Guarani	560
SUBTOTAL		560

Southern Region

States of Paraná, Santa Catarina, and Rio Grande do Sul

Paraná

Ethnie	Language family	Population
Guarani-Kaiowá	Tupi-Guarani	2,000
Guarani-Ñandeva	Tupi-Guarani	500
Kaingang	Jê	7,000
SUBTOTAL		9,500

Santa Catarina

Ethnie	Language family	Population
Guarani	Tupi-Guarani	600
Kaingang	Jê	3,500
Xokleng	Jê	2,000
SUBTOTAL		6,100

Rio Grande do Sul

Ethnie	Language family	Population
Guarani	Tupi-Guarani	800
Kaingang	Jê	10,000
SUBTOTAL		10,800

Indians living in cities such as Manaus, São Gabriel da Cachoeira, Boa Vista, Rio Branco, Porto Velho, Belém, São Luís, Recife, Rio de Janeiro, São Paulo, Cuiabá, Brasília, Goiânia, Campo Grande, Aquidauana, Dourados, and Corumbá

		40,000
TOTAL		352,266

Notes

Preface

1. A second edition came out in 1991. The present edition in English has been revised and updated to take into account a substantial portion of the literature in English pertaining to the topic of Indian ethnic survival.

2. The basis for most of the works on ethnic resistance and ethnic affirmation done in the 1970s and 1980s was laid out by anthropologist Fredrik Barth in his book *Ethnic Groups and Boundaries*. The subject is discussed in the introduction to this book.

Introduction

1. In a June 20, 1994, poll conducted by the highly regarded newspaper *Folha de São Paulo,* some 70 percent of Brazilians responded positively to the question of whether the Indians should have their territories guaranteed by the federal government.

2. Indian demography in 1500 has been the focus of various studies, calculations, and speculations. A summary can be found in John Hemming's *Red Gold.* Hemming considers the number he proposes—2.4 million—to be speculative. My rounded figure of 5 million is the product of several assumptions and is more fully explained in chapter 1. Other authors have proposed numbers that range from 800,000 (see Steward's analysis in his *Native Peoples of South America,* pp. 51–60), to a projected number that would certainly exceed 10 million (Pierre Clastres, *A Sociedade Contra o Estado,* pp. 56–70.). The smaller figure is clearly an underestimation, partly due to a disbelief regarding the descriptions and figures presented by chroniclers and missionaries in the sixteenth and seventeenth centuries. Today these descriptions are given more credit and consideration. The greatest difficulty lies in figuring out how many peoples, or rather, how many political-cultural units might have existed. In chapter 4 I discuss the various criteria for evaluating this question. If we correlate specific languages with political units, the number may vary from some 340 to 2,500. See, among others, J. Alden Mason's "The Languages of South American Indians," p. 163, which proposes a number of 5,000 languages/peoples

for all of South America; Nimuendaju's *Mapa Etno-histórico* totals 1,400 peoples; Loukotka's "Línguas Indígenas do Brasil" rounds up 237 languages for Brazil; Aryon Rodrigues's *Línguas Brasileiras* identifies 170 current languages and projects double this amount as a minimal number of Indian languages in 1500. The current figure of 350,000 Indians distributed among 220 nations comes from the latest statistics (May 1999) of FUNAI, the government agency for Indian Affairs, and the Indigenist Missionary Council (Conselho Indigenista Missionário—CIMI), with a calculated margin of error of less than 3 percent. See FUNAI's *Situação das Terras Indígenas do Brasil: Dados Estimativos;* CIMI's "Povos Indígenas no Brasil e Presença Missionária"; and *Povos Indígenas no Brasil,* edited by Beto Ricardo. This last work, though a comprehensive outline of many concrete aspects of the present situation of Indian ethnies in Brazil, uses mixed criteria to define an Indian ethnie. Thus it includes such distinct, self-identifying ethnies as the Xikrin and the Txukarramãe in the Kayapó group, while distinguishing the Krikati from the Gavião-Pukobye, the Canela from the Krahô.

3. By a convention established by Brazilian anthropologists and linguists in 1953, names of Indian groups are never pluralized, unless they are Portuguese words, and are always written with capital letters, unless they stand as adjectives. See *Revista de Antropologia,* Vol. 2, n. 2, pp. 150–2, 1954.

4. See Darcy Ribeiro, *Os Índios e a Civilização,* p. 236.

5. The Guató are canoe-dwelling Indians who were known since the seventeenth century to have lived on the banks of the upper Paraguay river. They had been last sighted in the 1930s and were thought to have become extinct. However, in the 1980s a surviving band was contacted by a Catholic mission, and they are now recognized as Indians by the Indian agency. Although few still speak their native language, they number some 700 people and are in the process of having their lands guaranteed. See Ricardo, ed., *Povos Indígenas no Brasil,* p. 762.

6. There is an extensive bibliography on the Old World-New World confrontation by Mexicans, Peruvians, Brazilians, North Americans, and Europeans. It may be pointed out here that one of the earliest and most pungent denunciations of the massacres perpetrated against the New World populations was made by Spanish Fransciscan friar Bartolomé de las Casas. For a comprehensive analysis of las Casas, including his mid-1500 debate with fellow countryman Sepulveda on the legitimacy of the conquest, see, for instance, Lewis Hanke's *Aristóteles e os índios americanos.* A still-useful general study done by a European on the Indian-white confrontation is Georg Friederici's *Caráter da Descoberta e Conquista da América pelos Europeus.* See also Darcy Ribeiro's *As Américas e a Civilização;* Leopoldo Zea's *América en la História;* and Tzestan Todorov's *A Conquista da América.*

7. These regulations contained the plans and recommendations of King John III for the colonization of Brazil. A selection of passages relevant to the Indians can be found in Georg Thomas's *A Política Indigenista.* My discussion of these regulations and indigenist policies is found in chapter 2.

8. The proposals contained in this text were first presented to the General Courts

of Lisbon in 1821, an assembly convened to reestablish the Portuguese monarchy after the expulsion of the Napoleonic troops and to keep Brazil within the Portuguese realm. Other Brazilians participated in this assembly and read papers dealing with the possibility of reconciling the Indians with the Luso-Brazilian polity. Among them are Francisco Muniz Tavares of Pernambuco; Francisco Ricardo Zane of Pará; and Domingos Borges de Barros of Bahia. Muniz Tavares and Borges de Barros, like Bonifácio de Andrade, had proposals to civilize the Indians. Francisco Ricardo Zane, who the previous year had been the administrative guide of the German scientists Karl Von Martius and Johann Baptist Von Spix along the Amazon River and its tributaries and had represented the mercantile interests of the region, proposed measures to enslave or wipe out the Indians. After independence was proclaimed, a Constituent Assembly was convened by the new Brazilian king, Pedro I, in 1823, but the proposals presented by Bonifácio de Andrade were rejected or ignored. At any rate, the idea of integrating the Indian into the Brazilian nation remained in the national liberal imagination and was later of great importance for the consolidation of a positive attitude with regard to the Indians. See Moreira Neto, "A Política Indigenista," and Cunha, ed., *História dos Índios*.

9. The estimated numbers of Indians massacred in this expedition and the following, in 1880, totaled 23,000 warriors. See Rubén's "Les Mapuches." For an overview of the Indian question in the United States, see Jacobs's *Dispossessing the American Indian* and Driver's *Indians of North America*. For Colombia, see Balcazar Pardo's *Disposiciones sobre Indígenas Baldios* and Uribe Misas's *Las Misiones Católicas*. For Venezuela, see Jimenez's "Análisis de Indigenismo Oficial en Venezuela" and Monsonyi's "La Situacion del Indigena en Venezuela."

10. Being at the core of this sentiment does not necessarily mean being in the official policy or discourse. Nor is it necessarily a positive feeling. It simply means being a constant and current motif of recognition, even if sometimes a negative one.

11. The life and work of Curt Nimuendaju, including his published bibliography, is summarized in *Textos Indígenas*. See also Maybury-Lewis's *Akwe-Shavante Society* and the collection of articles on Jê-speaking societies that he organized, *Dialectical Societies*.

12. The first volume was published in 1954 in São Paulo by the Commission for the Fourth Centennial of the City of São Paulo. The second, which encompasses materials of the first, was published in Germany in 1968 by the Kommisionsverlag Münstermann Druck GMBH. After Baldus's death, a third volume was compiled in 1984 by anthropologist Thekla Hartman and was published in Berlin by Dietrich Reimer Verlag.

13. Florestan Fernandes, *A Organização Social; A Função Social da Guerra; Investigação etnológica no Brasil*.

14. Darcy Ribeiro, *Os Índios e a Civilização*.

15. Galvão, *Encontro de Sociedades; Santos e Visagens*; Galvão and Charles Wagley, *The Tenetehara Indians*, 1949. About Galvão personally, see the preface written by Darcy Ribeiro in Galvão's *Encontro de Sociedades*.

16. Galvão and Wagley, *The Tenetehara Indians*. Intro. by Galvão, p. 10. Although the translation of the introduction was done in 1955, the Portuguese edition was not published until 1961. Italics mine.

17. Roberto Oliveira, *O processo de assimilação;* "Estudo de áreas de Fricção Interétnica no Brasil"; "Aculturação e Fricção Interétnica"; *O Índio e o mundo dos brancos; Urbanização e tribalismo; Identidade, Etnia e Estrutura Social.* Oliveira's most recent books deal with questions pertaining to theory and the history of anthropology.

18. See Brandão's *Etnia e Identidade* for an evaluation of various studies on ethnic identity in Brazil. For a view of the theoretical position on ethnic identity see Barth's *Ethnic Groups and Boundaries,* and *La Identidad,* edited by Claude Lévi-Strauss. See also Cunha's *Os Mortos e os Outros* and *Antropologia no Brasil.*

19. Moreira Neto, *Índios da Amazônia.*

Chapter 1. The Indian in History

1. Silvio Castro, ed., *A Carta de Pero Vaz;* see also Vespúcio, *Novo Mundo,* and Columbos, *Diário da Descoberta.*

2. Holanda, *Visão do Paraíso;* Franco, *O Índio Brasileiro.*

3. Roosevelt, *Moundbuilders of the Amazon.*

4. The bibliography on the Tupinambá Indians is the most extensive of all Indian peoples of Brazil. Florestan Fernandes' two main monographs include a large portion of the works to 1950 by chroniclers, missionaries, travelers, and anthropologists. See also Métraux's *Migrations Historiques* and *A Religião dos Tupinambá.* More recent works depend upon this bibliography, since there are no extant Tupinambá, or at least there is no longer a Tupinambá culture and society.

5. The idea that this type of anthropophagy could have anything to do with a complementary diet of protein is ludicrous, but it has certainly crossed the mind of many a cultural ecologist. See, for example, Pierre Clastres's "Guyaki cannibalism" and Dole's "Endocannibalism among the Amahuaca."

6. In a famous dialogue between Frenchman Jean de Léry and a Tupinambá chief at Guanabara Bay in present-day Rio de Janeiro, the Tupinambá wonders why French sailors travel from so far away and under such harsh conditions just to gather wood for a yellow dye. See Léry's *Viagem à Terra do Brasil.*

7. This is a value judgment that the author assumes, aware of its moral and scientific consequences, and certain that he can be challenged with technological, military, political, and religious arguments.

8. So writes Montaigne in his essay, in any case.

9. Gabriel Soares de Souza, *Tratado Descritivo do Brasil;* Thevet, *As Singularidades da França Antártica;* Cardim, *Tratados da Terra e Gente do Brasil;* Gandavo, *Tratado da Terra;* Vasconcelos, *Crônica da Companhia de Jesus;* Salvador, *História do Brasil.* These accounts list and locate most of the Indian peoples known in the sixteenth century. One cannot entirely trust either the names they give or their precise loca-

tions, since part of their information comes from vague accounts by other Indian peoples or adventurers passing through the regions. Demographic information on the Tupinambá peoples who inhabited the Brazilian coast is more trustworthy. The regions of São Paulo, Rio de Janeiro, Espírito Santo, Bahia, Pernambuco, Maranhão, and the lower Amazon concentrated reasonably large population contingents. Léry, for example, writes that in 1557 as many as 10,000 Tupinambá Indians were involved in war in the region surrounding Guanabara Bay. This may mean a population of 100,000 Indians between Cabo Frio and Santos, and another 50,000 in the Piratininga uplands. Mem de Sá, the third governor-general of Brazil (1555–70) is credited with the killing of some 30,000 Indians on the north-central coast of Bahia in 1558. When one adds the estimated 20,000 to 30,000 dead from the previous epidemics, as well as the survivors, it is possible that the Tupinambá population of this region exceeded 100,000. There were probably some 50,000 in the region of Espírito Santo and southern Bahia. For the northeast coast, which includes the present states of Alagoas, Sergipe, Pernambuco, Paraíba, Rio Grande do Norte, and the lower São Francisco River, we calculate a population of 150,000–200,000. In Maranhão, at the beginning of the seventeenth century, there were 50,000 Tupinambá. In the region of Belém and the lower Tocantins River, another 50,000. The Tupinambá south of Cananéia, near São Paulo were called Carijó and later Guarani; they may have totaled 500,000. Pierre Clastres calculates their number at 1,500,000. Thus, a total of 1 million can be arrived at for the Tupinambá. The concentrations of Indians in the interior or the country's savannas and gallery forest were located on the middle São Francisco and the backlands of Bahia, Goiás, São Paulo, and Mato Grosso. But even in the semi-arid *caatinga* regions of the northeast there were Indians in considerable concentrations. It is possible that no distinct region of Brazil's interior was without an Indian group. One million is not an exaggerated estimate for all the inland populations. As for the Amazon, especially along the river itself, Indian settlements were large and extensive, according to all early chroniclers. For the earliest accounts see Acuña, Carbajal, and Rojas's *Descobrimentos do Rio das Amazonas;* see also Porro's *As Crônicas* for a recent appraisal of these early sources. Father Antônio Vieira, based on the testimony of an important witness to the early decades of colonization, accused the Portuguese of having wiped out some 2 million Indians in the lower Amazon between 1616 and 1652. Notwithstanding this undeniable exaggeration, it is known that there were population concentrations of 20,000 to 30,000 persons in riverside villages of the Amazon, some of them extending upwards of nine kilometers along the river. Three million individuals seems to be a reasonable estimate for the whole valley.

10. There is an interesting and heated debate over whether these previous cultures were endogenous to the region or were brought from other places to the west. The first position is defended by Roosevelt in *Moundbuilders of the Amazon;* the second is argued by Meggers in *Amazonia: Man and Nature in a Counterfeit Paradise.*

11. Porro, *As Crônicas.*

12. Clastres, *A Sociedade Contra o Estado.*

13. See, for example, the pioneering study by Australian anthropologist R. F. Salisbury, *From Stone to Steel;* see also Sahlins's *Stone Age Economics.* For an example on the Amazon, see the observations of Carneiro in "Slash-and-Burn Cultivation among the Kuikuru and its Implications for Cultural Development."

14. The famous "Diary of the Ship *Bretoa*" is published in Varnhagen's *História Geral do Brasil.* The French expeditions are recounted in Gaffarel's *Histoire du Brésil Français.* The French colony established in Rio de Janeiro kept Indian slaves obtained from rival groups of their allies. See Léry's *Viagem à Terra do Brasil.*

15. See Varnhagen's *História Geral do Brasil,* volume 1, section 12, pp. 192–211.

16. Marchant, *Do Escambo à Escravidão.*

17. The work that best describes Antarctic France after the arrival of the second levy of settlers is an account made by an eyewitness, Léry's *Viagem à Terra do Brasil.*

18. Abbeville, *História da missão dos padres capuchinhos* and Evreux, *Viagem ao Norte do Brasil.*

19. Mello, ed., *Fontes para a História do Brasil Holandês;* Baro and Moreau, *História das Últimas Lutas;* Jonge, "Relatórios e Cartas."

20. Mello, *Tempo dos Flamengos.*

21. Souto-Maior, "Fastos Pernambucanos."

22. Taunay, "A Guerra dos Bárbaros."

23. Francisco Rodrigues de Prado, "História dos Índios Cavaleiros."

24. Taunay, *História Geral das Bandeiras,* pp. 290–5; Ennes, *As Guerras dos Palmares.*

25. On the extermination of the Indians of Piauí and the role of *bandeirantes,* Casa de Torre, and Casa de Ávila, as well as the land and cattle domains of the Jesuits, see Costa's *Chronologia Histórica;* Sobrinho's *O Devassamento do Piauí;* Ennes's *As Guerras dos Palmares;* Taunay's *História Geral das Bandeiras,* volume 8; and Mott's "Estruturas demográficas."

26. Because of this bloody exploit Mem de Sá was considered "below God, the man of the catechism" by Jesuit priest Rui Pereira in 1560 (Mecenas Dourado, *A Conversão do Gentio,* p. 85). It is interesting to note that one of the main reasons Jesuit priest José de Anchieta—who worked with the Tupinambá between 1551 and 1597 and is credited not only with the foundation of the town of São Paulo but also with saintly miracles—has never been designated a saint by the Vatican is the resonance of his poem "De gestis Mens de Saa," which praises Mem de Sá for his role in subduing by force of arms the Tupinambá.

27. For the extermination of the Tupinambá after the expulsion of the French, see Vasconcelos's *Crônica da Companhia de Jesus* and Leite's *Cartas dos Primeiros Jesuítas.*

28. For the conquest of Paraíba, see J. F. de Almeida Prado's *A Conquista da Paraíba.*

29. For the destruction of the Tupinambá in Maranhão, see Berredo's *Annaes históricos.* See also the new facsimile edition of the first edition, published in 1992

in the Coleção Monumenta Amazônica by the Centro de Estudios Amazonicos in Iquitos, with notes and preface by Carlos de Araújo Moreira Neto.

30. Father Antônio Vieira flaunted this number on various occasions, declaring he had heard it from an eyewitness to the conquest of Maranhão, who swore to the truth of his account on his deathbed. See Antônio Vieira's "Direcções a respeito da forma que se deve ter no julgamento e liberdade no cativeiro dos índios no Maranhão." See also Azevedo's História de Antônio Vieira, especially the chapters "O Missionário" and "O Revoltado." See also, by the same author, Cartas do Padre Antônio Vieira.

31. See the analysis made by Porro in As Crônicas.

32. These colonies were destroyed circa 1630, but Irish ships continued to trade with Indians until much later. See Hemming's Red Gold, pp. 223–228.

33. Moreira Neto, Índios da Amazônia.

34. On the Timbira of Maranhão, see Francisco de Paula Ribeiro's "Memória sobre as nações gentias," pp. 184–97, 297–322, and 442–56. See also Moreira Neto's "A Política Indigenista Brasileira" and "Alguns dados para a história recente," in Grünberg's La Situación del Indígena, pp. 381–419.

35. Moreira Neto, "Alguns dados," pp. 395, 399. Santos, Índios e Brancos no Sul.

36. Darcy Ribeiro, Os Índios e a Civilização, pp. 42–47; Caspar, Tupari, Aquino and Iglesias, Kaxinauá do rio Jordão.

37. See Darcy Ribeiro's Os Índios e a Civilização. See also Melatti's Índios e Criadores and Nimuendaju's The Eastern Timbira.

38. A fictional account of this case, titled Avaeté, was filmed by Brazilian movie maker Zelito Viana in 1984.

39. Willey, An Introduction.

40. Hemming, Red Gold, pp. 139–148.

41. Dias ("Colonização da Amazônia," pp. 471–490) cites a report estimating the number of deaths in Belém alone at 40,000. Azevedo (Os Jesuítas no Grão Pará, p. 199) states that the Indian population in Jesuit villages dropped in this period from 50,000 to 30,000.

42. Darcy Ribeiro, Uirá vai à procura de Deus.

43. Darcy Ribeiro, "Memórias sobre as nações gentias"; see also Francisco de Paula Ribeiro's "Descripção do Território," pp. 41–86.

44. Barbosa, A Pacificação dos Caingangs.

45. See chapter 2 for a full analysis and definitions of these colonial themes and institutions. For Father Antônio Vieira, see Azevedo's História de Antônio Vieira and Os Jesuítas no Grão Pará. See also Vieira's Obras Escolhidas de Vieira, especially volume 5, which contains various documents on the Indians of Amazonia, Maranhão, and Ceará, including the author's opinions on slavery, colonists, and the councils of missions.

46. Malheiro, A Escravidão no Brasil.

47. There is a controversy regarding the character of Indian labor in administra-

tive villages and Jesuit missions. While Marxist historian Nelson Werneck Sodré considers such labor as part of a "semi-feudal system," the equally Marxist historian Jacob Gorender (*O Escravismo Colonial,* pp. 124–133, 468, and 485) believes it was a part of the prevailing slavery system, although in an "incomplete" form. My own view on this question is being worked out in a forthcoming work on the Tenetehara Indians. Generally I tend to think more along the lines of Sodré's work than of Gorender's.

48. Nóbrega, "Diálogo sobre a conversão do gentio"; see also Métraux, *A Religião dos Tupinambá.*

49. Galvão, *Santos e Visagens.*

50. See, for example, Métraux, *A Religião dos Tupinambá,* and Wagley, "Xamanismo Tapirapé."

51. Dourado, *A Conversão do Gentio.* These observations are commonly found in the letters of the first Jesuits, including Nóbrega, Anchieta, and Aspicuelta. See Leite, *Cartas dos Primeiros Jesuítas.*

52. See the analysis by Lévi-Strauss in *Tristes Tropiques,* part 6.

53. Gomes, "The Ethnic Survival of the Tenetehara Indians."

54. Roberto, "Salvemos nossos Índios."

55. Azevedo, *Os Jesuítas no Grão-Pará.*

56. Lugon, *A República "Comunista."*

57. The Cabanagem Rebellion (1835–41), a major uprising in the Amazon, had the effective participation of many Indian ethnies as well as several of the towns that had formerly been Jesuit villages. With regard to the repression promoted by the official forces against the Indians, see Moreira Neto's *Índios da Amazônia.*

58. Moreira Neto, "A Política Indigenista Brasileira."

59. See Galvão's introduction to Wagley and Galvão, *Os Índios Tenetehara.*

60. Davis, *Victims of the Miracle;* Martins, *Não há terra para plantar.*

61. See the summaries of journalism on these struggles in documents published by the Ecumenical Center for Documentation and Information (CEDI), *Povos Indígenas do Brasil,* for the years 1981–86 and 1987–90, as well as Ricardo, *Povos Indígenas no Brasil,* for the years 1991–95.

62. It is shameful for Brazil that this should be so, considering that the protection of the Indians is derived from constitutional law. Worse yet is when the World Bank threatens the Brazilian government with breaking off contracts and suspending funding because of nonfulfillment of the clauses requiring demarcation of Indian lands, or lack of proper assistance.

63. Souza, ed., *Os Índios vão à luta;* Bamonte and Della Marina, eds., *La Festa degli Indios.*

Chapter 2. Indian Policies

1. Friederici, *Caráter da Descoberta;* Baião et al., *História da Expansão.*

2. Julien, *Les voyages de découverte.*

3. The bull *Romanus Pontifex* can be found in Baião et al., *História da Expansão;* the bull *Inter Coetera* is in Julien, *Les voyages de découverte.*

4. Hanke, *Aristóteles e os Índios Americanos.*

5. Dourado, *A Conversão do Gentio;* this cites a 1553 letter by Jesuit Luiz de Grão to the founder of the Society of Jesus, Fr. Ignatius Loyola, which reads: "This Gentile, father, is not converted by being given things of the faith, nor by reasons, nor by the words of preaching."

6. The complete text of this royal charter and the majority of the documents cited in the following pages are found in Hemming's *Red Gold.* For a more detailed analysis of the Portuguese Indian policiy in the first century of colonization, see Thomas's *A Política Indigenista.* See also Beozzo's *Leis e Regimentos,* Kiemen's *The Indian Policy,* and Moreira Neto's "A Política Indigenista Brasileira." I am entirely responsible for the analysis that follows.

7. Azevedo, *Os Jesuítas no Grão-Pará.* On the Pombal period in particular, see Mendonça, *A Amazônia na Era Pombalina.* On the Jesuits in general, see Leite, *História da Companhia.*

8. A well-documented example of these disputes was recently published by Cedeam as *Autos de Devassa contra os Índios Mura do Rio Madeira e Nações do Rio Tocantins, 1738–1739.* It includes details of the proposals made by the Jesuits, as well as official administrators, to destroy the "ferocious and uncivilizable" Mura Indians, who were said to be menacing Jesuit missions and private farms in the Madeira river region. Similar disputes are found throughout the colonial period both in the Amazon and the other regions of Brazil.

9. The role of Indian labor in colonial times is frequently underestimated by historians, as they allege that African slavery was initiated from the beginning of the colonization of Bahia and Pernambuco, that is, by the 1560s. Recent studies, such as Schwartz's *Sugar Plantations in the Formation of Brazilian Society,* however, demonstrate that Indian labor was indispensable in the sugar-rich region until at least the early 1600s. In the Amazon it continued to be important throughout colonial times and practically until the rubber boom, beginning in 1870, which attracted a massive influx of northeastern Brazilians. As warriors, the Indians were important in the expulsion of the French, Dutch, Irish, and English—the last two from the lower Amazon. The disputes over land began with the donations that the king, the governors, and the captains-general made to the Portuguese in Indian territories. Lands were also "granted" to Indians, always in smaller dimensions than those they had actually controlled as territory. For the role of Indian labor in São Paulo, see Monteiro's *Negros da Terra.*

10. *Lugares* would be the modern-day equivalent of villages or independent districts.

11. Moreira Neto, *Índios da Amazônia;* Gomes, "The Ethnic Survival of the Tenetehara Indians."

12. This royal charter explicitly states that the Indians are to be considered as orphaned children to be tutored by the state. This judicial condition is reconfirmed

by the regency in 1831. In the republic, the Civil Code of 1916 slightly modified this status to that of a minor in age who is "relatively capable." The principle of the state's guardianship is nonetheless maintained.

13. On the Jesuit missions in Paraguay and southern Brazil, see Furlong's *Missiones,* Hernández's *Missiones del Paraguay,* and Mürner's *Actividades politicas y económicas.*

14. Moreira Neto, "Alguns dados para a história recente."

15. I consider it a far-fetched and pro-Portuguese interpretation to think that the Portuguese crown treated Indian peoples as "sovereign nations" simply because one finds an occasional use of this expression in official administrative discourse, as Cunha asserts in *Os Direitos do Índio.*

16. This is a somewhat speculative estimate. There is evidence only that there were some 250,000 people living on the lower Amazon before the Cabanagem Rebellion in 1835, and the great majority must have been Indians, that is, *tapuios;* see Moreira Neto's *Índios da Amazônia.* Malheiros's *A Escravidão no Brasil* presents the following statistics on Indian populations for the years 1817–18:

> Statistics of the Governors
> Total Brazilian population: 3,817.000; village Indians: 250,400.

> Henry Hill
> Total population: 3,300,000; village Indians: 100,000; wild Indians: 500,000.

> Counselor A. R. Veloso de Oliveira
> Total population: 4,396,132; wild Indians: 800,000.

In the latter two cases the ratio of Indians to the total population is 18:100.

17. The Indian policy of the empire was first studied by Moreira Neto in his unpublished doctoral dissertation; see also Cunha's "Política indigenista no século XIX." I have analyzed the policy as applied in Maranhão in my unpublished doctoral dissertation "The Ethnic Survival of the Tenetehara Indians of Maranhão, Brazil." See also Arnaud's "Aspectos da Legislação."

18. See the report of Pinto Mendonça, the vice president of the province of Ceará, and of other provincial presidents in Moreira Neto's "A política indigenista brasileira."

19. See Haring's classic study, *Empire in Brazil.*

20. In the "Statistical Map of the Villages of Indians of Which There Is Notice in the *Repartição Geral das Terras Públicas,*" published by this agency on April 20, 1856, the demarcation of the following tracts of land is noted:

> Abrantes Village (Bahia)—2 square leagues.
> Santo Antônio Village (Bahia)—10 square leagues.
> Nossa Senhora da Saúde Village (Bahia)—1/2 square league.
> Soure Village (Bahia)—1/2 square league.
> Pombal Village (Bahia)—1/2 square league.
> Mirandela Village (Bahia)—1/2 square league.

Bom Jesus da Glória Village (Bahia)—1 square league.
Santarém Village (Bahia)—1 square league.
Barra do Salgado Village (Bahia)—1 square league.
Mamanguape Village (Paraíba)—12 square leagues.
Iacoca Village (Paraíba)—5 square leagues.
Urucu Village (Alagoas)—4 square leagues.

The number of recognized villages reaches 160, all of which should have had their lands demarcated. None of them, however, can be found in the registrars of later maps and reports. At any rate, the official statistics of the empire related to Indians are generally of a very poor quality, lacking in clarity and reliability on many points.

21. Paula, *Terras dos Índios.* The recent literature on this matter is very clear in defining Indian lands as a special type of land not to be confused with untenanted lands. See in this regard the pronouncements made by Supreme Court Minister Francisco Rezek in a seminar convened by the public attorney's office in September 1993. See also Juliana Santilli's *Os Direitos Indígenas.*

22. Lemos and Mendes, "Bases de uma Constituição, 1890"; see also Humberto de Oliveira, *Coletânea de Leis.* On the position of Justice Marshall, see McNickle, *The Indian Tribes.*

23. On Rio Grande do Sul, see Dutra, "Extrato do Parecer"; see also Simonian, ed., *A defesa das terras indígenas.* The Salesian missionaries went to Mato Grosso in 1890; see SPI's "Relatório Anual," which contains Darcy Ribeiro's letter to Bishop Helder Câmara, as well as the SPI documents accusing the Salesians established in Mato Grosso and the upper Rio Negro. This report also gives information about other religious missions including Protestant, installed up until that point among the Indians. The Capuchin suborder of Milan went to Pará and Maranhão in 1895; the Dominicans set up in Goiás and southern Pará during the same decade; the Franciscans founded a mission on the upper Tapajós at the beginning of the century. The positivists—above all Teixeira Mendes in Rio de Janeiro and the Center for Sciences, Arts, and Letters, of Campinas—published several articles on Indians and on the need for protecting them by state action. As examples, the following should be mentioned: J. Mariano de Oliveira's "Pelos Indianos Brazileiros"; Mendes's "Ainda os indígenas do Brazil e a política moderna," "O sientismo e a defesa dos indígenas brasileiros," "A civilização dos indígenas," and "Em defesa dos selvagens brasileiros"; and Lemos's "José Bonifácio."

24. Ihering, "A Antropologia do Estado de São Paulo"; see also the rejoinder by Mendes, "O sientismo e a defesa."

25. As a matter of fact, the SPI was also established for the "national workers," that is, poor, landless Brazilians, especially blacks and mestizos, who needed land and other economic incentives to make a living in the countryside. A few years later, however, this part of the service was abandoned altogether.

26. Rondon, "Relatórios dos Trabalhos" and "Conferências realizadas."

27. Darcy Ribeiro, *A Política Indigenista Brasileira;* see also J. Mariano de Oliveira, "Pelos Indianos Brazileiros," and Mendes, "A proteção republicana." A different

view concerning the origins and the purposes of the SPI has been propounded in recent years by Lima in his *Um grande cerco da paz*. He argues that the Brazilian state created the Indian agency to better control the Indians and the marginal populations of the country. In his analysis Lima overplays the military character of the SPI and the role of the state as a monolith of consensus and teleological sense of purpose. At the same time, he underplays the role of the SPI and its paragons in defending the Indians within the state and greatly ignores that the Indians have had traditionally many powerful enemies in both the state and the society at large.

28. This prestige was recognized by, among others, Collier, who was the director of the U.S. Bureau of Indian Affairs during the Roosevelt administration, and also at the First Interamerican Indian Congress held in 1943 in Patzcuaro, Mexico; see Darcy Ribeiro's *Política Indigenista Brasileira*.

29. For a discussion on these articles and the subsequent Brazilian constitutions by the great Brazilian jurist Pontes de Miranda, see Cunha's *Os Direitos dos Índios*, pp. 89–94.

30. See SPI, "Boletim Anual, 1955"; see also Ribeiro, *Línguas e Culturas Indígenas*, 1957. Ribeiro comments that the data he obtained from the SPI posts and inspectorships for the year 1953 pointed to a number of 150,000 Indians. He later found it necessary to correct some of these numbers, and finally, by a typological computation of the Indian populations, he reached a number that varied from 68,100 to 99,700. If 100,000 is a possible number, we can conclude that the Indian populations slowly began their growth process shortly after this nadir, accelerating in the seventies.

31. Darcy Ribeiro, *Os Índios e a Civilização*.

32. The state of utter desolation in which the Indians were said to be living, as well as the administrative scandals, had national and international repercussions. Norman Lewis's "Genocide" appeared in 1969 in the *Sunday Times Magazine* as well as in various European magazines. In 1970, at the invitation of the Brazilian government, a commission of the Red Cross traveled across the country and visited several Indian areas for a few months. The results of their investigations were published in several articles and books. If they did not confirm the accusations of genocide and ethnocide, they did leave the SPI and FUNAI with a very poor image of carelessness, irresponsibility, ignorance, and lack of determination in defense of the Indians. The following year, a commission of the Aborigines Protection Society also visited Indian areas across the country. See Akerren, Bakker, and Habersang's *Report of the ICRC* and Hanbury-Tenison's *Report of a Visit*. National repercussions flared up with reports in the major newspapers denouncing these occurrences. In June 1971, a group of eighty Brazilian anthropologists and scientists drafted a document titled "Os Índios e a Ocupação da Amazônia," in which they denounced the final solution plans of the military government with regard to the Indians. This document is included in Grünberg's *La Situación del Indígena*, pp. 449–53.

33. A journalistic description of the emancipation project and the opposition movement that was aroused by various segments of Brazilian civil society is in-

cluded in the Comissão Pró-Índio's *A Questão da Emancipação.*

34. Many of these programs were prepared by linguist-missionaries of the Summer Institute of Linguistics (SIL), a North American organization that maintains missions among Indians in Brazil and elsewhere. A few were prepared by FUNAI's own education staff, and others by Brazilian universities. For an evaluation of the education issue, see the Comissão Pró-Índio's *A Questão da Educação Indígena.* For one of the most successful cases of bilingual education, see Monte's "Educação indígena."

35. Nutels, "Plano para uma campanha" and "Medical Problems of Newly Contacted Indian Groups," Hern, "Saúde e demografia."

36. Demographic data on the Urubu-Kaapor come from D. Ribeiro's *Os Índios e a Civilização* and *Diários Índios;* from FUNAI reports written by Fred Spatti, former chief of the post among these Indians; and from the present author, who visited these Indians in the 1970s and 1980s. See also Balée's *Footprints of the Forest.* For two cases of Indian ethnies analyzed by a physician with long experience among Indians, see Vieira Filho's "Aumento demográfico."

37. For a general analysis, see Santos's *Educação e Sociedades Tribais.* For particular cases, see Viertler's "O projeto Tadarimana" and Mindlin's "A nova utopia indígena."

38. The notion of internal colonialism was developed by Mexican anthropologist Bonfil Batalla in his "El concepto del índio en América."

39. Brazilian attorneys and jurists have long been interested in Indian rights in relation to civil and political rights of the general population. In the last ten or fifteen years a new generation of young attorneys has come forward with new lines of argumentation that have enlarged the special character of Indian rights. See, for example, Juliana Santilli's *Os Direitos Indígenas e a Constituição.*

Chapter 3. What We Think about the Indians

1. Montaigne, "Os Canibais."

2. In this regard, Lévi-Strauss's *O Pensamento Selvagem,* citing the example of a Kwakiutl man taken to New York City in the beginning of this century by pioneer anthropologist Franz Boas, concludes that the curiosity of a "primitive" intellectual is usually in the direction of things that are close to his own culture. It is interesting to note that Montaigne's view on this matter seems broader and does not restrict the native's curiosity to focusing on cultural similarities.

3. Léry, *Viagem à Terra do Brasil;* Évreux, *Viagem ao Norte do Brasil;* José de Anchieta, *Arte de grammatica.* On the use of the Tupinambá lingua franca, see Ayrosa, *Primeiras noções;* Freire, "Da 'Fala Boa'"; and Navarro, *O método moderno de Tupi Antigo.*

4. Barléu, *História dos fatos;* Nieuhof, *Memorável Viagem;* Baro and Moreau, *História das Últimas Lutas.*

5. In the eighteenth century, the descriptions begin to fit the mold of the Enlight-

enment. See H. Clastres's "Primitivismo e Ciência," Nantes's *Relação Sucinta,* and Mamiani's *Arte de grammatica da língua.*

6. Eight of these letters were published in Souto-Maior's "Faustos Pernambucanos,"* pp. 403–14.

7. Castillo, *Historia verdadera* and Cortez, *A Conquista do México.* For an internal vision of the Indians, see Leon-Portilla, ed, *A Conquista da América Latina.*

8. Lévi-Strauss, *Antropologia,* pp. 334–35; Todorov, *A Conquista da América.*

9. It is interesting to note that the Tapirapé Indians call whites by the term *maíra,* whereas the Guarani use *juruá,* while the great majority of Indians in the Tupi-Guarani language group use the term *caraíba* or variations thereof. This last term apparently meant "great shaman." See Wagley's *Welcome of Tears.*

10. These cases are cited by Dourado in *A Conversão do Gentio,* in which he also analyzes some of the reasons for the difficulties the missionaries had in converting the Indians. For the ideas of Lévy-Bruhl, see his *Le Surnaturel.*

11. Rousseau, "Ensaio sobre a origem da desigualdade" and Hobbes, *Leviatã.*

12. Hélène Clastres, "Selvagens e Civilizados."

13. Rousseau, "Ensaio sobre a origem da desigualdade," p. 183.

14. Varnhagen, "Os Índios perante a Nacionalidade Brasileira" and "Os Índios Bravios e o Sr. Lisboa," in Varnhagen, *História Geral do Brasil,* cites the American example, contests the defenders of the Indians, and presents the anti-Indian arguments proposed in Congress by senators Vergueiro and Dantas de Barros Leite.

15. Cardim, *Tratado da Terra e Gente do Brasil* and Vasconcellos, *Crônica da Companhia.* Father Vieira's main Indian works have already been cited in chapter 1.

16. Évreux, *Viagem ao Norte do Brasil.*

17. The works of Darwin and Spencer constitute the foundations of what came to be called "social Darwinism," which justified the European political status quo of class domination and racism. See Darwin's *A Origem das espécies* and Spencer's *Principles of Sociology.* The works of Marx and Engels on primitive peoples are summarized in *Origem da Família* and *Formações Econômicas Pré-Capitalistas.* Their ethnological notebooks were edited and commented on by Krader in *Marx's Ethnological Notebooks.* There are also sparse comments in other books, such as Marx's *German Ideology,* the *Economic and Philosophical Manuscripts,* and in *Capital.* Morgan, author of *Ancient Society,* was the great American anthropologist of the nineteenth century who influenced Marx's vision of primitive peoples. From the 1930s on, the term *acculturation* became widely used among both scholars and journalists thanks to the article written jointly by Redfield, Linton, and Herskovitz, "Memorandum on the Study of Acculturation." It avoided any discussion of social evolution, as this concept had been badly criticized by most anthropologists in the preceding decade. The authors considered acculturation to be the general process of the passage of one social or cultural form to another. This process was caused mostly by the influence of the contact and the relationship established between two population groups. As two different cultures meet, the more powerful one influ-

ences the weaker one more strongly, making the dominated culture adopt its customs, ideas, and views. In theory the process could be reversed, but only in reference to certain items and not at the same level of intensity. The theory of acculturation was widely disseminated, and *acculturation* is one of the few terms in modern anthropology that is used by other social scientists and the public. It fits into the general expectation that a strong culture tends to dominate less powerful ones and that the world is moving toward the creation of a single culture. The concept weakens the perception of the political nature involved in the cultural relations between different peoples. By emphasizing that the passage from one form to another was a universal, cultural phenomenon, the concept of acculturation served the purpose of placating the liberal guilt feelings aroused when the process of extermination of Indian peoples was examined. In this sense acculturation carries a more ideological ring than social evolution. That is why I have chosen it to name the paradigm, that is, the general views on the destiny of Indian peoples since the eighteenth century. Other anthropologists who have theorized about the concept of social evolution taking into account the original ideas of Darwin and Morgan are Childe, in *What Happened in History* and *Man Makes Himself;* White, in *The Evolution of Culture;* and Steward, in *Theory of Culture Change.*

18. Lisboa, *Obras,* 1865. On Indians, see volume 1, book 5, and volume 4, note C, pp. 462–515. The most explicit indigenist text in Gonçalves Dias is his preface to the second edition of the chronicle of Berredo, *Annaes históricos.*

19. Varnhagen, "Memorial Orgânico" and *História Geral do Brasil.*

20. Manoel Almeida, "Civilização dos Indígenas," in *Jornal do Comércio,* cited in Rabelo, *Vida e Obra.*

21. The second edition was published by Editora Vozes in 1976.

22. Malheiro, *A Escravidão,* p. 249.

23. See in a recent edition Couto de Magalhães's *O Selvagem;* also his *Viagem ao Araguaia,* in which he comments on the Indians he visited and on how they might be used to the greater good of the national economy.

24. See Ottoni's "Carta ao Dr. J. M. de Macedo" and Marlière's "Notas e Documentos."

25. Rodrigues, *A Pacificação dos Crishanás.*

26. Veríssimo, *Interesses da Amazônia.*

27. This is the most influential journal of the empire, which published many articles on Indians up to the beginning of the twentieth century.

28. Lins, *O Positivismo no Brasil.*

29. Abreu, *Correspondência,* "Os Bacaerys," and *Rã-txa hu-ni-kuaim.*

30. Alípio Bandeira, *A Mystificação* and *A Cruz Indígena.*

31. The major works were published or republished in the Collection of the National Council for Protection of the Indians (CNPI), beginning in 1941. One can clearly detect the academically pretentious, dogmatic flavor of the SPI in a 1947 book commemorating Indian Day for the years of 1944 and 1945 (Publication

number 100 of the CNPI). From that point on, the SPI began to revitalize its activities and renew its research, which included a rich debate with anthropological knowledge. This process lasted until the middle of the following decade, when it finally succumbed to political anti-intellectualism.

32. Collier, *Los Indios de las Américas*, p. 273.

33. Freud, "Totem and Taboo," and *Psicologia de Grupo*.

34. Piaget, *O Raciocínio*.

35. Piaget (*Structuralism*, pp. 115–118) discusses his comparison between the primitive and the child in relation to the concepts of Lucien Levy-Bruhl and Claude Lévi-Strauss.

36. Boas, *The Mind of Primitive Man*; Evans-Pritchard, *Bruxaria, Oráculos e Magia*; Lévi-Strauss, *O Pensamento Selvagem*.

37. Carl Jung, *O Homem e seus símbolos*.

38. Piaget, *O Raciocínio*.

39. See, for example, Léclerc's *Crítica da Antropologia*. Incidentally, almost all of Mexican and Brazilian anthropology is marked by such a sentiment of self-criticism.

Chapter 4. Who Are the Indians?

1. Nimuendaju, *The Eastern Timbira*. The Kayapó could also be categorized in the same vein; see Vidal's *Morte e vida*.

2. For the notion of cultural compression, see Galvão's "Indigenous Culture Areas." For a description of two Xinguano cultures and societies, see Gregor's *Mehinaku* and Agostinho's *Kwarup*.

3. For the Suyá, see Seeger's *Os Índios e Nós*; for the Kayabi and Juruna, see B. Ribeiro's *Diário do Xingu*; for the Txukarramãe, see CEDI's *Povos Indígenas*.

4. Chernela, *The Wanano Indians*; Berta Ribeiro, *Os Índios das Águas Pretas*; Moran, *Through Amazonian Eyes*.

5. Both Meggers and Roosevelt agree on this.

6. Smith, "Anthrosols and Human Carrying Capacity."

7. D. Ribeiro and Berta Ribeiro, *Suma Etnológica*.

8. Moran, *Through Amazonian Eyes*; Milton, "Protein and Carbohydrate Resources," and "Comparative Aspects."

9. Cultural ecologists have made it their lifelong purpose to find the ecological rationale behind such choices. For a good collection of articles, see Hames and Vickers's *Adaptive Responses*.

10. Silverwood-Cope, "A Contribution to the Ethnology"; Ramos, *Hierarquia e simbiose*.

11. Daniel, "Tesouro descoberto do rio Amazonas."

12. Fernandes, *A Função Social da Guerra*.

13. Métraux, "The Paressi."

14. For the Bororo, see Colbacchini and Albisetti's *Os Bororo Orientais*; for the

Munduruku, see Spix and Martius's *Viagem pelo Brasil,* and Murphy's *Headhunter's Heritage.*

15. Moreira Neto, *Índios da Amazônia.* Today the Maué number some 10,000 people.

16. Darcy Ribeiro, *Kadiwéu.* The document presented to the Brazilian Supreme Court to prove the illegitimacy of the farmers over Kadiwéu lands can be found in Darcy Ribeiro, "Documento."

17. Pierre Clastres, *A Sociedade contra o Estado;* Hélène Clastres, *Terra sem Males.*

18. Early discussions on Jê population concentration can be found in Gross's "Protein Capture and Cultural Development" and in Zarur's "Ecological Need and Cultural Choice."

19. On the number of Indian languages, see chapter 1, note 2, above.

20. Aryon Rodrigues, in "Evidence of Tupi-Carib Relations," also suggests that the Carib and Tupi stocks may possibly have constituted a single one in the past. See also the discussion by Urban in his "A história da cultura brasileira."

21. Eduardo Castro argues in his *From the Enemy's Point of View,* as well as in other articles, for the validity of this comparion.

22. This argument can be found in Vidal's *Morte e Vida* and was anticipated in Nimuendaju's *The Eastern Timbira.*

23. On the Aruak as culture brokers and middlemen, see Métraux's "The Paressi."

24. Aquino and Iglesias, *Kaxinauá do rio Jordão;* Kensiger, *How Real People Ought to Live;* Lévi-Strauss, *Tristes Tropiques,* part 5; Melatti, *Javari.*

25. For the Guajá, see Gomes's "O povo Guajá"; for the Aché, also known as Guayaki, see Clastres's *Chronique des indiens Guayaki;* for the Xetá, see Helm's "Os Xetá"; for the Yuqui, see Steadman's *The Yuqui;* for the Maku, see Silverwood-Cope's "A Contribution to the Ethnography." For the little known tribes of the Javari Park, see Melatti and Ricardo's *Javari* and Cavucens's "A Situação dos Povos Indígenas."

26. Aquino and Iglesias, *Kaxinauá do rio Jordão;* Schmink and Wood's *Contested Frontiers* has several articles on the social consequences of the early twentieth-century rubber exploitation.

27. For a summary of newspaper articles on charges of corruption against FUNAI's president Romero Jucá, see CEDI's *Povos Indígenas,* pp. 41–47.

28. These cases have been widely publicized in the press. On the Gavião Indians, see Iara Ferraz's "Mãe Maria: Em Estado de Guerra." On Rondônia and the Suruí, see Mindlin's more general study, *Nós Paiter.* On the Cintas-Largas, see Chapelle's *Os Índios Cintas-Largas* and Junqueira, Mindlin, and Lima's "Terra e Conflito."

29. Cecília Helm, "A Integração do Índio"; Simonian, "Terra de Posseiros."

30. Silva, "Os Kaiowá."

31. Nimuendaju, "O Fim da tribo Oti," pp. 33–44. The Oti-Xavante should not be mistaken for the Ofaié-Xavante. In 1992 a family of highly acculturated Indians were found living in this region, where a hydroelectric power plant was to be built.

They were later recognized to be descendants of Ofaié-Xavante Indians, who were thought to have become extinct in the 1950s.

32. Edgar de Assis Carvalho, *As Alternativa dos Vencidos*.

33. Nasser, "Sociedade Tuxá."

34. IPARJ, "Quatro estudos de caso."

35. Amorim, "Índios Camponeses"; Moonen, "Os Potiguara."

36. Maria Rosário Carvalho, "Os Pataxó de Barra Velha"; Paraíso, "Caminhos de ir."

37. Maria de Lourdes Bandeira, *Os Kiriri de Mirandela;* Hohenthal, "As tribos indígenas."

38. Dantas and Dallari, *Terra dos Índios Xocó.* On the Maxakali, see Rubinger, Amorim, and Marcato's *Índios Maxakali.* On the Indians of the northeast, see Estêvão Pinto's *Os Índios do Nordeste,* Studart Filho's *Os Aborígenes do Ceará,* and Anaí/ Bahia's *Os Povos Indígenas.*

39. Arruti, "Morte e vida."

40. I have visited the caboclos of Taquaritiua and have personal information about those of São Miguel through anthropologist José Luiz dos Santos. As for the caboclos do Canto, the information comes from interviews I have carried with local residents.

Chapter 5. The Indians Today

1. Regarding the Kayapó and the presence of mining activity in their area, see the early news reports in *Jornal do Brasil* on May 31 and July 1, 1987. Since there are still a few gold mining sites in operation in Kayapó land, this problem continues. For a comprehensive analysis of the many socioeconomic aspects involving the Kayapó, see Fisher's "Megadevelopment, environmentalism." Regarding Paranapanema and its intervention over the Waimiri-Atroari Indian area, see Marewa's *Resistência Waimiri-Atroari,* and Baines's "The Waimiri-Atroari" and *Revista Veja.* For the Guajá and the Vale do Rio Doce Company, see Gomes's "Programa Awá" and "Sétimo Relatório."

2. Oilian's *Indígenas de Minas Gerais* documents the destruction of Indians affected by the traditional mining fronts.

3. See news report in *Jornal do Brasil,* June 12, 1987.

4. The Kayapó frequently appear in the written and television media due to their high journalistic visibility. See, for example, the news reports in the June 5, 1985, and December 12, 1987, *Jornal do Brasil.* In the 1990s the press has been less favorable toward the attitude of Kayapó leaders who manage the relationship between their society and the outside economic interests. Brazilians have become accustomed to TV reports that show Indians splurging easy money from mining and lumber royalties. For an anthropological view of this situation, see Turner's "Kayapó on Television." The Gaviões have acquired national fame due to their disposition to protest against the passage of the Carajás Railway through their lands, as well as

for the large sums of indemnities they have received. See Arnaud's "O comportamento dos índios Gaviões."

5. See Sandess's *Native Peoples,* which analyzes the difficulties these peoples face with hydroelectric projects and the flooding of their lands. On Alaskan Eskimos' indemnities for the passage of the oil pipeline through their lands and later problems, see Yarrow's "Alaska's Natives Try a Taste of Capitalism."

6. On the SPI's economicist ideology, see Darcy Ribeiro's *A Política Indigenista Brasileira.* In the process of extinguishing the SPI and creating FUNAI, various proposals for a new indigenist policy arose that exacerbated even more the previous economicist spirit. The very concept of "Indian income," found in the Statute of the Indian of 1973, implies the idea of enterprise for an Indian post.

7. See Helm's "A Terra, a Usina e os Índios," which discusses this question, presents maps, and brings to the surface the first problems with the building of a hydroelectric dam that will affect part of this area.

8. Westphalen, "Reforma Agrária nas Terras dos Índios." In 1975 the Kaingang Indians of Nonoai Indian land began their struggle to expel these squatters. By 1978 they had achieved success, but in the 1990s an unexpected conflict arose among the Kaingang over whether they should lease land for agriculture to non-Indians.

9. These data were shown during a 1984 television program focusing on the destructive power of the timber companies in Espírito Santo. See also the data presented in the report "Devastação da Mata Atlântica no Espírito Santo" in *Jornal do Brasil,* May 6, 1987, pp. 7–8. For an overall vision of the question, see Valverde's *O Problema Florestal.*

10. In September, 1987, the Guajajara of the Araribóia Indian Land reached the point of taking several FUNAI employees hostage, forcing the agency into a deal by which the Indians were allowed to invite lumber companies into their land (see the summary of several news reports in CEDI, *Povos Indígenas,* pp. 366–68). For a while several Indian leaders had good deals with the lumber companies and made money enough to buy houses in the nearby towns. Ten years later most of that land's hardwoods had been cut down, and the Indians were no better off than before the process had started.

11. Pinto, *Carajás.* It is interesting to note that the superintendent for the environment of the Vale do Rio Doce Company reached the point of writing a report contrary to this plan for utilizing charcoal, but no positive result came from his position. See "Usinas de carvão na Ferrovia Carajás" in *Jornal do Brasil,* July 19, 1987, pp. 8–9.

12. See the interview of World Bank economist Hans P. Binswanger in *Jornal do Brasil,* September 6, 1987.

13. The sale of these 8,000 cubic meters of timber was arranged by FUNAI to the SEVAT company. The Indians were to receive no share of it until they found out what was going on; see Vidal's "Xikrin do Cateté."

14. Between October 30 and November 20, 1987, several reports appeared in

Jornal do Brasil analyzing this problem and showing that one of the reasons leading the Indians to sell timber was the pressure put on them by FUNAI, which alleged that only in this way would it be able to meet the basic needs of the post and the Indians. On the other hand, the nature of the contracts made between FUNAI and the timber companies is so full of illegality that a minister of the Federal Accounting Court, upon analyzing a few of those contracts, requested an intervention in FUNAI by the Executive Office.

15. Minc, *A Reconquista da Terra;* Carelli and Severiano, *Mão Branca contra o Povo Cinza;* Ianni, *Colonização e Contra-Reforma.*

16. Velho, *Capitalismo Autoritário.* See also Ianni, *A Luta Pela Terra;* Santos, *Bandeiras Verdes;* and Luna, *A Terra era Liberta.*

17. Gomes, "Por que o índio briga com o posseiro." In the 1990s the World Bank financed the Small Producer Assistance Program (PAPP) in the region that included this Indian land and the village of São Pedro dos Cacetes. After many years of dispute, the village was evacuated and its population moved to a nearby area.

18. Data collected by the author during research carried out in 1985.

19. Santos, "Segundo Relatório sobre os Krikati" and "A Demarcação do Território Krikati." Both reports were presented to the Vale do Rio Doce Company and FUNAI. Between 1985 and 1994 the judicial process was supervened by legal advisers of the Vale do Rio Doce Company, since FUNAI seemed to be slackening on its responsibility to take action. In 1995 the Krikati came on the scene and threatened to burn down the power lines crossing their territory if FUNAI would not demarcate their land. After much tension, in March 1998, a tract of 146,000 hectares was demarcated with the help of three daring FUNAI staff and some 160 Indians from several lands nearby. However, most of the farmers and squatters who had established themselves in the process have not been removed.

20. Ladeira's "Algumas Observações" and Antônio Carlos Magalhães "Aldeamentos Indígenas," both reports presented to the Vale do Rio Doce Company and FUNAI.

21. Ferraz, "Mãe Maria: Em Estado de Guerra."

22. Regarding the struggle for land in northeast Pará, see Furtado's "Alguns aspectos do processo." Regarding the Tembé Indians and their lands, see Arnaud's "O Direito Indígena."

23. There is an extensive journalistic literature on the TransAmazon. For a geopolitical contextualization of its implantation, see Becker's *Geopolítica da Amazônia;* in relation to the Indians, see Davis's *Victims of the Miracle.* Regarding the Assurini, their history of pacification, their material culture, and their demographic problem, see Berta Ribeiro's "A oleira e a tecelã." On the colonization plans, see Smith's *Rainforest Corridors;* see also the April 27, 1986, news report in the *Jornal do Brasil.*

24. Edilson Martins, *Nossos Índios,* pp. 83–88. This study, however, does not include the later consequences of the transference. A more complete account can be found in Beltrão's *O Índio,* pp. 97–126.

25. Cota, *Carajás;* Vidal, "A Questão Indígena"; and Pinto, *Carajás.*

26. Gomes's "Programa Awá," a report presented to the Vale do Rio Doce Company and to the National Indian Foundation in 1985, provides an analysis of the different Guajá groups and a proposal for demarcation of their territory and the defense of the physical and cultural integrity of this people.

27. The anthropologists who prepared reports in this regard were Lux Vidal, Iara Ferraz, Antônio Carlos Magalhães, José Luiz dos Santos, Mara Luz, Lúcia Andrade, Maria Elisa Ladeira, and Mercio Pereira Gomes. Special reports were written by the physicians João Paulo Botelho Magalhães and Fernando Alves de Souza. Several of those reports, presented to CVRD (Companhia Vale do Rio Doce) and to FUNAI, are cited in this work.

28. The anthropologists who worked on surveys of Indian peoples and their needs in these areas were Carmen Junqueira, Betty Mindlin, Mauro Leonel, Rinaldo Arruda, and Ezequias Heringer Filho. They wrote reports incorporated in major documents for the Economic and Social Planning Institute of the Ministry of Planning, through the "Project for the Protection of the Environment and the Indian Communities," known by the acronyms PMACI I and PMACI II.

29. On the Guarani, see Edgar de Assis Carvalho's *Avá-Guarani;* on the CAPEMI scandal and the fraudulent reasons for tranferring the Parakanã, see J. Carlos de Assis's "O Escândalo Capemi."

30. Santos and Aspelin, *Indian Areas;* Carvalho, "Um Estudo de Caso."

31. Marewa, *Resistência Waimiri-Atroari,* 1983. These data are also available in newspaper reports and internal FUNAI reports. With regard to the Balbina hydroelectric project, the scandal is of such dimensions that even Roberto Messias Franco, the director of the Special Secretariat for the Environment, an agency connected to the office of the President of the Republic, considered it "the greatest stupidity of the Brazilian energy program"; see *Jornal do Brasil,* May 10, 1987.

32. Eletrobrás, *Plano Nacional* and *Plano Diretor.*

33. For a history of this movement, including the main public manifestations and journalistic coverage, see the Comissão Pró-Índio's *A Questão da Emancipação.*

34. Santilli, "Projeto Calha Norte." See also reports in *Jornal Gazeta Mercantil,* August 19, 1986, *Jornal do Brasil,* October 31, 1986, and *Jornal de Brasília,* November 1, 1986.

35. D. Ribeiro, *A Política Indigenista.* It is interesting to note that in this book, written in 1961, the author also analyzes the Indian issue with regard to the territorial frontiers, a problem that has always constituted a strategic state problem. In many ways the Calha Norte project is a recurrent national preoccupation very dear to the military.

36. A. Bandeira's *Antiguidade,* as well as other of his works cited in the bibliography.

37. See SPI's "Relatório Anual," which includes Darcy Ribeiro's letter to Dom Helder Câmara and the documents in which the SPI accuses the Salesians installed in Mato Grosso and the upper Rio Negro and gives information on religious missions, including Protestant ones, established among the Indians up to that period.

38. Roberto, "Salvemos nossos Índios."

39. American journalist Gerard Coby, in *Thy Will Be Done,* presents massive evidence to demonstrate that the founder of the Summer Institute of Linguistics (SIL) worked in conjunction with Rockefeller interests to map out mineral ores in the Amazon in the 1930s and 1940s. Later, SIL missionaries were charged with spying for the CIA in the areas surrounding their missions.

40. Suess's *Em defesa* includes these and other documents of great importance to understanding the new meaning of Christianization.

41. Besides the seven Indian assemblies, promoted between 1975 and 1981, CIMI has, since 1978, published a bimonthly journal, *O Porantim,* dedicated exclusively to Indian matters.

42. Analyzing the question of ethnicity and nationhood for the Indian peoples of the Americas, especially the great Mexican ethnic populations, Bartolomé considers that an *ethnic group* becomes a *nation* when it creates a political project which it can impose with regard to the world around it; see his article "Afirmación Estatal."

43. Gomes, "Por um Pacto Indigenista Nacional."

Chapter 6. The Future of the Indians

1. João Magalhães, "A Saúde dos Índios Xikrin." For the increase in the incidence of malaria and the appearance of new strains, see the report in the *Jornal do Brasil,* July 5, 1987. For a general overview, see Hern's "Saúde e demografia."

2. These data are not scientifically proven but appear in reports presented to FUNAI by post chiefs and indigenists.

3. In the 1985 document "A UNI e a Sua Organização" the organization outlines the bases of its political action and recounts the history of its formation. For a list of Indian organizations and their activities from 1987 to 1995, see CEDI's *Povos Indígenas,* pp. 69–72, and Ricardo's *Povos Indígenas,* pp. 89–100.

4. For a journalistic analysis of the rise of Juruna up to 1982, see Hoffmann's *O Gravador.*

5. In mid-1997 Juruna was taken to a hospital in Brasília, where he spent two months receiving treatment for diabetes and a kidney infection. In May 1999, he was suffering from the same problems and seemed to be very ill.

6. For the overall picture of the economic development of the Amazon and the environmental costs thereof, see the various studies in Salati's *Amazônia,* Moran's *The Dilemma,* and Sutlive's *Where Have All the Flowers Gone?* For a recent overview of alternatives to that kind of exploitation, see Anderson's *Alternatives to Deforestation.*

7. Lúcio Flávio Pinto, *Jari.*

8. Asselin, *Grilagem.*

9. The Carajás project and the installation of cast-iron plants in this area could reverse this situation to the detriment of Indian areas, since they would be powered

by vegetable charcoal; see *Jornal do Brasil,* July 5, 1987, for a complete analysis of these plans. As of October 1998, three such plants had been installed, but at least one had been closed down. The other two were in operation but were being challenged by IBAMA, the national environment agency.

10. The idea of the model of plants for the diversification of human cultures was inspired by Cronquist's *The Evolution and Classification.*

11. Anderson, *Imagined Communities.*

12. It has been reported by newspapers and FUNAI that between 1990 and 1996 over two hundred Guarani teenagers and young adults commited suicide, mostly by hanging. See Meihy's "Suicídio Kaiowá."

13. Marx and Engels, *The German Ideology,* p. 53. Part of this quote has been used previously by Siskind as the title of her 1973 book on the Sharanahua.

Bibliography

Abbeville, Claude d'. *História da missão dos padres capuchinhos na ilha do Maranhão e terras circunvizinhas.* Second Portuguese edition. Belo Horizonte and São Paulo: Ed. Itatiaia and Edusp, 1975.

Abreu, João Capistrano de. *Correspondência.* 3 vols. Edited by José Honório Rodrigues. Rio de Janeiro: Instituto Nacional do Livro, 1954.

———. *"Os Bacaerys."* In *Ensaios e Estudos (Crítica e História).* Rio de Janeiro: Sociedade Capistrano de Abreu and Livraria Briguiet, 1938: pp. 217–74.

———. *Rã-txa hu-ni-kuaim: a língua dos Caxinauás do rio Ibuaçu, afluente do Murú.* Rio de Janeiro: Sociedade Capistrano de Abreu and Livraria Briguiet, 1941.

Acuña, Cristóbal de, Gaspar de Carbajal, and Alonso Rojas. *Descobrimentos do Rio das Amazonas.* São Paulo: Companhia Editora Nacional, 1941.

Agostinho, Pedro. *Kwarup: Mito e Ritual no Alto Xingu.* São Paulo: EPU and Edusp, 1974.

Akerren, Bo, Sjouke Bakker, and Rolf Habersang. *Report of the ICRC Medical Mission to the Brazilian Amazon Region.* Geneva: International Committee of the Red Cross, 1970.

Almeida, Maouel Antônio de. "Civilização dos Indígenas." *Jornal do Comércio,* February 12, 1852.

Almeida, Jr., José Maria Gonçalves de. *Carajás, Desafio Político, Ecologia e Desenvolvimento.* São Paulo and Brasília: Brasiliense and CNPq, 1986.

Amorim, Paulo Marcos. "Índios Camponeses: os Potiguara da Baía da Traição." *Revista do Museu Paulista,* n.s. 19 (1970–71): pp. 7–95.

Anaí/Bahia. *Os Povos Indígenas na Bahia.* Salvador: n.p., 1981.

Ancheita, José de. *Arte de grammatica da língua mais usada na costa do Brasil.* São Paulo: Editora Anchieta, 1946.

Anderson, Anthony B., ed. *Alternatives to Deforestation. Steps towards Sustainable Use of the Amazon Rain Forest.* New York: Columbia University Press, 1990.

Anderson, Benedict. *Imagined Communities: Reflections on the Origin and Spread of Nationalism.* Revised edition. New York: Verso, 1991.

Aquino, Terri Vale do, and Marcelo Iglesias. *Kaxinauá do rio Jordão: história, território, economia e desenvolvimento sustentado.* Rio Branco: Comissão Pró-Índio, 1994.

Arnaud, Expedito. "Aspectos da Legislação sobre os Índios do Brasil." *Boletim do Museu Paraense Emílio Goeldi*, n.s. no. 22 (1973): pp. 1–18.

———. "O Comportamento dos índios Gaviões do Oeste face à Sociedade Nacional." *Boletim do Museu Paraense Emílio Goeldi*, Série Antropologia 1 (July 1984): pp. 1–24.

———. "O Direito Indígena e a Ocupação Territorial: o Caso dos índios Tembé." *Revista do Museu Paulista*, n.s. no. 28 (1981–82): pp. 35–49.

Arruti, José Maurício. "Morte e vida no nordeste indígena." *Estudos Históricos* 8, no. 15 (1995): pp. 57–94.

Asselin, Victor. *Grilagem, Corrupção e Violência em Terras de Carajás*. Petrópolis: Vozes, 1982.

Assis, J. Carlos de. "O Escândalo Capemi." In *Os Mandarins da República*. Rio de Janeiro: Paz e Terra, 1984: pp. 79–99.

Ayrosa, Plínio. *Primeiras noções de tupi*. São Paulo: Typografia Cupolo, 1933.

Azanha, Gilberto. "A Forma Timbira: estrutura e resistência." Master's thesis, Universidade de São Paulo, 1984.

Azevedo, João Lúcio de. *Cartas do Padre Antônio Vieira*. 3 vols. Coimbra: Imprensa da Universidade, 1925–1926.

———. *História de Antônio Vieira*. 2 vols. Second edition. Lisbon: Livraria Clássica Editora, 1931.

———. *Os Jesuítas no Grão Pará, suas missões e a colonização*. Coimbra: Imprensa da Universidade, 1930.

Baião, Antônio, et al. *História da Expansão Portuguesa no Mundo*. 3 vols. Lisbon: Editorial Ática, 1939.

Baines, Stephen. *É a FUNAI que sabe: a Frente de Atração Waimiri-Atroari*. Belém: MPEG, 1991.

———. "The Waimiri-Atroari and the Paranapanema Company." *Critique of Anthropology* 11, no. 2 (1991): pp. 143–53.

Balcazar Pardo, Marino. *Disposiciones sobre Indigenas Baldios y Estados Antisociales (vagos, maleantes e rateros)*. Popayan: Editora Universidad, 1954.

Baldus, Herbert. *Bibliografia crítica da etnologia brasileira*. São Paulo: Comissão do 4o. Centenário, 1954.

———. *Bibliografia crítica da etnologia brasileira*. Vol. 2. Hanover: Kommisionverlag Munstermann Druck GMBN, 1968.

Balée, William. *Footprints of the Forest: Ka'apor Ethnobotany. The Historical Ecology of Plant Utilization by an Amazonian People*. New York: Columbia University Press, 1994.

Bamonte, Gerardo, and Giulia Della Marina, eds. *La Festa degli Indios: Il quinto centenario visto dagli indigeni dell'America Latina*. Rome: Vecchio Faggio Editrice, 1992.

Bandeira, Alípio. *Antiguidade e Atualidade Indígenas*. Rio de Janeiro: Tipografia do Jornal do Commercio, 1919.

———. *A Cruz Indígena*. Porto Alegre: Livraria do Globo, 1926.

———. *A Mystificação Salesiana*. Rio de Janeiro: Lithotipo Fluminense, 1923.

Bandeira, Maria de Lourdes. *Os Kiriri de Mirandela: um grupo indígena integrado*. Salvador: Universidade Federal da Bahia and Secretaria de Educação e Cultura, 1972.

Barbira-Scazzochio, Françoise, ed. *Land, People, and Planning in Contemporary Amazon*. Cambridge: University Center for Latin American Studies, 1980.

Barbosa, L. B. Horta. *A Pacificação dos Caingangs Paulistas: Hábitos, Costumes e Instituições desses Índios*. Rio de Janeiro: n.p., 1913.

Barléu, Gaspar. *História dos fatos recentemente praticados durante oito anos no Brasil*. Belo Horizonte and São Paulo: Ed. Itatiaia and Edusp, 1974.

Baro, Roulox, and Pierre Moreau. *História das Últimas Lutas no Brasil entre os Holandeses e os Portugueses e Relação da Viagem ao País dos Tapuias*. Belo Horizonte and São Paulo: Ed. Itatiaia and Edusp, 1985.

Barth, Fredrik. *Ethnic Groups and Boundaries*. London: Little, Brown, 1969.

Bartolomé, Miguel. "Afirmación Estatal y Negación Nacional: El caso de las minorías nacionales en América Latina." Mexico City: Instituto Nacional de Antropologia y História, 1983. Unpublished ms.

Becker, Bertha K. *Geopolítica da Amazônia*. Rio de Janeiro: Zahar Editores, 1982.

Beltrão, Luiz. *O Índio, um Mito Brasileiro*. Petrópolis: Vozes, 1977.

Beozzo, José Oscar. *Leis e Regimentos das Missões*. São Paulo: Edições Loyola, 1983.

Berredo, Bernardo Pereira de. *Annaes históricos do Estado do Maranhão*. Second edition. São Luiz: Typographia. B. de Mattos, 1849.

Boas, Franz. *The Mind of Primitive Man*. Revised Edition. New York: Macmillan, 1938.

Boggiani, Guido. *Os Caduevos*. Belo Horizonte and São Paulo: Ed. Itatiaia and Edusp, 1975.

Bonfil Batalla, Miguel. "El concepto del índio en América: una categoría de la situación colonial." *Anales de Antropologia* 9 (1972): pp. 105–24.

Brandão, Carlos Rodrigues. *Etnia e Identidade*. São Paulo: Brasiliense, 1985.

Cardim, Fernão. *Tratado da Terra e Gente do Brasil*. Vol. 168, *Brasiliana*. São Paulo: Companhia Editora Nacional, 1978.

Carelli, Vincent, and Milton Severiano. *Mão Branca contra o Povo Cinza*. São Paulo: Brasil Debates, 1980.

Carneiro, Robert. "Slash-and-Burn Cultivation among the Kuikuru and Its Implications for Cultural Development." In *Man in Adaptation: The Cultural Present*, edited by Y. Cohen. Chicago: Aldine, 1968: pp. 157–66.

Carvalho, Edgard de Assis. *As Alternativas dos Vencidos*. Rio de Janeiro: Paz e Terra, 1979.

———. *Avá-Guarani do Ocoí-Jacutinga*. Curitiba: CIMI and Comissão de Justiça and Paz, 1981.

Carvalho, José Porfírio. *Waimiri-Atroari, a história que ainda não foi contada.* Brasília: Edição do Autor, 1982.

Carvalho, Maria Rosário. "Os Pataxó de Barra Velha: seu subsistema econômico." Master's thesis, Universidade Federal da Bahia, 1977.

———. "Um Estudo de Caso: Os Índios Tuxá e a Construção da Barragem em Itaparica." In *Os Índios Perante o Direito,* edited by Silvio Coelho dos Santos. Florianópolis: UFSC, 1982: pp. 117–28.

Caspar, Franz. *Tupari.* London: G. Bell, 1956.

Castillo, Bernal Dias del. *Historia verdadera de la conquista de la Nueva España.* México City: Editora J. Ramirez Cabañas, 1944.

Castro, Eduardo Viveiros de. *From the Enemy's Point of View: Humanity and Divinity in an Amazonian Society.* Chicago: University of Chicago Press, 1995.

Castro, Silvio. *A Carta de Pero Vaz de Caminha.* Porto Alegre: L & PM Editores, 1985.

Cavucens, Silvio. "A Situação dos Povos Indígenas do Vale do Javari." In *Pova Indígenas no Brasil, 1991–1995,* edited by Beto Ricardo. São Paulo: Instituto Socioambiental, 1996: pp. 333–42.

Cedeam (Comissão de Documentação e Estudo da Amazônia). *Autos de Devassa contra os Índios Mura do Rio Madeira e Nações do Rio Tocantins, 1738–1739.* Manaus: Universidade do Amazonas and INL, 1986.

CEDI. *Povos Indígenas no Brasil, 1987, 1988, 1989, 1990.* São Paulo: CEDI, 1991.

CEDI and Museu Nacional. *Terras Indígenas no Brasil.* São Paulo: Editora Tempo e Presença, 1987.

Chapelle, Richard. *Os Índios Cintas-Largas.* Belo Horizonte: Itatiaia, 1982.

Chernela, Janet. *The Wanano Indians of the Brazilian Amazon.* Austin: University of Texas Press, 1993.

Childe, V. Gordon. *Man Makes Himself.* New York: New American Library, 1951.

———. *What Happened in History.* Hardmondsworth, England: Penguin, 1964.

CIMI. "Povos Indígenas no Brasil e Presença Missionária." Map, 1985.

Clastres, Hélène. "Primitivismo e Ciência do Homem no Século XVIII." *Discurso* no. 13 (1980): pp. 21–39.

———. "Selvagens e Civilizados no Século XVIII." Manuscript, Campinas, SP, n.d.

———. *Terra sem Males.* São Paulo: Brasiliense, 1979.

Clastres, Pierre. *Arqueologia da Violência.* São Paulo: Brasiliense, 1982.

———. *Chronique des indiens Guayaki.* Paris: Plon, 1972.

———. "Guayaki Cannibalism." In *Native South Americans,* edited by Patricia Lyon. Boston: Little, Brown, 1974: pp. 210–37.

———. *A Sociedade Contra o Estado.* Rio de Janeiro: Francisco Alves, 1978.

Coby, Gerard, and Charlotte Dennet. *Thy Will Be Done. The Conquest of the Amazon: Nelson Rockefeller and Evangelism in the Age of Oil.* New York: Harper Collins, 1995.

Colbachini, Antonio, and Cesar Albisetti. *Os Bororo Orientais Orarimogodógue do Planalto Oriental de Mato Grosso.* São Paulo: Companhia Editora Nacional, 1942.

Collier, John. *Los Indios de las Américas.* Mexico City: Fondo de Cultura Economica, 1960.

Colombo, Cristóvão. *Diário da Descoberta da América.* Porto Alegre: L & PM Editores, 1984.

Comissão Pró-Índio. *A Questão da Educação Indígena.* São Paulo: Brasiliense, 1984.

———. *A Questão da Emancipação.* Caderno, no. 1. São Paulo: Global Editora, 1979.

———. *A Questão da Terra.* São Paulo: Global Editora, 1981.

Cortez, Hernan. *A Conquista do México.* Porto Alegre: L & PM Editores, 1986.

Costa, Francisco Augusto Pereira da. *Chronologia Histórica do Estado do Piauí.* Recife: n.p., 1909.

Cota, Raymundo Garcia. *Carajás: A Invasão Desarmada.* Petrópolis: Vozes, 1984.

Couto de Magalhães, General. *O Selvagem.* Belo Horizonte and São Paulo: Ed. Itatiaia and Edusp, 1975.

———. *Viagem ao Araguaia.* Vol. 28, *Brasiliana.* São Paulo: Companhia Editora Nacional and Instituto Nacional do Livro, 1975.

Cronquist, A. *The Evolution and Classification of Flowering Plantes.* London: Thomas Nelson, 1968.

Cunha, Manuela Carneiro da. *História dos Índios no Brasil.* São Paulo: Companhia das Letras/SMC/FAPESP, 1992.

———. *Os Direitos do Índio.* São Paulo: Brasiliense, 1987.

———. *Os Mortos e os Outros.* São Paulo: Hucitec-Edusp, 1977.

———. "Política indigenista no século XIX." In Cunha, ed., 1992: pp. 17–42.

———, ed. *Antropologia no Brasil: mito, história, etnicidade.* São Paulo: FAPESP/ SMC and Companhia de Letras, 1992.

Daniel, Padre João. "Tesouro descoberto do rio Amazonas." In *Anais da Biblioteca Nacional,* 2 vols, no. 95, 1975. Rio de Janeiro: Biblioteca Nacional, 1976.

Dantas, Beatriz Góis, and Dalmo de Abreu Dallari. *Terra dos Índios Xocó.* São Paulo: Comissão Pró-Índio, 1980.

Darwin, Charles. *A Origem das Espécies.* São Paulo: Hemus, n.d.

Davis, Shelton. *Victims of the Miracle. Development and the Indians of Brazil.* Cambridge, England: Cambridge University Press, 1977.

Denevan, William, ed. *The Native Populations of the Americas.* Madison: University of Wisconsin Press, 1976.

Dias, Manoel Nunes. "Colonização da Amazônia (1755–1778)." *Revista de História* 34 (1967): pp. 471–90.

Dole, Gertrude. "Endocannibalism among the Amahuaca Indians." In *Native South Americans,* edited by Patricia Lyon. Boston: Little, Brown, 1974: pp. 185–209.

Dourado, Mecenas. *A Conversão do Gentio.* Rio de Janeiro: Livraria São José, 1958.

Driver, Harold E. *Indians of North America.* Chicago: University of Chicago Press, 1969.

Dutra, Plínio. "Extrato do Parecer do Dep. Plínio Dutra, Relator do Inquérito que investiga a situação dos Toldos Indígenas do Estado." In *Anais da Assembléia Legislativa Estadual do Rio Grande do Sul.* Porto Alegre: Imprensa Oficial, 1967: pp. 240–49.

"Editorial sobre nomes indígenas." *Revista de Antropologia* 2, no. 2 (1954): pp. 150–52.

Eletrobrás. *Plano Diretor para Proteção e Melhoria do Meio Ambiente nas Obras e Serviços do Setor Elétrico*. Brasília: Eletrobrás, 1986.

——. *Plano Nacional de Energia Elétrica, 1987/2010*. Brasília: Eletrobrás, 1986.

Ennes, Ernesto. *As Guerras dos Palmares*. Vol. 127, *Brasiliana*. São Paulo: Companhia Editora Nacional, 1938.

Evans-Pritchard, E. E. *Bruxaria, Oráculos e Magia entre os Azende*. Rio de Janeiro: Zahar Editores, 1978.

Évreux, Yves d'. *Viagem ao Norte do Brasil feita em 1613 e 1614*. São Luís: Typographia do Frias, 1874.

Fernandes, Florestan. *A Função Social da Guerra na Sociedade Tupinambá*. São Paulo: Livraria Pioneira Editora, 1970.

——. *Investigação etnológica no Brasil e outros ensaios*. Petrópolis: Vozes, 1975.

——. *A Organização Social dos Índios Tupinambá*. São Paulo: Difusão Européia do Livro, 1963.

Ferraz, Iara. "Carajás dez anas depois: vitrine de ambientalismo." In CEDI, *Povos Indígenas no Brasil*. São Paulo: CEDI, 1991: pp. 87–91.

——. "Mãe Maria: em estado de guerra, proteção do território e da vida tribal." Report presented to the Companhia Vale do Rio Doce, February 1985.

——. "Os Parkatejê das matas do Tocantins: a epopéia de um líder Timbira." Master's thesis, Universidade de São Paulo, 1983.

Fisher, William. "Megadevelopment, Environmentalism, and Resistance: The Institutional Context of Kayapó Indigenous Politics in Central Brazil." *Human Organization* 53 (1994): pp. 419–30.

Folha de São Paulo, June 20, 1994.

Franco, Afonso Arinos de Melo. *O Índio Brasileiro e a Revolução Francesa*. Rio de Janeiro: Livraria José Olympio Editora, 1937.

Freire, José Ribamar Bessa. "Da 'Fala Boa' ao Português na Amazônia Brasileira." *Ameríndia* no. 9 (1983): pp. 39–83.

Freud, Sigmund. *Psicologia de Grupo e Análise do Ego*. Rio de Janeiro: Imago, 1976.

——. "Totem and Taboo." In *The Basic Writings of Sigmund Freud*. New York: Modern Library, 1938: pp. 807–930.

Friederici, Georg. *Caráter da Descoberta e Conquista da América pelos Europeus*. Rio de Janeiro: Instituto Nacional do Livro, 1967.

FUNAI. *Situação das Terras Indígenas do Brasil*. Brasília: FUNAI, 1998.

——. *Situação das Terras Indígenas do Brasil: Dados Estimativos*. Brasília: FUNAI, 1984.

Furlong, Guillermo. *Missiones y sus Pueblos Guaranis*. Buenos Aires: Imprenta Balmes, 1962.

Furtado, Lourdes Gonçalves. "Alguns aspectos do processo de mudança na região do Nordeste Parense." *Boletim do Museu Paraense Emílio Goeldi*, Série Antropologia 1 (June 1984): pp. 67–123.

Gaffarel, Paul. *Histoire du Brésil Français au Seizième Siècle*. Paris: Maisonneuve et Cie. Libraires-Editeurs, 1878.

Galvão, Eduardo. *Encontro de Sociedades: Índios e Brancos no Brasil.* Rio de Janeiro: Paz e Terra, 1979.

———. "Indigenous Culture Areas of Brazil: 1900–1959." In *Indians of Brazil in the Twentieth Century,* edited by Janice Hopper. ICR Studies, 2. Washington, D.C.: Institute for Cultural Research, 1967: pp. 169–205.

———. *Santos e Visagens.* São Paulo: Companhia Editora Nacional, 1955.

Gandavo, Pero de Magalhães. *Tratado da Terra do Brasil.* Vol. 1. *História da Província de Santa Cruz.* Vol. 2. Bibliographical note by Rodolfo Garcia and introduction by Capistrano de Abreu. Rio de Janeiro: Edição Anuário do Brasil, 1924.

Giaccaria, Bartolomeu, and Adalberto Heide. *Xavante, Povo Autêntico.* São Paulo: Editorial Dom Bosco, 1972.

Gomes, Mercio Pereira. "The Ethnic Survival of the Tenetehara Indians of Maranhão, Brazil." Doctoral dissertation, University of Florida, 1977.

———. "Por que o índio briga com posseiro." In Comissão Pró-Índio, *A Questão da Terra.* São Paulo: Global Editora, 1981: pp. 51–56.

———. "Por um Pacto Indigenista Nacional." Paper presented to the National Constituent Assembly, April 29, 1987.

———. "Programa Awá." Report presented to FUNAI and the Companhia Vale do Rio Doce, 1985.

———. "O povo Guajá e as condições reais para a sua sobrevivência." In CEDI, *Povos Indígenas no Brasil, 1987, 1989, 1990.* São Paulo, 1991: pp. 354–60.

———. "Sétimo Relatório sobre a Problemática Indígena no Maranhão, sobretudo em relação ao Projeto Ferro Carajás." Report presented to the Companhia Vale do Rio Doce and FUNAI, 1986.

Good, Kenneth, and David Chagnoff. *Into the Heart: One Man's Pursuit of Love and Knowledge among the Yanomama.* New York: Simon & Schuster, 1991.

Gorender, Jacob. *O Escravismo Colonial.* São Paulo: Ed. Ática, 1978.

Gregor, Thomas. *Mehinaku.* São Paulo and Brasília: Companhia Editora Nacional and Instituto Nacional do Livro, 1982.

Gross, Daniel. "Protein Capture and Culture Development in the Amazon Basin." *American Anthropologist* 77, no. 3 (1975): pp. 526–49.

Grünberg, Georg. *La Situación del Indígena en América del Sur.* Montevideo: Tierra Nuova, 1971.

Hames, R., and W. Vickers, eds. *Adaptive Responses of Native Amazonians.* New York: Academic Press, 1983.

Hanbury-Tenison, Robin. *Report of a Visit to the Indians of Brazil.* London: Primitive Peoples Fund, 1971.

Hanke, Lewis. *Aristóteles e os índios americanos.* São Paulo: Livraria Martins Editora, n.d.

Haring, C. H. *Empire in Brazil.* New York: W. W. Norton, 1958.

Hartman, Thekla. *Bibliografia crítica da etnologia brasileira.* Vol 3. Hanover: Volkerkundliche Abhandlugen, 1984.

Helm, Cecília M. V. "A Integração do Índio na Estrutura Agrária do Paraná: O caso Kaingang." Doctoral dissertation, Universidade do Paraná, 1974.

———. "A Terra, a Usina e os Índios de P. I. Mangueirinha." In Os Índios Perante o Direito, edited by Silvio Coelho dos Santos. Florianópolis: UFSC, 1982: pp. 129–42.

———. "Os Xetá: a trajetória de um grupo tupi-guarani em extinção no Paraná." Anuário Antropológico no. 92 (1994): pp. 105–12.

Hemming, John. Amazon Frontier. The Defeat of the Brazilian Indians. London: Macmillan, 1987.

———. Red Gold: The Conquest of the Brazilian Indians, 1500–1760. Cambridge: Harvard University Press, 1978.

Hern, Warren. "Saúde e demografia de povos indígenas amazônicos: perspectiva histórica e situação atual." Cadernos de Saúde Pública 7, no. 4 (1991): pp. 451–80.

Hernández, P. Pablo. Missiones del Paraguay: Organización Social de las Doctrinas Guaranis de la Companhia de Jesus. Barcelona: Gustavo Gili Editora, 1913.

Hobbes, Thomas. Leviatã, ou Matéria, Forma e Poder de um Estado Eclesiástico e Civil. Coleção "Os Pensadores." São Paulo: Editora Abril Cultural, 1974.

Hoffmann, Assis. O Gravador do Juruna. Porto Alegre: Global Editora, 1982.

Hohenthal, W. "As tribos indígenas do médio e baixo São Francisco." Revista do Museu Paulista, n.s. 12 (1960): pp. 37–86.

Holanda, Sérgio Buarque de. Visão do Paraíso. Vol. 333, Brasiliana. São Paulo: Companhia Editora Nacional, 1977.

Hopper, Janice, ed. Indians of Brazil in the Twentieth Century. ICR Studies, 2. Washington, D.C.: Institute for Cultural Research, 1967.

Horta, L. B. Pelo Índio e pela sua Proteção Oficial. 1923. 2nd edition. Preface by Major Alípio Bandeira. Rio de Janeiro: Departamento de Imprensa Nacional, 1947.

Ianni, Octávio. Colonização e Contra-Reforma Agrária na Amazônia. Petrópolis: Vozes, 1979.

———. A Luta Pela Terra. Petrópolis: Vozes, 1979.

Ihering, Hermann von. "A Antropologia do Estado de São Paulo." Revista do Museu Paulista 7 (1907): pp. 202–57.

Instituto de Pesquisas Antropológicas do Rio de Janeiro (IPARJ). "Quatro estudos de caso." Report presented to Eletrobrás, Rio de Janeiro, 1989.

Jacobs, Wilbur. Dispossessing the American Indian: Indians and Whites on the Colonial Frontier. New York: Charles Scribner's Sons, 1972.

Jimenez, Nelly Arvelo de. "Análisis del Indigenismo Oficial en Venezuela." In La Situacíon del Indígena en América del Sur, by Georg Grünberg. Montevideo: Tierra Nuovo, 1971: pp. 31–42.

Jonge, Gedeon Morris de. "Relatórios e Cartas." Revista do Instituto Histórico e Geográfico Brasileiro 58 (1886): pp. 237–319.

Jornal de Brasília, November 1, 1986.

Jornal do Brasil, Rio de Janeiro. June 5, 1985; April 27, 1986; October 31, 1986; May 6, 1987; May 10, 1987; May 31, 1987; June 5, 1987; June 12, 1987; July 1,

1987; July 5, 1987; July 19, 1987; September 6, 1987; September 23, 1987; October 5, 1987; October 30, 1987; November 11, 1987; December 12, 1987.

Jornal Gazeta Mercantil, São Paulo. August 19, 1986.

Julien, Charles André. *Les voyages de découverte et les premiers établissements XV–XVIe siècles.* Paris: Presses Universitaires Françaises, 1948.

Jung, Carl. *O Homem e seus símbolos.* Rio de Janeiro: Nova Fronteira, 1981.

Junqueira, Carmem, and Edgar de Assis Carvalho, eds. *Antropologia e Indigenismo na América Latina.* São Paulo: Editora Cortez, 1981.

Junqueira, Carmen Betty Mindlin, and Abel Lima. "Terras e Conflito no Parque do Aripuanã." In *Os Índios Perante o Direito,* edited by Silvio Coelho dos Santos. Florianópolis: UFSC, 1982: pp. 111–16.

Kensiger, Kenneth. *How Real People Ought to Live: The Cashinahua of Eastern Peru.* Prospect Heights, Ill.: Waveland Press, 1995.

Kiemen, Mathias. *The Indian Policy of Portugal in America with Special Reference to the State of Maranhão, 1500–1755.* Washington, D.C.: Catholic University Press, 1955.

Krader, Lawrence. *Marx's Ethnological Notebooks.* Assen, Netherlands: Van Gorcum, 1972.

Ladeira, Maria Elisa. "Algumas Observações sobre a Situação Atual dos Índios Apinayé." Report presented to Companhia Vale do Rio Doce and FUNAI, June 1983, 66 pp.

———. "A Troca de Nomes e a Troca de Cônjuges: uma contribuição ao estudo do parentesco Timbira." Master's thesis, Universidade de São Paulo, 1982.

Léclerc, Gerard. *Crítica da Antropologia.* Lisbon: Editorial Estampa, 1973.

Leite, Serafim Padre. *Cartas dos Primeiros Jesuítas no Brasil.* 3 vols. São Paulo: Comissão de Publicação do 4° Centenário, 1954.

———. *História da Companhia de Jesus no Brasil.* 12 vols. Rio de Janeiro: Instituto Nacional do Livro, 1938–50.

Lemos, Miguel. "José Bonifácio: a propósito do novo Serviço de Proteção aos Índios." *Publicação* no. 305 (1910).

Lemos, Miguel, and R. Teixeira Mendes. "Bases de uma Constituição política ditatorial federativa para a República Brasileira, 1890." In *Anais da Assembléia Nacional Constituinte.* 2 vols. Rio de Janeiro: Imprensa Nacional, 1892: pp. 99–105.

Leon-Portilla, Miguel. *A Conquista da América Latina vista pelos índios: Relatos astecas, maias e incas.* Porto Alegre: L & PM Editores, 1987.

Léry, Jean de. *Viagem à Terra do Brasil.* 3rd Portuguese edition. São Paulo: Livraria Martins Editora, 1960.

Lévi-Strauss, Claude. *Antropologia Estrutural II.* Rio de Janeiro: Biblioteca Tempo Brasileiro, 1976.

———. *O Pensamento Selvagem.* São Paulo: Companhia Editora Nacional, 1970.

———. *Tristes Tropiques.* São Paulo: Anhembi Editora, 1955.

———, ed. *La Identidad.* Barcelona: Ediciones Petrel, 1981.

Lévy-Bruhl, Lucien. *Le Surnaturel et la Nature dans la Mentalité Primitive.* Paris: Presses Universitaires de France, 1963.

Lewis, Norman. "Genocide." *Sunday Times Magazine* (London), February 22, 1969, pp. 27–28.

Lima, A. C. de Souza. *Um grande cerco de paz: poder tutelar e indianidade no Brasil.* Petropolis: Vozes, 1995.

Lins, Ivan. *O Positivismo no Brasil.* São Paulo: Companhia Editora Nacional, 1964.

Lisboa, João Francisco. *Obras.* 4 vols. São Luís: Typographia B. de Mattos, 1865.

Loukotka, Chestimir. "Línguas Indígenas do Brasil." *Revista do Arquivo Municipal de São Paulo* 54 (1939): pp. 41–61.

Lugon, C. *A República "Comunista" Cristã dos Guarani, 1610–1768.* Rio de Janeiro: Paz e Terra, 1977.

Luna, Regina. *A Terra era Liberta.* São Luís: Editora da UFMA, 1985.

Lyon, Patricia, ed. *Native South Americans: Ethnology of the Least Known Continent.* Boston: Little, Brown, 1974.

Magalhães, Antônio Carlos. "Aldeamentos Indígenas Parakanã: Apuiterewa, Marudjewara e Paranati." Report presented to Companhia Vale do Rio Doce and FUNAI, March 1985, 41 pp.

Magalhães, João Paulo Botelho de. "A Saúde dos Índios Xikrin do Bacajá." Report presented to the Companhia Vale do Rio Doce and FUNAI, January 1985.

Malheiro, Perdigão. *A Escravidão no Brasil.* Vol. 2. Petrópolis: Vozes, 1976.

Mamiani, Luis Vicencio. *Arte de grammatica da língua brasilica da naçam Kiriri.* Rio de Janeiro: Biblioteca Nacional, 1877.

Marchant, Alexander. *Do Escambo à Escravidão.* Vol. 225, *Brasiliana.* Rio de Janeiro: Companhia Editora Nacional, 1943.

Marewa. *Resistência Waimiri-Atroari.* Itacoatiara: n.p., 1983.

Marlière, Guido. "Notas e Documentos." *Revista do Archivo Público Mineiro,* brochures 3 and 4 (1906), brochures 1, 2, 3, and 4 (1907).

Martins, Edilson. *Nossos Índios, Nossos Mortos.* Rio de Janeiro: Codecri, 1978.

Martins, José de Souza. *Não há terra para plantar neste verão.* Petrópolis: Vozes, 1986.

Martius, Carl Von. "Como se deve escrever a História do Brasil." *Revista do Instituto Histórico e Geográfico Brasileiro* 7, no. 24 (1845): pp. 35–48.

———. *O Estado do Direito entre os Autóctones do Brasil.* Coleção Reconquista do Brasil, n.s., vol. 58. Belo Horizonte and São Paulo: Ed. Itatiaia and Edusp, 1982.

Marx, Karl, and Friedrich Engels. *Capital.* 3 vols. New York: International Publishers, 1964.

———. *Economic and Philosophical Manuscripts.* New York: International Publishers, 1967.

———. *Formações Econômicas Pré-Capitalistas.* Rio de Janeiro: Paz e Terra, 1975.

———. *The German Ideology.* Pt. 1, with excerpts from pts. 2 and 3. New York: International Publishers, 1970.

———. *Origem da Família, da Propriedade Privada e do Estado.* Rio de Janeiro: Editora Civilização Brasileira, 1974.

Mason, J. Alden. "The Languages of South American Indians." In *Handbook of South American Indians,* edited by Julian Steward. Vol. 3. New York: Cooper Square, 1963: pp. 157–317.

Matta, Roberto da. *Um Mundo Dividido*. Petrópolis: Vozes, 1976.

Maybury-Lewis, David. *Akwe-Shavante Society*. Cambridge: Harvard University Press, 1974.

————. *Dialectical Societies: The Jê and Bororo of Central Brazil*. Cambridge: Harvard University Press, 1979.

McNickle, D'Arcy. *The Indian Tribes of the United States*. London: Oxford University Press, 1964.

Meggers, Betty. *Amazonia: Man and Nature in a Counterfeit Paradise*. Chicago: Aldine Atherton, 1971.

————. *América pré-histórica*. Rio de Janeiro: Paz e Terra, 1979.

Meihy, José Carlos Sebe Bom. "Suicídio Kaiowá." *Carta'* no. 9 (1993): pp. 53–60.

Melatti, Júlio César. *Índios e Criadores*. Rio de Janeiro: Instituto de Ciências Sociais, 1967.

————. *O Messianismo Krahó*. São Paulo: Editora Herder and Edusp, 1972.

————. *Ritos de uma Tribo Timbira*. São Paulo: Editora Ática, 1978.

Melatti, Júlio César, and Beto Ricardo, eds. *Javari*. São Paulo: CEDI, 1979.

Mello, José Antônio Gonçalves de. *Fontes para a História do Brasil Holandês*. Vol. 1, *A Economia Açucareira*. Recife: Parque Histórico Nacional dos Guararapes, 1981.

————. *Tempo dos Flamengos*. Coleção Documentos Brasileiros, vol. 54. Rio de Janeiro: José Olympio Editora, 1947.

Mendes, R. Teixeira. "Ainda os indígenas do Brazil e a política moderna." *Boletim do Apostolado Positivista Brasileiro* no. 253 (1907): 23 pp.

————. "A civilização dos indígenas brasileiros e a política moderna." *Boletim da Igreja do Apostolado Positivista Brasileiro*. no. 294 (1910): 21 pp.

————. "Em defesa dos selvagens brasileiros." *Boletim do Apostolado Positivista Brasileiro* no. 300 (1910): 17 pp.

————. "A proteção republicana aos indígenas brasileiros e a catequese católica dos mesmos indígenas." *Boletim do Apostolado Positivista Brasileiro* no. 349 (1912): 21 pp.

————. "O sientismo e a defesa dos indígenas brasileiros: a propósito do artigo do Dr. Hermann von Ihering 'Extermínio dos indígenas ou dos 'sertanejos'." *Jornal do Commercio*, December 15, 1909.

Mendonça, Marcos Carneiro de. *A Amazônia na Era Pombalina*. 3 vols. Rio de Janeiro: Edição da Revista do Instituto Histórico e Geográfico Brasileiro, 1963.

Métraux, Alfred. *Migrations Historiques des Tupi-Guarani*. Paris: Maison Neuve Frères, 1927.

————. "The Paressi." In *Handbook of South American Indians*, edited by Julian Steward. Vol. 3. New York: Cooper Square, 1963.

————. *A Religião dos Tupinambá e suas Relações com as demais Tribos Tupi Guarani*. Translated, with preface and notes, by Estêvão Pinto. São Paulo: Companhia Editora Nacional, 1950.

Milton, Katherine. "Comparative Aspects of Diet in Amazonian Forest-Dweller." *Philosophical Transactions of the Royal Society of London* no. 334 (1991): pp. 253–63.

———. "Protein and Carbohydrate Resources of the Maku Indians of Northwest Amazon." *American Anthropologist* 86 (1984): pp. 7–27.

Minc, Carlos. *A Reconquista da Terra*. Rio: Jorge Zahar Editor, 1985.

Mindlin, Betty. *Nós Paiter: Os Suruí de Rondônia*. Petrópolis: Vozes, 1985.

———. "A nova utopia indígena: os projetos econômicos." In *Antropologia e Indigenismo na América Latina*, edited by Carmem Junqueira and Edgar de Assis Carvalho. São Paulo: Editora Cortez, 1981: pp. 25–35.

Monsonyi, Esteban E. "La Situacion del Indígena en Venezuela: Perspectivas y Soluciones." In La Situación del Indígena en América del Sur, by Georg Grünberg. Montevideo: Tierra Nuovo, 1971: pp. 43–63.

Montaigne, Michel de. "Os Canibais." In *Ensaios. Coleção "Os Pensadores."* São Paulo: Editora Abril Cultural, 1972: pp. 205–235.

Monte, Nietta. "A construção de currículos indígenas nos diários de classe: estudo do caso Kaxinauá, Acre. Master's thesis, Niterói, Universidade Federal Fluminense, 1994.

Monteiro, John. *Negros da Terra: índios e bandeirantes nas origens de São Paulo*. São Paulo: Companhia das Letras, 1994.

Moonen, Francisco. "Os Potiguara: índios integrados ou deprivados?" *Revista Ciências Sociais* 4, no. 2 (1973): pp. 131–54.

Moran, Emílio, ed. *The Dilemma of Amazon Development*. Boulder, Colo.: Westview Press, 1983.

———. *Through Amazonian Eyes: The Human Ecology of Amazonian Populations*. Iowa City: University of Iowa Press, 1993.

More, Thomas. *Utopia*. New York: Penguin, 1970.

Moreira Neto, Carlos de Araújo. "Alguns dados para a história recente dos índios Kaingang." In *La Situacíon del Indígena en América del Sur*, by Georg Grünberg. Montevideo: Tierra Nuovo, 1971: pp. 381–419.

———. *Índios da Amazônia: De Maioria a Minoria*. Petrópolis: Editora Vozes, 1988.

———. "A política indigenista brasileira durante o Século XIX." Doctoral dissertation, Faculdade de Filosofia, Ciências Humanas de São Carlos, 1971.

Morgan, Lewis Henry. *Ancient Society*. Gloucester, Mass.: Peter Smith, 1974.

Mörner, Magnus. *Actividades politicas y económicas de los jesuítas en el Rio de la Plata*. Buenos Aires: Paidos, 1968.

———, ed. *The Expulsion of the Jesuits from Latin America*. New York: Alfred A. Knopf, 1965.

Mott, Luiz de Barros. "Estruturas demográficas das fazendas de gado do Piauí colonial." *Ciência e Cultura* no. 30 (1978): pp. 1196–1210.

Murphy, Robert. *Headhunter's Heritage: Social and Economic Change among the Munduruku Indians*. Berkeley: University of California Press, 1960.

Nantes, Martinho de. *Relação Sucinta de uma Missão no Rio São Francisco*. Vol. 368, *Brasiliana*. Translated, with notes, by Barbosa Lima Sobrinho. São Paulo and Brasília: Companhia Editora Nacional and Instituto Nacional do Livro, 1979.

Nasser, Elizabeth. "Sociedade Tuxá." Master's thesis, Universidade Federal da Bahia, 1975.

Navarro, Eduardo. *O método moderno de Tupi Antigo. A língua do Brasil nos primeiros séculos.* Petrópolis: Vozes, 1998.

Nieuhof, Joan. *Memorável Viagem Marítima e Terrestre ao Brasil.* Belo Horizonte and São Paulo: Ed. Itatiaia and Edusp, 1981.

Nimuendaju, Curt. *The Eastern Timbira.* American Archaelogy and Ethnology, vol. 41. Berkeley and Los Angeles: University of California Press, 1946.

———. *Mapa Etno-histórico.* Rio de Janeiro: IBGE, 1982.

———. *Textos Indigenistas.* Edited by Paulo Suess. São Paulo: Edições Loyola, 1982.

Nóbrega, Padre Manuel da. "Diálogo sobre a conversão do gentio (1557)." In *A Conversão do Gentio*, by Mecenas Dourado. Rio de Janeiro: Livraria São José, 1958: pp. 25–165.

Nutels, Noel. "Medical Problems of Newly Contacted Indian Groups." *Biomedical Challenges Presented by the American Indian*, no. 165. Washington, D.C.: Pan American Health Organization, 1968, pp. 68–76.

———. "Plano para uma campanha de defesa do índio brasileiro contra a tuberculose." *Separata of the Revista Brasileira de Tuberculose* 20 (1952): pp. 5–17.

Olian, José. *Indígenas de Minas Gerais.* Belo Horizonte: Edições Movimento/Perspectiva, 1965.

Oliveira, Humberto de. *Coletânea de Leis, Atos e memórias referente ao Indígena Brasileiro.* Conselho Nacional de Proteção aos Índios, Publication no. 94. Rio de Janeiro: Imprensa Nacional, 1947.

Oliveira, J. Mariano de. "Pelos Indianos Brasileiros." *Boletim da Igreja do Apostolado Positivista Brazileiro.* Rio de Janeiro, 1894, 17 pp.

Oliveira, Roberto Cardoso de. "Aculturação e Fricção Interétnica." *América Latina* 6, no. 3 (1964): pp. 17–32.

———. "Estudo de Áreas de Fricção Interétnica no Brasil." *América Latina* 5, no. 3 (1963): pp. 43–71.

———. *Identidade, Etnia e Estrutura Social.* São Paulo: Livraria Pioneira Editora, 1976.

———. *O Índio e o mundo dos brancos: A situação dos Tikuna do Alto Solimões.* São Paulo: Difel, 1967.

———. *O Processo de assimilação dos Terena.* Rio de Janeiro: Museu Nacional, 1960.

———. *Urbanização e tribalismo: A integração dos índios Terena numa sociedade de classes.* Rio de Janeiro: Zahar Editores, 1968.

Ottoni, Theophilo B. "Carta ao Dr. J. M. de Macedo em 1858 sobre os selvagens do Mucuri." *Revista do Instituto Histórico e Geográfico Brasileiro* 21 (1858): pp. 193–97.

Paraíso, Maria Hilda Baqueiro. "Caminhos de ir e vir e caminhos sem volta: índios, estradas e rios no sul da Bahia." Master's thesis, Universidade Federal da Bahia, 1982.

Paula, José Maria de. *Terra dos Índios*. Serviço de Proteção aos Índios, Bulletin no. 1. Rio de Janeiro: Imprensa Nacional, 1944.

Piaget, Jean. *O Raciocínio na Criança*. Rio de Janeiro: Editora Record, n.d.

———. *Structuralism*. New York: Harper & Row, 1970.

Picchi, Debra. "Impact of an Industrial Agricultural Project on the Bakairi Indians of Central Brazil." *Human Organization* 50, no. 1 (1991): pp. 26–38.

Pinto, Estêvão. *Os Índios do Nordeste*. 2 vols. Vols. 44, 45, *Brasiliana*. São Paulo: Companhia Editora Nacional, 1935–38.

Pinto, Lúcio Flávio. *Carajás, o Ataque ao Coração da Amazônia*. Rio de Janeiro: Editora Marco Zero, 1982.

———. *Jari: Toda a Verdade sobre o Projeto de Ludwig*. Rio de Janeiro: Editora Marco Zero, 1986.

Porro, Antonio. *As Crônicas do Rio Amazonas: notas etno-históricas sobre as antigas populações indígenas da Amazônia*. Petropolis: Vozes, 1993.

Prado, Francisco Rodrigues de. "História dos Índios Cavaleiros ou da Nação Guaykuru." *Revista do Instituto Histórico e Geográfico Brasileiro* 70 (1908): pp. 21–44.

Prado, J. F. de Almeida. *A Conquista da Paraíba (séculos XVI e XVII)*. Vol. 321, *Brasiliana*. São Paulo: Companhia Editora Nacional, 1964.

Rabelo, Marques. *Vida e Obra de Manuel Antônio de Almeida*. São Paulo: Livraria Martins Editora, 1943.

Ramos, Alcida. *Hierarquia e simbiose. Relações intertribais no Brasil*. São Paulo: Hucitec/INL, 1980.

Redfield, Robert, Ralph Linton, and Melville Herskovitz. "Memorandum on the Study of Acculturation." *American Anthropologist* 38 (1936): pp. 149–52.

Reichel-Dolmatoff, G. *Amazonian Cosmos*. Chicago: University of Chicago Press, 1971.

Revista Veja, September 5, 1984.

Ribeiro, Berta. *Amazônia Urgente: cinco séculos de história e ecologia*. Belo Horizonte: Editora Itatiaia, 1990.

———. *Diário do Xingu*. Rio de Janeiro: Paz e Terra, 1979.

———. "A oleira e a tecelã: o papel social da mulher na sociedade Assurini." *Revista de Antropologia* 25 (1982): 25–62.

———. *Os Índios das Águas Pretas*. São Paulo: Companhia das Letras, 1995.

Ribeiro, Berta, and Darcy Ribeiro. *Suma Etnológica Brasileira*. Petrópolis: Vozes, 1986.

Ribeiro, Darcy. *As Américas e a Civilização*. Petrópolis: Vozes, 1977.

———. *Diários Índios*. São Paulo: Companhia das Letras, 1996.

———. "Documento sobra as terras dos Kadiwéu." *Carta* no. 9 (1991): pp. 268–69.

———. *Kadiwéu*. Petrópólis: Vozes, 1980.

———. *Línguas e Culturas Indígenas do Brasil*. Rio de Janeiro: Centro Brasileiro de Pesquisas Educacionais, 1957.

———. *Os Índios e a Civilização*. 2nd edition. Petrópolis: Vozes, 1977.

———. *A Política Indigenista Brasileira.* Rio de Janeiro: Ministério da Agricultura, 1962.

———. *Uirá vai à procura de Deus.* Rio de Janeiro: Paz e Terra, 1974.

Ribeiro, Francisco de Paula. "Descripção do Território de Pastos Bons, nos sertões do Maranhão." *Revista do Instituto Histórico e Geográfico Brasileiro* 12 (1849): pp. 41–86.

———. "Memória sobre as nações gentias que presentemente habitam o continente do Maranhão." *Revista do Instituto Histórico e Geográfico Brasileiro* 3 (1841): pp. 131–47.

Ricardo, Beto, ed. *Povos Indígenas no Brasil, 1991–1995.* São Paulo: Instituto Socioambiental, 1996.

Roberto, Fátima. "Salvemos nossos Índios." Master's thesis, Universidade Estadual de Campinas, 1983.

Rodrigues, Aryon Dall'Igna. "Evidence of Tupi-Carib Relationships." *South American Indian Languages: Retrospect and Prospect,* edited by H. E. M. Klein and L. R. Stark. Austin: University of Texas Press, 1985: pp. 371–404.

———. *Línguas Brasileiras.* São Paulo: Edições Loyola, 1986.

Rodrigues, João Barbosa. *A Pacificação dos Crishanás.* Rio de Janeiro: Imprensa Nacional, 1882.

Rondon, Cândido Mariano da Silva. *Relatórios dos Trabalhos realizados de 1900 a 1906.* Conselho Nacional de Proteção aos Índios, Publication, nos. 69–70. Rio de Janeiro: Imprensa Nacional, 1949.

———. *Conferências realizadas nos dias 5, 7 e 9 de setembro de 1915.* Da Comissão de Linhas Telegráficas Estratégicas de Mato Grosso ao Amazonas, Publication no. 42. Rio de Janeiro: Imprensa Nacional, 1946.

Roosevelt, Anna. *Moundbuilders of the Amazon: Geophysical Archaeology on Marajó Island, Brazil.* San Diego: Academic Press, 1991.

———. "The Rise and Fall of Amazonian Chiefdoms." *L'Homme* 33, nos. 126–28 (1993): pp. 255–83.

———, ed. *Amazonian Indians from Pre-history to the Present: Anthropological Perspectives.* Tucson: University of Arizona Press, 1994.

Rousseau, Jean-Jacques. "Ensaio sobre a origem da desigualdade entre os homens." In *O Contrato Social.* São Paulo: Editora Cultrix, 1977: pp. 41–115.

Rubén, Guillermo. "Les Mapuches: l'Illusion de l'Indianité." Doctoral dissertation, University of Paris, 1980.

———. *O que é Nacionalidade.* São Paulo: Brasiliense, 1984.

Rubinger, Marcos Magalhães, Maria Stella de Amorim, and Sonia de Almeida Marcato. *Índios Maxakali: Resistência ou Morte.* Belo Horizonte: Interlivros, 1980.

Sahlins, Marshall. *Culture and Practical Reason.* Chicago: University of Chicago Press, 1976.

———. *Stone Age Economics.* Chicago: Aldine, 1972.

Salati, Eneas, et al. *Amazônia: desenvolvimento, integração e ecologia.* São Paulo and Brasília: Brasiliense and CNPq, 1983.

Salisbury, R. F. *From Stone to Steel.* Melbourne: University of Melbourne Press, 1962.

Salvador, Frei Vicente do. *História do Brasil, 1500–1627.* New edition. Revised by Capistrano de Abreu. São Paulo and Rio de Janeiro: Editores Weiszflog Irmãos, 1918.

Sandess, Douglas Esmond. *Native Peoples in Areas of Internal National Expansion: Indian and Inuit in Canada.* Copenhagen: IWGIA, 1973.

Santilli, Juliana, ed. *Os Direitos Indígenas e a Constituição.* Porto Alegre: NDI and Sergio Antonio Fatris Editor, 1993.

Santilli, Márcio. "Projeto Calha Norte, tutela militar e política de fronteiras." *Tempo e Presença* no. 223 (September 1987): pp. 17–19.

Santos, José Luiz dos. "A Demarcação do Território Krikati: Situação Atual." Report presented to Companhia Vale do Rio Doce and FUNAI December 1985, 15 pp.

———. "Segundo Relatório sobre os Krikati." Report presented to Companhia Vale do Rio Doce and FUNAI, March 1985, 45 pp.

Santos, Murilo. *Bandeiras Verdes.* São Luís: CPT/MA, 1981.

Santos, Silvio Coelho dos. *Educação e Sociedades Tribais.* Porto Alegre: Editora Movimento, 1975.

———. *Índios e Brancos no Sul do Brasil.* Florianópolis: EDEME, 1973.

———, ed. *Os Índios Perante o Direito.* Florianópolis: UFSC, 1982.

Santos, Silvio Coelho dos, and Paul Aspelin. *Indian Areas Threatened by Hydroelectric Plants in Brazil.* Copenhagen: IWGIA, 1981.

Schmink, Marianne, and Charles Wood, eds. *Contested Frontiers in Amazonia.* New York: Columbia University Press, 1992.

———. *Frontier Expansion in Amazonia.* Gainesville: University of Florida Press, 1984.

Schubart, Herbert. "Ecologia e Utilização das Florestas." In *Amazônia: desenvolvimento, integração e ecologia,* by Eneas Salati et al. Sao Paulo and Brasília: Brasiliense and CNPq, 1983: pp. 101–43.

Schwartz, Stuart. *Sugar Plantations in the Formation of Brazilian Society. Bahia, 1550–1835.* Cambridge, England: Cambridge University Press, 1985.

Seeger, Anthony. *Os Indios e Nós.* Rio de Janeiro: Editora Campus, 1980.

Serviço de Proteção aos Índios (SPI). "Relatório Anual, 1954." Rio de Janeiro: SPI, 1955.

Silva, Aracy Lopes da. *Nomes e amigos: da prática Xavante a uma reflexão sobre os Jê.* São Paulo: Edusp, 1987.

Silva, Aracy Lopes da, and Luís Grupioni, eds. *A Temática Indígena na Escola.* Brasilia: Mec/Mari/Unesco, 1991.

Silva, Joana A. Fernandes. "Os Kaiowá e a Ideologia dos Projetos Econômicos." Master's thesis, Universidade Estadual de Campinas, 1982.

Silverwood-Cope, Peter. "A Contribution to the Ethnography of the Colombian Maku." Ph.D. dissertation, Cambridge University, 1972.

Simonian, Lígia T. L. *A defesa das terras indígenas. Uma luta de Moysés Westphalen.* Ijuí: Cadernos do Museu Antropológico "Diretor Pestana," 1979.

———. "Terra de Posseiros: um estudo sobre a política de terras indígenas." Master's thesis, Museu Nacional, 1981.

Siskind, Janet. *To Hunt in the Morning.* London: Oxford University Press, 1973.

Smith, Nigel. "Anthrosols and Human Carrying Capacity in Amazonia." *Annals of the Association of American Geographers* 70 (1980): pp. 553–66.

———. *Rainforest Corridors: The Transamazon Colonization Scheme.* Berkeley: University of California Press, 1982.

Sobrinho, Barbosa Lima. *O Devassamento do Piauí.* Rio de Janeiro: Companhia Editora Nacional, 1946.

Souto-Maior, Pedro. "Fastos Pernambucanos." *Revista do Instituto Histórico e Geográfico Brasileiro* 75, pt. 1 (1912): pp. 414–26.

Souza, Gabriel Soares de. *Tratado Descritivo do Brasil em 1587.* Vol. 117, *Brasiliana.* São Paulo: Companhia Editora Nacional, 1971.

Souza, Lincoln de. *Os Xavante e a Civilização.* Rio de Janeiro: IBGE, 1953.

Souza, Marcio, ed. *Os Índios vão à luta.* Rio de Janeiro: Editora Marco Zero, 1981.

Spencer, Herbert. *Principles of Sociology.* New York: D. Appleton, 1986.

———. "Boletim Anual, 1955." Rio de Janeiro: SPI, 1956.

Spix, Johann Baptis von, and Karl von Martius. *Viagem pelo Brasil.* 3 vols. Belo Horizonte and São Paulo: Ed. Itatiaia and Edusp, 1976.

Steadman, Janet. *The Yuqui.* New York: Holt, Rinehart, 1986.

Steward, Julian. *Native Peoples of South America.* New York: McGraw-Hill, 1959.

———. *Theory of Culture Change.* Urbana: University of Illinois Press, 1955.

———, ed. *Handbook of South American Indians.* 6 vols. New York: Cooper Square, 1963.

Studart Filho, Carlos. *Os Aborígenes do Ceará.* Fortaleza: Editora "Instituto do Ceará," 1965.

Suess, Paulo. *Em defesa dos Povos Indígenas. Documentos e Legislação.* São Paulo: Edições Loyola, 1980.

Sutlive, V. H. *Where Have All the Flowers Gone? Deforestation in the Third World.* Williamsburg, Va.: College of William and Mary Press, 1981.

Taunay, Afonso d'Escragnole. "A Guerra dos Bárbaros." *Separata da Revista do Arquivo Municipal de São Paulo* 22 (1936): pp. 11–253.

———. *História Geral das Bandeiras Paulistas.* 11 vols. São Paulo: H. L. Canton, pp. 1424–50.

Thevet, André. *As Singularidades da França Antártica.* Coleção Reconquista do Brasil, vol. 45. Belo Horizonte and São Paulo: Ed. Itatiaia and Edusp, 1978.

Thomas, Georg. *A Política Indigenista dos Portugueses no Brasil, 1500–1640.* São Paulo: Edições Loyola. 1982.

Todorov, Tzestan. *A Conquista da América. A descoberta do outro.* São Paulo: Livraria Martins Fontes, 1988.

Turner, Terence. "Kayapó on Television: An Anthropological Viewing." *Visual Anthropology Review* 8, no. 1 (1992): pp. 107–12.

Urban, Greg. "A história da cultura brasileira segundo as línguas nativas." In *Antropologia no Brasil*, edited by Manuela Carneiro da Cunha. São Paulo: FAPESP/SMC and Companhia de Letras, 1992: pp. 87–102.

Uribe Misas, Alfonso. *Las Misiones Catolicas ante la Legislación Columbiana y el Derecho Internacional Público.* Bogotá: Editorial Lumen Christi, s/d.

Valverde, Orlando. *O Problema Florestal da Amazônia Brasileira.* Petrópolis: Vozes, 1980.

Varnhagen, F. A. *História Geral do Brasil.* 5 vols. Revised, with notes, by Rodolfo Garcia. Rio de Janeiro: Editora Melhoramentos, 1962.

———. "Memorial Orgânico." *Revista Guanabara* 1 (1851): pp. 5–17.

Vasconcellos, Simão de. *Crônica da Companhia de Jesus.* 2 vols. Petrópolis: Vozes, 1977.

Velho, Otávio. *Capitalismo Autoritário e Campesinato.* São Paulo: DIFEL, 1976.

Veríssimo, José. *Interesses da Amazônia.* Rio de Janeiro: Typographia do Jornal do Commercio, 1915.

Vespúcio, Américo. *Novo Mundo. Cartas de Viagens e Descobertas.* Porto Alegre: L & PM Editores, 1984.

Vidal, Lux. *Morte e vida de uma sociedade indígena brasileira: os Kayapó-Xikrin do rio Cateté.* São Paulo: Hucitec/Edusp, 1977.

———. "A Questão Indígena." In *Carajás, Desafio Político, Ecologia e Desenvolvimento,* by José Maria Goncales de Almeida. São Paulo and Brasília: Brasilense and CNPq, 1986: pp. 222–64.

———. "Xikrin do Cateté: Segunda viagem a campo." Report presented to the Companhia Vale do Rio Doce and FUNAI, July 1983.

Vieira Filho, João Paulo Botelho. "Aumento demográfico das populações indígenas Xikrin e Suruí." *Revista Paulista de Medicina* 79, nos. 1, 2 (1972): pp. 1–27.

Vieira, Padre Antônio. "Direcções a respeito da forma que se deve ter no julgamento e liberdade no cativeiro dos índios no Maranhão." *Obras Escolhidas.* Vol. 5. Lisbon: Livraria Sá de Cortes, 1851: pp. 33–96.

Viertler, Renate. "O projeto Tadarimana e suas conseqüências sociais entre os índios Bororo." In Comissão Pró-Índio, *A Questão da Terra.* São Paulo: Global Editora, 1981: pp. 112–22.

Villas-Boas, Orlando, and Villas-Boas, Cláudio. *Xingu, os índios, seus mitos.* Rio de Janeiro: Zahar Editores, 1970.

Wagley, Charles. *Welcome of Tears.* New York: Oxford University Press, 1977.

———. "Xamanismo Tapirapé." *Boletim do Museu Nacional* no. 3 (1943): pp. 1–18.

Wagley, Charles, and Eduardo Galvão. *Os Índios Tenetehara: Uma cultura em transição.* Rio de Janeiro: Ministério da Educação e Cultura, 1961. Original edition, *The Tenetehara Indians.* New York: Columbia University Press, 1949.

Westphalen, Moysés. "Reforma Agrária nas Terras dos Índios." *Correiro do Povo,* March 7, 1963.

White, Leslie. *The Evolution of Culture.* New York: McGraw-Hill, 1959.

Willey, Gordon R. *South America.* Vol. 2, *An Introduction to American Archaeology.* Englewood Cliffs, N.J.: Prentice-Hall, 1971.

Yarrow, Andrew L. "Alaska's Natives Try a Taste of Capitalism." *New York Times Magazine,* March 17, 1985.

Zarur, George. "Ecological Need and Cultural Choice in Central Brazil." *Current Anthropology* 20 (1979): pp. 649–53.

———. *Parentesco, Ritual e Economia no alto Xingu.* Brasília: FUNAI, 1975.

Zea, Leopoldo. *America en la História.* Mexico City: n.p., 1957.